Orthography and Word Recognition in Reading

Orthography and Word Recognition in Reading

LESLIE HENDERSON

Psychology Group
School of Natural Sciences
The Hatfield Polytechnic
Hatfield, Hertfordshire
England

1982

ACADEMIC PRESS
A Subsidiary of Harcourt Brace Jovanovich, Publishers
London New York
Paris San Diego San Francisco
São Paulo Sydney Tokyo Toronto

ACADEMIC PRESS INC. (LONDON) LTD.
24/28 Oval Road
London NW1

United States Edition published by
ACADEMIC PRESS INC.
111 Fifth Avenue
New York, New York 10003

British Library Cataloguing in Publication Data

Henderson, L.
Orthography and word recognition in reading
1. Reading, Psychology of
I. Title
428'.4'019 BF456.R2

ISBN 0-12-340520-3

LCCCN 81-69587

Typeset by Gloucester Typesetting Services
and printed in Great Britain by
T. J. Press (Padstow) Ltd., Padstow, Cornwall

Preface

In writing this book my primary intention was to interest those concerned with research in the psychology of reading. The main focus is on experimental investigations of word perception in the fluent reader, but I have also touched upon the problem of how we learn to read and upon recent work on patients with dyslexia as a consequence of brain damage. Perhaps the least orthodox aspect of the coverage is the inclusion of a considerable amount of material on the nature of orthographies and on the different problems that various types of writing system pose for the reader. In this I have hoped to engage, or at least provoke, those in linguistics and education who share an interest in visible language and also to interest English-speaking psychologists in a broader testing ground for theories of reading.

Part One of the book deals at a largely descriptive level with the nature of orthographies and the ways in which they reflect speech and meaning. This material is presented for its own sake as an exploration of the borderline between linguistic and psychological enquiry but it also serves another purpose, that of introducing the nonspecialist reader to many of the formal properties of written language round which psychological interpretations revolve.

In Part Two, we enter territory that is more obviously psychological. We begin with a fundamental question. When confronted with a word, what strategies does the reader employ to decide upon its pronunciation? Two chapters are devoted to this apparently simple question, partly in acknowledgement of recent progress on the topic, and partly because work in this area serves to illustrate a remarkable number of important trends in current research—normal and neuropsychological data, the influence of linguistic characterizations of the task and, not least, in dual-process and lexical analogy theories, two worthy rival accounts. A third chapter deals with other aspects of the mechanics of translating print into sound, and a fourth reviews evidence from the reading of other scripts, notably oriental ideographs.

Part Three is, perforce, slightly less thematically cohesive. Two chapters treat the detection and identification of letters and words. A third chapter deals with attention and awareness in word recognition. The final chapter deals with the influence of context on word recognition and with models of access to the mental lexicon.

Within the areas outlined the treatment is fairly comprehensive. However, I stop short of two topics that might possibly have been expected—the control of eye-movements and comprehension. The eye-movement literature is competently covered in other recent sources. Comprehension eluded me, as it has done so often.

There are two aspects of the treatment that may be worth commenting on. First, my central concern has been with the nature of argument in cognitive psychology. For this reason, I have not rested with a report of what *X* found or *Y* asserted. Often arguments are examined, picked at, and weighed at a length that is not often encountered in works of this sort. On this I plead premeditation. It has, however, concerned me that an innocent reader might become depressed by the impression that this scrutiny leaves nothing standing firmly on which we might hope to build. I have certainly been hesitant about the role of the manic dentist making a circuit of the great cognitive grin and testing each tooth to destruction with his little pick. I can only affirm that the exercise of writing this book strengthened rather than diminished my own affection for cognitive psychology. The second idiosyncrasy is this: there are almost no flow diagrams in the book.

The Social Science Research Council have provided financial support for much of the research leading to this book. I am especially indebted to the Council for a Personal Research Grant which released me from my other duties during the session 1978–79, when a first draft of the book was written. I would not like the imaginative nature of these awards to pass unremarked.

I am grateful to Alan Allport, Derek Besner, Max Coltheart, Uta Frith, Tony Marcel and Karalyn Patterson who have commented on portions of the work and especially grateful to Rod Barron and Sheila Henderson who have commented on almost all of it.

Stevie Hibbard typed the manuscript expertly.

Leslie Henderson

Old Hatfield
January 1982

Acknowledgements

Material is quoted from the following sources with permission.

Liberman, A. M., Cooper, F. S., Shankweiler, D. P. and Studdert-Kennedy, M. (1967). *Psychological Review* **74**, 431–461.

Kavanagh, J. and Mattingly, I. G. (Ed.) (1972). *Language by Eye and by Ear.* Cambridge, Massachusetts Institute of Technology Press.

Haas, W. (Ed.) (1976). *Writing without Letters.* Manchester, Manchester University Press.

Scragg, D. G. (1975). *A History of English Spelling.* Manchester, Manchester University Press.

Frith, U. (Ed.) (1980). *Cognitive Processes in Spelling.* London and New York, Academic Press.

Chomsky, N. and Halle, M. (1968). *The Sound Pattern of English.* New York, Harper and Row.

Reber, A. S. and Scarborough, D. (Ed.) (1977). *Towards a Psychology of Reading.* Potomac: Laurence Erlbaum Associates.

Underwood, G. (Ed.) (1978). *Strategies of Information Processing.* London and New York, Academic Press.

Laberge, D. and Samuels, S. J. (Ed.) (1977). *Basic Processes in Reading: Perception and Comprehension.* Potomac, Laurence Erlbaum Associates.

Marshall, J. C. and Newcombe, F. (1973). *Journal of Psycholinguistic Research* **2**, 175–199.

Requin, J. (Ed.) (1978). *Attention and Performance VII.* Potomac, Laurence Erlbaum Associates.

Gibson, E. J. and Levin, H. (1975). *The Psychology of Reading.* Cambridge, Massachusetts Institute of Technology Press.

Huey, E. B. (1968). *The Psychology and Pedagogy of Reading.* Cambridge, Massachusetts Institute of Technology Press.

McClelland, J. L. (1978). *Journal of Experimental Psychology: Human Perception and Performance* **4**, 210–223.

Haas, W. (1970). *Phonographic Translation.* Manchester, Manchester University Press.

Figures and tables are reproduced from the following sources with permission.

Figure 1. From Pulgram, E. (1976). The typologies of writing systems. *In* W. Haas (Ed.) *Writing without Letters.* Manchester, Manchester University Press.

Figure 2. From *The Highway Code*. Her Majesty's Stationery Office.
Figure 3. From Gardiner, A. H. (1950). *Egyptian Grammar*. (2nd Edit.). Oxford, Oxford University Press.
Figure 4. From Fossey, C. (1927). *Notices sur les Caractères Etrangers Anciens et Modernes, Redigées par un Groupe de Savants*. Paris, Imprimerie National.
Figure 5. From Liberman, A. M., Cooper, F. S., Shankweiler, D. P., and Studdart-Kennedy, M. (1967). *Psychological Review* **74**, 431–461.
Table 4. From Taylor, I. (1980). The Korean Writing System: An Alphabet? A Syllabary? A Logography? *In* P. A. Kolers, M. Wrolstad and H. Bouma (Ed.) *Processing of Visible Language Vol. 2*. New York, Plenum Press.
Figure 11. From Vesey, G. (1973). *Perception*. Milton Keynes, Open University Press.

Contents

for Sheila

Try not to think of understanding as a "mental process" at all—
for *that* is the expression which confuses you

LUDWIG WITTGENSTEIN
Philosophical Investigations

Part One

Orthography

Introduction

The primary purpose of the four chapters comprising Part I is to examine the nature of written language through the range of writing systems that have evolved. The material in these chapters is, on the whole, more linguistic than psychological, although Chapter 2 deals in a general way with the psychology of speech recognition and Chapter 3 includes a brief examination of the child's perception of speech as a preliminary to his understanding of the relationship between print and sound.

To begin with material that is, at least in a broad sense, linguistic is not to attribute any logical primacy to linguistic analysis in the study of reading. My reasons for beginning this way are largely ones of expository convenience. Thus Part I serves as an introduction to certain descriptive terms and concepts that pervade the wider study of reading. In particular, Chapter 1 can be used to glean some notion of the variety of written languages. As Coltheart *et al.* (1980) pithily observe: "Brains may be similar from one culture to another but orthographies certainly are not" (Preface to *Deep Dyslexia*, 1980). Chapter 2 also includes some introductory descriptive material in the form of a discussion of the units of sound that are employed in the formal analysis of spoken language. The expert reader may choose to skip this material, though at a theoretical level it is worth contemplating the possibility that the perception of speech and of print involve processes that differ in important ways. In Chapter 3 I treat some speculations about the functional consequences of the formal differences between orthographies. This material is intended to cast further light on the linguistic taxonomy of scripts reviewed in Chapter 1 and also to expose, from the standpoint of psychological prejudice, the differences between linguistic and psychological arguments. (Psychological experiments that involve contrasts between types of orthography are discussed in Chapter 8.) Chapter 4 treats the structure of English orthography in some detail, serving as a background to later psychological discussion of strategies for the translation of print into speech and, incidentally, illustrating both the extent and the limitations of purely descriptive approaches.

Taken together, Part I probably contains more descriptive and linguistic matter than is typically found in books on perceptual processes in reading.

While some of this is intended to make this work relatively self-contained, clearly I have gone beyond that objective. Essentially, there are three reasons for this. First, if the study of reading is to illuminate cognitive processes in some general way then we must strive for a clearer view of what is universal in reading and what is specific to a type of script, or indeed to a method of reading pedagogy. Secondly, I believe that an important ingredient of recent progress in reading research has been an increased attention to the nature of the stimulus and to what encoding strategies it allows or encourages. Perhaps the best example of this is to be found in work on mechanisms for assigning sound in the reading of irregular orthographies such as English (see Chapters 5 and 6). As a third point, I have been interested in the contrast of the formal and psychological approaches to reading. This point may be worth enlarging.

Epistemologists have always found it difficult to adhere to a philosophical concern with the nature of our knowledge of the world without slipping into psychological speculation about the mechanisms of perception. Indeed, it has even been suggested (Craik, 1948) that it is absurd to expect a theory of knowledge that is not psychologically informed. Similarly, the linguistic student of orthography has often strayed into the psychology of reading. Of course there is nothing intrinsically objectionable about linguists engaging in psychological speculation, or in psychologists discussing language. We are concerned here not with a trades dispute but with the failure to notice that one has passed from one realm to the other, a failure, in particular, to observe that psychological propositions require a different sort of justification from linguistic ones. Thus we must be alert to the distinction between claiming that Chinese script refers directly to meaning as a formal, descriptive statement about a writing system and, on the other hand, as a psychological hypothesis about the strategy that Chinese adopt when reading their language. Or, taking another issue from Chapter 3, if we wish to assert that maximal "analyticity" is a desirable feature in a writing system (for example, having a written symbol for each elementary sound rather than, say, a symbol for each syllable or word), we must be clear either that our preference for analyticity is a purely aesthetic one or that it requires to be justified in terms of some psychological criterion, such as the ease with which a child can learn to read a language or the speed with which a fluent reader can comprehend what is written.

In this respect, the transgressions are by no means all committed by linguists. Often it happens that psychologists, impressed by some piece of linguistic analysis, have imported it without regard to its psychological plausibility. It is arguable that the notion of reading by grapheme–phoneme correspondences became incorporated into the psychological nest in this way. The general problem here is well described by Glushko (1979). We need, he argues, to distinguish carefully between three conceptions of orthographic rules (or indeed any linguistic rule): rules as *linguistic* descriptions, rules as *knowledge of the structure of a language*, and rules as *procedures*, e.g. for arriving at pronunciations of print.

Chapter 1

Writing Systems

Spoken language precedes written language in the evolution of cultures and also in the development of the individual. From this observation comes the simplest theory of the nature of writing systems. This theory holds that script serves as a cipher or notation for the sounds of spoken language. In such a view, all written language is essentially phonographic, a quality epitomized by *phonetic transcription*, the system of notation by which the lexicographer or phonetician records the stream of sounds in speech. A refinement of the phonetic transcription view holds that the major differences among writing systems are in the size of the sound unit that they represent by their elementary symbols. Thus in the logograph of Classical Chinese it is the word that is the unit of reference. In alphabetic language it is the phoneme that is represented. In yet other, intermediate, systems the syllable is the unit. The most minute unit is of course the phone, as represented in the specially designed writing system for phonetic transcription. The perspective presented in this view is an orderly one in which the evolution of writing systems generally proceeds from logographic scripts, containing a very large number of basic symbols each representing a large unit of sound (the word), to alphabetic scripts, which use a small set of elements to represent relatively microscopic constituents of speech.

It may seem but a short journey from this position to the view that reading must therefore consist in the translation of these various sorts of ink-marks into sounds, at a level determined by the size of the basic units. However, in this apparently short and innocent journey we have strayed from a rather over-simplified bit of descriptive linguistics into a quite different domain, one that is inhabited by the hypotheses of psychology.

This particular act of sleepwalking from the description of a linguistic state of affairs to the assertion of a psychological doctrine passes two unmarked junctions. The first can be recognized when we find ourselves talking about the "function" of linguistic entities, such as the elements of a writing system. The second arises when we use words like "reading" to describe both a linguistic performance and psychological theories about the underlying means by which it is accomplished. In a more psychologically neutral word like "translation" we can more readily distinguish the linguistic usage from the psychological one.

1.1 CLASSIFICATION OF WRITING SYSTEMS

A variety of classifications of writing systems have been proposed by linguists. These have been the subject of learned dispute, and much of this disputation has been about terminology. For example, the terms "pictograph", "ideograph" and "logograph" have sometimes been used in overlapping and sometimes exclusive senses. Furthermore, some writers have felt it necessary to invent their own terminology in protest at the debasement of established terms (e.g. Gelb, 1963, in which the three terms above are eschewed in favour of "semasiographic" and "word-syllabic").

Such proliferation of terminology will not be unfamiliar to the psychologist. It does not signal perversity on the part of the linguists but rather serves to illustrate the fact that even linguistic descriptions are not theoretically neutral. Classifications of writing systems are influenced by, among other factors, views about what can properly be called "language", theories of the historical evolution of writing, and theories of the relationship between written and spoken languages.

Many of these difficult issues need not concern us here, but it will be useful to examine classifications in a brief and general fashion for three reasons. First, this will provide a rationalized glossary for some of the terminology that we shall be unable to avoid using. Secondly, a consideration of the relationships between spoken and written languages will serve to remind us of some fundamental aspects of the structure of spoken language to which we shall be referring throughout this book. Finally, and most generally, this enquiry should provide a simplified conceptual framework into which we can introduce the discussion of particular language systems.

One widely influential classification is that proposed in Gelb's (1963) classic survey of the history of writing. The basic elements of Gelb's classification are shown in Table 1. The classification starts from pictures considered as objects of expressive art. It is often suggested that it is in such pictorial representations that

Table 1 Classification of writing systems, adapted from Gelb (1963)

1 NON-WRITING *Pictures*

2 FORERUNNERS OF WRITING *Semasiography* (the direct expression of meanings without reference to speech)

- 2.1 Descriptive-representational signs
- 2.2 Identifying-mnemonic signs

3 FULL WRITING *Phonography* (the representation of speech)

- 3.1 Word-syllabic
- 3.2 Syllabic
- 3.3 Alphabetic

writing systems have their origin. Yet their purpose is not the communication of a linguistic message, and they lack an explicit framework of conventions in the choice of symbols. This is not to gainsay that there is an element of literary symbolism in much sophisticated art. In certain periods of art "iconology"—the pictorial representation of meaning—became the subject of quite complex conventions. Certain Italian Renaissance paintings (consult, for example, Panofsky, 1939) can be "read" for such meaning.

As forerunners of writing, Gelb proposes those pictures that are specifically intended to communicate messages. These he has subdivided into two loosely defined sub-classes. The "descriptive-representational" pictures resemble works whose primary purpose is aesthetic, but they are generally stripped of irrelevant decoration. Their intention is to express an entire thought (hence the German *Gedankenschrift*).

What Gelb calls "identifying-mnemonic" pictures have progressed a little further toward writing by virtue of their more specific reference to language forms, including names. These devices are intended to aid memory by tagging an object for ownership or by providing a retrieval cue for an event or episode.[1*] Salient examples of these intentions are embodied, respectively, in the Old Sumerian ledger tablets and in the calendar of the Dakota Indians, the so-called "winter counts". An important characteristic of these systems is the move towards a conventionalized representation.

We now come to a curious feature of Gelb's taxonomy: there is a hiatus between the pictorial prewriting category and the first stage of writing proper, the *word-syllabic* category. Another way of describing this pecularity of the taxonomy is to say that, for Gelb, all true writing is phonographic, that is, it refers directly to units of sound in speech. Thus, scripts which others have described as logographic and which contain signs that correspond with whole words, Gelb regards as phonographic (Gelb, 1963, p. 193). Since many logographic languages consist largely of monosyllabic words (notably Chinese), a sign corresponds equally to the word and the syllable level, hence Gelb's term "word-syllabic".

Gelb's remaining categories of phonography are orthodox, consisting of the *syllabic* (or syllabary) and the *alphabetic*. In the syllabary there is an economical and systematic set of signs representing syllable sounds independently of their meaning. A consequence of the interpretation of logographs is that the syllabary is viewed as no more than a simplification of the word-syllabic system (Gelb, 1963, p. 162).

Gelb's taxonomy is essentially one of the sort in which all true writing systems are held to be direct representations of speech sounds which can be ordered according to the size of the sound unit represented. The guiding principle of the

* Notes will be found at the end of the volume.

taxonomy appears to be that of providing a description of the *evolution* of particular scripts.

By way of contrast, the classification proposed by Pulgram (1976) takes a less phonographic view. Pulgram's taxonomy differs from Gelb's in two principal ways. One concerns its extension: Pulgram's consideration of phonographic systems extends through the syllabic and alphabetic down to the deliberately contrived systems for representing phonemes (*phonemic*), phones (*phonetic*), to the most elementary unit, the acoustic feature (*spectrographic*). The other difference relates to Pulgram's treatment of logographic systems: whereas these are treated in the category *word-syllabic* by Gelb, Pulgram clearly regards their primary correspondence as with *morphological* structure, that is, meaning rather than sound. This is most clearly shown in his discussion of the "signalling" property of writing systems, where he classifies pictographs and logographs as "signs" in contrast to the "figurae" of all the phonographic systems. This distinction is between signals composed of meaningful units (signs) and those composed of meaningless units (figurae) which have to be combined to yield meaning.

The development from pictures to phonography is attractively illustrated by

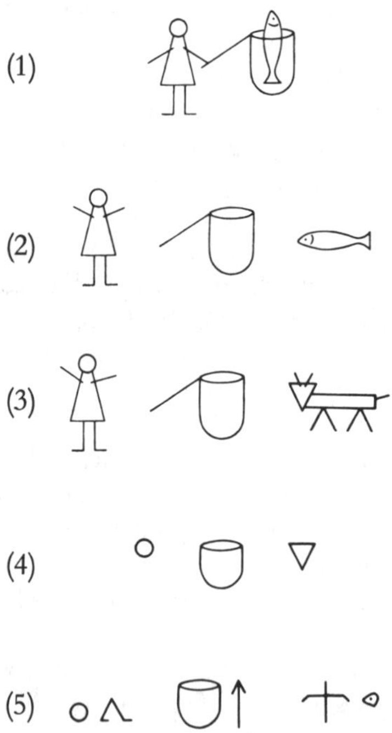

Fig. 1 Hypothetical example of the development from pictography to phonology. From Pulgram (1976).

Pulgram in the manner of Fig. 1. At the top (1) is a drawing intended to convey a whole utterance such as "man catches fish" (the pictograph actually refers to the meaning of a whole set of equivalent utterances). The next development (2) preserves the same code but segments the pictorial elements into a linear sequence, to express a sort of picture grammar, by analogy with the grammar of language. Stage 3 involves a subtle shift. Here the representation is of the meaning "man catches cow". But cows are not caught in nets. So the net refers logographically rather than pictorially to the concept of "catching". In Stage 4, stylization of the representation leads to graphs that are now devoid of any recognizable pictorial reference. Finally, in Stage 5, these pure logographs are emptied of semantic reference. The sign for "man" comes to stand for the syllable /man/. Permutation of such figurae then gives us man-goes, ketch-up and sel-fish.

In this example what we see combined are two levels of taxonomy. In the superficial level we find described the stages of historical evolution. These are accidental and continuous, with the gradual replacement within a system of old constituents by new ones. Underlying this historical level there is a logical level characterized by discrete shifts in the nature and status of the representations. These have a linguistic reality even though no historical system may fall exclusively into one category at a given time.

An even more abstract classification has been attempted by Haas (1976). His scheme is based on the combination of three binary choices to yield a theoretical maximum of eight types of script. The first choice involves the relationship of graphemes to speech, which can be either *derived* or *original*. For a script to be derived there must exist rule-governed correspondences between the written and spoken language. In original scripts, such as pictographs, there exists a set of quite different, but equivalent, utterances in the spoken language that expresses the meaning of a given representation.

The second choice concerns the relationship of the graphemes to the *message* conveyed by a passage of script. This relationship can be either *empty* or *informed* according to whether or not the grapheme contributes directly to the meaning of the message of which it is a constituent. Thus the *3* in $3+4 = 7$ is informed, but the *t* in three is empty.

The third choice concerns the relationship between graphemes and the extra-linguistic world of "things". This can be said to be *motivated* or *arbitrary* according to whether or not the relationship is pictorial.

This classification is somewhat scholastic, because although the categorical choices are logically independent, not all of the resultant options are real. In fact one cannot ask of empty scripts whether they be motivated or not, so there are only six final types possible. Furthermore, a script that was both original (no correspondence with speech) and semantically empty would make no sense. So we are left with five realistic types, for which the classification is shown in Table 2.

Returning to actual scripts, we can now see that the pictograph can be

Table 2 Summary of Haas's (1976) classification of scripts

Categories	Relationship of the graphemes of a script to speech	to meaning	to things
Alternatives	+ derived − derived (original)	+ informed − informed (empty)	+ motivated − motivated (arbitrary)
Type 1 Major pictograph	−	+	+
Type 2 Ideographic pictograph	−	+	−
Type 3 Lexical pictograph	+	+	+
Type 4 Logograph	+	+	−
Type 5 Syllabary/Alphabet	+	−	−

described as being semantically informed, motivated in its relationship to "things", and underived in relation to speech. Such Type 1 pictographs may be supplemented by a subsidiary Type 2 script which differs only in being arbitrary in its relationship to "things", as when a pictographic reference in a roadsign is supplemented with an arbitrary visual convention such as a red circle to indicate that the message expresses a prohibition. Such a script is confined to its subsidiary role by virtue of the fact that the conventions, having no relation either to speech or to the world of things, are difficult to memorize.

Another variant of the basic pictograph is also based on the change of state of a single binary choice, this time a change from *original* to *derived* in the relationship to speech. The resultant Type 3 script is, in itself, a trivial variant of the pictograph. In it, elements of the picture space are extracted from that space to stand on their own, often as quasi-lexical representations. For example, the roadsign for "hump-backed bridge" has a fairly direct reference to the words, whereas the eventful roadsign for quayside or river bank (much loved by linguists) is not derived, since its meaning can be expressed in many equivalent utterances, constrained only by the semantics and syntax of the picture (see Fig. 2).

However trivial this last distinction might seem at the pictographic level, the extraction of pictorial units from the picture context is an important stage in the development of the relationship of scripts to speech. We have already seen this in Pulgram's illustrative example (Fig. 1, Stages 2 and 3). For this reason, Haas (1976) describes the Type 3 script as "transitional".

Once the derived relationship between script and speech is established, further developments inevitably involve the discarding of motivated (depictive) reference to objects (Fig. 1, Stage 4). Finally, as the size of the speech unit that is represented contracts to less than that of the morpheme, *informed* status is lost and the individual grapheme, whether standing for a syllable or phoneme, became, on its own, semantically empty, as in scripts of Type 5.

Fig. 2 Roadsigns exhibiting various properties within the Haas classification system. The sign on the left exemplifies script of Type 1, conveying a general idea without strongly implying one particular form of words. The red triangular surrounds of the signs conform to an arbitrary convention expressing the notion of *warning* and is therefore a Type 2 device. The sign on the right contains an element of Type 3, insofar as the pictograph for "hump bridge" could be said to suggest those particular words.

A characteristic of Haas's scheme is that it permits fine distinctions in the pictographic realm, whereas in the phonographic realm once informed (or logographic) status is lost no distinction is made according to the size of the sound unit represented (i.e. syllable, phoneme, phone, acoustic feature).

1.2 HISTORY OF WRITING SYSTEMS

The study of the evolution of writing systems is one of the more fascinating detective stories of our times. The archaeological evidence is beautifully presented in the book by Gelb (1963) which has become a basic reference in this field. As with other evolutionary processes, vestiges of more primitive antecedents have survived into the present, in varying states of purity. As we shall see, languages such as Japanese, which preserve the traditions of logographic representation alongside that of the syllabary, represent a fruitful source of data for the student of reading.

Many cultures believed the origin of their writing system to be mysterious or divine. Pei (1965) has noted that the name of the Sanskrit alphabet means "pertaining to the city of the gods". The ancient Egyptians held that writing had been invented by their god of wisdom. These legends probably have their motivation partly in the sacred functions which early writing often served, but it is also probable that they were inspired by the sort of awe at the achievement of written language which led Plato to liken the power of science to the condensation of speech into the symbols of the alphabet.

Pictographs

The most primitive writing system, which Gelb and others prefer to describe as a prewriting system, was the pictographic system in which concepts were represented by simple pictorial symbols. This rather loose category is bounded on one side by drawings for magical or artistic purposes, of which the communicative function may be remote from any verbal form, and on the other by such precise reference as is conveyed by the three stylized, pictographic fingers in the Roman numeral (III).

The pictographic system suffers from a variety of fairly obvious problems. To the extent that it becomes conventionalized, there are a great many signs to remember. Writing demands considerable skills in draughtsmanship. Moreover, the representation of abstract concepts is problematic. This can be achieved by combinations of symbols, but these tend to become formidably complex. Eventually this complexity leads to stylization and, by stages, a logographic system is born.

Pictographic systems of representation have in common with sign languages, such as those used by the deaf (Bellugi and Fischer, 1972), a very impoverished syntax. Partly for that reason they do not raise problems of literacy, nor of translatability between language. These very factors, perhaps magnified by an irrational component of fashion, have lead to a second flowering of pictography in our contemporary culture. Pictographs, in internationally agreed form, decorate our roads and our underwear, warning against falling rocks or drycleaning.

Rather than regarding pictures as a visual embodiment of verbal information, the view is often taken that alternative verbal and imaging representational systems are available as distinct forms of code. Long ago pictorial and verbal codes were posited as the alternative vehicles for all thinking. Although this view is no longer tenable, images do seem to have a peculiar potency as representations of consequences or of concrete possibilities. A literary version of this idea dominates William Golding's classic novel about Neanderthal man, *The Inheritors*, in which the characters' attempts to envisage possible states of affairs are usually heralded by the announcement: "I have a picture".

> "I am by the sea and I have a picture. This is a picture of a picture. I am"—she screwed up her face and scowled—"thinking" (William Golding, *The Inheritors*, 1955).

The popularity of the term "scenario" amongst inhabitants of think-tanks may be symptomatic of the survival of at least a quasi-pictorial mode of representing consequences.

Logographs

Two of the more important factors governing the development from pictographs to logographs were, as noted above, the increasing stylization of the representation and the tendency to adopt the convention of using one sign to represent one word.

Stylization, or the move away from a literal pictorial treatment, was the inevitable product of the tendency to combine pictographs to extend the range of possible referents. In ancient Chinese the pictographs for "eye" and "water" were combined to represent "tear". Progressively more abstract concepts could be rendered by conjunctions of pictographs. However, this served to complicate the rendition in such a way as to encourage the development of a more simplified and idealized representation. This process of simplification was probably accelerated by the tendency, evident in contemporary language, for frequency of usage to lead to the abbreviation and simplification of forms.

Logographic script (sometimes referred to by the ambiguous term "ideographic") seems to have been developed fairly independently by the Sumerians in Mesopotamia, the Egyptians, the Hittites, and the Chinese. The Sumerians appear to have invented cuneiform, the writing constructed from wedge-shaped marks products by the application of a stylus to soft clay. Cuneiform writing is therefore composed from a modular basic shape. This sort of constraint imposed by the writing medium may have given further impetus to the change from the pictograph to the more stylized logograph.

Another constraint imposed by the mechanical problems of writing occurs in the development of cursive script. Such a system is designed for informal and speedy communication, and its fluency of line leads to the loss of pictographic reference. In ancient Egyptian, for example, the hieroglyphic writing was reserved for official purposes, and for informal use a hieratic and subsequently a demotic cursive script were developed. An example of hieratic is shown in Fig. 3, together with its hieroglyphic transcription. To the innocent eye all pictorial reference is lost in the cursive script, although the association with the hieroglyphic form is clear enough. Even this visual association between scripts becomes obscure with the demotic form.

With the tendency for a logograph to represent a single word in the spoken language it becomes reasonable to regard the script as speech-derived, that is, as referring to units of the spoken language more or less directly. The directness of this reference to spoken forms was increased, owing to a variety of pressures. For example, Gelb has remarked that the Sumerians were an urbanized people with a highly developed economy which required the keeping of inventories subsumed under a personal name. The requirement of exactly rendering the name of a person led to the development of a phonographic representation.

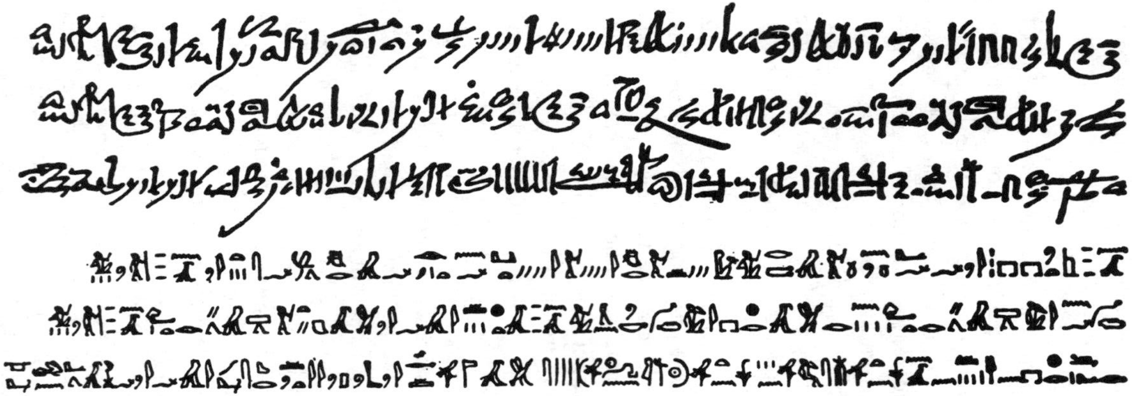

Fig. 3 Specimen of hieratic writing showing the equivalent pictographic hieroglyphs. From Gardiner (1950).

This was especially so because Sumerian names, unlike American Indian names, were seldom based on picturable objects.

Furthermore, as soon as the logograph is conceived of as representing, in a direct fashion, a word in the spoken language, then this sort of phonological reference can be generalized. The ancient Egyptian pictograph for the sun *re* came to be used for the spoken syllable *re*, occurring as part of a longer word. A similar tendency was manifest in Chinese where a single logograph developed out of the combination of a *radical*, the component indicating the semantic field in which the concept lay, and the *phonetic complement*, which indicates the appropriate sound by means of an analogy. It is as if we represented *corn* by means of a complex sign combining a semantic pointer to cereal crops and a phonological cue: rhymes with "horn". Eventually this combination of pictography with phonography resulted in a single logographic unit which was read as referring directly to the spoken word.

In modern Chinese it is usual to regard the characters as belonging to five main categories: (*i*) *pictographs*, albeit highly stylized; (*ii*) *ideographs*, representing a concept or relationship, such as a pointer indicating *up*; (*iii*) *compound ideographs* such as eye+water = tear; (*iv*) *phonetic loans*, in which, given two words with the same sound, the character representing one comes to be used also to represent the other (with an outcome resembling the English homographs such as *post*); and (*v*) *phonetic compounds*, combining a semantic clue (the radical) with a phonetic clue based on a similar sounding word.

The term "logographic" was probably first used in Du Ponceau's early discussion of Chinese writing, and he used it interchangeably with "lexigraphic" (Martin, 1972). These terms imply an absence of explicit reference to phonology which is clearly gainsaid by the introduction of the characters in categories (*iv*) and (*v*). Phonetic loans, and to a lesser extent phonetic compounds, are evidence of a tendency for a pure logographic system—which represents meaning directly—to incorporate an increasing component of phonological reference.

From a linguistic point of view it is probably fair to regard logographs as direct representations of morphemes (units of meaning). This does justice to the pictographic or ideographic parentage of the logograph. It is also consistent with the fact that in phonetic loans and phonetic compounds the reference to phonology is indirect. However, when we speak in this context of direct and indirect reference, it is important to be clear that our criterion is linguistic or historical. The way in which the characters are actually treated by the reader is a quite different question. It is evident that logographic systems could be treated as representations of sound, just as alphabetic systems might be read as unitary visual representations of word-meanings.

Traditionally, the Chinese character constituted a much more complex shape than the graphemes of alphabetic language. This was particularly true of the phonetic compound, with its combination of radical and phonetic elements. Because each character has to occupy the same amount of space, the evolution of compound characters inevitably led to more tightly packaged detail. This in turn lead to simplification, so that in many compounds it may be doubted whether the phonetic element continues to serve its original purpose. In such characters there may be a reversion to purely logographic status, i.e. an arbitrary sign representing a unit of meaning.

In the simplified contemporary Chinese calligraphy each character is composed of about five strokes, not unlike an English letter (Wang, cited in Martin, 1972), but the combination of these strokes forms a more complex spatial design than in our letters and imposes a characteristic rhythm on the writing of a given logograph. Perhaps this rhythm facilitates communication when Chinese sketch a character in the air, as they are said to do when disambiguating speech. Sasanuma (1974) describes a dyslexic Japanese patient who, when confronted with a logograph (Kanji) that he could not read, would trace its strokes over and over again with his finger as if trying to evoke a proprioceptive memory of writing it.

As the reference of the logographic system becomes extended to include its phonological implications, as in the case of phonetic loans, so a system develops in the direction of the *rebus*, in which a word is constructed from pictographs of the accidental semantic referents of its component syllables. For example, *cannot* could be represented by pictures of a (tin) *can* and a *knot*. An amusing instance of this is described by Martin (1972) for the case of foreign politicians' names. As we have already seen, proper names pose problems for non-phonographic languages. The Chinese solution is to transliterate the name phonetically, using characters that have the appropriate sound, whilst setting aside their original meaning. This of course presents the opportunity to select characters that have a particularly abusive original meaning. Thus is born the soundless pun.

Syllabaries

The increasing incorporation of phonological pointers into a logographic system creates a condition which is conducive to the development of the syllabary. In the syllabary, phonology is directly represented by the graphic character, at the level of the syllable. Most syllabaries occurred as intermediate stages in the development of alphabetic systems and they commonly existed as supplements to a more ancient logographic system.

In classical Chinese the use of the syllabary was restricted by two major factors. First, the spoken language was monosyllabic. This meant that a word tended to be at once monomorphemic and monosyllabic. Therefore little economy was to be achieved by using a character to represent the syllable (syllabary) rather than the morpheme (logography). Secondly, the representation of syllables was more economical because of the existence of large numbers of homophones (the Chinese equivalent of *crews/cruise*). Clearly a sign that represents word meaning rather than sound serves to avoid the ambiguity that is present in the spoken language. The existence of large numbers of homophones is sometimes given as the reason why Japanese has preserved the Chinese logographs alongside the Japanese syllabaries (Pei, 1965). It is claimed that Japanese /ka/ has over 200 lexical meanings, each with a separate logograph.

The example of Japanese script

The logographic component of Japanese script was borrowed directly from Chinese. The Chinese word-signs were taken over to represent the same meanings in Japanese, although the spoken form was usually quite different. This logographic system is known as *Kanji*.

Various difficulties arose out of the wholesale adoption of these Chinese logographs. Multiple readings of one character arose from different forays into Chinese. There are now four different, derivational systems of readings of Kanji script, and often context must be used to decide which is appropriate.

To add to the confusion, for many characters there is an option of a *kun* or *on* reading. The *kun* reading is based on Japanese pronunciation of a word and the *on* reading comes from the spoken Chinese form of the borrowed character. Nowadays these two spoken forms have come to express quite different meanings. Again context has to provide the basis for choice.

The correspondence between Kanji characters and meanings is therefore not one to one. Like the correspondences between letters and sounds in English, there are diverging options in both directions of translation. One spoken word can have several meanings, each with its Kanji representation. One Kanji character can stand for several spoken words, each with its individual meaning.

To supplement the logographic Kanji, the Japanese evolved two types of syllabary which had become formalized by about the ninth century. These syllabaries were developed in order to transliterate foreign loan words, especially proper names, and also to represent grammatical forms, which are expressed in very different ways in Chinese and Japanese.

One syllabary is known as *Katakana*, the other as *Hiragana*. Katakana is generally reserved for foreign loan words; Hiragana is used for grammatical formatives. The two syllabaries are, however, totally equivalent and both systems are *complete* in the sense that each on its own is capable of representing all the forms of the spoken language. They are collectively known as *Kana*, and it is with Kana that the child first learns to read. In fact, Kana is generally mastered by the end of the first grade (Sasanuma, 1975). There are 47 basic signs in either form of Kana, though these are sometimes combined with additional markings which provide redundant phonetic detail. This number of signs is typical for a syllabary,

ア	カ	サ	タ	ナ	ハ	マ	ヤ	ラ	ワ	ガ	ザ	ダ	バ	パ
a	ka	sa	ta	na	ha	ma	ya	ra	wa	ga	za	da	ba	pa
イ	キ	シ	チ	ニ	ヒ	ミ		リ	井	ギ	ジ	ヂ	ビ	ピ
i	ki	si	ti(tsi)	ni	hi	mi		ri	wi(i)	gi	zi	di	bi	pi
ウ	ク	ス	ツ	ヌ	フ	ム	ユ	ル		グ	ズ	ヅ	ブ	プ
u	ku	su	tu(tsu)	nu	hu	mu	yu	ru		gu	zu	du	bu	pu
ヱ	ケ	セ	テ	子	ヘ	メ	エ	レ	ヱ	ゲ	ゼ	デ	ベ	ペ
e	ke	se	te	ne	he	me	ye	re	we(e)	ge	ze	de	be	pe
オ	コ	ソ	ト	ノ	ホ	モ	ヨ	ロ	ヲ	ゴ	ゾ	ド	ボ	ポ
o	ko	so	to	no	ho	mo	yo	ro	wo	go	zo	do	bo	po
ン	(n)													

Fig. 4 The Japanese katakana syllabary. From Fossey (1927).

many falling in the range of 40–60 signs. The Katakana signs are shown in Fig. 4.

The coexistence of a logographic system with the syllabaries in written Japanese is a typical state of affairs. A purely logographic script is rarely, if ever, encountered. It is this fact about whole writing systems which leads Gelb to abandon a logographic category in his classification of scripts. Accordingly, it is his insistence on classifying a script as a whole that leads him to the idiosyncratic conclusion that all non-pictographic script must be phonographic.

Gelb also observes that all syllabaries employ signs that are either identical to, or simplified from, the word signs of the parent writing systems. The development from logography to syllabary is therefore a gradual and overlapping one. The question of whether a culture divested itself wholly of the logographic system appears to have depended partly on linguistic peculiarities, such as the prevalence of homophones, but largely on extra-linguistic factors, such as those that arise during the transmission of a writing system between cultures. In historical terms it is unclear to whom the first invention of a purely syllabic script should be attributed (see, for example, Grumach, 1976).

Alphabets

The transition from syllabary to alphabet is the subject of some disagreement. Certainly some syllabaries also included markers for phonetic information at a sub-syllabic level. We have already observed that Japanese includes some of these, notably indications of voicing and nasality of consonants.

A much more radical example can be found in the native Korean script, *Hangul*. This extraordinary script might have been designed especially to confound linguistic taxonomies, for it appears that certain of the original signs were pictographs that depicted the process of articulating the sound to which they corresponded. For example sibilants were represented by a stylized tooth. Thus the script was both pictographic and alphabetic.

In terms of historical development, however, a crucial stage was reached when in the Near East the traditional syllabographic signs started to be marked for vowel identity. This development departed from a long-standing practice in the Egypto–Semitic tradition for phonographic signs to neglect vowel-reference. For example the Ancient Egyptian phonography which supplemented their pictographic script contains 24 signs for CV syllables. But each sign stood for a syllable consisting of a particular consonant followed by any vowel.[2]

The reason for the indifference to vowels in the Semitic languages is, I suspect, that they play a less critical role than in Indo-European languages. This argument is derided by Gelb, who claims contrariwise that English is as readable without vwls. However, Gelb makes no empirical test of this assertion. Short of doing a reading experiment, what we need to know linguistically is whether vowel changes generate as many different unrelated words in either type of language. In English, for example, vowel information matters to the extent that it is crucial to lexical decisions as in *hat*, *hit*, *hot*, *hut*. The question is this: is such a crucial role equally common in Semitic languages?

Consider, on the other hand, vowel changes that lack morphological significance such as those that occur in the English strong verbs (e.g. *ring*, *rang*, *rung*). In such a situation the vowel is only required to make a relatively fine distinction. This is quite rare in English but is extremely common in the Semitic languages.

The reason why the dispute about the precise status of the Semitic consonantal scripts has assumed such importance is of course the significance attached to the invention of the alphabet proper. It is now generally agreed that this arose out of the modification of the Phoenician consonantal script to produce the Greek alphabet, the precursor of all modern alphabetic scripts.

Little is known about the circumstances or the date of this crucial development from Phoenician to Greek. It was clearly born out of the requirement in Greek for a set of critical vowel indicators to signify those functional word-suffixes which frequently consisted of a single vowel in Greek. To achieve this, the Greeks appear to have transformed those Phoenician consonantal signs that were not needed to represent Greek phonology, using them instead as vowel signs.

Historically what is unique about the Greek alphabet is that it is systematic. This must be understood in order to appreciate the distinction between Greek script and various Semitic scripts which had occasional resort to vowel markers as an optional afterthought for the removal of ambiguities in the consonantal script. Moreover, the Greek alphabet is not only systematic in its level of phonography, it was also accompanied by a new order of phonological awareness which is at least logically independent of writing. *This awareness consisted of the explicit idea that something like the phoneme was the basic element of spoken language*, rather than the syllable. This idea appears to arise in Greek philosophy for the first time about 500 B.C. (Grumach, 1976).

The relationship between script and phonological awareness is a crucial one from a psychological point of view. As we shall see later, it has been given a crucial role in theories of the child's development of reading skills as well as in a culture's development of a writing system. Some linguists have assumed that because we utilize phonemic contrasts we must therefore have *explicit* knowledge of the phonemic level of analysis. A remarkably clear example of this unquestioning assumption is to be found in Pulgram's (1976) excellent little essay on the taxonomy of scripts, referred to earlier. Pulgram speculates as to why there are no instances of a society jumping several stages in the development of script, say from pictographic straight to alphabetic. He writes:

> There seems to be no theoretical obstacle to this: any speaker is aware . . . of the discrete character of all units at all levels actually in the language, hence should be able to devise a writing system that operates on any one of these levels (Pulgram, 1976, p. 16).

Semitic consonantal script

Returning for a moment to the Semitic consonantal scripts, let us take up some observations made by Barr (1976). He notes that in scripts such as Arabic and Hebrew, vowel markers were added at a late stage, and their accidental status is attested by the fact that even then their use was optional and they were added apart from (above or below) the line of text. Marking of vowels was achieved by the use of a subset of the consonant signs, mainly *h*, *w*, *y*, and *aleph*. When so used, these signs carried a different sense from that of their normal consonantal role. In old Hebrew this script with vowel marking was known as *scriptio plena* and was the script used in Biblical texts. The vowel markings were called *matres lectionis*.

As noted in the discussion of Japanese, the development of a script is influenced by the phonological structure of the spoken language. So it was with the Semitic languages, because the reading of the three bands of scripts (diacritic markers above and below the consonantal skeleton) was facilitated by their simple CV syllabic structure. Generally the syllable consisted of a simple consonant followed by a single vowel. This must have made it easier for the reader to move systematically between the bands of script.

Because of the property of Semitic languages that internal vowel changes are used to indicate different syntactic forms of a base-word, vowel marking often has the function of specifying syntax as much as pronunciation. Thus the unpointed (i.e. lacking vowel marking) Hebrew *'klb* can be translated "she ate", "to eat", "eating" or "I shall eat" (Barr, 1976). It follows that we might equally well mark the consonant skeleton of a word according to grammatical category in order to disambiguate it, and this, Barr tells us, is exactly what the Syriac language does. This mediation of the pronunciation by a prior stage of grammatical decision-making should not, on reflection, seem odd to the reader of English, since much the same process occurs in the assignment of stress to English words (Smith and Baker, 1976). Thus we have the noun *ém-ber*, but the verb *em-béd*. In this case, the final letter alone adjudicates the lexical identity and syntactic class of the word, and this in turn provides the information about which syllable to stress.

An interesting observation made by Barr (1976) is that it is not possible to generate readable pseudowords in unpointed script. Unpointed text can only be read out in circumstances where it is possible to come to a lexical interpretation of the text: the lexical decision brings with it the specification of phonetic form. This leads Barr to speculate whether pointed and unpointed text might be read according to quite different procedures and to question whether these possibilities set Semitic languages apart from a language such as English.

In Table 3 we can see diagrammed the procedures which Barr considers might characterize the reading of semitic consonantal script with a parallel

Table 3 Possible procedures for reading Semitic, depending on whether vowels are pointed, and English, depending on whether grapheme–phoneme correspondences are "regular"[a]

ENGLISH REGULAR WORDS ⟨FEAR⟩→ "feeyr" SEMITIC POINTED TEXT ⟨d*b*r⟩ → "deber"	Script ⟶	Full phonemic interpretation	⟶	lexical interpretation
ENGLISH "IRREGULAR" WORDS ⟨PEAR⟩ → "peeyr"? SEMITIC UNPOINTED TEXT ⟨dbr⟩ → "?"	Script ⟶	lexical interpretation	⟶	full phonemic interpretation

[a] Following a common, though unsatisfactory, practice a correspondence is defined as "regular" if it is the most frequently encountered translation of the grapheme. See text for a disclaimer of any psychological imputation in this diagram. The Semitic script is, of course, simulated.

description for English. This does no more than illustrate how a script as superficially dissimilar as that of English might involve, at a gross level of analysis, similar strategic decisions. However, it must be stressed that in diagramming some logical possibilities that arise out of the nature of various scripts we are not "doing" psychology. We have already observed that English *might* be read logographically. In the context of Table 3 we can contemplate this possibility for Semitic and English script by considering that only the *lexical interpretation → phonemic interpretation* ordering might be used, even when the nature of the script (pointed or regular) permits the alternative ordering. Contrariwise, something like the reverse ordering of mental operations could serve as the invariable procedure if it were modified so as to be adaptive. For example, a partial phonemic description of an unpointed consonantal text might be derived and used to search a mental dictionary until an "appropriate" lexical entry was located. Similarly, for English a stack of the legally possible phonemic interpretations might be assembled and then tried out in order of diminishing "regularity". Intuitively, this might seem an implausibly clumsy procedure, but the point is that no amount of contemplation of the script alone, even in conjunction with our intuitions about efficiency, will constitute a psychological examination of the theory.

The Greek alphabet

Our discussion of Semitic script serves to illustrate the fact that the invention of the fully alphabetic writing by the Greeks is unprecedented only in so far as it involves a complete and systematic rendition of vowels; this in turn, however, seems to have led to a new awareness of the hierarchy of phonological constituents of language.

Curiously, the Phoenician script from which the Greek seems to be derived was a purely consonantal one, so the Greeks may have been faced with the problem of developing their systematic vowel representation from nothing. However, even the theory of Phoenician origin is circumstantial in its evidence: it is quite possible that although the names of the letters are Phoenician, the principle of vowel marking was acquired from some other Semitic source and adapted by the Greeks to suit the phonology of their language and the set of letter signs at their disposal.

Whatever its inspiration, this development seems to have taken place some time between the seventh and ninth centuries B.C. As Gelb remarks in closing his review of the evolution of scripts: "In the last twenty-five hundred years use of alphabetic script has pervaded the whole of civilisation, worldwide, but during all this period no significant further reforms have taken place in the principles of writing." Although this assertion is broadly true, as we shall see when we examine phonographic translation in English, there are tendencies in modern English for the written forms to deviate from direct reference to sound in order to reflect the etymological history of the language. However, it would be more reasonable to describe this as a property of English spelling rather than as a revision of the alphabetic principle of the script as a whole. In large measure this property of English was due to the fact that English spelling was the product of deliberate planning (consequent on the invention of printing), and this sets it apart from the more usual products of cultural evolution.

Chapter 2

Speech

In this chapter we shall consider the structure of spoken language both from a linguistic (phonology) and a psychological (speech perception) point of view. With regard to the problems of speech perception, it will be necessary to review in summary form a difficult and frequently technical literature. However, we cannot usefully consider the correspondences between written and spoken language without first examining the speech signal in some detail. The substantial differences between the way in which information is carried in speech and in print make this task at once difficult and crucial. At the heart of this difficulty are a variety of expository problems. It is probable that many individuals without prior training can form helpful intuitions about the features involved in the recognition of letters. Indeed, students of visual perception have only recently begun to consider alternatives to the definition of letters in terms of fragments of lines, curves, and angles. Furthermore, we can readily point to these features in the course of explanation and manipulate them for the purpose of experimentation. The same is not true of the sounds that carry speech information. Again, in non-technical fashion we can isolate and comprehend units of written language such as the letter and word, whereas the levels of analysis in spoken language are not so transparent. Moreover, units such as the acoustic feature, the phone, the phoneme and the syllable involve us in disconcerting shifts between definitions founded in physics, in linguistics, and in psychology. In our discussion of writing systems we referred to views such as Gelb's that scripts could be ordered on a phonographic continuum according to the size of the phonological unit represented by each graphic unit. These units were the word (word-syllabic), the syllable (syllabary) and the phoneme (alphabet). In Pulgram's taxonomy this range is extended downwards through the phone (phonetic transcription) to the acoustic feature (spectrography). We can no longer leave the definition of these units to intuition. More especially, we cannot begin to consider the psychological problems involved in translating between spoken and written language until we have examined, at least in outline, the process of speech perception, the functional units in speech, and our awareness of these constituents.

Accordingly, in this chapter we turn our attention first to fundamental problems in the perceptual analysis of speech. These include the perceptual categorization of speech sounds, the attempt to find isolatable segments of sound that correspond to these perceptual categories, and the search for invariant features to serve the identification of these segments. This leads to a consideration of the various units of analysis into which speech may be classified. Finally, we consider a collection of issues that bear upon the "efficiency" of some of these units from a phonographic point of view. This includes the number of units required to form a representation at a given level and the availability of the units to psychological awareness.

2.1 SPEECH RECOGNITION

The translation problem

We can consider the problem of getting from the messy and continuous physical stream of sound to the perceptual categories that mediate successfully identified speech as a problem in translation. Generally our first inclination in dealing with such a translation problem is to attempt the following procedure. Given that the problem is to get from an unknown language (the acoustic signal) to a fixed set of perceptual categories (speech sounds of English), we should: (*i*) identify the elementary speech sounds of English, (*ii*) identify the segments, or units, of the acoustic signal that correspond to these perceptual categories of speech, and (*iii*) identify the invariant features of each acoustic segment that define it, in terms of its correspondence with a specific category of speech sound. The formulation of this simple procedure is helpful in an unexpected way: the examination of the difficulty or even the impossibility of attaining the objective stated in each of these stages turns out to be a good way of summarizing the problem itself.

Consider first the simplest stage, that of identifying the speech sounds of English. Here we encounter two questions. Into what size of speech unit shall we attempt to translate our raw sounds? (The word? The syllable? Something more elementary?) From what perspective shall we define this unit? (Linguistics? Perceptual psychology? Physics?)

Throughout most of the 1950s and 60s is was tacitly assumed that the answer to these questions was a unit intermediate between syllable and acoustic feature in size and linguistic in definition, the *phoneme*. This was the view taken by the most influential school of thought, that prevailing at the Haskins Laboratory (see, for example, Liberman, *et al.*, 1967). Later we shall be introduced to a formidable definition of the phoneme. For the moment it suffices to consider the phoneme as *an abstract unit of spoken language something like a letter*.

This decision to try to explain speech recognition in terms of the mapping of the acoustic signal into phonemes led to the rejection of the entire procedure set out above. Once step (*i*) had yielded a decision to treat the phoneme as the elementary unit of speech perception then the outcome of stage (*ii*) was a failure to discover any rules that would reliably segment the continuous acoustical signal, on the time dimension, into discrete physical units that could be translated on a one-for-one basis into phonemic categories. Furthermore, even if we postponed this search for a segmentation rule, the object of stage (*iii*) appeared to be unrealizable, in so far as it had not proved possible to specify a fixed set of acoustical features that would uniquely define a phoneme in physical terms. Liberman *et al.* (1967) begin their classic discussion of these problems with the rejection of what I have called stages (*ii*) and (*iii*). Thus, having stated their intention to study the problem with respect to the translation of sound into phonemes (stage (*i*)) they go on to say:

> The acoustic cues for successive phonemes are intermixed in the sound stream to such an extent that definable segments of sound do not correspond to segments at the phoneme level. Moreover, the same phoneme is most commonly represented in different phonemic environments by sounds that are vastly different. There is, in short, a marked lack of correspondence between sound and perceived phoneme. This is a central fact of speech perception (Liberman *et al.*, 1967, p. 431).

It is worth noting in this context that Liberman *et al.* describe the translation procedure that we are discussing as "alphabetic", that is, they take the correspondence of alphabetic script with speech as a paradigm of unit-by-unit translation. We shall savour the irony of that choice of analogy in Chapter 4, when we discuss the structure of English orthography.

What is the source of the difficulty of translating sound into perceptual categories? The basis of the problem is to be found in the process of articulation, for speaking is about the swiftest and most intricate gymnastic activity of which most of us are capable. The acoustical patterns of speech are generated by a complex repertoire of articulatory movements ("gestures"), most of which are automatically controlled, but of which we can be made aware by training. In highly simplified terms, expiration of air from the lungs provides a source of energy which can be given acoustical form by the vibration of the vocal cords through which the air passes and by the resonant cavities of the throat, mouth and nose through which the air then passes. Vibration of the vocal cords yields a quality called "voicing", which can be understood in the contrast of /b/ and /p/. In both, the resonant cavities are similar in shape but /b/, which is voiced, has a low, grunting quality that can be felt as a vibration in the base of the throat.

The most spectacular array of speech gestures, however, consists in the ways in which we continually alter the shape of the resonant cavities. Much of this work is done by the tongue, supplemented by the lower lip. For example, /p/ is produced by sealing the cavity at the two lips and then opening them to release the air explosively. An explosive release of the tip of the tongue from the front of the palate produces /t/. An explosion further back produces /k/, this time using the rolled back of the tongue as an air-dam.

Further sorts of gestures produce further types of sound. In the fricatives, air is forced through a narrow gap such as that between the upper teeth and tip of the tongue, as in /th/, or the upper teeth and the lower lip, as in /f/. In the nasals the oral cavity is dammed and the air diverted through the nose, as in /ng/.

We must now consider the rate at which the normal speaker can produce these delicate and controlled vibrations, explosions and diversions of the air column. If we were to regard the process of articulation as involving one of these "actions" for each phoneme, we would have to admit to a maximum rate of such acts of about 12–15 per second. This rate is so high that it has led one noted theorist of communication to reject the phoneme as a basis for the *perception* of speech, since such a small, elementary unit would require an implausibly high rate of identification decisions (Miller, 1962). (In fact we can recognize artificially compressed speech at rates up to about 30 phonemes per second.) A crucial consequence of the rate of articulatory events and their continuity is that the individual actions become incomplete, and as the flow of action moves from one event to the next, successive events exercise an influence each on the other. When we say "do", the oral cavity is already taking up the position for the vowel before we utter the initial consonant. (Freeze on the point of saying "do" and again on the point of saying "die". Notice the different mouth shape through which the /d/ was to be expelled.) In this phenomenon, known as *coarticulation*, what is happening is that the tongue and lips are failing to get to their *target* destination, which would result in the ideal, context-free sound, or the consonantal explosion of air is resonating in an oral cavity of which the shape is determined by the requirements of the vowel that follows. Where the articulators actually succeed in getting to depends upon where they have been for the last sound. We can now see why the sequence /st/ is relatively easy. The tongue has a short journey from the half-closure behind the teeth, producing the /s/, to the explosion created by flicking the tip up against the roof behind the teeth. (Compare the feeling of saying /st/ and attempting /sg/.)

The result of all these compromises in the pursuit of the sequence of articulatory targets is rather like a "rolling average" graph, in which the position of each point is constrained by the value of its predecessor. This in turn means that the particular acoustic signal produced by a given gesture will vary in quite major ways as a function of the context of articulatory gestures from which it arises.

There is, I think, a helpful analogy to be made here with hand-writing (though I have never encountered this comparison in the speech perception literature). In cursive script often the physical form of a letter is dependent on its context. To take a very simple instance, the lead-in stroke in the letter *o* will vary when preceded by *t* and by *r* because of the different height of the terminating stroke of these letters. Thus, we write

 and 

This may seem a trivial example, but as writing speeds up, these context-dependent transformations magnify and proliferate.

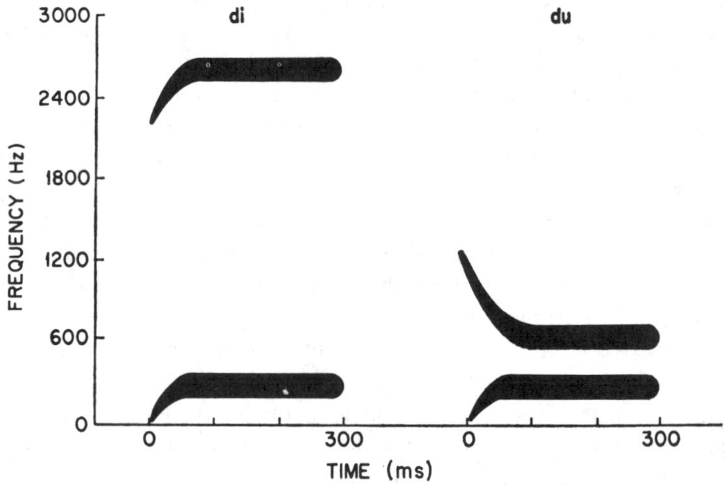

Fig. 5 Spectrographic patterns sufficient for the synthesis of /d/ before /i/ and /u/. Figure reprinted from Liberman *et al.*, 1967 with permission. The spectrograph displays bands of energy at particular frequencies over time. Actual speech results in similar but more complex spectrographic patterns. Abstract representations like that displayed above contain the minimum amount of information that requires to be programmed into a speech-synthesizing device to yield syllables that can be clearly identified by a listener.

In the same way, the context-dependent transformations in speech are exaggerated by the speed of production, but it is arguable that any speech that is naturally articulated, so as to be continuous, will manifest these contextual effects. Liberman *et al.* (1967) use a classic example (Fig. 5). Here are shown idealized spectrograms of the syllables /di/ and /du/. At the left of each pattern are the rising or falling *formant transitions* which contain information about the consonant. These turn into the steady-state horizontal bands of acoustic energy which correspond to the vowels. The striking feature of these spectrograms is the difference between the two acoustical patterns which yield the experience of /d/ in different phonemic contexts. When we contemplate the way in which the second (upper) formant transitions seem to be so grossly influenced by the frequency of the following vowel formant it is difficult to conceive how we could discover a *fixed set of physical characteristics that formed a necessary condition for the experience of /d/.*

Segmentation

Nor is it obvious, turning to the segmentation problem, how we are to decide where on the time axis the segment corresponding to /d/ stops and the vowel starts. In fact, there are two sorts of demonstration of the impossibility of such segmentation. The first is logical in nature and appeals to the aforementioned fact that the physical form of the pattern that renders /d/ is wholly dependent on the vowel pattern. The implication this carries for the attempt at segmentation can be brought out more strongly by stating that every portion of the second formant transition is carrying indivisible information about *both* the consonant and the vowel. The second demonstration is experimental and involves the actual attempt to cut the signal at various points along the time axis and to play back the resulting parts separately. There is no point at which we can cut to produce a pure, vowelless /d/. As we cut into the second formant transition, first no perceptual change occurs, and then beyond a critical point the experience of any speech-like sound is suddenly lost and we are left with a glissando. As Liberman *et al.* (1967) note about Fig. 5, this glissando reveals the physical differences underlying the common experience of /d/ arising from the two syllables, for once we have lost the categorical perception of /d/, we are left with clearly distinct glissandos. The /di/ pattern produces a rising, and the /du/ a falling whistle.

The attempt at physical segmentation that we have just considered serves to make an ancillary point. It reveals the tendency for continuous changes of physical parameters of the acoustic signal to be correlated with categorical changes in perceptual experience. As we gradually change a parameter, first nothing changes perceptibly, then there is a critical shift to a categorically different perceptual experience. This can be a shift from one perceived speech sound to another or from speech sound to a nonspeech noise.

My primary purpose at this stage has been to illustrate the translation problem by treating it in the context of the classical Haskins-group formulation. This, as we saw, defined the problem in terms of translation into phonemic categories. What we have seen is that units smaller than the syllable do not appear to be marked by physically definable boundaries. Furthermore, for units like the phoneme, the segmentation problem cannot be considered apart from the problem of specifying their defining features in the acoustic signal; even if we could reliably isolate phonemic segments along a time scale, their physical constituents would grossly change according to the context of other segments.

There are two ways of coming to terms with this difficulty. One is to abandon the pursuit of temporally defined segments as a preliminary to translation of the sound stream. This is the approach taken by Liberman *et al.* (1967), who assumed instead that phonemic information is encoded *in parallel* in the sound stream but that it is *recovered* by using the production rules in reverse. That is, because the encoding of phonemes in parallel is determined by the limitations of the process of articulation and because these articulations were the result of our phonemic "intentions", so to speak, we can recover the ideal phonemic identities by running the process backwards. The listener can simulate the translation of a set of phonemic intentions into articulatory responses in order to test whether these would result in a sound pattern that matches the unknown, in-coming acoustic signal. This very difficult idea treats segmentation, if at all, at the level of these simulated articulatory acts rather than at the acoustic level.

An alternative approach retains the notion of temporally defined segments but locates the search for these at a higher level than the phoneme. Thus Massaro (1975b), for instance, takes the syllable as the elementary unit of identification. This is the level at which he supposes the acoustical pattern to be translated into the speech-sound categories that are listed in long-term memory. Massaro is motivated in his choice of unit by a variety of reasons, the principal of which concern the availability of an invariant set of defining features, but an important part of his argument is that the syllable presents less of a segmentation problem than the phoneme. Simple syllables tend to be bounded by silent or steady-state periods. Of course, syllabically based theories concede that we can become aware of phonemes, or at least, phonemic contrasts. What they deny is that the segmentation or identification of phonemes constitutes a preliminary stage in the perceptual analysis of speech. Just because a unit is composed of smaller units does not mean that it has to be introduced at a later stage of perceptual analysis. As we shall see, a superficially similar debate exists in the realm of written language. It has often been asserted that the letters of a word are "perceived" by decomposition of the word, which is first identified as a whole. As with the case of speech, such an ordering of processes is entirely logically possible.

Invariant defining features

We have already touched upon the difficulty of finding a fixed set of acoustic features that will define an acoustical pattern in the sense that it allows it to be assigned uniquely to a phonemic category. We saw that at the phonemic level this problem was inseparable from the problem of segmentation.

Some psychologists have not abandoned hope of specifying invariant features in the acoustic signal. The speech categories for which this problem has generally been assumed to be most intractable consist of the stop consonants. The difficulty has been located, in particular, with those stop consonants that are distinguished by their *place of articulation*. *Place* refers here to the point in the oral cavity at which the air flow is blocked and released to produce the sound. Place of articulation has systematic effects upon the shape of the formant transition. But as we have seen with the example of /di/ and /du/ (Fig. 5) the formant shape is also determined by the following vowel.[3]

Neither bursts nor transitions can serve as invariant (context-free) features for the definition of phonemes. However, in so far as the effect on the consonant of the following vowel is systematic, there is hope of defining this consonant–vowel (CV) *conjunction* by means of a set of invariant acoustic features. This would make the CV (or simple syllable) into an elementary "perceptual unit"—to use a much abused term. We can form a sort of visual analogy to this by considering the possibility that the letter bigram KA could be recognized by means of the unique conjunction of contours </ at the boundary between K and A. (In fact this has been considered as a mechanism serving visual word recognition, although a little reflection reveals that it provides a very limited and unstable set of features.) At the price of complicating the notion of an acoustic feature, there is some prospect of arriving at a system of fixed correspondences between the acoustic and *syllabic* levels. What, then, are the objections to such a solution of the translation problem? There are two principal objections, but neither is totally persuasive.

The first objection to the syllable as the elementary unit of perceptual matching is that "no theory can safely ignore the fact that phonemes are psychologically real" (Liberman *et al.*, 1967). This objection lacks force for several reasons. First (as we shall see in the following section) the phoneme is by definition a linguistic abstraction, and moreover it turns out to be difficult to find an independent test of its "psychological reality". Secondly, a theory which asserts that the syllable is the unit against which the sound stream is compared does not thereby deprive smaller units of perceptual reality. We might still be able to *attend to* the smaller unit even if it were derived from the syllabic unit by further analysis. To deny this is to confuse the order of encoding information with its availability for subsequent recovery in awareness.

The second objection to the syllable is on grounds of parsimony. There are about forty phonemes in English but over a thousand syllables. In this, English is exceptionally luxuriant, largely owing to the occurrence of a great number of permissible consonant clusters within the syllable. Syllabically "regular" languages, like Japanese, may have only 40–60 syllables. Arguments from the principle of parsimony do not, however, have a happy history in psychology.

A radical alternative to the search for invariant features which are acoustically defined has been advanced by Liberman *et al.* (1967) and centres round the assertion that the invariant features in speech are to be found at the level of speech production. This view, alluded to above in the context of *segmentation*, holds that the listener matches the acoustic input to categories stored in permanent memory by attempting to produce what he hears and comparing the outcome of that production with the unknown input. The reason can be seen by returning to Fig. 5. It is the physical difference between the acoustic features required for the perception of /d/ in /di/ and in /du/ which characterized the translation problem. What might be common to those two versions of /d/ is the *phonemic intention* that serves as the starting point for articulation, even though the actual results of these intentions are shaped by the particular itinerary taken by our articulatory organs. (This expresses a general truth of motor programming. For example, at a high level of the control of movement we might have the intention to jump forward one metre. What we actually do at a muscular level will depend on the precise disposition of our bodies at the moment of execution.)

It certainly seems that the most economical way of specifying a feature-set to describe speech is in terms of the articulatory gestures required (see, for example, Jakobson *et al.*, 1961). However, there is a considerable leap from the demonstration that our articulatory intentions can be classified in this way to the explanation of how this information can be brought to bear on the analysis of the sounds that reach the ear. Such a "motor" theory of speech perception has encountered increasingly damaging criticism in recent years. It is unclear whether the concept of translation of the acoustic steam into phonemic categories can outlive the motor theory.

Levels of speech processing and their accessibility

Perception of speech sounds is often said to be categorical. Consider the sounds /b/ and /d/. Why do we find it so difficult to imagine an intermediate sound between these two? We cannot produce possible compromise sounds in real speech but we can synthesize speech that varies along the physical dimension by which the two spectrographic patterns differ. When we play such synthesized compromises to a listener we find only the perception of an unambiguous /b/ or /d/, the one categorical percept changing suddenly to the other at the midpoint of the physical dimension. In fact speech perception can be said to be categorical both in the weak sense that we map continuous acoustical variables into an exhaustive and non-overlapping set of perceptual categories and in the stronger sense that our ability to discriminate physical differences is poor within and good between these subjective categories. Moreover, these perceptual categories appear to be present at birth (see, for example, Eimas, 1975; for a readable general account of categorical auditory perception, see Cutting, 1977).

Two questions arise from the demonstration of categorical speech perception. The first concerns the fate of the precategorical acoustic information. The second concerns the correspondence of the perceptual categories with the various units of speech, such as the phoneme or the syllable.

Is the acoustical information which distinguishes between patterns that fall within a speech category discarded in the act of categorization? That is, when we move from one level of processing to the next, is information at the previous level irretrievably *transformed*? Several strands of evidence suggest that it is not. Barclay (1972) and Pisoni and Lazarus (1974) have shown that acoustic variations within a speech category are discriminable even in stop consonants, when the task is simple enough and a suitable discrimination criterion is induced. This suggests that raw acoustic information remains available to the listener and the main problem is in attending to this level of information. Interestingly enough, the subject in these tests often has to be persuaded to attempt a discrimination which he believes to be impossible.[4]

Can these perceptual categories be identified as speech units of a particular size? In particular, do they invest the phoneme with the psychological reality claimed for it by Liberman *et al.* (1967)? The short answer to this question seems to me to be "no". Nothing in these experiments favours the phoneme over the syllable as the basis of categorization. The matter is expressed succinctly by Paap (1975, p. 178):

> Since the studies of consonant discrimination are actually asking whether consonant–vowel clusters are perceived categorically or continuously, we agree that the results imply nothing about the units of which those syllables may be composed.

Perhaps the most direct test of the correspondence of the perceptual categories with linguistic units was that of Ades (1974), who used a procedure known as *selective adaptation* in which a sound is repeated again and again until sensitivity to this particular sound is diminished. Ades found that adaptation of a given CV syllable transferred slightly but imperfectly to a syllable commencing with the same consonant followed by a different vowel. This might be thought to offer limited support for the notion that the consonant phoneme was what had been adapted. However, there was no transfer at all to the VC inversion of the original syllable. This is as if adaptation of "day" transfers slightly to "die" but not at all to "aid". If the perceptual category adapted had been truly phonemic, it would not have been affected by the position of the phoneme within the syllable. An alternative conclusion might be that the effective category in adaptation is syllabic and that the probability of transferring adaptation to another syllable decreases along with decreases in the overall similarity of the two syllables, but even this linguistic interpretation is threatened by Cutting's demonstration that similar adaptation effects obtain for musical sounds (Cutting, 1977).

Another attack on the "perceptual reality" of the phoneme occurs in a much-discussed recent literature on the reaction-time to syllable and phoneme targets embedded in continuous speech. This literature began with Savin and Bever's

(1970) report that syllable targets could be detected more rapidly than phoneme targets and that therefore phonemes must be perceived by the analysis of syllables. This claim was quickly echoed by Warren (1971). This argument is totally invalid, because it depends upon the untenable assumption that the order of encoding in perception must be directly reflected in the speed of subsequent conscious recovery of the various levels of information. If we could search a picture faster for *books* than for *blue rectangles*, would this entail the conclusion that perceptual analysis first dealt with real world entities and then proceeded to an analysis of their colour and shape? Cast in this general form, we can see how absurd the argument is. In the case of phonemes and syllables subsequent authors showed the inconsistencies to which the order-of-perception argument led (Foss and Swinney, 1973; McNeill and Lindig, 1973). Elsewhere (Henderson, 1980a) I have criticized similarly constructed arguments about the order in which letter and word information is first encoded.

The question of the relative priority of phonemes and syllables in speech perception probably first interested theorists as a question about the ordering of the preliminary stages on the route to word recognition because of the central position occupied by questions about the *architecture* of the pattern-recognition system. From this point of view the discovery that some of the evidence from phoneme-monitoring tasks merely showed that syllables were more readily attended to than phonemes—that whatever the layout of the encoding stages, the syllabic level of analysis was subsequently more accessible to conscious inspection—might seem to rob these phenomena of any major theoretical interest. Such a dismissal would be ill-founded, however. It is by no means clear whether structural questions about the information processing system represent the most promising contemporary line of enquiry. Furthermore, if syllables turn out to be more readily attended to than phonemes, this might have other important implications, such as for the translation of print to sound in reading. This last point is well made by Savin (1972), who argues:

> What is important for the teaching of reading, however, is not whether phonemes play any part at all in speech perception, but whether they play any conscious (or potentially conscious) part—whether, that is to say, the child can be aware of enough of them to make any sense of the things his teacher tells him about the sounds of the letters (Savin, 1972, p. 323).

One thing that emerges from research on the levels of processing in speech perception is the utility of distinguishing between a *prelexical* speech code, which functions as a preliminary to word identification, and a *postlexical* speech code, which holds abstract information about a word's sound that becomes available once a word's entry in the mental lexicon has been located and scrutinized. Some authors have termed the prelexical code a *phonetic* representation and the postlexical code a *phonological* representation (Foss and Blank, 1980).

The prelexical code used to address the lexicon probably consists of a pragmatic mixture of various levels of code, containing some syllabic and some featural information. What seems generally agreed is that the prelexical code typically consists of a very incomplete specification of a word's sound. This information has to be supplemented by various sorts of contextual information in order to maximize the likelihood of correct lexical identification. It is worth noting that the currently most successful simulation of speech identification operates on a blend of "bottom-up" phonetic information and "top-down" contextual information in which the phonetic code is fairly crude and impoverished (Reddy and Newell, 1975).

Foss and Blank (1980) have persuasively argued that performance on most speech processing tasks (e.g. phoneme monitoring, shadowing and mispronunciation detection) calls upon a mixture of prelexical and postlexical codes, the ratio depending on circumstances. For example, background noise or powerful contextual information both favour the postlexical code.

What is remarkable about this literature is its close analogy with issues in the study of visual word processing. Here, too, we find attempts to identify the priority of such units as letters and letter clusters by means of search tasks (Chapter 8), we find use made of the distinction between prelexical and postlexical sound codes (Chapter 11), and we find emphasis on the distinction between tacit and explicit knowledge of a level of analysis (Chapter 10). However, a curious and disappointing feature of this parallelism is the lack of cross-reference between the literatures on speech and print. On the other hand, where contact is made, as in Neisser's (1967) wholesale importation of the notion of analysis-by-synthesis into the visual domain, the analogy has not been tempered by sufficient consideration of the possible differences between the auditory and the visual signal.

2.2 UNITS OF ANALYSIS IN SPOKEN LANGUAGE

In the preceding section we examined the problem of translating between the acoustic signal and the categories of perceived speech. This involved mention of speech units that might be functional in segmenting the acoustic stream and defining its correspondences with the content of speech. However, it was possible to rely on very sloppy, intuitive definitions of such units as the phoneme and syllable. We must turn now to a rather more formal definition of the various units of analysis in spoken language. This will not only serve to clarify certain additional difficulties inherent in the phoneme from the point of view of speech perception, it will also equip us with concepts necessary to consider other levels of translation that involve spoken language: the translation between speech and meaning and between speech and script.

Words and phrases

Although from the reader's point of view there may seem to be nothing mysterious about the isolation or definition of words as linguistic units, this has not always been true. Most alphabetic scripts designate word boundaries by the use of a space, which might be considered as a blank letter, but early versions of alphabetic script may not have used word spacing. Syllabaries often used a special sign for word boundaries, such as the vertical division line of the Phaistos disk found in Crete (Gelb, 1963, fig. 83) or the small symbol employed in Ugaritic cuneiform (Gelb, fig. 68). Similarly it has been suggested that the auxiliary, semantic classifying markers that often accompany logographic script serve the incidental purpose of indicating word boundaries.

By way of contrast, in speech there is generally no systematic marking of word boundaries. We owe to the spectrogram the discovery that the segmentation of the speech stream into words is a perceptual achievement rather than a physical fact. In the present state of our knowledge, caution dictates the assumption that there exists no wholly reliable phonetic feature to signal word boundaries. The definition of a word in the context of the speech stream is therefore a problem in phonology, considered as the study of the formal relationship between sound and meaning. It is also an independent problem for psychology from at least two points of view: empirically, we are concerned with the extent to which speech can be segmented into words, including, notably, the development of this ability by the child; theoretically, we are concerned to understand the means by which this segmentation is accomplished.

The phonological problem is illustrated by the highly technical discussion of what constitutes a "word" to be found in Chomsky and Halle's monumental *The Sound Pattern of English* (1968, pp. 366–371). Chomsky and Halle specifically eschew the assumption that word boundaries are systematically indicated by phonetic effects; in their model, words are segmented by a complex process of syntactic analysis. One property of this analysis is that the "words" it yields sometimes consist of phrases in which a preposition and/or article are compounded with a following noun. This, the authors note, follows the orthographic convention of Semitic scripts.

Interestingly enough, empirical investigations of the segmentation abilities of very young children also find a tendency to group function words along with associated content words (Holden and MacGinitie, 1972). However, such studies rely on verbal questioning of the child, and it is far from clear how the explicit definitional knowledge that they call for relates to *implicit* phonological competence.

Models of the psychological processes underlying word segmentation sometimes assume that primary segmentation is into syllables and that these syllabic segments are organized into word units by semantic and syntactic analysis using contextual constraints and also gross physical features of the speech stream (e.g. Massaro, 1975a).

Curiously, although the speech stream lacks any obvious, systematic physical marking of word boundaries, it does contain highly important acoustic indications of higher level segments. In particular, intonation and stress carry information about syntactic boundaries and also some content information, such as the rising and falling intonation contours of interrogatives and commands, respectively. We may therefore summarize this state of affairs with the assertion that spoken language marks phrase information in rich but complex ways but often leaves word boundaries without acoustical markers. The isolation of word segments has to be achieved both by building up from syllabic segments and by decomposition of phrases. On the other hand, most written languages mark word boundaries clearly but do not mark syllabic boundaries at all, and contain impoverished marking (by means of punctuation, for example) of syntactic units larger than the word. Given that it is often an unquestioned assumption that alphabetic writing is the ultimate refinement in the representation of spoken language, it is salutary to consider whether a syllabary, accompanied by auxiliary syntactic and semantic markers, might not provide a better reflection of speech. (Of course this begs the question of whether the most efficient form for script is one that mimics speech.) Furthermore, this line of speculation is given an ironic twist by one psychological theory of visual word recognition which holds that alphabetic information is composed into syllabic groups at an early stage of perceptual analysis. (We shall discuss this theory of Spoehr and Smith in some detail later.)

The acoustical cues to syntactic boundaries in speech include intensity changes, frequency changes (the contour of the voice's fundamental frequency) and *disjuncture* (the temporal interval between vowel centres). The role of these cues in assisting the syntactic analysis of such extraordinary sentences as "The good flies quickly by" has been reviewed by Scholes (1971) and by Freund (1975).

In addition to these cues, in English there is a characteristic pattern of stress at the syllabic level. The temporal structure formed by the sequence of stressed and unstressed syllables creates a higher-order pattern, known as "prosody". Prosodic pattern in speech is highly recognizable even when word intelligibility is low (Freund, 1975), and recent research on response preparation in speaking has suggested that the stress pattern may be represented at a high level of motor programming (Sternberg *et al.*, 1978). Such phrase prosody is probably an important source of information about word boundaries.

Syllables and morphemes

The syllable is a strange creature, the workhorse of psychological studies of speech perception yet neglected or disowned by linguists. Syllables belong to the interesting category of "fuzzy sets". The existence of syllables is not doubted; they can be readily defined ostensively; they can even be counted without dispute. However, dictionaries disagree about the location of syllabic boundaries within a word, phonologists often seem to attempt to phrase their discussions of structural units without explicit mention of syllables (see Anderson, 1974, chapter 14 for a discussion), and no clearly agreed definition of the concept of a syllable exists.

What does seem to be agreed is that syllables are built round vowel nuclei. The vowel may exist on its own or, in English, may be preceded, followed or surrounded by consonants, either singly or in clusters. The most prevalent attempts to define the concept of a syllable have been, broadly speaking, psychological and have focused on articulation (an individual chest pulse) or on speech perception (the smallest invariant or context-free feature).

The ambiguity of syllabic boundaries is not as marked in all languages as it is in English. In languages such as Japanese the syllabic structure is simple and determinate, consisting of a V or CV unit (sometimes known as the a-ta syllabaries). In our discussion of speech recognition we noted that such "simple syllables" are readily segmented in the acoustic stream. Syllabic script, which by its very nature has visually defined syllable boundaries, is most commonly encountered in such languages. Other scripts, while being basically alphabetic, represent syllabic boundaries. French (1976) calls these latter scripts *syllable-delimiting* in contrast to *syllable-representing* (they include Tibetan and modern Korean). Despite the extraordinary claim by Lindsay and Norman (1977, p. 270) that the syllable and the letter constitute the elementary units of printed English, no explicit marking of syllabic boundaries exists in our writing.

Psychological studies of speech perception usually assign a fundamental role to the syllable. A particularly strong assumption is made by Massaro (1975b), who asserts that the syllable is the basic unit in speech perception. Thus Massaro supposes that the syllable is the output of the first stage of speech recognition and that this syllabic code is the one used to search the lexicon in order to identify words.

In contrast to the syllable, the morpheme is a unit of meaning rather than sound. Yet morphemic structure has implications for orthography. This can easily be illustrated through the different pronunciation of the letters *ph* in *morpheme* and in *shepherd*. Stated simply, the sounding of *ph* in *shepherd* is anomalous because, while *ph* is usually treated as a digraph corresponding to a single phoneme, in *shepherd* the adjacency of *p* and *h* is accidental. In this case it is not a digraph but rather the consequence of the conjunction of two independent morphemes, one ending in *p* and the next commencing with *h*. English orthography is at pains to conserve morphological information, and so the conjunction of *p* and *h* at the morphemic boundary does not provide grounds for changing their sounding. The morphology-conserving rule overrides the generalization that *ph* be sounded as /f/.

This is but a single example of a widespread pattern of morphemic influence upon phonology. What, then, is a morpheme? Conventionally it is defined as the smallest unit of meaning in a language. Thus *telephones* is held to consist of three morphemes, *tele* meaning "at a distance", *phone* meaning "sound" and *s* meaning "more than one". So far, morphology might seem to be the study of etymology, an enquiry into the history of a word. However, it is more than this.

Morphemes may be 'free" if they have meaning by themselves. Otherwise they are said to be "bound", as in the plural suffix *s*. In addition, there are two systems of morphology. "Inflectional" morphology varies greatly across languages. In English it is extremely simple, involving the use of the affixes *-s*, *-es*, *'s*, *-ed* and *-ing* to indicate plurality, third person singular verbs, the possessive form and verb tense. The amount of inflection in English is intermediate between that of highly inflected languages like Latin, with its declensions and conjugations, and uninflected languages like Chinese, which, as we have seen, are largely monomorphemic. Grumach (1976) has suggested that languages which are agglutinative (that is, express more complex meanings by stringing together basic words) can get by quite well with logographic scripts, whereas inflective languages tend to require phonographic representation to render their affixed bound morphemes.

The inflectional morphemes in English do not add appreciably to the complexity of English phonology, but the same is not true of the system of "derivational" morphology. Derivational morphology, simply described, is the process whereby affixes are added to a word to yield different grammatical forms. This is an illustration of the fact that morphemes are the minimal units upon which the grammar of a language operates. Thus we have *phóto-graph*, *photó-graph-er*, *photo-gráph-ic*. As this example shows, the process of arriving at derived forms by the use of affixes is not, from a phonological point of view, simply additive. Instead there is a systematic change in the pattern of stress within the word as it is transformed. These systematic changes in the sounding of morphemes as a function of their morphological environment within a word have received considerable attention from phonologists (e.g. Chomsky and Halle, 1968). The study of these transformations is sometimes known as *morphophonemics*. Clearly these "readjustments" of the phonetic form taken by a given morpheme disturb the correspondences in the written language between script and sound. This consequence is of interest to students of orthography. As we shall see, it has led to the suggestion that English orthography does not represent sound directly but instead represents morphology. On this view the sound of a word is arrived at, once these abstract morphemic segments have been identified, by applying the morphophonemic rules. By no means all alphabet scripts are morphophonemic in reference, however: some, like Finnish, do not vary the sound of a morpheme. Therefore the script corresponds directly to both the phonology and the morphology of the language. On the other hand, Turkish phonology is like English in so far as the derived forms frequently change the sound of their constituent morphemes. Turkish orthography is unlike that of English in that the spelling changes with the sound so as to preserve a regular correspondence between the two. Obviously this has to be achieved at the expense of the correspondence between spelling and morphology. This state of affairs in Turkish orthography can be envisaged by considering the equivalent in English, which might consist of the spellings: *pho-ti-graph, phi-to-grapher*.

Phones and phonemes

We turn our attention now to those subsyllabic units which were frequently invoked in our discussion of speech recognition without ever being defined. We saw that at the level of the physical signal, researchers found it useful to deal with a spectrographic representation of the signal in which the complex waveform is analysed into its sine wave components and the presence of energy within each frequency band is recorded over time. This information can be transformed or manipulated by filtering out components of real speech or by artificially synthesizing a spectrogram which can be played back to yield perceived speech. As a result of such experimentation we can arrive at a proposed set of *acoustic features* which are sufficient to yield an experience which, observers agree, falls into a perceptual category of basic speech sound. The notion of an acoustic feature is the point of departure from the realm of physics in our journey towards the cognition of language. The acoustic feature is anchored in physical acoustics but bears a theoretical relationship to the psychology of perception. This relationship consists of the inferences of sufficient cause linking acoustic features to the categories of speech perception. These categories are called *phones*. The phone is essentially a perceptual rather than a linguistic concept.

At this point we must enter into a terminological disgression. This is a matter of some delicacy which involves us in picking our way through the confusing and inconsistent usage of the terms *phone* and *phoneme* as they occur in the literatures of psychology, phonology and orthography. In an attempt to be concise I shall expose myself to the risk of seeming dogmatic.

(*i*) We require a term for the basic perceptual categories involved in speech discrimination. I proposed to call these *phones*. This is consistent with the agreed definition of the phone as an elementary speech sound. What I have added to this definition is an implied procedure for determining phones by the ultimate use of psychological discrimination functions, and this anchors the phone in the realm of perception.

As a matter of history, which is incidental to this psychologically framed definition, it may be noted that the term originated in the intuitive attempts made by descriptive linguists (phoneticians) to classify all the *distinguishable* speech sounds of a language. This resulted in a transcription such as that of the International Phonetic Alphabet (IPA), which in a sense is a record of the perceptual experiences of phoneticians. (The full IPA in fact specifies, in addition to phones, larger and noncategorical features such as intonation and stress.)

(*ii*) We also require a term for the basic linguistic elements involved in the specification of meaning by speech. This is the *phoneme* and it is an abstract, linguistic entity. The phoneme is defined with respect to an abstract phonological level of analysis of language. This consists of a string of segments (the phonemes) which have the property that a change in the identity of one of these elementary segments is capable of changing the lexical significance of the string. This is usually explicated by reference to *minimal contrasts*. For example, "bad" is held to be describable in terms of three abstract phonemic entities /b/, /æ/ and /d/ each of which can be changes so as to yield a different word (e.g. "*c*ad", "*b*ed" and "ba*g*"). It must be stressed that these *minimal contrast* tests do not consist of auditory discrimination experiments. The phoneme is an abstract, linguistic fiction, and the tests are actually purely speculative "thought experiments" conducted on these abstract entities. We could say that phones are discovered but phonemes are invented.

(*iii*) *Phonemes* relate to *phones*, as linguistic entities to psychological entities, in the following way. Phonemes are represented in experience by specific perceptual tokens, the phones. A single phoneme may be represented by different phones, the particular phone depending on the phonetic context. This family of phones capable of representing a particular phoneme consists of similar sounds, called *allophones*. Let us take the example of the phoneme /t/ in English. This can be represented by one of four allophones, according to context. Thus, in "tip" the allophone [t′] is used, whereas in "pit" the same phoneme is represented by the allophone [t⁻]. At first these two phones may seem identical, putting at risk our definition of "phones" in terms of perceptual discriminability. But this is because their close family resemblance has been exaggerated by the linguistic requirement that we ignore a phonetic distinction that is literally "insignificant". Allophonic variation reflects only the convenience of articulation, determined by the context of articulatory gestures. However, it is possible to draw attention to the distinction between these allophones of /t/. In "tip" the [t′] has a breathy follow-up almost like saying "tih-hip". In contrast, the [t⁻] of "pit" is barely sounded at all (at least, in a normal stream of speech). The explosive release of air from behind the tongue is barely accomplished before the next sound in the stream ensues.

The distinction between phones and phonemes is frequently glossed over in the literature on speech perception, and the innocent reader in particular could often conclude that the phoneme was a perceptual category. The apparent correspondence between phonemes and letters adds to this misleading impression of tangibility on the part of the abstract phoneme. It is too easy to come to believe that a phoneme must be audible in the same sense that a letter is visible. In part, this illusion that the phoneme is actually perceptible may be a product of a desire to ignore the inconvenient complexities of the relationship between phone and phoneme. It would be understandable if the researcher on speech perception, having struggled with the problem of getting from the acoustic signal to perceived speech sounds (phones), were to wish to take for granted the next climb, from speech sound to meaning (via phonemes). But there is another accidental reason for the blurring of the distinction, arising from the fact that experiments on categorical perception of speech sounds *are typically designed to exclude allophonic variation.* Consider the example of /ba/, /da/ which we used in our discussion of categorical perception in the previous section. The consonant contrast is deliberately embedded in the same syllabic context, for obvious reasons of experimental control. Consequently, however, it is never necessary in these experiments to consider different allophones of the consonants, since such phonetic variations are caused by differences of syllabic context. Accordingly, the perceptual categories revealed in the discrimination experiments give a misleading impression of being of phonemic size.

So far the relationship between phonemes and phones might seem quite simple. It would be easy to jump to the conclusion that both kinds of unit belonged to different levels of the same taxonomic system, that in practice there was no force to the assertion that the two concepts belonged to different universes of discourse, the linguistic and the perceptual, that phones could be mapped into a smaller set of phonemic categories in which each similar set of phones (allophones) nested within a single phonemic category, and that translation in the opposite direction simply required a set of phonetic context rules (e.g., for /t/ use [t′] in word-initial positions). Such a simplifying set of assumptions, however, would be quite wrong. We can see why by using an example taken from a cogent discussion of the problem by Gleitman and Rozin (1977) and which holds true for most American speakers of English.

Consider the pair of morphologically related words GRATE, GRATER in contrast to the pair GRADE, GRADER. Focus, in particular, on the medial vowel and its following consonant, written AT and AD. Phonetically we can write these: [ăt⁻] in GRATE, [ăd̂] in GRATER, [ād⁻] in GRADE and [ād̂] in GRADER. The first thing to note is that each of these two-phone patterns is in some way distinct from the other. However, contrary to our intuitions and to our spelling system the consonant sound in GRATER and GRADER is not discriminably different in American English, thus we assign the same phone [d̂]. This differs slightly from the phone [d⁻] in GRADE in a lawful allophonic way, determined by the phonetic context (as in the /t/ of PIT and TIP). So, too, the slight variation in vowel length is the product of a phonetic-context rule that dictates a lengthening of the vowel preceding a voiced consonant (e.g. rĭp/rīb, săfe/sāve). Yet how can that work for GRATER/GRADER, which utilize the same stop consonant phone but preceded by a short and long vowel, respectively? The only reasonable answer is that the vowel-length convention is carried over from the morphologically simpler relatives GRATE/GRADE, where the consonants did differ on the voicing dimension.

We have now assembled enough evidence to see the structure of the dilemma facing us in arriving at a phonemic description. If we insist on trying to map phones directly into phonemes, using only phonetic context guidelines for deciding amongst allophones, we face one of the following consequences.

(*i*) We represent the phone [d̂] in GRATER and GRADER by one or other of the phonemes /t/ or /d/ as in GRATE or GRADE. Let us say /d/. The choice is arbitrary.

(*ii*) We create a third phoneme /?/ to represent the [d̂]. This is uneconomical and not warranted by the doctrine of minimal contrasts, i.e. /?/ could never be required to contrast with /t/ or /d/ to distinguish otherwise identical words.

(*iii*) If we adopt any solution such as (*i*) or (*ii*) which involves the same phonemic sign for the [d̂] in GRATER and GRADER, we would have to admit two different phonemic signs for the preceding vowel phones [ă] and [ā]. These *are* phonetically distinct (listen carefully!) and the burden of contrasting GRATER and GRADER would fall upon these vowel phonemes. But this proliferation would raise further problems like those in (*ii*).

(*iv*) We can give up trying to devise rules at the phonetic level for translation between phones and phonemes, conceding that these two conceptual systems do not exist in the same taxonomic space. Instead we can opt for a phonemic representation which is closely allied to the morphological level. Such a system would conserve the morphological relatedness of GRATE and GRATER by using the same phonemic representation. This would incidentally preserve the relationship between spelling and phonemic representation in this and many other examples. These relationships with spelling and with morphology were, of course, early casualties of the attempts to derive phonemes directly from phones.

An advantage of this alliance between phonemes and morpheme is that it emphasizes the role of the phoneme as the mediator between sound and meaning. We are still left with the task of translating between our morphophonemic level and the phonetic level. To achieve this we have to employ powerful rules that appeal to syntactic consideration. These syntactic variables can only be described at the lexical (morphophonemic) level to which we have raised our phonemic representation.

The major theory that sets out to describe translation between the lexical and the phonetic domains is that of Chomsky and Halle (1968). The approach of these authors is often loosely referred to as "morphophonemic", and I have used the word here because I have been intent on tracing the fate of the concept of phonemes. However, Chomsky and Halle specifically eschew the term along with any other reference to a phonemic level. They write:

> The term "morphophonemic representation" seems to us appropriate only if there is another linguistically significant level of representation, intermediate in "abstractness" between lexical (phonological) and phonetic. . . . We feel, however, that the existence of such a level has not been demonstrated and that there are strong reasons to doubt its existence. We will make no furhter mention of "phonemic analysis" or "phonemes" in this study (Chomsky and Halle, 1968, p. 11).

This leaves us with our final option for the assignment of phonemes in GRATER/GRADER.

(*v*) We can stop talking about "phonemes". But if we do *that*, where does this leave the alphabet as the culmination of an orderly evolution of phonographic representation by script?

Chapter 3

Reference and Efficiency in Scripts

Having examined the units in terms of which spoken language can be described, we can now return to the topic of orthography to enquire into the relative merits of these units as a basis for representation in orthographies. This is a question which admits both linguistic and psychological answers. There is no requirement that aprioristic linguistic considerations of the efficiency of an orthography will be consistent with psychological evidence about either the ease of acquisition of an orthographic convention or the efficiency with which it can be employed by the skilled reader.

In Section 1 we shall examine the criterion of efficiency most commonly invoked by the linguists—the number of signs required by a given form of script. In this context we shall also touch upon another virtue sometimes cited in linguistic treatments of script—that of analyticity, otherwise described as the property of representing in script the most "elementary" segments of spoken language.

In Section 2 we shall return to the more general question of what levels of language a script represents, or refers to. First, we shall examine this question from a linguistic point of view, distinguishing direct reference to meaning from phonography, or reference to speech segments. Within these two forms of reference we shall distinguish various levels of representation. Then we shall upturn this apple-cart by showing that these linguistic classifications do not tell us anything about how a script is actually processed by the reader. We shall see that most highly evolved scripts can be decoded in a variety of quite different ways, so as to make a nonsense of any a prioristic classification of the script. We shall also provide a reminder of the extent to which a given written language may use mixed forms of script.

In Section 3, we shall attempt to make a specific connection with our discussion of speech in Chapter 2 by considering phonographic efficiency in terms of the unit of speech that is referred to by the script. Here the primary consideration will be the immediacy of the various units in the perception of speech and the development of our tacit and explicit knowledge of these speech components.

3.1 LINGUISTIC CRITERIA OF ORTHOGRAPHIC EFFICIENCY

The notion that the alphabet is, in some absolute sense, the optimally efficient writing system for any language often comes close to being the fundamental dogma in treatments of the history of writing systems. I think that we can find several understandable but nevertheless inadequate reasons why this assumption has achieved such currency. Before attempting to fathom these implicit assumptions it is worth pointing out that the notion of efficiency as applied to a script makes most sense when interpreted psychologically. Accordingly I shall assume here that when speaking of "efficiency" a commentator is using a sort of shorthand for a hypothetical set of psychological tests which would have to include, at the least, the ease of acquisition of a script by the child, for his own language, and the speed and accuracy with which a script can be read and produced as spelling by the skilled adult. These issues in turn are potentially capable of analysis in terms of particular properties of the script and the implications of these properties for a human operator with limited abilities to discriminate, attend to and remember various sorts of linguistic entities. Unfortunately, though we know a little about the relevant physical characteristics of typeface design, we know almost nothing about the interaction between fundamental psychological limitations and the more abstract linguistic properties of the various writing systems. Thus our discussion of efficiency must of necessity be superficial and inconclusive, and its main function must be to question aprioristic assumptions, especially the absolutist doctrine of the alphabet as the optimal form of representation, thereby opening the topic to the psychological examination that it requires.

Probably the simplest justification for the belief in the alphabet as optimal is based upon the presentation of the alphabet by linguistic historians as the culmination of an evolutionary process. In Gelb's (1963) influential and vigorously asserted formulation we have already noted two assumptions that carry particular force, in this regard. First, Gelb holds all true writing systems to be phonographic, that is, to make direct and immediate reference to speech sounds. Thus, Gelb cites with approval Aristotle's words, from *De Interpretatione*: "Spoken words are the symbols of mental experience and written words are the symbols of spoken words." Clearly, this first assumption acts as a constraint upon the sort of efficiency that we might look for in an orthography. Secondly, Gelb is at great pains to present the history of writing systems as an evolution that progresses through an invariable sequence of stages toward the alphabet. It is but a short step from the contemplation of this sort of historical pattern to the assumption that development invariably signals progress. The tacit adoption of this assumption raises some questions for Gelb. For instance, he feels called upon to explain why some contemporary languages appear to remain fixated at an intermediate stage of development and remarks almost reproachfully that "even with their two fully developed syllabic systems the Japanese could not persuade themselves to give up the old Chinese logography" (Gelb, 1963, p. 162). Such atavism has to be explained for Gelb in terms of conservatism, insulation from external pressure, and social, political or religious vested interest. In such a view no account seems to be taken of the possibility that, say, Japanese acquires some flexibility from the use of a mixed (logographic and syllabic) script, or that the simple, syllabic structure of spoken Japanese might be peculiarly well adapted to a syllabary, with little to be gained from the adoption of an alphabet.

Gelb also comments on the obvious fact that developments in primitive scripts which have been provoked by contact with more developed cultures have commonly halted at the level of the syllabary. He supposes this to be caused by the fact that "this sequence of the stages of writing reflects the stages of primitive psychology . . . the division of syllables into single sounds usually lies beyond their capacity" (Gelb, 1963, p. 203). Presumably children in our own society may be expected to be at a psychologically "primitive" stage, but the implications that this might have for the acquisition of alphabetic reading are not pursued.

Economy and analyticity as criteria of efficiency of representation

One assumption about efficiency that appears to have some currency in linguistic writings is that analyticity is of itself a Good Thing. That is to say, it is assumed that up to some limit (usually the phoneme) it is desirable for an orthography to transcribe the minimal units of the spoken language. This view is proposed, but not justified, by Pulgram (1976, p. 26), who stops short of advocating a spectrographic script only on the basis that it is too cumbersome for writing by hand. Pulgram does, however, exclude a phonetic level of transcription (representing phones) because it makes distinctions that are linguistically meaningless.

A more balanced view of analyticity is taken by French (1976). As he points out, if degree of analyticity were taken as the criterion of excellence, the Korean *Hangul* script would excel by virtue of its representation of articulatory gestures as part of some of its signs. However, French continues:

> The assumption that syllabaries are more primitive than alphabets seems to be not unconnected with the historical fact that the Greek alphabet developed from a type of writing system which some have termed syllabic. But it is surely inappropriate to speak in the abstract, as many Western surveys of writing-systems do, of the inferiority of syllabaries to alphabets, since it is only with reference to a particular language that one can assess the relative merits of an alphabetic and a syllabic type of writing-system (French, 1976, pp. 118–119).

French goes on to consider the second conventional criterion of efficiency, that of economy in the number of different signs required. Here it is generally agreed that logographic script is inefficiently prolific. Gelb estimates the total number of logographs in Chinese at about 50,000, and Martin (1972) cites estimates as high as 80,000. However, these estimates can be misleading. As Gelb points out, the Chinese logograph is often compound, and the compounds are reducible, in theory at least, to a few hundred basic "keys". Moreover, as far as the principle of logographic representation is concerned, there seems no reason why a system as highly organized as human semantic memory appears to be should not be accessed by a highly organized corpus of signs. It is certain that our internal lexicon is better indexed than the alphabetic system of the English dictionary reveals, and there is no reason why a logographic system should not capitalize on such organization.

It is also necessary to bear in mind, in considering the number of signs, more factors than the number of different possibilities. We also must have regard to the total number of signs per utterance and the number of different signs per utterance. For example, given the distribution of frequency of usage of words it is estimated that a thousand Chinese characters account for 90% of text occurrences (Alleton, cited in Martin, 1972). For the content words represented by Japanese *Kanji* logographs, Martin reports the statistics provided by the Japanese National Language Research Institute. These show that 99% of occurrences in running text are accounted for by a set of about 2,000 Kanji characters. According to Gelb, the logographic systems of ancient Egyptian, Sumerian and Hittite evolved toward a set of about 400–600 distinct signs.

There seems no doubt that a wholly logographic system makes excessive demands of the reader and writer, owing to the number of signs required. By the nature of such systems the set of signs is an open one, forever subject to additions, and this would seem to be another unsatisfactory feature. However, in an ideal, semantically *organized* logographic system the nature of a new sign would have a high degree of predictability. The known instances of the employment of semantic-field indicators (*radicals*) probably do not represent anything like the full potential for such semantic organization in a logographic script.

A recent development of some interest is the logographic system invented by Charles Bliss (Bliss, 1965). Bliss was an eccentric inventor who visited China and was impressed by Chinese logography. In particular he admired the way that logographic script could be decoded by the reader into any spoken language by virtue of its lack of phonographic reference. Motivated by the ideal of a Universal Symbolism, as Leibniz had been before him, Bliss devised a logographic writing system from scratch. Perhaps on account of its highly idiosyncratic exposition the system has received little scientific attention, but it has attracted interest as a means of providing the verbally handicapped (aphasic adults and cerebral palsied children) with an expressive medium (see, for example, Bliss, 1976).

The main features of the system are the simple geometrical design of the symbols, the rentention of pictographic reference where possible, and the combination of symbol elements to express new meanings. For example, *train timetable* is expressed by three pictographic symbols: book, clock and train. Abstract ideas, however, often require a clumsy agglomeration of symbols.

Generally it would appear that the primary objective of the Bliss logography is ease of acquisition, and this has been sought at the expense of economy and fluency. This may be an acceptable tradeoff when the system is used with non-verbal children.

Another way of reducing the memory demands of a logographic system is to incorporate it into a mixed system. To some extent this is achieved by the Chinese supplementary syllabary, but this development is carried further in Japanese with the logographic Kanji, which is reserved for context words. The fact that although Japanese possesses a complete syllabary in the *Kana* it is only used exclusively by children and the naïve suggests that such a mixture is functional, unless the retention of *Kanji* is to be ascribed to purposeless conservatism. The possible advantages of mixed scripts should not surprise the user of English: as Edgerton (1941) and others have pointed out, written English makes use of a number of pictographs (the X in Xmas) and logographs (cwt, 2, and !, for example).

The number of signs required by the great majority of syllabaries lies in the range 40–100. The Japanese *Kana* provides a typical example of a syllabary serving a language that is simple and regular in its syllabic structure. The *Kana* syllabaries have 74 distinct signs but some of these indicate phonetic features by combining signs. For example *voicing* in the articulation of stop consonant syllables is indicated by a general purpose sign, so that in *Katakana* unvoiced コ (ko) and ト (to) become, when voiced, ゴ (go) and ド (do). The number of basic signs can therefore be regarded as about 50. Five of these represent vowel syllables, and the remainder, simple CV syllables, save for a phonemic sign that permits the closing of syllables with a nasal consonant (n).

According to Gelb, the West Semitic syllabaries, which lie in the mainstream of development from Egyptian to the Greek alphabet, were among the most economical systems, the Phoenician version having as few as 22 signs and the others fewer than 30.

Even for languages with a greater variety of syllable types than the V and CV types, a modified syllabary may be a better solution than total conversion to a phonemic alphabet. The 'fan-ch'ieh principle in Chinese represents the more complex syllabic structure of Chinese with 62 signs. Fifty of these are syllable-initial CV signs and the remaining 12 are final V or VC signs. This carries somewhat further the use in *Kana* of the nasal phonemic sign for closing of syllables. More recent Chinese scripts display an even more mixed style (see, for example, French, 1976, pp. 120–122 for a discussion of the National Phonetic Script, which is about equally phonemic and syllabic in its level of representation).

Accordingly, there are two basic options for representing closed syllables and syllables with consonant clusters by means of a script whose basic signs are CV syllable signs. Either certain additional subsyllabic V, C, and VC segments are represented and often restricted to syllable-final positions, or the basic CV syllabary is retained but some of the signs are employed occasionally as consonant indicators, with their vowel values ignored. This latter option is probably more commonly exercised in languages which rarely pose the problem. Using Gelb's example, the *Kana* rendering of tapt would be *ta-p*(u)-*t*(u).

In a case such as Kana there is really very little economy to be gained by changing to a phonemic alphabet. Phonemic representation would require about 20 signs, compared with the 47 syllabic signs which Gelb describes as "basic". Probably what offends the advocates of alphabetization is not any lack of economy but a lack of analyticity. The fact is that there is no evidence in the design of, say, the 15 signs for syllables containing /o/ that they have anything phonemic in common (though, as we have seen, the consonants do indicate the similarity of stops which differ only in voicing). Given the restricted choice of vowel phonemes, however, it is not at all clear whether this omission carries any psychological penalty. It might equally well be argued that in Japanese a representation of phonemic segments would discard information about powerful regularities created by the constraints upon the sequencing of phonemes, in a language largely composed of V and CV syllables.

It seems clear, however, that in a language with a syllable structure as complex and unconstrained as English even a mixed syllabary would have to contain a formidable number of distinct signs. On the other hand, attempts to treat written English as a representation of surface phonemes are less economical than the existence of 26 alphabetic characters would suggest. For example, Hanna *et al.* (1966) report a painstaking attempt to inventory the correspondences between a 52 phoneme analysis of English and the graphemic representations of these phonemes. This showed, for instance, that /a/ sounded as in *a*ngel can be represented in sixteen ways (A, AI, AIGH, etc). Although the consonant correspondences are simpler, /k/ has thirteen different graphemic representations (C, CQ, CK, etc.). Thus, in terms of a purely phonographic analysis English contains many more representational units than the 26 alphabetic signs.

A different solution to the phonographic representation of a language with a complex syllable structure is manifest in Hangul, the Korean alphabet. Korean has syllables of the V, VC, CV, CVC and CVCC types. The writing system accommodates this complexity by constructing syllabographs out of 24 alphabetic characters. These alphabetic elements are arranged in a two by two matrix, forming the syllabograph. It might seem that all that is gained by this device is the visual segmentation of a fundamentally alphabetic representation into syllabic groups. However, more than that is achieved, because a syllable is frequently a morpheme. The most complex syllabographs (CVCC) are, in fact, invariably morphemes. Accordingly, such characters can be read as logographs that signal a meaning directly by the use of a single, distinctive sign, while at the same time the sign provides a complete phonographic specification of the syllable/morpheme. (See Taylor, 1981, for further details. Examples of the various types of syllabographs in Hangul are shown in Table 4, from Taylor, 1980.)

Table 4 Examples of Korean Hangul syllabic writing[a]

Complexity level[b]	Linearly arranged C	V	C	C	Packaged in block[c]	Syllable	Morpheme (native)
I		ㅏ			아	V/a/	suffix; ah
I	ㄷ	ㅏ			다	CV/da/	all
II		ㅏ	ㄹ		말	VC/al/	egg
II	ㄷ	ㅏ	ㄹ		달	CVC/dal/	moon
III	ㄷ	ㅏ	ㄹ	ㄱ	닭	CVCC/dalg/	hen

[a] All the letters in this table, except the level III letter, could represent both native morphemes and Chinese loan morphemes: only the native ones are given here.

[b] "Complexity" is based on visual complexity, which is partly confounded with syllabic complexity.

[c] In V and VC letters, the empty circle is required to show that a vowel is alone in a syllable. The circle depicts the shape of the throat in vowel production—it is empty and wide open.

3.2 ORTHOGRAPHIC REFERENCE: SPEECH OR MEANING

We must not think of the option, for a script, of making distinct reference to speech or to meaning as exclusive, all-or-none alternatives. To understand this, it may be helpful to return to the linguistic classifications of scripts considered in Chapter 1. Taking Haas's taxonomy as an example, we saw that a script might be described as exercising three binary options according to: (1) whether the graphemes were semantically *empty* or *informed*; (2) whether, when semantically *informed* they were *motivated* (i.e. pictorial); (3) whether the graphemes were *derived* from the spoken language or *original*. We are now ready to qualify the application of this sort of linguistic taxonomy. We shall set out these qualifications in three stages, characterized by increasing generality. First, in examining the formal relationship of script to spoken language, I shall attempt to show that derivedness is usually a matter of degree, largely because, as we have seen, speech can be described at various levels, and the more minute the level which is reflected in a script, the more constrained the script by the spoken language. Secondly, we shall turn to the relationship of script to meaning, and I shall argue that direct reference to meaning cannot be wholly dealt with in terms of the question as to whether or not individual graphemes are semantically *empty*. Thirdly, as a development of the first two points, I shall show that whatever the formal relationship of script to speech or meaning, the question of how script is used by the reader is a psychological one. Most scripts can be processed in alternative ways, and the way in which a script is handled is constrained by its formal linguistic properties but certainly not wholly determined by them.

Reference to speech: a matter of degree

The closest a script comes to being totally free of correspondences with spoken language is in the pictograph or ideograph which expresses a phrase-meaning. A large set of equivalent utterances could stand for this meaning and so any reference of the script to spoken forms is very imprecise. As we saw in Pulgram's example (Fig. 1), even pictographs can be invested with a grammatical structure by laying out pictorial segments in a linear array with a significant order.

In the logograph the pictorial sort of reference to meaning is lost, but direct reference to morphemic units of meaning is substituted. This often results in a correspondence between graphemes and individual words of the spoken language, as in Chinese. This creates ambiguity of reference because in Chinese the logograph might equally be said to correspond to the morpheme of meaning or to the spoken word that represents that morpheme in speech. Such ambiguity is reflected in Gelb's classification of the logograph as a word-syllabic grapheme, constituting the first of his stages of phonographic representation.

The closeness of correspondence between speech and script is increased in the syllabary, since syllables owe their conception to the analysis of speech perception and production. However, this increase in the closeness of correspondence with speech is not continued consistently as we descend the hierarchy to the level of alphabetic script. In languages such as English the correspondence between the script and the phonetic surface of the spoken language is irregular. This in itself justifies the assertion that the correspondence with speech is less close than might be true of a syllabary, but in addition these irregularities of phonography in English can be shown to be *systematic*, that is, they can be shown to be due to the sacrifice of phonetic information in favour of morphological information. This can be understood for the moment by the example of the silent grapheme in *damn* which serves no phonographic function but preserves a morpheme which can be seen to recur in *damnation*. (A more extended discussion of this issue can be found in Chapter 4.) This morphophonemic characteristic of English leads us naturally to our second issue.

Direct reference to meaning

The principal reason for preferring the "visual morpheme" interpretation of the logograph to Gelb's phonographic one can be understood by considering the frequently homophonous nature of Chinese words. The famous story constructed by the Chinese linguist Y. R. Chao consisted of repetitions of an identical syllable which would be unintelligible in speech but when written would consist of a comprehensible series of differing written graphemes. A feeble sample of this experience can be gleaned from the English wordplay: "How much *wood would a woodchuck chuck* if a *woodchuck would chuck wood*". (As I write this I have caught myself in several writing errors, such as ending with a *would*, and this suggests, along with other evidence, that even if reading is not necessarily mediated by implicit speech, writing may be.) The point of this Chinese example is that the correspondence of the logographs with morphology is more informative than the correspondence with sound. This in turn illustrates the general thesis enunciated by Haas (1976) that the more a script is constrained by correspondences with speech, the fewer the distinctive advantages of writing over speech.

For the sort of reason adduced above I have chosen to regard the pictograph and the logograph as directly referring to meaning. Notice that this has not required us to appeal to the fact that in these forms of script the graphemes are also semantically *informed*, that is, each grapheme has meaning on its own. When we turn to a morphophonemic script like English this last condition is no longer fulfilled. Alphabetic graphemes are semantically *empty*. A grapheme by itself has no significance, yet combinations of these graphemes that represent morphemes and form words seem to reflect meaning more efficiently than they reflect sound, not only because they disambiguate homophones (*crews/cruise*) more often than they obscure lexical distinctions present in speech (*lead* meaning the metal, *lead* meaning the present tense of led), but also because they tend to refer to morphology rather than speech sound, when a choice has to be made (*damn/damnation*).

The reader's options

However we choose to describe a script in formal terms, it remains open to the reader to treat it in different ways. Written Chinese expresses more meaningful distinctions than the spoken language. In principle, therefore, this linguistic fact makes it more efficient to translate the graphemes directly into meaning rather than into spoken forms and thence to meanings, although this does not tell us what the Chinese actually do when they read.

Erickson *et al.* (1973; see also Chapter 7) have reported acoustical confusions in the immediate recall of Japanese subjects presented with *Kanji* logographs, just like the errors reported as evidence of phonetic recording when alphabetic material is given to Western subjects. Clearly the result of this memory test tells us nothing about the first translations performed in reading, but it serves to emphasize the fact that the script does not deprive the reader of options.

Carroll (1972) discusses the problem of teaching Classical Chinese to American students. Apparently some students learn to translate the characters directly into meanings but more are taught correspondences between Classical script and modern spoken Chinese. Still others appear to translate directly from the Chinese script into spoken English.

Despite these strands of evidence based on short-term memory coding and second-language acquisition, there is a wealth of information to suggest that logographs are treated differently by the reader from alphabetic and syllabic signs. When a word is written in a phonographic script, its pronunciation is accessible to the reader, even if that particular combination of signs has not previously been encountered. It is therefore open to the reader to "sound out" this novel visual pattern to gain access to the meaning via his comprehension of the spoken language. (Indeed, some theorists have attempted to maintain that this procedure is followed in reading alphabetic script even when the words are familiar.) It therefore makes sense that Japanese children first learn to read using the *Kana* syllabaries. The number of these signs is relatively few, the phonological units (syllables) referred to are fairly obvious, and the correspondences between sign and spoken form are fairly regular. Accordingly, translation between script and the spoken language is rapidly acquired. Later, acquisition of the logographic *Kanji* progresses much more slowly, and we are told that the exact mixture of scripts used depends upon an individual's education and whim (Martin, 1972). This might still be the case even if logographs were treated as an inefficient phonographic system (inefficient because each correspondence would be unique and hence ungeneralizable), but clinical evidence suggests that the logographic and syllabic scripts are treated by the reader in fundamentally different ways. There exist forms of brain damage in which the ability to read and write either *Kanji* or *Kana* is selectively impaired. Furthermore, the type of error produced by these two forms of impairment seems to differ. Finally, there appear to be differences in the ability of the two brain hemispheres to process the two scripts. (We shall examine such evidence in more detail in Chapter 7.)

Curiously enough, this sort of comparison between the manner of processing logographic and phonographic script can also be performed using English. Among the most prevalent logographs used by readers of English are the arabic numerals. Once again the clinical literature offers the suggestion that brain damage may be selective in its effect on alphabetic and logographic (numeral) processing (Hécaen and Kremin, 1976). Such comparisons have been carried further by Besner and Coltheart (1979), using normal subjects. They asked subjects to judge which of two numbers was numerically the greater. Such judgements were influenced by the relative physical size of the pair of numbers when displayed logographically (e.g. 3) but not when displayed alphabetically (e.g. THREE). This might be taken to suggest that logographic numbers are processed in a manner that is closer to pictures than to alphabetic material, since Paivio (1975) has shown a relative display-size effect in judgements about animals when these are based on pictures but not when based on names.

The options in processing English are not confined to contrasting types of script. Even alphabetic English script could in principle be processed logographically or phonographically, and in fact there exist theories which assert that:

(*i*) English is processed logographically in the strong sense. Words are treated as if they comprised a single grapheme which can be directly translated into meaning (e.g. Smith, 1969).

(*ii*) Processing is logographic in the weak sense. Words are directly translated into meaning, but preliminary visual pattern analysis uses the constituent graphemes as a unit of analysis (e.g. Massaro, 1975c).

(*iii*) Processing is phonographic (syllabic). The grapheme array is segmented into syllabic units each of which is translated into a syllable in the spoken language (e.g. Spoehr and Smith, 1973).

(*iv*) Processing is phonographic (phonemic). Graphemes are translated into phonemes which give access to the spoken language and thence to word meanings (e.g. Rubinstein *et al.* 1971).

Thus, short of asserting that alphabetic script is processed as if it were pictographic, psychologists have variously described the reading of English as if the script were logographic, a syllabary or a phonemic alphabet. There exists some doubt as to whether option (*iii*) (the syllabic mode postulated by Spoehr and Smith) is a genuine logical possibility, since it is unclear how printed English is to be segmented into syllables, but the remaining options and numerous variants on them are certainly logically possible and indeed it is sometimes suggested that several of these processing operations are conducted simultaneously during reading.

We shall later examine particular psychological models in some detail. For present purposes it is sufficient to have demonstrated that no amount of contemplation of a script can tell us, *a priori*, how the script will be treated by the reader in pursuit of its meaning.

3.3 THE ACCESSIBILITY OF PHONOLOGICAL LEVELS

In Chapter 1, I observed that the relationship between script and phonological awareness is a crucial one from the psychologist's point of view. If an orthography is to be easy to learn, the phonological level to which it refers must be one of which the reader has cognizance. Many psychologists have gone beyond this to assert that the phonological units into which we map a script, whether they be syllables, phonemes, phones, or whatever, must be units of which we are capable of *explicit* awareness. This point was glossed over in Pulgram's assertion that a script could as well represent any level of spoken language, since any speaker must be "aware . . . of the discrete character of all units at all levels". The fundamental questions are these: what sort of phonological awareness does a phonographic script require of the reader and what sort of awareness do the child and adult have of the various units that have been implicated in phonographic translation?

Status of phonemes

In practice, much of the debate about the accessibility of phonological units has centred on the status of the phoneme. This is due not only to the assumption that the alphabet corresponds with the phonemic level but also to a certain fragility in the status of the phoneme as a unit. I have already discussed the uncertainties about the role of the phoneme in speech perception in Section 2.1. These difficulties can be summarized in the following points.

(*i*) By definition, the phoneme is a linguistic abstraction. Moreover, even amongst linguists there is some dispute about the necessity to postulate a phonemic level intermediate between the mental lexicon and the phonetic surface of speech (Chomsky and Halle, 1968).

(*ii*) No algorithm exists for mapping phones, the categorical percepts of speech sounds, into the abstract phonemes.

(*iii*) In many theories of speech perception it is held that the acoustic signal is translated at the level of the syllable and that any phonemic analysis is subsequent to syllable identification and dependent upon it (Cole and Scott, 1974; Massaro, 1975b).

(*iv*) Some attempts have been made to evaluate the "psychological reality" of the phoneme by direct test, for example by comparing the time taken to search for phonemic and syllabic targets. These are tests of *explicit* knowledge, in terms of our ability to attend to units of various sorts. They have usually been used to argue against the psychological reality of phonemes, but this conclusion is not secure.

Explicit knowledge

It has usually been assumed that for a unit to be used in phonographic translation the reader must have explicit knowledge of the existence and attribute of such units. This point is clearly expressed by Savin (1972) in the passage quoted on p. 36. The distinction at issue here between *tacit* and *explicit* knowledge has played an increasingly important role in recent treatments of the psychology of language. For example, it is evident that children of a certain age have tacit understanding of the concepts of noun and verb. This is implied by their correct production and comprehension of utterances in which these forms play their syntactical roles. Nevertheless, they are unable to abstract this understanding from the context of its normal use and make it explicit, for example by categorizing words as nouns or verbs. Furthermore, this lack of explicit understanding does not consist in a failure to grasp the relevant terms. It can be demonstrated in tasks where the requirement is defined ostensively, without resort to words like "noun".

The prevailing assumption that phonographic translation depends upon a degree of explicit knowledge of phonological units has been challenged by Coltheart (1977), who starts from the assumption that

> in studying language development, or learning to read, or skilled reading, it is the listener-reader's tacit knowledge which is of primary importance, since the fundamental processes involved in speaking and reading, and the store of knowledge drawn upon by these processes, may not be accessible to introspection, and so may not be explicitly known by the listener-reader (Coltheart, 1977, p. 159).

Coltheart then goes on to criticize experiments, such as those of Calfee *et al.* (1972), in which children's phonological preparedness for reading is evaluated by asking them questions such as: "Does 'look' begin with l-l-l?".

Although Coltheart's original point that implicit knowledge is of primary importance in linguistic tasks is not in dispute, the extension of this argument, in his claim that explicit knowledge of phoneme-like segments is irrelevant to the question of readiness to learn alphabetic correspondences, is highly disputable. The *prima facie* case is that put by Savin (1972):

> There is evidently no point in trying to teach a child who cannot make himself aware of phonemes that the letter *s* has the sound /s/. Such conversations are futile, whether or not his perceptual processes involve phonemes at some unconscious level.

This argument for the crucial status of explicit phonological knowledge is taken even further by Rozin and Gleitman (1977), who assert specifically that: "Good and poor readers differ not in their underlying phonological organisation, but in their ability to make judgements based on this" (Rozin and Gleitman, 1977, p. 95).

A more general aspect of the tacit–explicit distinction as applied to reading is that whereas speech recognition gets picked up by the child without formal tuition—often indeed despite his linguistic environment—reading usually requires formal tuition. This leads Gough and Hillinger (1980) to call learning to read "an unnatural act". The rules of phonics, they point out, have to be taught verbally and explicitly. This formal and propositional aspect of reading tuition is also discussed by Marcel (1978a).

What, then, is the evidence on the role of phonological awareness in reading readiness?

Accessibility of phonological levels

The literature on phonemic awareness in relation to reading ability has been reviewed recently by Liberman *et al.* (1977), Rozin and Gleitman (1977), and Ehri (1979), and the reader is directed to these reviews and their source material for details which will only be summarized briefly here. More general treatments of linguistic awareness in children can be found in a recent book edited by Sinclair *et al.* (1978).

Generally speaking, it is not difficult to find statements of the view that lack of phonemic awareness is a major stumbling block in the acquisition of reading skill (see, for example, Bradley and Bryant, 1978; Liberman *et al.*, 1977; Rozin and Gleitman, 1977; Savin, 1972). We have already seen that such suspicions rest on a strong base of intuition. What is surprising, therefore, is the relative paucity of data which might reasonably be said to bear upon this claim.

One sort of observation which is sometimes invoked in support of the claim consists of no more than the demonstration that pre-school children are deficient in a variety of tasks that require explicit phonological analysis. In this vein, Calfee *et al.* (1972) have shown that five-year-olds are very deficient at the recognition and production of rhymes (a task requiring a sub-syllabic level of analysis). Similarly, Liberman *et al.* (1977) showed that four- to six-year-olds were poor at tapping out phonemes when presented with short utterances. At age four, none of their subjects could enumerate phonemes, whereas about half could enumerate syllables. A related observation was made by Rozin *et al.* (1974). They showed children pairs of printed words such as MOW and MOTORCYCLE, told them that one word was *mow* and the other *motorcycle*, and asked which was which. Despite the obvious correlation between written and spoken length of the words, a sample of educationally disadvantaged children performed very poorly on the test. Only 60% of second graders could meet a criterion of 7 out of 8 correct. Such studies tell us much that is useful, and even surprising, about the child's explicit understanding of speech sounds, but they are incapable of supporting causal inferences about the role of such knowledge in the acquisition of reading skill. As Liberman *et al.* (1977) have observed, it is quite possible that phonological awareness is itself brought about by reading experience or that it depends on some independent, maturational factor.

Rather more compelling findings might be expected from studies in which the ability to analyse speech sounds is compared in good and poor readers. Even this sort of evidence is purely correlational, but at least reading ability is a more pertinent correlate than mere age or educational opportunity. Early studies which show some predictive success by measures of phonological awareness are reviewed in Dykstra (1966). More recently, Savin (1972) has made strong claims about the role of speech analysis in the acquisition of alphabetic phonography. "In the present author's experience," he writes, "everyone who has failed to learn to read even the simplest prose by the end of the first grade has been unable to analyse syllables into phonemes." The tests on which Savin bases this claim include perception of rhyme, of shared initial phonemes and of the ability to learn Pig Latin—a word game which requires the transposition of certain phonemes.

Savin presented no data in support of his claim, but such evidence is forthcoming from other studies. Rosner and Simon (1971) reported findings with the Auditory Analysis Test. This involves problems such as saying "boy" without the "buh". One might of course object to this task on the basis that "boy" doesn't actually contain "buh". Presumably the reply would be the somewhat circular justification that the test nevertheless predicts reading attainment fairly well. Using a less problematic task, Liberman (1973, reported in Liberman *et al.*, 1977) has found that her phonetic segmentation test (tapping out the phonemes in a spoken word) predicts poor word recognition performance in second grade.

Liberman has also advanced a different, rather technical, argument in favour of the thesis that phoneme segmentation ability plays a fundamental role in reading acquisition. In Liberman *et al.* (1977) it is suggested that lack of ability to analyse syllables into their phonemic constituents should result in fewer reading errors in the first phoneme of monosyllabic words than in later phonemes. This predication appears to be supported in quite a large number of studies. For example, Shankweiler and Liberman (1972, table 6) reported percentage errors in reading aloud which, when collapsed over the nonclinical groups, read as follows: initial consonant 7%, medial vowel 18%, final consonant 13%. There are, however, at least three sources of difficulty in the argument that these positions effect within the syllable support the segmentation ability theory.

First, it is never actually made clear why the theory predicts these position effects, nor is attention paid to the possibility that other theories might make the same prediction of superior translation of the first phoneme. Yet it is not difficult to conceive of various "guessing" models which might have just that property, for example those based on the assumption that lexical memory is organized on the basis of initial phonemes (Smith and Jones, 1975).

Secondly, Shankweiler and Liberman's results quite clearly suggest that the position effect in error frequencies is independent of the good/poor reader distinction. They acknowledge this but make no attempt to reconcile this finding with their original thesis about the role of segmentation ability.

Thirdly, the most impressive "position" effect arises from the poor performance on medial vowels. Furthermore, vowel errors do appear to distinguish good and poor readers. Shankweiler and Liberman (1972) discuss vowel errors rather carefully, coming to the conclusion that these errors are due to orthographic complexity: the letter–sound correspondences are more ambiguous for vowels. Now, if ambiguity of letter–sound correspondence were greater for final than initial consonants then the error position effect might be entirely due to letter–sound ambiguity. I know of no direct test of this possibility, but inspection of Table 5, showing "graphemic options representing phonemes by position in syllables" for 30 consonant phonemes, in Hanna *et al.*'s (1966) monumental tabulation, reveals that the ambiguity of consonant correspondences, at least in the phoneme to grapheme direction, is much larger at the end than the beginning of a syllable. The suggestion that poor readers have particular difficulties with ambiguous letter–sound correspondences is not novel, nor is it equivalent to the phonological awareness issue. Taking these three points together, I believe we are obliged to reject the error-position evidence as an argument for the role of phonemic segmentation in reading acquisition.

It would be wrong to conclude that the direct comparison of segmentation ability with reading achievement is necessarily a fruitless enterprise. Perhaps the best way to determine the direction of causal influence is to compare backward readers with younger children *of the same reading age*. This is what Bradley and Bryant (1978) did.[4] They used a rather clumsy task of detecting the odd sound among four similar-sounding words and found the poor readers to be worse than the younger, good reader controls. The operation of matching groups on reading age is intended as a control of reading experience, in order to preclude this as a cause of phonological awareness. This type of matching has probably been insufficiently exploited, although of course it cannot be safely assumed that just because they have the same *reading age* a ten-year-old backward reader and a six-year-old good reader have had the same amount of *reading experience*, as it might bear upon the induction of phonological awareness.

An interesting study which casts a different light on the relationship between phonetic awareness and reading performance has been reported by Morais *et al.* (1979), who studied two groups brought up in a backward peasant community. Neither group had learnt to read in childhood, but one group had remained illiterate and the other had received literacy training as adults. It was found that the illiterate group were unable to delete or add a single phone at the beginning of a nonword, while the literate group could do so fairly readily. If we assume that the groups did not differ in their phonological potential in the first place, it would seem to follow that their accidental encounter with adult literacy training induced the phonological skills that distinguish the literate group. Furthermore, the implication may be drawn that ability to attend to phonetic segments does not necessarily develop spontaneously. From these grounds the authors move to the conclusion that we should assert not that phonological awareness is a precondition for reading but rather that the "capacity for becoming aware" is the precondition. This means that the appropriate predictive test of a child's reading success should be to find whether we can teach him phonetic segmentation rather than merely to determine whether he already exhibits that phonological skill.

A quite different sort of argument that bears upon the role of phonological awareness is based not upon the difficulty of acquiring the alphabetic principle but instead upon the relative tractability of alternative orthographies. Rozin *et al.* (1971) have issued the remarkable claim that American children with reading difficulties can easily learn to read English words represented by Chinese characters. This finding is certainly provocative, but it is unclear what particular conclusion should be drawn with respect to the nature of the children's previous difficulty with alphabetic script.

Another rather open-ended demonstration is that of Gleitman and Rozin (1973). They invented a very limited syllabary for English, representing 60 simple syllables. The script was highly eclectic, using pictographs (a *bee* for /be/) and logographs (4 for /for/) according to the rebus principle. Generally, they characterize their approach as recapitulating the historical development of scripts. Again, the demonstration that kindergarten and first grade children learned the script with ease is interesting. It might indicate that learning phonemic segmentation and grapheme–phoneme correspondences presents the crucial difficulty to the child, but it might equally well indicate that visual distinctiveness of the graphemic elements was crucial. As a system it could have advantages by providing some early success. (This argument and its various counter-arguments are often made about the Initial Teaching Alphabet.) In any case, the application of syllabic script to English is likely to be severely restricted due to the large number of content syllables in the language and to their complexity.

In languages possessing a natural syllabary, reading may require much less formal instruction and reading backwardness may be remarkably rare (see, for example, Makita's (1968) claim about Japanese *Kana*[5]). However, such cross-cultural comparisons are notoriously hedged with qualifications. Gibson and Levin (1975) provide a useful review of some of the findings on different orthographies, together with the difficulties of interpretation which any such findings pose.

In conclusion, the evidence from linguistic analysis and from psychological studies of speech perception suggests that the phoneme may be a peculiarly difficult speech segment to isolate and attend to. However, when we turn to attempts to demonstrate by direct means that such phonological awareness plays a major role in the acquisition of alphabetic reading we find a curious lack of secure argument. Despite the attractive and committed advocacy by Rosin and Gleitman (1977) and others, the central role of phonological awareness remains as yet no more than a plausible hypothesis.

Chapter 4

English Orthography

This chapter examines the relationship between spelling and speech sounds in English. In keeping with the purpose of Part I I shall attempt to keep the treatment as psychologically neutral as possible. The central problem will be the description of English orthography, and one way to approach this problem is to consider it in terms of three sorts of regularities: those within the script, those between script and sound, and those between script and lexical meaning. These issues will be dealt with in three of the four sections of this chapter; the first section deals with the history of English spelling.

The examination of the three forms of relationship is fundamental to the psychological study of the reader's and speller's performance. As with other linguistic questions we have considered, such as the efficiency of a script, or the level of language to which a script refers, I shall emphasize the distinction between the linguistic and psychological realms. However, although it is true that no amount of contemplation of the nature of the correspondences between script and sound or script and meaning can provide the answer to psychological questions about what strategies we actually follow when we read or spell, such psychological issues cannot be clearly formulated in a linguistic vacuum. As psychologists we often need to be reminded of the details of what is done when we use language. Furthermore, it is important to be clear about precisely what it is that we are asserting when we claim that the subject is capitalizing upon some form of regularity.

Let us consider, in anticipation, some examples of psychological issues informed by linguistic considerations. Spelling reformers often assume that the irregularities in the correspondence between sound and spelling in English are arbitrary and unsystematic, and that the desirability of changing spelling into a regular representation of sound is therefore self-evident. The inadequacy of this argument is illuminated by the demonstration that many of the phonographic irregularities of English are due to the conservation of a different sort of regularity, that between script and lexical meaning (morphemes). In the absence of this information, any discussion of spelling reform is ill-informed. However, the other aspect of the relationship between linguistics and psychology can also be noted here, because demonstration of the existence of a form of regularity in no way entails that it is used, or even can be used, by the reader or speller. This is the problem for advocates of the teaching of spelling by morphological rule. Although their scheme is linguistically well-informed, it assumes that the child is a competent linguist and that he possesses and can explicitly use the requisite morphological information.

Another issue illuminated by the linguistic facts is grapheme-to-phoneme translation. It is often treated as an obvious truth that written English can be translated directly into speech without considering morphology, that is, it is asserted that translation can be achieved at a prelexical level of grapheme-to-phoneme correspondences without recourse to higher-level information that is represented in the mental lexicon. What linguistic study does, in this case, is to make clear just how complex and clumsy such a procedure would be. There are difficulties in deciding at the grapheme level what segment to use as the translation unit. For example, there are two units to be translated in the TH of FATHEAD but one in the TH of FATHER. Furthermore, the low-level translation rules contain many options. Even if we worked through the options starting with the most usual correspondence, for many words this first attempt would fail and we would have to experiment with a number of correspondence and their combinations. Moreover, each possible translation would have to be checked against the correct pronunciation, stored in memory. So even if we do not use the linguistic (e.g. morphological) information in our memory to help us choose the pronunciation, we still must check our attempts against the stored representation of the correct sound. To do this, we cannot just discover whether there exists a word with that sound. Consider the attempt to read LEAD (the metal). When eventually we get round to trying out /e/ as the sounding of EA, we find that there is indeed a word in our lexicon with the sounding /led/. However, most occurrences of that word-sound are actually spelt LED (the verb), so in fact what we have to do is check whether /led/ is a genuine pronunciation for the spelling LEAD. Although this example was deliberately chosen for the difficulties it revealed, there are, nevertheless, general conclusions to be drawn from it about the difficulties confronting direct grapheme–phoneme translation. Furthermore, we have not yet touched upon the problem of assigning syllabic stress, as in the contrast of *ém-ber* and *em-béd* (cf. Baker and Smith, 1976).

The point of these examples—which by no means exhaust the issue—is to demonstrate how much clarification of the psychological problem can be achieved before we have done a single experiment. Indeed, it seems to me folly to take up a psychological position before examining in some detail what the language allows and encourages. The linguistic evidence does not provide the psychological answers, but it goes a long way toward clarifying the questions.

4.1 A HISTORICAL NOTE ON ENGLISH SPELLING

Before commencing an examination of the relationships between English script and either sound or meaning, it may be helpful to consider how the orthography evolved. Historical analysis often allows us to distinguish between those irregularities of the spelling–sound correspondence that are arbitrary, usually owing to faulty analogy or mistaken etymology, and those that are motivated by some linguistic principle.[6] Furthermore, it is instructive to find current debate about spelling reform and assumptions about the nature of an optimal orthography foreshadowed in the disputes of the sixteenth-century reformers. For much of this historical account I have borrowed from the excellent monograph by Scragg (1974).

Around 600 A.D., Irish missionaries converted the Anglo-Saxons to Christianity and to the Roman alphabet. Previously, the Angles and Saxons had used the Runic alphabet, which had been widely used by the Germanic peoples. Some Runic elements continued to influence English spelling into the period of Middle English (12th–16th C.). Their replacement in Middle English (ME), by Roman letters had consequences for the relationship of letters to sound.

The most important Runic influence was the use of the thorn, a letter resembling lower-case *y*. Thorn represented the initial consonants in *th*e and *th*in. The first word in such archaisms as **Ye Olde Inn**, usually ignorantly pronounced as /ji/, is actually our old friend *the*, merely spelled to suit the printer's convenience with the Roman letter that looks most like the Runic thorn (þ). In the Runic, a single letter corresponded to a single phoneme, but when the Roman transliteration TH became adopted, two letters became a single, functional segment. (Scragg calls TH, used in this way, a single *grapheme*, taking the grapheme as that which corresponds to a unit of sound. Another influential source (Hall, 1961) similarly refers to "compound graphemes". This usage encounters difficulties in the case of silent "graphemes". I have therefore tied the term grapheme to the letter and I refer to "digraphs" when two letters correspond to a single sound.)

The best records of Old English are of the West Saxon scribal tradition and reveal the spelling as remarkably stable and as coming nearer than Modern English to a one-to-one relationship with sound. Scragg documents a number of these correspondences, including an absence of unsounded consonants (like that in *debt*) and a larger number of unambiguous mappings of consonants. However, a consequence of a stable spelling system is that changes in the phonetics of the spoken language will gradually weaken the orthographic correspondences. Phonological drift, towards the end of the Old English period, yielded this outcome. It was at this time, for example, that the short vowels in unstressed syllables converged on the single sound /ə/, as in Modern English:

ca nál, ré *bel*, cár *ton*. The price of the stability of spelling in Old English was an inevitable lack of responsiveness to changing pronunciation. Moreover, as a result of this conservatism the orthography came to consist of coexisting layers of fossils from each wave of innovation. These innovations had diverse sources, of which perhaps the most notable was the Norman conquest.

A primary consequence of the Norman invasion was the decline of the scribal tradition in English. In Middle English the stability of the West Saxon spelling is lost, partly through lack of the practice of writing English and partly through Latinization of English. Above all, what was lost was a pervasive standard. As a result, the tradition was only maintained in terms of regional orthographies, and orthographic consistency, even within a given text, became extremely lax. For many scribes, the copying of English was secondary to French and Latin.

If the early period of Middle English spelling was characterized by instability and Anglo-Norman borrowings, the transition from Middle to Modern English was dominated by the etymological influences on spelling. One entertaining form of this influence described by Scragg was that an important determinant of accepted spelling was to be found in the writing of legal clerks. Their writing was paid for by the inch, so lengthy spellings were lucrative! Thus *poor* became *pauper* by a process of rediscovering the Latin derivation. A more general factor motivating the etymological movement was the revival of interest in Greek and Latin which was so characteristic of the Renaissance. "As a result," Scragg remarks of the sixteenth century, "both of the increase of Latinate vocabulary in English (and of Greek vocabulary transcribed in Latin orthography) and of the familiarity of all literate men with Latin, English spelling became as affected by the etymologising process as French had earlier been" (1974, pp. 53–54). Moreover, this movement happened to take place shortly before spelling became stabilized in Modern English, so that the new etymological spellings generally became fixed.

Another characteristic of the advent of Modern English was the great spread of literacy, which had an interesting consequence for pronunciation. The interaction between trends in spelling and pronunciation is usually conceived in the form of continuous and autonomous changes in pronunciation coursing ahead of an unresponsive and inertial spelling system. However, the implication of spreading literacy, which Scragg brings out, was that the new awareness of spelling served to check phonological drift. Indeed, the effect was more than a checking, for pronunciation actually moved toward correspondence with the newly etymological spellings. Some of these changes have been very slow. *Nephew* (ME *nevew*) is only now changing its pronunciation to /nefju/ to regularize the sounding of PH. Silent consonants are also increasingly tending to be sounded, as in the /t/ of *often*, but phonotactic constraints will probably prevent the sounding of silent B, such as in *debt* and *doubt*. This tendency toward what Scragg calls "spelling-pronunciation" raises the question of why the vociferous advocates of spelling reform (in the direction of phonographic regularity) have never turned their attention to pronunciation reform.

The impact of the etymologizing movement was to shift the correspondence of spelling toward "meaning" as represented by morphology, at the expense of sound—at least until pronunciation caught up. For this reason we can argue that the spelling–sound irregularities introduced are, in principle, *systematic*. (This theme is developed in Section 3 of this chapter.) But this principle nevertheless admits many realizations which are entirely arbitrary. A major source of error in application of the principle involved mistaken etymology. Thus *scissors* (ME *sisoures*) acquired a silent C on the mistaken assumption that it derived from Latin *scindere* "to cut" rather than *cisorium* "a cutting instrument". Etymologizing, whether mistaken or not, became a major source of silent consonants in English (e.g. in *thyme*, *crumb*, *scent*).

Another source of arbitrariness in the orthography, acting as a sort of extention of mistaken etymologizing, was the mistaken analogy. Thus OE *coude* became *could*, with a silent L, by analogy with *would* (OE *wolde*).

In contrast to the theoretically motivated changes that characterize the etymologizing, there existed also in the sixteenth century less extensive, pragmatically motivated changes. These were essentially psychological in character, having such aims as the avoidance of homographs (in which a single spelling represents two unrelated meanings). Thus it may be that the historically unjustified W became added in *whole*, to distinguish it from *hole*.

Not only did the Renaissance bring extensive changes to English spelling, it also brought the invention of printing. Unfortunately, the early printers were careless and out of touch with the new developments in spelling. Caxton had spent much of his life in the Low Countries, and many of his type-setters were foreigners. In addition, the limitation of foreign type to Roman elements consolidated the loss of the Irish ⟨ð⟩ in favour of the digraph ⟨th⟩, with a consequent complication of the grapheme–phoneme correspondence. The printers' spelling was inconsistent, and a word might be lengthened to fill up the line or consonants doubled for decorative effect.

Out of this flux, there began to grow pressures for the reform of English spelling. Perhaps the earliest attempt to reform English spellling into a model of phonographic consistency was that of *The Ormulum*, an early thirteenth-century manuscript (Venezky, 1970), and there is no evidence of further attempts at reform until the Renaissance. For the sixteenth-century reformers of spelling–sound correspondence, written language amounted to no more than it had been in Aristotle's opinion, "the symbol of spoken words". This was the view taken by Sir Thomas Smith, a Cambridge don, who published his argument for phonographic consistency in a book, *De Recta et Errendata Linguae Anglicae* (1568). Smith's reform revolved around a major expansion of the English alphabet. In the following year John Hart published *An Orthographie*, in which he set out a reformed alphabet, using only the Latin characters. For Hart writing was above all a form of phonetic transcription, and it has been claimed (Venezky, 1970) that his chief contribution lay in his recording of the speech of Renaissance England.

Before the century was out, the case against the phonetic transscription model had been put, and the lines along which four centuries of dispute would continue were drawn. In 1582 Richard Mulcaster, a prominent schoolmaster, published *The First Part of the Elementarie*, setting out the case for a historically and etymologically based spelling. It must be conceded, however, that the traditionalist viewed often amounted to little more than an élitist conservatism. As Haas (1969) has observed, "It was enjoyable to discover in one's script some fossils of an earlier age. Also, to be able to spell correctly came to be a welcome sign of 'class', and of more than average education." Moreover, a salient attribute of English spelling is that its design is not adapted to the capacities of the child. As Chomsky and Halle (1968) put the matter, in a much-cited remark: "Orthography is a system designed for readers who know the language". In fact, there are two senses in which this is so: one is the sense intended by Chomsky and Halle, that the orthography does not express phonetic variations when these are predictable from general phonological rules; the other is the sense alluded to by Bradley (1919), who stressed the utility of etymological cues to the cultured reader.

4.2 SPELLING–SOUND CORRESPONDENCES

In this section we shall examine what is involved in direct translations between spelling and sound. By "direct" I mean translation which does not involve consultation of a mental dictionary or lexicon in which whole words are listed and their spelling and pronunciation specified. Direct translation moves between low-level graphic and phonetic elements without taking account of lexical factors, and so I shall call it a "single-level" process.

There are two problems confronting the single-level phonographic translator. One is the problem of *segmentation.* (Yet another problem of segmentation!) As in the translation of the acoustic signal into the categories of speech sounds, a preliminary stage requires the segmentation of both the "languages" between which we are to translate into *functional units*, that is, segments which are to be related via the correspondence rules. The problem of segmentation at the phonographic level is often attributed to the fact that the correspondences are not always one-to-one, with a single grapheme representing a single phoneme; however, it is more precise to treat the problem as consisting in the unreliability of the functional units. Thus PH functions as a single unit (a "digraph") in *morpheme* but as two independently functional graphemes in *uphill*. Conversely, the single grapheme U corresponds with a single sound /u/ in *rude* but with two sounds /ju/ in *cube*.

The second problem is the more notorious. Even when the segmentation is determined, the correspondences between the graphic and phonetic units are not invariant. This is illustrated by an example taken from Haas (1970) and shown in Fig. 6. Here we see optional correspondences in both directions of translation. The grapheme C can be translated as /s/ or /k/. The phoneme /k/ can be translated into K or C.

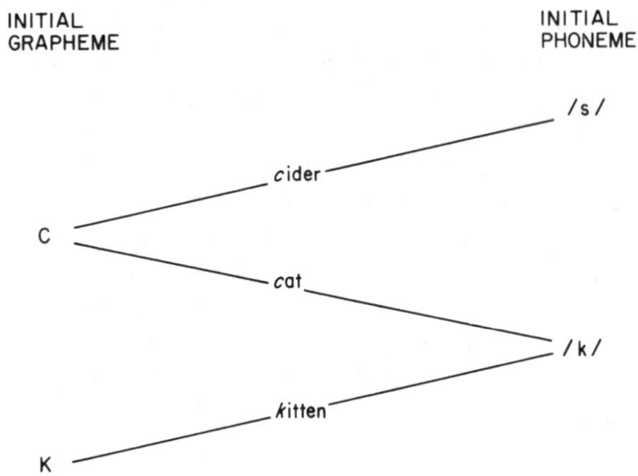

Fig. 6 Optimal correspondences in translating in either direction between phonemes and graphemes. An example taken from Haas (1970).

Segmentation in phonographic translation

We have already established that a grapheme cluster may function as a single unit corresponding to one phoneme and that a single grapheme may correspond to more than one phoneme. The former (graphemic segmentation) problem is quite common and occurs in both vowel and consonant doubling (*odd*, *food*). In such cases the segmentation is generally unambiguous (but cf. *cool* v. *co-ordinate*). There are a large number of digraphs involving a pair of different vowels, such as those in *read*, *raid*, *road*. Some of these vowel combinations are ambiguous, since the vowels can also function as separate units (*react*, *coarticulation*). There are also large numbers of consonant digraphs, notably the family of ones involving H (CH, PH, SH, etc.), some of which are segmentally ambiguous (*uphill*, *morpheme*). Many other consonant digraphs are segmentally invariant (QU, CK, etc.). Some consonantal units are even larger than the digraph, such as the final clusters in *yacht* and *watch*.

Other graphemic segmentation problems arise through so-called "silent" graphemes. Some of these are historically unjustified and phonographically irregular, as in the example of the C in *scissors*. Are we to treat this SC as a digraph, in which case the segmentation is ambiguous, or shall we assume that segmentation should be into single graphemes with C as a silent grapheme? The choice is arbitrary. A quite different sort of silent grapheme is the final E which lengthens an earlier vowel (*hate* v. *hat*). From a segmental point of view this forces us to analyse *hate* as (H)(A+consonant+E)(T). Finally, there are silent graphemes such as the final B in *bomb*. We could segment *bomb* treating MB as a digraph, but we would have to treat it as two graphemic units in *bombard*. In the absence of lexical information (unavailable in "direct" translation) we cannot readily decide on the more reasonable method of segmentation. Nor does an appeal to a nonlexical rule such as "B is a silent grapheme following M in word-final position" help, since B is sounded in *bombard* but silent in *bombed*.

Evidently graphemic segmentation problems are much more common than phonemic segmentation problems, but the latter do exist. Most often noted is the representation of /ks/ by the single grapheme X.

Various listings of the functional units in English spelling have been compiled. In his *Rules of Pronunciation for the English Language* (1966) Axel Wijk listed 46 different speech sounds corresponding to 102 functional spelling units. Wijk's major preoccupation was translation of spelling into sound. This concern was shared by Venezky (1970), who also offered a listing of functional graphemic units and their correspondences with sound. In contrast, Hanna *et al.* (1966) produced their inventory of units and their correspondences out of concern with the problem of translating sounds into spelling.

We owe to Haas the analogy between lexical segmentation and phonographic segmentation. Figure 7 shows examples drawn from Haas (1970, p. 49),

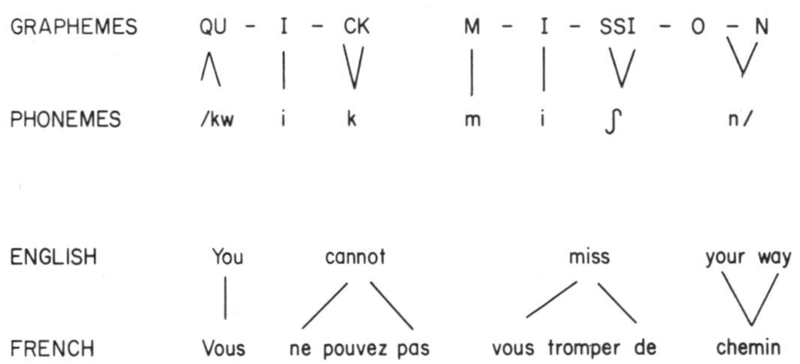

Fig. 7 Segments and their correspondences in translation between French and English, and translation between spelling and sound within English.

illustrating the segmentation problem for phonography and for translation between spoken languages.

Haas (1970) and Venezky (1970) have shown that uncertainty about the appropriate way to segment a grapheme string can be reduced by taking into account various rules. Unfortunately the most powerful of these rules draw upon morphological information which is denied to the process of direct translation by virtue of the fact that such translation, by definition, takes no account of lexical knowledge. In the absence of such morphological constraints it seems clear that no segmenting procedure can be formulated so as to result in a correct translation of all English words. We shall defer an examination of these constraints until they can be discussed together with the problem of choosing the correct correspondences between segmental units.

Correspondences in phonographic translation

Even if we took the solution to our segmentation problem for granted, we would still be left with the major difficulty in translation, that of determining the appropriate correspondences between spelling and sound units. As Venezky (1970) has pointed out, some correspondences are invariant (or nearly so) in the grapheme-to-phoneme direction. Thus we can regularly assign /f/ to F (save in *of*) and the appropriate phonemes can also be readily assigned to M, Y, Z and CK. Similarly, translating from phonemes to graphemes, /θ/ and /ð/ (as in *th*in and *th*en) can invariably be spelled TH (Hanna *et al.*, 1966). It should already be clear from the foregoing, as it is from the mapping of correspondences shown in Fig. 6, that ambiguity differs between the two directions of translation. What is predictable in the reading direction, need not be so in the spelling direction; and the converse is also true. Clearly this fact has considerable practical implications, and we shall return to a consideration of this asymmetry at the end of this section.

The most detailed examination of English orthography, from the viewpoint of grapheme-to-phoneme translation, has been that of Venezky (1970), which was based on a computer analysis of the spelling–sound correspondences in the 20,000 commonest English words. These correspondences were tabulated according to the position in the word in which they occurred (initial, medial, final) and for each correspondence a list was derived of the words in which it occurred. These data allowed Venezky to arrive at his main descriptive aim. For each grapheme or graphemic functional unit he was able to describe its distribution over word-positions, its possible phonemic correspondents, and a third attribute, which he termed "graphemic alternations". This term refers to a fairly predictable source of variation in the correspondences whereby two graphemes may substitute one for the other depending upon the graphemic context. For example, in the case of I and E, the suffix *-ity* becomes *-ety* when preceded by the letter I (e.g. *society*) but its sounding does not change. Here there is a complication of the spelling–sound correspondence, but the resultant disjunctive mapping need not create real ambiguity, since the choice is predictable from the graphemic context. In this example the context is defined in terms of a particular graphemic environment; in others it may be word-position that matters (e.g. the alternation of I with Y).

Venezky devoted some space to the traditional preoccupation with the "regularity" of correspondences. He has remarked upon the looseness of the prevailing usage of the term "regularity", commenting: "The true problem faced here is deciding what to count" (Venezky, 1970, p. 124). In place of the gross concept of regularity, Venezky offered a more detailed classification, shown in Table 5. The major division is into *predictable* and *unpredictable* correspondences, and Venezky makes an important distinction between predictability and variability (the existence of disjunctive mappings).

Table 5 Venezky's classification of English spelling-to-sound correspondences (from Venezky, 1970, p. 126)

(I) PREDICTABLE

Patterns which can be predicted upon the basis of regular graphemic, morphemic or phonemic features of the word or sentences in which they occur

- (A) *Invariant.* Patterns which admit no (or very few) variations or exceptions
- (B) *Variant.* Patterns which have predictable variations or exceptions (variant patterns could be divided further on the basis of the features needed to predict each pattern)

(II) UNPREDICTABLE

All patterns which do not fit into (I)

- (A) *Affix-aided.* Patterns which could be derived by relating the word to one of its prefixed or suffixed forms, e.g. *sign–signal*
- (B) *High-frequency.* Occurs frequently (frequently enough to allow an association group to be profitably employed in teaching)
- (C) *Low-frequency.* Occurs too infrequently to merit the formation of an association group

Let us consider some examples. The sound correspondence of F is invariant (ignoring *of*) and therefore also predictable. The sound of C, on the other hand, is variant. Nevertheless, many of these variations are predictable. Most instances can be accommodated by the graphemic context rule that C is sounded /s/ before the spellings I, Y or E, but otherwise sounded /k/. C in *call* and in *cell* can therefore be said to be predictable but variant (Venezky's category IB). In contrast, the C in *cello* is unpredictable and low in frequency (category IIC). Although there is a reason for the sounding in *cello* (the regular correspondence in Italian from which the word is borrowed), such a reason, however certain, cannot be considered as a source of predictability in Venezky's scheme.

Now, Venezky's classification scheme was designed with the problem of teaching reading in mind. For example, the distinction between categories IIB and IIC is purely pragmatic, depending upon whether an exceptional pattern occurs often enough for it to be worth developing a mnemonic for that group of instances. But the trouble is that Venezky's taxonomy derives from an arbitrary mixture of linguistic and pedagogic criteria. For example, why should the morphological rule enabling us to translate the PH in *shepherd* be regarded as predictable (category IB), when the morphological rule relating *sign* to *signal* to elucidate the G correspondence is regarded as unpredictable (category IIA)?

Let us see whether we can tidy up the issues. Consider, first, the linguistic criteria bearing upon predictability. Broadly speaking there are three types of source for predictive rules: morphology, phonemic context, and graphemic context. We have seen that the sounding of PH in *shepherd* and of G in *sign* is governed by coherent morphophonological rules. The silent B in *debt* is derived from a phonemic context rule and the soft C in *cell* from a graphemic context rule. However, the concept of a "rule" is not clearly defined: powerful rules, such as those just cited, shade off gradually into predictabilities of other sorts. The point here is that most spelling–sound mappings have an *explanation*. (We have considered a range of historical explanations in Section 4.1.) Such explanations come in varying shades of rulelikeness. At one extreme there are explanations that appeal to historical accidents, such as the C erroneously added to *scissors* after the pronunciation had been fixed. At a slightly greater level of generality, there are foreign borrowings. For instance, a silent S frequently occurs in words adopted from the French (*corps*, *bourgeois*, etc.). Even in words no longer thought of as foreign loans, pronunciation often reflects their origin. *Soup* and *group* owe their exceptional sounding of OU to their French origin.

There are, therefore, various sort of linguistic justifications for particular spelling–sound correspondences. It is quite another matter to decide which of these justifications can usefully be employed in teaching the child to read. We cannot determine *a priori* what rationale will be memorable to the child, and many of the more powerful linguistic rules depend upon subtle and complex variables that may be inaccessible to the child.

So far we have seen that such concepts as "regularity" or "predictability" can have a basis in linguistic rules and linguistic justifications and a different basis in the pedagogy of reading. In Chapter 5 we shall have to consider a third usage which overlaps with the linguistic but is logically distinct. This concept of regularity is psychological and has to do with theories that postulate a prelexical channel for translating print into sound using only nonlexical correspondence rules. Such a strategy, by stopping short of lexical information, cannot call upon morphological or syntactic rules but can draw on nonlexical rules like graphemic context rules.

The primary aim of Venezky's work was to cast light upon the process of reading, and he is careful to distinguish the correspondences required for reading from those for spelling. For an analysis of the predictability of correspondences in the phoneme-to-grapheme direction we must turn to the work of Hanna and his associates (Hanna *et al.*, 1966). They conducted a computer search of a 17,000 word corpus drawn largely from Part 1 of the Thorndike–Lorge *Teacher's Word Book*. These items were then described in terms of 52 phonemes, enabling a list of the graphemic correspondents of each of these phonemes to be compiled. The decision as to what constituted a functional graphemic unit caused Hanna *et al.* some difficulty, and some of their solutions seem rather odd. In the case of silent final E they invented a silent phoneme as a specific correspondent with this grapheme. A more conventional and linguistically sensible solution is that which treats the E as part of a single functional unit that specifies a "long" vowel. For example, in *make* the medial vowel phoneme would be assigned the graphemic unit: A(consonant)E.

The main substance of Hanna *et al.*'s study consists of this listing of the frequency distribution of the various graphemic options corresponding to each of the 52 phonemes. When compared with the fairly refined linguistic analysis offered by Venezky, the Hanna *et al.* study appears rather more basic. Morphological constraints, for example, are not considered. The only predictive factors that are used in the classification are syllable position (initial, medial, final) and whether or not the syllable is stressed. Nevertheless, Hanna *et al.* are able to claim that these constraints enable correspondences to be predicted with 84% accuracy. In the absence of stress and position information, predictability fell to 73%. That is the performance level arrived at by choosing the most common graphemic correspondent for each phoneme.

Hanna *et al.* went on to develop an algorithm for translating phonemes into their spellings. To the factors of stress and position they added information about phonemic context (i.e. the identity of surrounding phonemes) and thus ended up with a system of about 200 "rules". They then tested the power of the algorithm to deal with the 17,000 words. The result of this test (see Hanna *et al.*, 1966, table 22) indicated that 50% of the words could be spelled without error. A further 36% contained no more than one error. This performance is not particularly impressive. In fact, Simon and Simon (1973) have shown that a group of nine-year-olds can conclusively outperform the computer algorithm: the algorithm generated on the test corpus 27% errors, but the children averaged less than 3%.

At least the power of the Hanna *et al.* spelling algorithm is known. No equivalent statistics seem to be available for translation rules in the grapheme-to-phoneme direction. Venezky (1970) provides no quantiative data on the frequencies of particular correspondences. Wijk (1966), however, does provide some estimates for the power of his rules. These are based on the proportion of words which require to be changed in order to accord with his *Regularized Inglish*. These changes, he claims, need be applied to less than 10% of the total vocabulary (see also Wijk, 1969). However, the rules work relatively poorly for the most common words. Of the commonest 3000 words as many as 21% violate the rules.

Recently, the concept of the predictability of correspondences has played an increasing role in psychological experimentation. Thus, for example, Baron and Strawson (1976), Stanovich and Bauer (1978), and Coltheart *et al.* (1979) have compared the latency of naming "regular" and "exception" words. The employment of this concept out of context has certain dangers. First, although it is easy to fall into the habit of speaking of regularity as if it were an absolute and categorical attribute, regularity is only interpretable with respect to some set of hypothetical rules. By adding to the rules we can always increase the size of the "regular" category, although, of course, each new rule tends to apply to a diminishing number of instances. Moreover, the complexity of the rules tends to increase. (In the *reductio ad absurdum* a "rule" only embraces a single instance.)

A second difficulty arises in the interpretation of the power of a system of rules. We have seen that although the Hanna *et al.* system only spelled 50% of English words correctly, the accuracy of this algorithm is often cited as 80%, on the basis of individual correspondences. Again, Coltheart (1978) cites a number of estimates in the 80–95% range as evidence of the considerable regularity of English. As we have seen, such figures, without further qualification, can be misleading.

Finally, a difficulty occurs when estimates of regularity are brought to bear on the question of *direct* phonographic translation, that is, translation which does not involve consultation of the mental lexicon. Thus, Coltheart (1978) supposes regular words (defined by the Wijk–Venezky rules) to be amenable to *direct* translation, but the difficulty here is that some of these rules appeal to morphological considerations. (No estimate of how much of their power depends on morphology seems to be available.) Yet it is unclear how a process that is nonlexical can gain access to morphological information.

We shall turn to a psychological examination of the hypothesis of direct translation in Part II, but it is appropriate in the present context to consider what the orthography allows. Imagine a simple translating device. In order to spell, this device scans the speech sound, segmenting it into phonemes and translating each phoneme (or occasionally a functional unit comprising a pair of phonemes) into graphemic correspondents, one by one. Oral reading is obtained by the reverse of this process. For such a plodding device the only method of minimizing errors is to base decisions on a frequency criterion. Thus segmentation and translation are based upon choosing the solution that works correctly in the largest number of words. (Other, slightly more complicated frequency criteria are also possible, but such distinctions are not germane here.)

As we have seen, the performance of such a device can be greatly improved by allowing it to utilize contextual constraints. But if the device is limited to *direct translation*, as psychological theorists have often had need to suppose, the device cannot be influenced by rules whose applications depend upon knowledge of morphological and syntactic features of the word. In direct translation, the input can only be treated as a nonlexical string of sounds or letters. For this reason, it is convenient to distinguish *same-level* constraints from *higher-level* constraints. Generally speaking, same-level constraints take account of regularities at the graphemic or phonemic level (for example, the fact that /k/ is never translated as CK in word-initial positions). Higher-level constraints have to do with morphological or lexical factors, that is, with regularities which occur when phonemes or graphemes are composed together into significant units (for example, TH is pronounced with voicing in functors such as *the* and without voicing in contentives such as *thin*).

The predictability introduced by these two forms of constraint is considerable. Haas (1970) has examined the constraints by means of the example of Bernard Shaw's alternative spelling of *fish* as GHOTI (GH as in *tough*, O as in *women*, TI as in *nation*). Using only same-level regularities we can establish that GH is never sounded /f/ in word-initial position nor TI as /ʃ/ in word-final position. In fact Haas goes so far as to claim that "according to the rules of English orthography /fiʃ/ *can* only be written FISH".

Same-level constraints

What sorts of same-level constraint can we distinguish? Broadly speaking, we can distinguish constraints upon position (in syllable or word) and constraints upon sequences. Furthermore, we can apply the constraints both to phonemes and to graphemes, giving four possible types of constraint. Phonemic contextual constraints are usually known as *phonotaxis*. The best known of these consist of prohibition of certain sequences of stop consonant sounds. The implications that these have for spelling-sound translation are brought out by Venezky (1970), using the example of *subpoena*. The sequences /pb/ and /bp/ do not occur in English, so when their normal graphemic correspondents occur the first grapheme is silent. Other phonotactic regularities combine sequential with positional constraints. MB is sounded fully where it straddles a syllabic boundary (*ambit*) but the B is silent when the cluster closes a word (*bomb*). In fact, a full description of the correspondents of MB probably requires a higher-level rule, since the B is also silent before inflexional affixes (*bombing*), but not before other morphemes (*bombard*). This introduction of morphological considerations removes the regularity to a higher level.

Phonotactic constraints are often spoken of as "rules" as if they derived their force from something more powerful than the observation that certain patterns do not in fact occur. I suppose that I have flirted with this view by using the word "prohibition" above. Perhaps such a view gains strength from the fact that the prohibited sequences are generally difficult to articulate. Nevertheless, pronunciation is subject to conventions which are mobile, so it would be more cautious to regard these constraints as regularities that just happen to be universal.

This component of arbitrariness is more obvious in graphotactic patterns. Borrowing another example from Venezky, word-final V (and U) has been avoided in English since the late Middle English period. Where final /v/ occurs, the V is followed by a silent E. To take another example, the digraph CK is never found in word initial position. Therefore, when a word starts with /k/, this graphemic correspondent is not an option.

The distinction between phonotactic and graphotactic constraints in these examples is a clear one. For example, it is CK and not /k/ that is prohibited in word-initial position. However, some writers have used such phrases as "orthographic rules" in ways which obscure and even confuse the distinction. Thus Gibson and Levin (1975, pp. 172ff.) distinguish "phonological" from "orthographic" rules, defining the latter as "the legal letter sequences". Yet the examples they provide of these rules are sometimes curiously ambiguous: some, like the prohibited initial CK and final BL are clearly graphotactic; others, like initial RT and ND, seem to be prohibited on phonotactic grounds.

Another set of constraints, this time purely positional, are those which Venezky calls *graphemic alternations* (Venezky, 1970, pp. 37–38). In this set, two letters occur in what is known by linguists as "complementary distribution". That is to say, whichever of two alternative graphemes occurs depends on position in the word, rather as allophones substitute one for another according to the articulatory context. The major example of graphemic alternation involves the letter I and Y. The general form of the rules is that Y substitute for I in final position. However, thus formulated, there are many exceptions (*dying*, *taxi*). Some can be accounted for by additional, same-level context rules; others require appeal to a higher-level attribute, such as foreign borrowing (*confetti*, *ski*).

The phonotactic and graphotactic constraints examined so far can be described without mention of the translation between spelling and sound. They refer to purely phonemic contextual conditions for the occurrence of a given phoneme and purely graphemic conditions governing grapheme occurrences. However, I have concentrated on examples which have implications for translation. Clearly many phonotactic constraints do not bear upon the spelling or reading of particular words (the avoidance of initial /nd/, say). However, in an example like *subpoena* where the graphemes would normally indicate phonemes of which the sequencing is prohibited, the resultant suppression of the sound of the first grapheme does have implications for translation. These implications are determinate for reading (Don't sound the P) but vague and unhelpful for writing (There could be a B before the P). Graphotactic constraints appear invariably to have implications for spelling. This may be because graphotactic constraints have been subject to less comment, and so we only identify them when they predict translations from sound to spelling that could have been otherwise. In Section 4 of this chapter we shall examine probabilistic regularities of pattern amongst graphemes which have been studied by psychologists interested in the visual identification of words rather than their translation into sound.

Before we leave same-level constraints we must take note of a further species of constraint that differs subtly from those already discussed. To mark this distinction I have reserved the terms "graphotactic" and "phonotactic" for constraints upon the occurrence of graphemes and phonemes. Although these often have implications for phonographic translation, the constraint nevertheless operates upon the *occurrence* of the unit and not upon the nature of its *translation*. However, there also exist constraints upon the translation (correspondence). Thus C is sounded /k/ before A, O and U but /s/ before E, I, and Y. Haas has called constraints of this sort "graphotactic rules for the reader" (1970, p. 59), but this usage obscures the difference between prohibited occurrence (e.g. of initial CK) and prohibited translation (e.g. of CE as /ke/). The true class membership of Haas's "graphotactic rules for the reader" is with the *markers*. Examples of markers are the silent final E that lengthens a preceding vowel (*mat*, *mate*), or the silent U that intervenes between G and E or I to prevent the softening: G→/j/. Unfortunately, linguists have reserved the term *marker* for graphemes that indicate the appropriate correspondence of another grapheme while being themselves silent. As a consequence of this definition the final E that softens the C in *peace* may be called a marker, whereas the E in *cent* may not because, although it softens the C in identical fashion, it also is itself sounded. In this latter case the linguists permit us to say that the E "performs marking functions" (e.g. Venezky, 1970, p. 52). These marker functions constrain translation in both directions, though not necessarily to the same extent.

In summary, we can note that there are three broad classes of same-level constraint. Within a string of graphemes there may be contextual effects upon grapheme occurrence (graphotaxis) and contextual effects upon grapheme translation (marker functions). Within a string of phonemes there may be contextual effects upon phoneme occurrence. An equivalent of marker functions amongst phonemes does not appear to exist, so the possible fourth cell, in this two-by-two classification, remains empty.

Higher-level constraints

We turn now to higher-level constraints in which correspondences are predictable from morphological or etymological properties of the language. One such basis of prediction (discussed above) involves the consequences of morphemic boundaries for segmentation. The segmental ambiguity arises where we have a possible digraph, the conjunction of two graphemes that are generally sounded as a single functional unit (e.g. PH in *morpheme*, DD in *adder*, GN in *signer*). When these pairs of consonants straddle a morpheme boundary, they are segmented into single graphemes and translated separately (compare with the preceding: *shepherd*, *midday*, *ignore*).

Another source of morphological/syntactic influence is due to form class. Pronunciation of the digraph TH is voiced in functors such as *then*, but voiceless in contentives such as *thin*. (Most people who have no difficulty with translating this digraph are none the less surprised to discover that the rule is so simple. This suggests either that the rule is unconsciously used, or, more radically, that the correspondence used in functors is learned as a small, undefined group of exceptions to a general rule that initial TH is voiceless.) A major set of form class influences is mediated by stress, which we shall discuss separately.

A rather minor morphological determinant of pronunciation is to be found in the example of *bombard* v. *bombed*, which we have previously examined. Here the rules depends upon the class of suffix. The B is silent before inflectional suffixes but not before other morphemes.

The rules considered thus far have enabled the prediction of pronunciation. Morphological constraints upon spelling often involve whole affixes, rather than individual grapheme–phoneme correspondences. A major source of difficulty in English spelling stems from the existence of a set of affixes that cannot be distinguished on the basis of sound. Perhaps the most notorious occurs in the contrast between nominal *principle* and adjectival *principal*. Others, to which Haas (1970, pp. 66–67) draws attention, include the fact that /əl/ tends to be written as AL in derived nouns (*recital*) and adjectives (*herbal*), but with a variety of other spellings in underived nouns (*shovel*, *petrol*, *peril*).

Morphological constraints also operate at a similar level to disambiguate the pronunciation of homographs and to disambiguate the spelling of homophones. Thus the vowel correspondence in TEAR differs in sounding according to whether the sense is *weeping* or *ripping*. Conversely, the spelling of /teə/ depends on whether TEAR or TARE is intended. Where morphological factors act to disambiguate the spelling or pronunciation of whole, lexical items English is often said to operate logographically or logophonically. However, there is actually no great difference between the use of morphological information to predict the spelling of the second vowel in *herbal* and the medial vowel in *tare*. The fact that *tear* is also a word but that *herbel* is not is a lexical accident. In both cases it is ambiguous alphabetic correspondences that are constrained.

We turn now to the complex and important question of stress. It is well known that spoken English contains patterns of stress. On reflection it is clear that stress involves the accentuation of certain vowels and syllables. A little further thought reveals that some aspects of stress, at least, are lawful. In the noun *cón-vict* the stress falls on the first syllable. In the verb *con-víct* the stress shifts to the second syllable. When we turn out attention to whole utterances we find that the function words are unstressed. It is generally the content words that contain the stress, and the listener experiences something like: *in the CONtext of a WHOLE UTTerance*. So much is readily agreed. However, beyond these common intuitions lie uncertainty and disagreement. There is debate about the nature of the physical correlates of stress, though many writers postulate four features: fundamental frequency, intensity, duration, and vowel quality (MacNeilage and Ladefoged, 1976). There is also debate about how many degrees of stress require to be postulated. Finally, there is uncertainty about how representative *typical* patterns of stress are. (It is to *typical* patterns that phonological theories tend to address themselves.)

Phonological interest in stress-assignment rules received impetus from the proposals advanced by Chomsky and Halle (1968). The rules they set out involved a combination of same-level (phonetic) factors with higher-level factors. Stress assignment was predicted from number of syllables, phonetic aspects of the final syllable (e.g. lax v. tense vowel), and form class of the word (noun v. verb). In addition, appeal sometimes had to be made to internal morphemic boundaries.

An important experimental test of the factors influencing the reader's stress assignment was conducted by Baker and Smith (1976). They had subjects read aloud polysyllabic nonsense words. Their experiments were designed to adjudicate between two strategies: (1) pronunciation by analogy with a similar real word; (2) pronunciation by phonological rule. In fact, subjects appeared to draw upon both of these strategies. Baker and Smith were able to confirm that phonetic, morphological and syntactic properties of a word all tended to influence the stress assignment, though these properties did not always predict performance in the ways described by Chomsky and Halle's theory.

We have seen that higher-level constraints play a role in determining stress assignment, but we have treated stress somewhat vaguely, without considering its implications for the choice of grapheme–phoneme correspondences. Probably the most prevalent effect of stress upon correspondences in reading occurs in the translation of the primary vowels A, E, I, O, and U and certain vowel digraphs such as OU, in unstressed syllables. In this, the most striking example of convergent translation, all the correspondences are with the unstressed vowel sound known as *schwa* and transcribed /ə/. For the reader, it is only necessary to determine word stress in order to assign *schwa* to a vowel grapheme (Table 6).

For the speller, arriving at the correct graphemic correspondent of a *schwa* is perhaps the most notorious problem in English spelling. Frequently, however, the correct correspondent is predictable on the basis of form class or morphological derivedness (as in the /əl/ example treated above).

Table 6 Examples of the translation of a variety of vowel graphemes into the unstressed vowel phoneme schwa (ə). In these particular examples the words have two syllables with the stress falling upon the first. The unstressed second syllables all sound the same despite considerable variation in spelling

hon*our*
mart*y*r
act*o*r
bak*e*r
alt*a*r
nad*i*r
meas*u*re

In the probabilistic approach of Hanna *et al.* (1966), the addition of stress information increased the predictability of correspondences from 79% to 84%. Even if their stress rules are not optimally formulated, it seems clear that knowledge of the stress pattern has much less predictive value for correspondences in spelling than in reading.

Up to this point we have discussed higher-level constraints that are fairly straightforwardly syntactic or morphological. Before closing this account of these influences, I shall mention two further sources of predictability: transformations and origins. Both have a bearing on spelling.

Transformational information can be understood through the commonly cited example of disambiguation of the schwa in *photography*. The first vowel is ambiguous in a direct phoneme-to-grapheme translation. It might just as well be spelled as in the first vowel of *fatality*. However, apprehension of the relationship between *phótograph* and *photógraphy* serves to disambiguate matters. In *photograph*, the first vowel is stressed and its graphemic representation is therefore clear. But in this instance the second vowel is an ambiguous schwa, which in turn is disambiguated by a comparison with the stressed second vowel in *photography*.

The particular theoretical context out of which interest in transformational cues grew was that of generative phonology. Chomsky and Halle (1968) had suggested that morphologically related words like those in the *photography* family were associated through their possession of a common, abstract lexical base. This abstract structure is more closely related to the spelling than is the sound of the word. Accordingly, C. Chomsky (1970) has suggested that this relationship might be used to aid spelling. An important point to note is that the cues could, in principle, be used in two ways. First, if spelling matches closely some abstract lexical representation of the word's morphological and phonological structure, then that representation could be made to yield up spelling cues directly. Secondly, and this seems on the whole to be the strategy that C. Chomsky favours, the comparison could be confined to the relationship between the surface forms that are generated from the abstract representation, as in the *photograph–photography* example. Now, this second strategy could still be used even if the abstract lexical representation did not exist or if, while existing, it did not allow deliberate access to its constituents. Clearly, the fact that most people can see a relationship between two of the three words *numb*, *number*, *numbed*, does not, by itself, constitute proof of the theory of generative phonology.

Transformational cues depend upon the construction of related forms from morphological bases. Origin cues go back further to the etymological sources of a word. Both are distinctive in that they remove the search for information from the particular words in the utterance to be translated. Origin cues, in addition, remove the search from the language itself. Examples of eytmological origin cues are readily come by. The more obvious include the Greek PH for /f/ and numerous silent consonants, reflecting Latin origins (*debt*, *receipt*). In some cases cues for these spellings are also available from transformations (*recipient*). Origin also serves to disambiguate the *schwa* in *actor* and *baker*, *-or* indicating Latin and *-er* Anglo-Saxon derivation.

Although origin cues are obviously only available to the highly educated, a study by Smith and Baker (1976) does suggest that, at least among undergraduate subjects, perceived foreignness of a word may have systematic consequences. Smith and Baker presented subjects with nonsense words in context and required them to read aloud. They also had the subjects rate the foreignness of the nonsense words (the subjects proved to be remarkably creative, suggesting 56 different languages as sources). Where the nonsense form ended with an E there was a correlation between perceived origin and pronunciation. Silent E went with French attribution and sounded E with Italian attribution. Furthermore, in a related study, Smith (1980) required subjects to provide spellings for spoken, nonsense words. Once again perceived origin appeared to influence the subject's choice of forms. Smith summarized his hypothesis in a luminous example:

> The intuition we are expressing here is that a subject is more likely to regard *nodude* (Latin spelling) as a technical verb meaning (say) to weld metals in a certain way, whereas *nodood* (non Latin spelling) might refer to an article of clothing of a North American Indian.

Asymmetry of correspondences in reading and spelling

In the preceding discussion of correspondences and their predictability, I have several times remarked, in passing, upon the asymmetry of difficulties in reading aloud and spelling. This is a question of some practical concern for at least two reasons. First is the attitude of spelling reformers, who have commonly attempted to simplify the problem of reading without any concern for the problem of writing. This point is well made by Haas (1970) in his discussion of the *initial teaching alphabet*. Haas quoted Pitman to the effect that ambiguity in phoneme–grapheme translation "does no great harm" whereas in the grapheme–phoneme direction it represents an "intolerable burden on the child" (Pitman, 1961). Other spelling reformers appear to have held similar views (e.g. Wijk, 1969, p. 72). The second practical reason arises from the recent development of interest in the dissociation between the reading and spelling abilities of children (e.g. Frith, 1976; Bryant and Bradley, 1980).

An obvious, but gross, cue to the asymmetry of translation difficulty is evident in the disparity between the number of phonemes and of graphemic patterns to which they correspond. Estimates of the ratio of phonemes to graphemic correspondents vary according to each commentator's selection of phonemic and graphemic functional units. Wijk (1969) distinguishes 46 phonemes corresponding with 102 graphemic patterns, a ratio of about 4:9. Hanna *et al.* (1966) distinguish 52 phonemes with 170 graphemic correspondents, a ratio of 4:13. Few correspondences in either direction are one-to-one, although in reading N, Q, R, V and X are wholly unambiguous and several more digraphs are unambiguous if correctly segmented. In spelling only /ð/ and /θ/ are entirely without ambiguity. This, then, is the basis of the asymmetry: (*i*) the number of ambiguous correspondences and the amount of ambiguity are greater in spelling than in reading, and (*ii*) for particular pairs of correspondents and for particular words the predictability of translation in one direction cannot be deduced from the predictability in the other direction.

Elsewhere, I have drawn attention to various consequences of this asymmetry (Henderson and Chard, 1980). One such consequence is that a simple translation device that operated by working down an ordered stack of correspondence frequencies, starting with the most frequent, would encounter different difficulties for a given word, depending on the direction of translation. In accounts which define words as "regular" when the correspondences they use are the highest in relative frequency, a word like *chief* would have to be considered regular in pronunciation but highly irregular in spelling. (The most common pronunciation of IE is /i/ though this still only occurs in a minority of cases. On the other hand as a spelling of /i/, IE only occurs on about 2% of occasions.)

The asymmetry of translation difficulties is manifest not only in the divergent mapping of correspondences and the relative frequency of mapping options but also in the action of constraints upon translation in one or other direction. Clearly, in the realm of same-level constraints, the phonotactic rule that determines the pronunciation of *subpoena* does little to predict its spelling. As for higher-level constraints, there are examples of selective prediction of either pronunciation or spelling. We have seen that morpheme boundary information disambiguates pronunciation by specifying the appropriate graphemic segments to be translated. Form class predicts pronunciation of initial TH and spelling of various suffixes. Both morphology and form class affect stress, which is itself an attribute of pronunciation and which determines the mapping of divers vowel letters into *schwa*. Stress also has a slight and probabilistic effect on spelling predictability. Finally, both the transformational strategy and origin cues have their influence primarily on spelling.

Not only do these various linguistic factors yield asymmetries in translation into spelling and into sound, they also tend to result in greater difficulty of translation into spelling. (This bias in favour of reading is less marked in English than in French.) Nevertheless, the major determinants of the relatively greater difficulty of spelling are probably psychological. Foremost amongst these is the fact that we generally come to written language with an already existing command of spoken language, hence when we attempt to read a word, we already have the specification of the word-sound listed in our mental lexicon. It is only a question of translating into a sufficiently approximate form to lead us to this entry in memory. No equivalent store of orthographic specifications is already established in the lexicon of the child when he encounters script.

4.3 SPELLING–MORPHOLOGY CORRESPONDENCES

In the previous section our discussion of spelling–sound correspondences was deliberately held at a rather empirical level. It was as if we had accepted as a working hypothesis the premise that English orthography refers directly to sound, albeit in an irregular way, and had taken as our task the provision of the best description possible of the correspondences between spelling and sound, drawing where necessary on support from sources of constraint external to the spelling–sound relationship. In attempting thus to improve the predictability of sound from spelling we found that what we called higher-level constraints functioned as quite powerful predictors. In some ways these higher-level constraints seemed more rule-like than the various same-level co-occurrence constraints, many of which appeared more like probabilistic generalizations. (However, this is an intuition that I shall not attempt to justify.)

This approach, in which the orthography is regarded as a sort of system for phonetic transcription supplemented by some conveniently available cues from outside the system, treats the correlation between spelling and morphology as essentially fortuitous. However, such an approach not only yields an unsatisfactory account of orthography, it also takes insufficient cognizance of the complex relationship between sound and lexical meaning. To give a fuller account of orthography it is necessary to re-examine the entire system of relationships between all three factors—spelling, sound, and meaning.

The Aristotelian model

Stated systematically, Aristotle's rendering of the traditional view asserts that the relationship of speech sounds to meaning is one of direct correspondence. Script is but a visible record of speech sounds and hence the relationship between script and lexical meaning is indirect, being of necessity mediated by sounds. We can write this proposition thus:

$$\text{SCRIPT} \rightleftarrows \text{SPEECH SOUNDS} \rightleftarrows \text{LEXICAL MEANINGS}$$

This traditional model is the one implicit in most approaches to spelling reform from the sixteenth century onwards. Its view of script is that expressed by Voltaire in his characterization of writing as a sort of picturing of speech (*peinture de la voix*). It appears also to be the model to which Gelb subscribes, in his description of scripts as evolving toward a phonographic ideal, although Gelb does make important concessions to the view that writing may occasionally express more than speech sounds, giving the example of English homophones (*check–cheque*) wherein the ambiguity is removed in the spelling. Significantly, Gelb adopts Bolinger's (1946) term "visual morphemes" for these particular occurrences. However, nowhere does he attempt to subsume such cases in a systematic account of reference in written English.

The phonographic view of script was championed earlier in this century in the influential writings of Bloomfield, notably in his book *Language*, published in 1933. Bloomfield did not hesitate to use the traditional model as a basis for an approach to the teaching of reading, pursuing the implications of his central premise that "the letters of the alphabet are signs which direct us to produce sounds of our language" (Bloomfield, 1942). This can be regarded as a modern translation of the ancient notion of a grapheme's *potestas*, its power to evoke sound.

There are three general sorts of difficulty with this traditional model. First, it does not do justice to the relationship of orthography to morphological structure. Secondly, it implies an over-simple view of the relationship of sound to meaning (the central problem of phonology). Thirdly, it contains implications about the reader's actual performance which are paradoxical, for if script requires to be translated into sound in order to be interpreted lexically (i.e. to gain access to meaning), it is unclear how higher-level constraints can be used to help predict translation into sound. In the extreme case of reading a word aloud without context, translation into sound could not be influenced by higher-level constraints because information about morphemic structure and form class could not be available until translation had been completed and the resultant sounds used to gain access to the mental lexicon.

Re-evaluation of spelling–sound relationships in English

The idea that English orthography is more than an irregular system of phonography is not new. We have already seen the example of Mulcaster, the sixteenth-century opponent of spelling reform, rejoicing in the tendency of written English to preserve linguistic history in its spellings, although Mulcaster's desire to conserve etymological information in the spelling did not amount to a linguistic theory.

Important steps in the direction of a theoretical reappraisal of English orthography were taken some years ago by the Czech linguist, Vachek (e.g. Vachek, 1966). Vachek was particularly concerned with advantages that writing held over speech. One focus of his interest was the emancipation of writing from the limitation of serial access that characterizes speech. Of more concern to us was his adherence to the view that writing contrasted with phonetic transcription in referring directly to meaning, being "the sign of an outside world" (Vachek, 1966, p. 155). Furthermore, he established that Czech writing combined phonemic and morphemic correspondences and held this also to be a property of English.

The notion that English orthography tends toward conservation of morphological information was developed and systematically explored in the work of Venezky (1970; see also Weir and Venezky, 1968). Preservation of morphemic identity across variant lexical forms is the cause of graphemes alternating between sounding and silence, as in the celebrated B of *bomb* and *bombard* (see Section 2). It is the cause of phonographic divergence in certain inflectional suffixes, so that we have *dog-z* but *cat-s* and *tapp-t* but *tabb-d*. In these and many more cases a given morpheme takes varying phonetic forms, though these variants are predictable from the phonetic context. The morphographic spelling, however, remains constant, insensitive to phonetic variation. In Venezky's words, "the orthographic preservation of morphemic identity is predicted on the assumption that the reader knows the phonemic alternations that accompany derivational and inflectional formations" (1970, p. 120).

Venezky's work was essentially pragmatic, being aimed at the prediction of sound from spelling. For this reason, perhaps, he does not dwell on the implication of his analysis for views of the nature of English orthography. The very brief section of his book devoted to an explicit consideration of this question amounts to little more than a summary of the factors influencing the predictability of spelling–sound correspondences. This often involves him in stressing the simple phonographic predictabilities that exist, as when he asserts: "the spelling of the base form of a word tends to be phonemic" (p. 120), and he even qualifies his comments on the morphographic nature of the representation of derived and inflected forms with the observation that even in these forms the morphographic representation is often supplemented with "phonemic aids", such as the doubling of consonants before a suffix to indicate the quality of the preceding vowel (e.g. *labelling*). Nevertheless it is clear from Venezky's descriptive model of orthographic translation that he assumes the immediate referent of the orthography to be morphemic. The stages of the translation are illustrated in Table 7. The first stage involves the access to morphemic identities using the graphemic code. These morphemic units are then assigned a general morphophonemic form which is operated on by an ordered set of rules that specify first grammatical and phonotactic constraints and then graphemic constraints, until a final phonetic form can be realized.

Table 7 Venezky's model of orthographic translation illustrated using his example of generating the pronunciation of SIGNING

Input	Graphemic form (morpheme identification and segmentation)	SIGNING
Stage 1	Morphemic representation (rules for assigning morphophonemes)	*sign ing*
Stage 2	Morphophonemic representations (stress and phonotactic rules)	/sɪgn/ /ɪng/
		/sɪ́gnɪŋg/
	(graphemic translation rules)	
		/sáɪnɪŋ/
Stage 3	Phonetic form	[sáɪnɪŋ]

The status of Venezky's (1970) formal model is uncertain. It seems clear that the model is not intended to have psychological reality. Elsewhere (Venezky and Calfee, 1970), he appears to imply that letter–sound rules are rarely available "other than to some linguists and reading specialists". Instead, Venezky suggests, the reader may adopt a pragmatic trial-and-error approach to spelling–sound translation, influenced by analogies between words as distinct from abstract rules.[7] Moreover Venezky is silent on the processes which yield up the morphophonemic representation, processes I have called "morpheme identification" and "rules for assigning morphophonemes". It would, however, be unfair to dwell upon the summary form of the model, since Venezky's purpose is best regarded as the pragmatic one of giving a parsimonious account of the predictabilities in spelling–sound translation, rather than proposing a coherent theory of the marriage of orthography and phonology.

Developments in phonological theory

I have already suggested that the inadequacies of the traditional Aristotelian theory can best be understood in the context of a systematic re-examination of the relationships between writing, speech and lexical meaning. For a variety of reasons the impetus for such a re-examination came from phonology. Although it may seem at first sight odd that a new account of orthography should have its provenance in the study of the relation of sound to meaning, the reasons are not hard to find. Phonology has long been a vigorous discipline not only at a descriptive level but also in terms of theory. For much of the period over which modern linguistics developed (say, since the mid-nineteenth-century) the study of orthography was almost exclusively historical and had little or no connection with general linguistic theory. Indeed for some of those who were concerned with phonology or syntax, orthography had no independent existence as a field of study. This was always an implication of the traditional view of script as parasitic on speech. (Venezky (1970) contains a useful survey of studies of orthography by early grammarians.)

It is possible to trace much of the development in phonological theory since the beginning of the century in terms of the vicissitudes of the concept of the *phoneme*. In the problematic journey from the raw, acoustic signal to meaning, linguists have generally treated the phoneme as a bridge to be placed across the most forbidding gulf of which their survey informed them.

We have already examined that journey from the point of view of the psychologist's attempt to explain speech perception (Chapter 2). In the linguist's approach, speech perception has generally been taken for granted, if only because the linguist's analysis traditionally began with a thorough phonetic transcription of the speech sound. Such an analysis therefore starts from a point determined by the discriminative sensitivity of the transcriber.

Speech forms a continuum that is infinitely divisible. This conclusion is evident from physical measurement but it presents itself as a hard-won discovery for the enquiring transcriber. The notion that speech could be represented in terms of discrete segments probably had multiple origins. In part, it may have derived from introspection upon the process of articulation, or it may have been a purely auditory intuition. Certainly the demands of transcription seem to be most readily met by a representation in terms of discrete symbols. This in turn serves as a reminder that the alphabet represents an intuition about the segmental quality of speech and, once available, acts to reinforce the segmented perception. The objectives of phonetic transcription are different from those of natural writing, however, and the transcription is required to capture nuances that are less obviously discontinuous. Because there is no physical basis for a segmental description of speech, its justification must lie in the possibility of describing the sound stream in terms of a succession of ideal states, plus a set of rules that use the context of states to determine the particular form taken by a state (i.e. coarticulation) and the transition between states (Anderson, 1974).

Such a description will represent features which are irrelevant to the signification of lexical distinctions in a given language. In English, aspiration of voiceless stop consonants is such a feature, as we saw with the allophonic variations of /t/. Another favourite example in English is the initial consonant in *keep*, *coop*, and *cop*. Here the demands made by the articulation of the following vowel shift the place of articulating the /k/ forward on the roof of the mouth, as we progress through the three instances, so that an attentive phonetic transcriber would write something like [k1], [k] and [q] respectively. Many of these allophonic variations are entirely predictable from the phonetic context. This fact itself constitutes further grounds for the conclusion that such features play no role in signalling meaning. To the extent that such phonetic variation is not wholly predictable, this is largely due to vague but important influences such as the "carefulness" of speech.

The intuition about the existence of a deeper phonemic level was born out of the convergence of two principles: one that argued for the exclusion of phonetic features that were predictable and one concerned with the essential contrasts in speech that signified lexical meanings. The crucial distinction between phonemic theories consisted in the depth at which this phonemic level was located. In some early treatments, such as the work of Saussure, the phonemic level is discussed in very abstract terms which relate to the function of contrasting signs in a language system. Saussure's concern was limited to the internal workings of a system of contrasting signs, with no attention to the nature of such a representation and its relation to the phonetic domain. Other early theorists, however, tended to emphasize the derivation of the phonemic level in the physical reality of speech, as described in phonetic transcription. Such a conception is often called a "surface phoneme". It is the surface phoneme which poses the problem of translation from the phonetic level (phones) into phonemes. In our discussion of speech perception in Chapter 2 we saw that such translations forced us into arbitrary and inconsistent decisions about phoneme assignment (the *grater–grader* problem). In order to rationalize the assignment of phonemes, it was necessary to work forward from the morphemic level rather than backward from phones, and hence was born the notion of a morphophonemic level of representation. At such a level the common morphemic identity of forms is preserved in the phonemic representation, even though inflection or derivation may have changed the actual phonetic realization of these abstract phonemes. Thus for the problematic *t* and *d* in *grater* and *grader* we would write /t/ and /d/ to signal the relationships with *grate* and *grade* even though the phonetic distinction in the former pair lies often in the preceding *a* rather than the consonant.

The development of the phonemic intuition is described by Anderson (1974). A crucial stage in his account is represented by Bloomfield's conception in which the phoneme proper is correlated with the phonetic level, but in addition a deeper morphophonemic level is treated. This abstract level is, for Bloomfield, "nothing but a descriptive device invented by the linguist to keep things straight, and to organize his data" (Anderson, 1974, p. 24).

In the later development, which came to be known as "taxonomic phonemics", the attempt was made to specify the exact relationship between phonemes and phonetics. This approach, according to Anderson, was characterized by "absolute faith in the proposition that whatever distinguished one phoneme element from another was located in the phonetic event alone". He provides several reasons for the adherence to a phonetically anchored definition of the phoneme. In part it arose from the inductive strategy of the linguistic field worker when attempting to describe the phonology of unfamiliar languages. Clearly such an enterprise has to begin from the sound rather than the system of lexical contrasts. Interestingly, another reason offered by Anderson is due to a commitment to a certain psychological view of speech perception. Thus speech perception was widely held to be accomplished by a passive procedure in which the acoustic signal is sorted through a classification net by means of lists of defining features. The failure of such a translation algorithm to derive phones from the acoustic signal was used earlier as a way of examining the nature of the speech recognition problem.

The concept of a morphophonemic level, even if only as a linguist's fiction, had often coexisted with the doctrines of surface phonemes. We have noted that the former, deep level tended to be invoked in the context of attempts to work forward from meanings to sound. In a sense, such an attempt underlay the radical development of phonological theory by Chomsky and Halle (1968).

In *Syntactic Structures* (1957), Chomsky's principal objective had been to describe the process of arriving at a linguistic output in terms of a terminal string of morphemic units; however, Chomsky had seen the need to translate the string of abstract morphemes comprising surface structure into actual spoken forms. This process was outlined by positing morphophonemic rules for transforming morphemes into phonemes (e.g. *take*+*past*→/tuk/). At this stage in the theory the phonological problem received little more than acknowledgement of its existence, as Greene (1972) put it, "for the sake of completeness" in Chomsky's description of grammar.

Chomsky's major revision of his theory, presented in *Aspects of the Theory of*

Syntax (1965), dispensed with the notion of a morphophonemic level intermediate between the string of lexical morphemes and the physical realization of speech. Instead, the phonological component of his theory described procedures for translating morphemes directly into their spoken forms, and this set of proposals is examined in some detail in the specifically phonological volume, *The Sound Pattern of English* (Chomsky and Halle, 1968). In this work the authors set out to consider phonology in the context of general linguistic theory. For this reason they give more emphasis to phonetic features such as stress, which seem to carry general implications, in contrast to features such as degree of aspiration, which do not. Moreover, they are at some pains to justify their lack of any account of exceptions to the phonological rules they propose. This lack, is due to their interest in describing the principles of a universal grammar rather than any particular concern for the details of English phonology. Thus they assert that "exceptions to rules are of interest only if they suggest a different general framework or the formulation of deeper rules. In themselves they are of no interest" (Chomsky and Halle, 1968, ix).

In the theory it is proposed that the mental lexicon contains abstract morphemic units. These lexical entries express the ideal phonological form of the morpheme. However, sometimes these ideal forms are not ready for the application of phonological rules which are to translate them into a phonetic representation. Accordingly, their form must be subjected to a preliminary modification by the *readjustment rules*. For example, in forming the past tense these rules would be used to transform the lexical representations *sing+past* and *mend+past* into the (abstract) phonological representations *sang* and *mended*. It is the concern of the phonological rules to translate the abstract phonological representation into a phonetic form occurring in the context of an entire utterance. The phonological representation, even though it is abstract, takes the form of a set of phonetic features. However, these only relate to features of the eventual phonetic representation through the operation of the phonological rules. There is a division of responsibility between the lexicon and the phonological rules whereby it is a matter for the lexicon to specify irregular properties, such as the past form of *sing*, so that the phonological form on which the rules operate contains sufficient information for the rules to predict the phonetic form appropriate in a given context. The lexicon contains no indication of matters which are predictable by the rules. Thus, for example, the lexical representation of *telegraph* will be a morphemic string:

+tele+græf+

(where + designates a morpheme boundary and the symbols describe ideal phonetic forms). The phonological rules must be able to convert this underlying form into several different variants at the phonetic level, such as:

1 3 teləgr æ f	(in isolation)
3 1 teləgr æ f	(in *telegraphic*)
1 talegr əf	(in *telegraphy*)

(where the numerals indicate degrees of stress).

An important point to note is that Chomsky and Halle assign a lexical representation to a word by working backward from the phonetic representation. That is, the form the lexical representation takes is determined by the requirement that when the phonological rules are applied to it then this results in the appropriate phonetic realization. Therefore it is sometimes possible to posit alternative underlying, lexical representations, since the only criterion is that the phonetic form be derivable by applying the rules to the lexical form. Here we see the non-psychological character of the theory: neither the existence of lexical representations nor, *a fortiori*, the particular form they take is inferred from some aspect of behaviour; rather, these abstract representations are assumed because they permit a powerful description of phonological regularities in language.

At this point Chomsky and Halle introduce their provocative observation about English orthography. The crux of their argument is the claimed resemblance between the actual spelling of English words and their hypothetical, abstract lexical representations. They continue:

> The fundamental principle of orthography is that phonetic variation is not indicated where it is predictable by general rule. Thus stress placements and regular vowel or consonant alternations are generally not reflected. Orthography is a system designed for readers who know the language, who understand sentences and therefore know the surface structure of sentences. Such readers can produce the correct phonetic forms, given the orthographic representation and the surface structure by means of the rules that they employ in producing and interpreting speech (Chomsky and Halle, 1968, p. 48).

Chomsky and Halle extol the merits of an orthography that matches underlying lexical representations. Such an orthography should have a long life because of the stability of lexical representations. Dialect and historical change in pronunciation can be accommodated by changes in the phonological rules for transforming these underlying forms into particular dialects.

Reading aloud, in Chomsky and Halle's theory, begins as it does in Venezky's, with the use of the grapheme string to access the abstract lexical representation. The comprehension process then assigns a surface syntactic structure to the lexical representation. To this structured representation the phonological rules can be applied and a phonetic representation derived.

Some orthographic options for English

The rationale that Chomsky and Halle provide for English orthography has been considered in an interesting paper by Klima (1972), who examines a range of orthographic options, beginning with those that reflect surface phonemes and progressing to ones that reflect increasingly abstract levels of representation. The most superficial level of orthographic representation that Klima considers is quite similar to that of Turkish, Serbo-Croat and Finnish. It is worth noting that Klima starts from the assumption that the reader knows the phonological rules of the language. Accordingly, even his most superficial orthography is much more abstract than a phonetic transcription and might be liable to offend the majority of spelling reformers. In discussing this orthographic option, Lotz (1972) echoes one of Chomsky and Halle's points and comments on the problem that a superficial orthography encounters in dialect variation.

For Klima, the main objection to a superficial orthography is its lack of economy, by which he means the extent to which the indication of variation is left to the phonological rules. However, he is careful to add the proviso that the appropriate criterion for optimality would take account of the level of phonology that was "most readily accessible in the process of reading and writing" (Klima, 1972, p. 67). In effect, by asserting the primacy of psychological criteria, Klima has implicitly challenged the *aprioristic* basis of the Chomsky–Halle concept of optimality.

Klima turns to a consideration of orthographic options which maximize structural economy. Where such a letter assignment convention does not represent morphological boundaries, there results a system like that for English. This convention has the familiar property of preserving the underlying morphemic form of inflectional endings (*-ed*, *-s*, etc.), while ignoring their predictable phonetic variants ([d], [t], [əd], etc.). The convention described by Klima resembles, at least in principle, that which governs English, but he moves beyond this to consider a modification in which the orthography reflects internal word boundaries. Such a feature would be more substantial in its linguistic implications than in its effect upon the predictability of pronunciation. In practical terms it would only serve to resolve contrasts like that of *singer* with *finger* in which the *g* is silent before an internal word boundary (but not in various dialects in England). Using this convention, we might write something like: *sing'er*.

An interesting aspect of Klima's discussion of these and other modifications of a "deep" orthography is that as the orthographic representation is brought into closer correspondence with the abstract lexical representation so it becomes possible for the phonological rules to operate directly upon the orthographic representation. Yet all that Chomsky and Halle's view of an optimal orthography requires is that the orthographic representation be an efficient means of gaining access to the appropriate lexical entry. The question then becomes whether an orthography that represents word (or morpheme) boundaries can be more readily used to gain access to the lexical entry. Klima does not explicitly acknowledge this but apparently has it in mind when, for example, he speculates on the relative accessibility of word and morpheme boundaries. If it is correct to relate this speculation to the problem of identifying the lexical entry, an interesting consequence emerges: as soon as we start talking about the relative accessibility of various features of the abstract lexical representation postulated in Chomsky and Halle (1968), we lose the conception of that representation as a singular entry, subject to all-or-none retrieval. Instead, we have a conception more analogous to the in-depth search of semantic systems of representation. Clearly this issue is psychologically important. However, in so far as Chomsky and Halle confine themselves to a treatment of the linguistic issues, it is not incumbent on them to take a view on this question.

How principled is English orthography?

I believe there is some danger of overstating the case for a morphophonemic (or abstract lexical) basis to English orthography. Clearly the phonetic transcription model of orthography is a naïve one, and furthermore it is fun to discover that teachers, pupils and spelling reformers have all joined together in vilifying our orthography for the absence of regularities that were never a part of its design. Nevertheless, the alternative, morphophonemic thesis requires more examination in detail than it has hitherto received.

One rather indirect reason for doubting the view that English orthography is systematically morphophonemic is historical. This is the criticism put by Lotz (1972) in his argument that the underlying forms represented by orthography are not abstract, synchronic phonological structures but rather forms produced by the accumulation of evolutionary layers in the orthography. However, Lotz does not apply his argument to particular examples. Certainly it is clear enough that many of the phonographic irregularities of English have rather arbitrary historical origins, based as we have seen on etymologizing or analogy, both sometimes mistaken. Scragg (1974) has noted that the printer has had more influence on the details of English spelling than the philologist or lexicographer.

Another, related difficulty for the morphophonemic principle is that it applies rather better to the Romance part of English vocabulary. Halle (1969) has discussed this sort of restriction on the application of the rule for changing /k/ to /s/ before /i/.

Furthermore, even in conditions where morphology conservation might be expected, it does not invariably occur. Thus we have *delude* but *delusion* (Klima, 1972) and *idiot* but *idiocy* (Halle, 1969) despite the fact that the changes in sound are phonologically predictable. Moreover, Venezky (1970) points out examples where a predictable lack of change is indicated as in *can–canning* and *picnic–picnicking*, by adding a consonant to signal the absence of a marker effect. Exceptions such as these have led Halle (1969) to consider that there may be limitations on the validity of the principle that the orthography ignores predictable phonological variation. Klima (1972) goes further: "the Chomsky–Halle claim, I assume, is only that the *general principle* of English orthography is felicitous and not necessarily that the particular realization in the form of letters are as clear or as consistent as they could be."

How "optimal" is the morphophonemic principle?

We have already reviewed in general terms the difficulties with linguistically based notions of efficiency in scripts (Chapter 3, Section 1). What are we to make of Chomsky and Halle's claim that English possesses "a near optimal system"? A weak interpretation of this use of the concept of optimality is that it is devoid of psychological implications, being no more than a way of remarking upon the resemblance between spellings and the hypothetical, abstract lexical representations. However, on the face of it, Chomsky and Halle seem to be claiming more than this.

The most obvious limitation on their concept of optimality is the one that Chomsky and Halle themselves bring out. English orthography is a system "designed for readers who know the language". Chomsky and Halle discuss the question of the child's development of phonological rules rather carefully, concluding firmly that "these are open questions, and it is pointless to speculate about them any further" (Chomsky and Halle, 1968, p. 50). Certainly, it is often asserted that children "hear" more phonetically than adults or that "the child's phonology seems to be quite separate from his morphology" (O'Neil, 1972). The primary evidence on this question comes from children's use of the inflectional affixes (plural, past tense, etc.), and it suggests that even by first grade the child has abstracted these phonological rules with fair success. (See Gibson and Levin, 1975, pp. 125–128 for a brief review.)

The other side of this optimality argument consists of the question of whether orthographies that do not conserve morphology, such as Finnish and Turkish, thereby incur some penalty. I know of no formal evidence on this question, though Gibson and Levin (1975) report anecdotal evidence that bilingual Finnish adults read more slowly in Finnish than English. Surprizingly, the current state of knowledge bearing upon the ease of acquisition of various orthographic principles and the speed with which they can be processed by the skilled reader is little better than when *The Sound Pattern of English* was published. The linguist's intuition that a phonetic orthography might be easier for the child to acquire, whereas a morphophonemic orthography might be more suitable to the skilled reader remains untested. Like many tests of the relative efficiency of orthographic principles, this one is subject to many complexities, not least the difficulties of cross-language comparisons which are also cross-cultural, and the uncertainties of attempts to determine the child's tacit and explicit language competences. (See Liberman *et al.*, 1980, for a recent discussion of orthography and beginning reading.)

In the absence of direct performance tests for comparing orthographies we can still make some progress by enquiring into the assumptions underlying optimality claims. One such crucial assumption for Chomsky and Halle concerns the psychological reality of the underlying, abstract lexical representations, to which the orthography supposedly corresponds closely. The strength of the assumption about such representations was that they appeared to offer a powerful model for describing the phonological regularities of the spoken language. In a sense this model attempts to show what knowledge of phonology consists of. It is a bold step from asserting the power of a descriptive model to asserting that people actually follow the procedures in the model when they use language. The territory covered in this step has been examined by psycholinguists at some length, and I shall not pursue the general issue here.

An interesting and subtle comment has been made by Miller (1972, p. 127), who suggests that a writing system that refers to a morphological level affects our perception of the language system: "You think about words very differently after you know how to write them than before you know how to write them. Being literate has extensive effects upon one's cognitive processes that should be investigated." One can think of all sorts of implications of this insight of Miller's, but one inference one might draw is that experience with a morphophonemic orthography is actually active in constructing or rendering more accessible the abstract lexical descriptions.

This, in turn, raises the question of the accessibility of the information contained at the abstract lexical level. A strong interpretation of phonological competence in the generative theory is that the information at this level is readily, if tacitly, available to fluent speakers of the language. However, Klima's definition of optimality makes reference to the accessibility of various levels *to the consciousness of the reader and writer* and that is not necessarily the same thing. Not only is the requirement of conscious (explicit) access a more severe one, but also it may be the case that the codes used to gain access to the abstract lexical entries are different in speaking/listening from those in reading/writing.

One way to view the question is to ask why, if the abstract lexical level is so accessible, is spelling so difficult (cf. Klima, 1972, p. 60). Personally, I am convinced that my spelling has improved since gaining access to the description of my abstract lexical entries in the pages of *The Sound Pattern of English*! (Halle has also referred to a colleague of his who owed a similar debt to the book.)

In this debate about the accessibility of various phonological levels we have an obvious parallel with the debate about the relative accessibility of phonemes as compared to syllables. The latter was phrased in terms of the difference in segment size, but we can see that it might as well have been cast in terms of phonological data (if only phonological theories made reference to syllabic entities).

It might, I suppose, be asked why morphology should be conserved in writing but not in speech. After all, the whole apparatus of phonological theory has been constructed in order to establish contact between the morphological level and the phonetic level, at which morpheme constancy is lost. If speech communication can work with such a system, why cannot writing? This is really only another way of stating the question of what is optimal. Since writing is designed primarily to signify meaning and only secondarily to permit reading aloud, an arrangement that minimizes the distance from the deeper levels of meaning is felicitous. Furthermore, since writing is *designed* (in a vague but important sense which does not hold for speech) and since it is not constrained by the real-time production difficulties of speech, there is no evolutionary reason why it should not have optimized its proximity to the structure representing meaning.

In such a view, the only reason why a morphographic alphabetic script makes *any* reference to speech is to minimize what Klima calls "arbitrariness" in the assignment of written forms to lexical entries. That is, the use of an (abstract) phonological notation makes forms easier to learn than in a pure logographic system like Chinese.

4.4 REGULARITIES WITHIN THE GRAPHEME ARRAY

So far we have discussed the relationships between orthography and sound and orthography and meaning. For the sake of completeness it is worth mentioning regularities which exist within the orthographic representation, considered as an array of graphemes. Some such regularities were mentioned under the heading of graphotactic constraints upon the spelling–sound correspondence, for example, that /k/ could not be spelled CK at the beginning of a word. Although there are often historical explanations of how such constraints came about, most of them appear "lawful" only in a weak sense. Constraints which are even more obviously confined to a probabilistic level have been described and manipulated in experiments by psychologists over the last twenty-odd years.

Concern with probabilistic constraints on graphemic patterns in English probably had its origin in the interest in information measurement in the early 1950s. The classic manifestation of this sort of interest in graphemic patterns was the study of Miller *et al.* (1954) in which they measured the ability of subjects to identify briefly presented arrays of graphemes as a function of their resemblance to the statistical structure of English. Thus in a zero order approximation the letters are chosen randomly. A first order approximation consists of letters chosen with probabilities determined by their frequency of occurrence in English. A second order approximation does the same for pairs of adjacent letters; and so on. (The exact procedure for generating approximations is described in Shannon, 1948.) What Miller *et al.* were concerned to show was that the amount of uncertainty about letter identities was what determined the level of performance.

Interest in statistical measures of information, conceived as amount of uncertainty, has waned in psychology. And rightly so. However, some psychologists saw in these manipulations of letter probabilities ways of studying the *process* of recognition, especially the way in which the perceiver capitalized upon familiarity. Accordingly, compilations of the statistics of English grapheme arrays flourished. To the tables presented in Miller *et al.* were added the more detailed sequence norms of Underwood and Schultz (1960).

The focus of interest shifted, and psychologists lost an interest in letters simply as manipulable tokens and became more interested in the processes underlying word recognition. In one influential approach, Gibson *et al.* (1962) tried to define letter patterns in a manner which went beyond a simple frequency count. They sought to identify "the critical unit of language for the reading process" (p. 554) and speculated that these *spelling patterns* consisted of letters and letter clusters which possessed invariant sound correspondents. This definition would indeed result in a curious view of graphemic patterning, since the most common grapheme combinations are often those that lack invariant correspondences. This is especially true of the vowel letters, though Gibson *et al.* tend to ignore vowels. However, as it turns out, the invariant correspondence definition of spelling patterns has little to do with what Gibson *et al.* actually manipulated in their experiment, which contrasted orthographically "legal" strings like GLURCK with "illegal" strings such as CKURGL. There are two features worth noting in such transpositions of consonant clusters: (1) the effect achieved is actually the violation of graphotactic and phonotactic "rules" and has nothing to do with the invariance of correspondences; (2) the implied description of graphemic pattern is limited to an all-or-none classification. No continuous measure of regularity is made available.

In later work (Gibson *et al.* 1970; Gibson and Levin, 1975), Gibson concedes that what she calls "pronounceability" and "orthographic legality" have been confounded. However, no further proposals are advanced as to how orthographic legality is to be determined. As Coltheart (1977) has pointed out in a cogent critique, at the heart of Gibson and Levin's (1975) difficulties lies a confusion of rules and frequency counts. Thus they treat as synonymous the expressions "obeys the orthographic rules of English" and "contains no sequence of letters which do not occur in any English word". In sum, then, Gibson and Levin's concept of orthographic regularity equivocates between at least four definitions, founded in graphotactic rules, phonotactic rules, correspondence invariance, and zero-frequency sequences. Despite the low esteem in which they hold purely frequency-based measures, it seems likely that the major effect of their work has been to encourage the development of frequency counts that are positionally constrained.

The basic source for positionally constrained frequency counts is a series of papers by Mayzner, Tresselt and Wolin based upon a computer search of a corpus of 20,000 common words. This resulted in a tabulation of frequencies as a function of word position and word length for single letters and bigrams (Mayzner and Tresselt, 1965) and for trigrams, tetragrams and pentagrams (Mayzner *et al.*, 1965a, b, c).

Mason (1975) has distinguished two forms of regularity underlying these frequency counts. What she calls "spatial frequency redundancy" is represented in the single-letter counts. (Given that such regularities have nothing to do with metric space and given that "spatial frequency" has other accepted referents, I shall instead call this variable, *positional redundancy*.) In contrast, "sequential redundancy" is represented in the *n*-gram counts, although the fact that these are positionally constrained in Mayzner *et al.*'s tabulation means that positional and sequential redundancy are confounded.

McClelland and Johnston (1977) have raised some doubts about the psychological utility of the Mayzner and Tresselt tabulation. They rightly point out that the word sample was small relative to the extensive breakdown entailed by the classification. (For example, even for the simple, single-letter frequency tabulation there are 650 cells produced by the combination of 26 letters with 25 word lengths/word positions.) Furthermore, they suggest that a *type count* which registers the number of different words in which a graphemic pattern appears may be more psychologically relevant than a *token count* such as that of Mayzner *et al.* which is based on total occurrences in running text and is therefore highly influenced by common words. McClelland and Johnston therefore base their study on their own norms, which, however, they have not yet published.[8]

A new attempt to distinguish probabilistic measures from rule-based measures of regularity has been launched by Venezky and Massaro (1979) and Massaro *et al.* (1979), for whom a primary criterion for the evaluation of measure of regularity is the correlation between the intuitive wordlikeness of a pseudoword and the score obtained by summing the measure across the letters of the pseudoword. Thus they cite as examples of the inadequacy of Mayzner and Tresselt's (1965) bigram frequency norms, the fact that the plausible string *bipon* scores but 17 in summed frequencies whereas *thrsm* scores 417. (In addition, note that the real word *bison* only scores 24.) Similarly, they show that using single-letter frequencies to control positional redundancy it is possible to generate pronounceable items such as *juff* with low scores (371) and unpronounceable items such as *thrt* with high scores (3421).

It is not entirely clear what Venezky and Massaro believe to be established by such demonstrations. In fact, they appear to appeal to at least three criteria. First is intuitive wordlikeness. The trouble with intuitions is that they contain no way of dealing with contrary intuitions. Personally I find *thrt* more wordlike than *juff* and furthermore, I think I know why: I associate *thrt* with quite a lot of real words (*that*, *threat*, etc.) but *juff* hardly resembles any words (fluff?). Nor is this fortuitous. An important but unnoticed correlate of the total single-letter or letter-cluster positional frequency of a string is what I shall call *visual lexicon density*, by which I mean the number of graphemically similar real words. (Others have referred to a similar attribute as "orthographic neighbourhoods", cf. Landauer and Streeter, 1973.) One simple guide to this is the number of words that can be generated by changing a single letter in the letter string under investigation. It is an open question to what extent the wordlikeness associated with high summed positional frequencies is mediated by *visual lexicon density*.

Venezky and Massaro's second criterion is ease of recognition. They appear to take it for granted that *juff* is more readily recognized than *thrt*, remarking of these items: "thus, if orthographic regularity relates to recognition ease, spatial frequency counts are inadequate for defining it".

Their third criterion is not explicitly stated but appears to be pronounceability or perhaps conformity to phototactic rules. Such a criterion leads us naturally to the rule-governed approaches to regularity that Venezky and Massaro contrast with the probabilistic approaches.

Venezky and Massaro consider two sorts of rule. These amount essentially to the graphotactic and phonotactic constraints discussed under the heading of *same-level constraints* in Section 4.2. In that context, I remarked upon the difficulty of showing that a description of these regularities amounted to anything more than an empirical generalization. However, since Venezky and Massaro specifically contrast the concepts of rule and of probabilistic generalization, we must re-examine more carefully the possible grounds for assigning rule status. This task is made more difficult because Venezky and Massaro nowhere state a precise criterion for distinguishing rules from probability statements.

Notice first that there is a perfectly legitimate usage of the term "rule" as in "rule of thumb" which asserts no more than a generalization. Since these two concepts are contrasted in the present context, we must assume that a stronger sense of "rule" is intended. To understand this sense it may be useful to have regard to notions of "lawfulness" that might occur, for example, in the philosophy of science. The formulation of a distinction between scientific laws and empirical generalization is in fact central to a good many philosophies of science.

What these concepts of a law generally have in common is first the prohibition of exceptions (hence the "falsifiability" of theories) and secondly perhaps the derivation of the law from some higher level of abstractness.

For the most part the instances of rules cited by Venezky and Massaro (1979) quite obviously fail by these criteria to aspire to the condition of laws. The authors frankly acknowledge that many of their candidate rules do admit to exceptions, albeit infrequent ones (for example the rule prohibiting initial geminate (doubled) letters is violated by *eel*). Indeed, they make the curious remark about phonological constraints that "one implication of the constraints described above is that *different degrees of regularity* are possible".

With respect to the derivation of laws from a set of more abstract and systematic propositions (e.g. a "model"), it is a historical fact that many of the graphemic conventions of English arose from nothing less arbitrary than what Venezky and Massaro describe as "scribal practices, printing conventions, lexicographers' selections and occasional accident". Turning to phonological conventions, there might be some basis for the claim that certain phonotactic regularities can be derived from a more general description of articulatory constraints. However, as we observed in our discussion of *subpoena* in Section 4.2, the consequence of phonotactic constraints is generally to modify the *correspondence* rather than the *graphemic pattern*. Thus, since /wr/, /mn/, and /mb/ are illegal sound sequences, the normal grapheme–phoneme correspondences are modified in *write*, *hymn* and *lamb*. Such phonological rules therefore have no fixed implications for regularities of graphemic pattern.

A final feature of Venezky and Massaro's attempt to formulate a rule-governed description is that they believe probabilistic approaches to be restricted to a word token base, whereas the rule-governed approach is based on word types. However, as we have seen, McClelland and Johnston (1977) base their bigram frequency counts both upon word tokens and word types.

In summary, the psychological literature dealing with regularities of pattern within the graphemic array reveals a persistent intuition that such regularities are capable of description in terms of a set of linguistic rules. These rules are held to express regularities at a deeper level than mere probability statements which are based upon the positional and sequential frequencies of letter occurrences. I have concluded that this distinction has not yet received an acceptable formulation. Moreover, I do not even think that it is in principle capable of being systematically formulated.

We can get the debate into some perspective by enquiring into what motivated these various attempts to describe graphemic regularities. From their beginnings in information theory they were based on information-processing models of how the reader might use regularities to assist identification. This psychological question has been the underlying concern even when the attempt has appeared on the surface to be devoted to producing a neutral, linguistic description. It is important to acknowledge this, since it is by no means necessary that a description of regularities motivated by neutral criteria of consistency and parsimony will reveal those features of the regularity that are actually detected and used by the reader. From this perspective, measures of regularity are best viewed as implicitly reflecting psychological hypotheses about the detectability and utility of various forms of regularity by the reader. The capacity of the measure to generate consistently "wordlike" pseudowords is another matter, and one which requires a clarification of the notion of wordlikeness.

Part Two

From Print to Sound

Introduction

The four chapters that comprise Part II deal with different aspects of a central problem in the psychology of reading: how we translate printed or written symbols into spoken language. The treatment of these issues is, of course, informed by the linguistic material in Part I, for it would be foolish to take no account of what a language permits and even encourages by its formal relationships. Nevertheless, our purpose is psychological and we must travel beyond the description of linguistic regularities in an attempt to infer what strategies the reader is actually using. To do this, we rely on two main forms of evidence: that based on the performance of the skilled reader, and that based on the pattern of disabilities found in substantially impaired reading, notably in acquired dyslexia.

Chapters 5 and 6 deal with the mechanisms serving the fluent reader when he assigns a pronunciation to a printed word. In large measure we are concerned here with the processes underlying error-free performance. The paradigmatic task for this purpose is the word-naming reaction-time (RT) task, in which we measure the latency of a subject's naming response to a printed word. This simple task has been the battle-ground of competing accounts of the strategies for determining word pronunciation in fluent reading. The nature of the word-naming RT task also serves to illustrate certain limits on the discussion. Thus, we concern ourselves in these chapters with the translation of single words in isolation from their normal linguistic context. This simplification is in part a matter of convenience, for experimental and theoretical purposes, but it is also justifiable in other ways. Consider, for example, the fact that we usually commence the teaching of reading with isolated words. Moreover, the ability to arrive at the name of isolated words turns out to be a surprisingly powerful diagnostic test of backwardness in learning to read, as well as in various types of acquired dyslexia consequent on brain damage. Finally, decisions at the word level play a fundamental role in almost all theoretical models of reading and of speech perception. "Words", in the memorably unlovely phrase used by Cole and Jakanik (1978), "are where the action is."

A more subtle limitation of subject matter is also implicit in the example of the word-naming task: in studying largely error-free performance by the skilled reader we are concerned with rapid and automatic mechanisms for assigning pronunciation in the course of normal, fluent reading. We can distinguish such performance from the slow, deliberative, trial and error attempts at decoding whereby the novice reader, the dyslexic, and occasionally even the normal adult endeavour to arrive at a pronunciation of a printed word for which no ready solution materializes. Not only is this limitation to fluent word-naming brazenly confessed, I would even go so far as to cast doubt upon some of the uses to which the evidence on acquired dyslexia has been put, precisely on the grounds that the strategies of the severely impaired may be special, "problem-solving" inventions arising out of the unavailability of the mechanisms responsible for automatic, fluent performance.

My main reason for concentrating on fluent reading is, *tout court*, that this is the realm where most recent theoretical advances have taken place in the understanding of mechanisms for translating print into sound. Moreover, to concentrate on fluent performance is not to neglect the problem of the novice or impaired reader, because it is difficult to teach the novice without an understanding of the strategies that normally underlie fluency or to understand impairments without some independent evidence about what it is that is impaired.

Having declared this bias, it must be conceded that the neuropsychological literature has provided a major historical influence on theories of skilled reading (for example, Wernicke, 1874) and has recently become once again the vehicle for vigorous and ingenious investigations (see, for example, Coltheart *et al.*, 1980; Patterson, 1981). I have not been able to do full justice to this work, much of which is absorbing in its own right, by considering it only for the light it purports to cast upon normal reading.

Concerning my neglect of studies of the acquisition of "decoding" skills I am less penitent. First, there is a vexing disproportion between the volume of literature on beginning reading and the weight of the conclusions that have been reached about decoding processes. Secondly, much of this literature takes as its unquestioned starting point the (presumably self-evident) reality of one or other of the mechanisms which are under test here. At its extremes, the debate between adherents of translation of gross word shapes into word sounds and advocates of the hypothesis of serial grapheme-to-phoneme translation has been so formulated as to exclude any position which it is reasonable to take on the adult literature. I have, however, included some slight discussion of the development of reading skills where they seemed relevant to strategies postulated on other grounds. The reader interested in systematic reviews of the developmental literature might consult Barron (1981), Ehri (1980) or Gibson and Levin (1975, chapter 9).

In Chapter 7 we turn to matters that are not always considered part of the province of reading research. Here we deal with some of the production demands of reading aloud and the way in which translation from print to sound has to be combined with speech production in continuous oral reading. Although this chapter compels us to broaden our perspective to include the processing of continuous text, I stop short of a systematic treatment of the extensive literature on the control of eye movements.

Part II concludes with an examination of the psychological evidence for processing strategies that are specific to types of orthography. This research, discussed in Chapter 8, is at an early stage of development. Cultural evolution has presented us in the variety of orthographies with some exciting stimulus material. Unfortunately, however, these gifts do not come neatly packaged, and it has proved extremely difficult to incorporate type of orthography, as a variable, into rigorously controlled experiments. Moreover, conceptions of the way in which underlying processes might differ according to type of orthography have tended to be dominated by rather crude dichotomies, such as that between "pictorial" (logographic) and "verbal" (alphabetic) codes. Despite these present limitations this is a promising area of investigation and it has seemed worth sampling the aroma from the experimental kitchen.

Chapter 5

Possible Routes from Print to Sound

Experimental enquiry into the means by which the reader uses script to arrive at sound developed surprisingly late in the investigation of reading. This is the more curious because reading as an activity has often been equated with the translation of print into sound, by psychologists, by linguists, and by educators concerned with the teaching of reading. One reason for neglect has been the persistent tendency to confuse linguistic with psychological analysis. It seems frequently to have been assumed that, by scrutinizing the orthography and striving to achieve a systematic description of the relationship between script and sound, one was necessarily enquiring into what the reader did when he read aloud. This strange shyness about psychological experimentation is particularly evident in the formulation of theories about the pedagogy of reading. Most of the rival methods of teaching children to read concern themselves to some extent with developing the child's competence at oral reading. However, these methods have generally been arrived at simply by speculating about the "nature" of reading, as a competence. The chosen teaching methods generally reflect in a quite obvious way assumptions about the underlying strategy to be cultivated, though these assumptions are seldom formulated fully and explicitly. It rarely seems to have occurred to the pedagogic theorist to attempt to determine what strategies the reader follows when he has acquired the skill, although, to be sure, the strategies of the relatively skilled reader need not be those that are best suited to the apprentice reader. Where there is consistency in the evolution of cognitive strategies there may be implications to be gleaned about the constraints imposed by the nature of the cognitive machinery. After all, at a general level this supposition motivates most information-processing approaches to cognitive psychology. Furthermore, where individuals differ systematically in the strategies that they develop, this may cast some light on the constraints imposed by their particular abilities, as well, of course, as their history of training.

Even when psychological enquiry into the strategies used for orthographic translation did arrive upon the scene it did so riding on the coat tails of a separate question. Since the time of the earliest neuropsychological work on dyslexia (e.g. Wernicke, 1874) it has been suggested that the normal reader has two means of gaining access to the stored meaning of printed words: (*i*) a direct lexical route in which the visual information in the word specifies the relevant entry in the mental dictionary, and (*ii*) a phonological route in which the visual information is translated directly into a speech code and then this speech code is used to gain access to the relevant entry in the mental dictionary. Now, this two-route view of access to meaning contains the seeds of a related view of access to phonology, though for a long time these implications seem not to have been explicitly remarked upon. We can set out the implications as follows.

If route (*i*) from print to lexical meaning exists, it can also be used to gain access to word phonology. This must be so because we clearly have a mental dictionary that allows us to get from word meanings to word sounds; otherwise how could we voice our thoughts? If we can get from print to meaning, we can progress thence to sound. Moreover, if the visual, phonological and semantic information about words are all contained in a single mental dictionary with direct links between each pair of domains, we need not even detour via meaning to get from print to sound using entries in the dictionary.

Consider now the hypothetical route (*ii*) from print to meaning. If it is sometimes useful to translate print into sound in order to use that sound to gain access to the lexicon, this might seem to suggest the existence of a nonlexical route from print to sound. After all, if access to phonology in route (*ii*) were not *prelexical*, why should it serve as a useful preliminary to gaining access to meaning through the lexicon? In fact, despite the widespread acceptance of this implicit argument for a nonlexical route to phonology, its conclusions are by no means inevitable. It might be the case, for instance, that access to phonology in route (*ii*) is *lexical* but that due to some property of the indexing of the mental lexicon, gaining access to meaning is not a straightforward procedure, at least using visual information, so that it may sometimes be efficient to translate from print to sound using information about a word that is stored in the lexicon and then use the sound to search for the meaning of the word. In short, then, even if route (*ii*) has a role to play in reading for meaning, this leaves open the question of how we translate from print to sound and, in particular, the question of whether such translation utilizes the mental lexicon.

This little argumentative excursion illustrates how far one can travel over this terrain by the exercise of a little reasoning and in the total absence of psychological facts. If one believes, with Stevenson, that "to travel hopefully is a better thing than to arrive", then such excursions make commendable sport. However, since I have been at some pains below to *rebut* the two-route theories, I should explain my reason for starting with a discussion of this line of argument: it is, in short, its historical importance. The mechanisms serving access to meaning have always attracted more attention than those for gaining access to sound. Moreover, it has often seemed to be assumed that the solution to the second of these problems would emerge as a by-product of the solution of the first. Finally, the growth of interest in the translation from print to sound in the 1970s stemmed directly from work on access to lexical meaning. One particular focus of such work was on the "regularity" of spelling–sound correspondences The practical need to generate lists of "regular" and "irregular" stimulus words drove experimental psychologists to the work of linguists such as Wijk, Venezky and Chomsky, who had been concerned with the description of orthography.

In this chapter we consider some of the general strategies that might be applied to the translation of print into sound. We concentrate on evaluating the plausibility of three strategies: (*i*) prelexical translation according to grapheme–phoneme correspondence rules (GPCs), (*ii*) access to word-specific phonology in the lexicon, and (*iii*) the use of lexical analogies. In Chapter 6 we examine how these strategies might combine to yield pronunciations in fluent reading. Do the various methods of assigning a word-sound interact, do they engage in a horse-race, or is the notion of independent routes itself questionable?

5.1 SOME PRELIMINARY SPECULATIONS

We are able to conceive and produce speech as well as being able to hear and understand it. These facts suggest that there are processes linking our stored representations of word meanings to plans for the articulation of these words and also to pattern detectors for auditory identification of the words. Since we can pronounce words in a variety of ways and identify them spoken by others in a much larger variety of styles, the central specification of these articulatory and phonetic patterns must be rather abstract, or idealized. One possibility is that this central representation is so abstract that the same representation of word phonology underlies both the perception and the production of the word.

We may speculate as to the relationship of these phonological representations of words to their semantic counterparts. In the conventional flow diagram the possible relationships are expressed by containing both sorts of representation in the same box, in separate boxes that are directly linked or in separate boxes that are linked via an intermediate box. In arranging these boxes, we may seem to be deciding important theoretical matters but this is only true if we can unambiguously relate the arrangement to certain functional statements about what performance should be possible.

The question of how the meaning of a word is related to its spoken form has also been of interest to the linguist. The phonological theorist is concerned to describe in the most parsimonious way the relationship between various linguistic structures such as the abstract lexical representation of a word and its articulatory or phonetic realization. In recent work within the framework of generative phonology this relationship is conceived of as a general procedure for transforming lexical abstractions into realizations via a set of rules. The lexical entry used for this purpose takes the form of a string of abstract elements which include indicators of morpheme and word boundaries. The rules are applied in a fixed order to transform the string of abstract elements into a particular phonetic form. Linguistic theories of phonology do not concern themselves with the distinction between phonetics and articulation: their aim is to describe the rules of the language and they stop short of any attempt to account for variation of which the source is physiological or psychological.

It is important to notice how abstract the lexical base is in phonological theory, for the job of the phonological rules is not only to deal with phonetic matters such as vowel lternations (the lawful change in the vowel values between the *a* in prof*a*ne and prof*a*nity, for example) but also to transform the lexical base into, say, *take* or *took*, according to context.

It cannot be too often stressed that linguistic theory describes regularities in the language without carrying any necessary implications about psychological processes in the language user. It is quite possible, for example, that a language user might have *take* and *took* listed as two unrelated dictionary entries each with its associated articulatory programme. It is also possible that the speaker lists separately the phonetic form of *profane* and *profanity* without having available to him the general rule that predicts vowel alternation. Moreover, even if these rules are part of the tacit linguistic knowledge of the skilled language user, it might not be efficient to utilize the rule system each time a word is spoken. Instead, the speaker might by-pass the apparatus of rules after a number of passes through the system by a given word. This might result in the storage of the final articulatory form of the word, which could be retrieved directly.

We can now enquire as to how these hypothetical lexical systems might adapt to an input in the form of written language. Perhaps the simplest possibility consists of a development of the dictionary model. Just as the semantic lexicon acquired phonetic entries, so it comes to acquire graphemic entries. Once again this confronts us with subordinate options. In the *single-lexicon* version, these graphemic, semantic and phonetic/articulatory representations are directly linked, so that access to one automatically renders the others available. In the *separate-lexicon* view, each form of representation is independently stored. This separation does not necessarily imply anything about the spatial layout of the brain, it simply means that some processing is required to move between the various forms of representation of a word. One possible implication of the separate-lexicon view is that the reader might be able to move between graphemic lexical entries and phonetic/articulatory entries without encountering a semantic representation. We must bear this in mind when we come to consider particular approaches in the literature which refer to the "lexical code" from print to sound as if this necessarily implied contact with the appropriate entry in the *semantic* lexicon. (This question often lurks behind discussions of performance in the lexical decision task.)

As we have seen, the basis of Chomsky and Halle's (1968) claim that English possesses a near optimal orthography was that orthographic forms were frequently isomorphic with the abstract lexical representation, from which phonetic realizations could be generated by the rules. Therefore we could think of the graphemic forms as being used to access the abstract lexical representation directly, in order for the rules to be applied to generate the phonetic/articulatory form. We must also bear this in mind when we encounter particular approaches in which the "lexical route" is contrasted with a "grapheme–phoneme correspondence" (GPC) route which is regarded as necessarily non-lexical. In so far as phonological rules are used to translate morphophoneme-like elements into a pronunciation, and the morphophonemic representations is matched by an almost isomorphic graphemic form, we might speak of such a system as involving grapheme–phoneme correspondences. However, this particular GPC route is explicitly *lexical*, that being the essence of the Chomsky and Halle model.

All the possibilities reviewed so far are based on the assumption that the reader is dealing with a familiar word to which the system has already accommodated itself. The phonetic dictionary models assume that the print–sound association has already been encountered and stored. The generative phonology model assumes slightly less. The print–sound association for a given word need never have been encountered before, because once the lexical representation exists, its relation to both the graphemic form and the phonetic form is predictable. This is because of the isomorphism between the orthography and the lexical representation and because the phonological rules are capable of generating the phonetic form from the lexical representation. Nevertheless, the word requires to be familiar in spoken form: only then can an abstract lexical base have been constructed for the rules to operate upon. In the generative model, word learning can best be regarded as the development of an appropriately structured lexical representation. But clearly what a new word requires is a translation route which is nonlexical, in any of these various senses of "lexical".

We can distinguish several types of nonlexical translation routes. One class, which we shall call *nonlexical GPC* procedures, has been outlined in Section 4.2 dealing with "spelling–sound correspondences". The properties of such procedures can be understood by contrasting them with the generative phonology procedure; in the generative phonology procedure the graphemic form was first used to access an abstract lexical representation and then the phonological rules operated upon the lexical representation to translate it into a phonetic realization, but in the nonlexical GPC procedure the rules operate directly upon the graphemic information translating the graphemic elements into phonetic/articulatory elements. These rules might be very like the phonological rules of the generative theory, but because the procedure must, by definition, be nonlexical, higher-level rules must be precluded from consideration, since they make mention of variables such as morpheme boundaries and form class which cannot be known below the lexical level. (This assertion is in fact only generally true: there are sometimes purely graphemic grounds for guessing at the form class of a word. For example, words ending in AL tend to be adjectival. Similar grounds exist for inferring some morpheme boundaries.) The probabilistically formulated GPC rules of Wijk (1966), Haas (1970) and Venezky (1970) generally appeal to a type count. That is, the frequencies that they consider are based on the number of different words in the language that exhibit a given property. Thus they conform to a general tendency for linguistic analyses to follow type counts. Psychologically oriented approaches to language statistics have more often concentrated on token counts, which are based on occurrences in language use and are therefore sensitive to word frequency (see, for example, Section 4.4). The choice between a type and token count basis for GPC rules is of some consequence given that the most common words are often those which violate the type count rules.

A different class of nonlexical procedure is the *analogy* one. In this procedure a phonetic/articulatory form is assigned to a word by analogy with visually similar words of which the phonetic form is known. To use an example from Glushko (1979), HEAF might be assigned the pronunciation /hif/ by analogy with *leaf* or /hef/ by analogy with *deaf*. The analogy procedure differs from the GPC procedure essentially by not appealing to an independent corpus of "rules". Analysis may nevertheless be sensitive to frequencies of some sort. For example, it could plausibly be assumed that analogies tend to be made with common words. In addition to this essential difference between analogy and GPC procedures there may be other incidental ones. The GPC procedure is usually conceived of as operating on single graphemes (with the possible supplement of graphemic context constraints). The analogy procedure, on the other hand, can readily be thought of as operating upon larger clusters of graphemes; moreover it need not involve any precise segmental considerations. The global intuition that HEAF looks like a cross between *heal* and *leaf* may suffice to suggest /hif/ without more detailed analysis.

This closes our inventory of some of the possible strategies for assigning sound to print, and we now turn to an investigation of the claims made for each of the main classes of possibility.

5.2 EVIDENCE FOR A NONLEXICAL GPC STRATEGY

Several different reasons have been proposed for believing in the existence of a nonlexical strategy, including the effects of orthographic "regularity", the symptoms of a form of brain damage known as "surface dyslexia", and the very fact that we can assign a pronunciation to invented pseudowords. Despite the ready acceptance these various arguments have received, I shall try to show that none of them can stand close scrutiny.

Surface dyslexia

Perhaps the strongest claim of support based on the symptoms of surface dyslexia has been made by Coltheart (1978), who describes these findings as a "line of evidence implying that GPC procedures have psychological reality". Others have made less specific claims, asserting that patients with surface dyslexia rely upon "prelexical, phonological coding" (Allport, 1979) or "assign meaning . . . solely via a phonological coding of the visual stimulus" (Marshall, 1976).

There are several reasons for examining these interpretations of surface dyslexia in some detail. Neuropsychological investigations of acquired dyslexia have recently been pursued with renewed vigour (see for example, Coltheart *et al.*, 1980; Patterson, 1981). While much of this work is absorbing in its own right, proponents of the neuropsychological approach have made strong claims concerning the bearing of this work on our understanding of normal reading. Although I share the enthusiasm for this work, my own view has been that the implications that have been drawn for normal reading are not quite so compelling as has been supposed. The claims made on the basis of surface dyslexia provide an opportunity to see these arguments from the abnormal to the normal at work. To be fair, however, it should be stressed that surface dyslexia is one of the least investigated of the acquired dyslexia syndromes.

Surface dyslexia was the name given to a clinical syndrome by Marshall and Newcombe (1973) in an important discussion of acquired dyslexia. Other case reports have been presented by Holmes (1978) and by Shallice and Warrington (1980), who call the syndrome "semantic dyslexia". A possibly related disorder in a Japanese reader has been reported by Sasanuma (1980).

Whereas in the more extensively described syndromes of deep dyslexia and phonological dyslexia errors in reading aloud isolated words seem to be largely determined by semantic and syntactic features of the word (hence the descriptive term "deep"), in surface dyslexia errors seem more related to the length of the word and its spelling–sound regularity (hence the description "surface", implying impairment at a level which is linguistically superficial, however debilitating to the reader).[9]

Other syndromes have been posited that appear to share some of the symptoms defining surface dyslexia. Thus, in word-form dyslexia (sometimes called letter-by-letter reading or, most confusingly, spelling dyslexia) performance deteriorates on longer words but is apparently unaffected by spelling–sound regularity (Patterson, 1981). One or other of surface and word-form dyslexia is referred to in the French literature as "verbal alexia" (Hécaen and Kremin, 1976).

The conventional interpretation of surface dyslexia which we are concerned with here is roughly as follows (see Coltheart, 1978; Marshall and Newcombe, 1973). There are two routes to word phonology from print: a lexical route in which visual information is used to specify an entry in the lexicon from which whole-word phonology is retrieved, and a nonlexical route in which graphemes are translated into phonemes by means of GPC rules. When a surface dyslexic makes an error in oral reading it is assumed that he has failed, on this occasion at least, to operate the lexical route which would have provided whole-word phonology and has had to rely instead upon the nonlexical GPC route. Errors should therefore result when a word contains irregular GPCs. However, because many regular words are also read incorrectly and because some of these errors can be seen as arising from the use of correspondences which are not the appropriate "regular" ones but are nevertheless correspondences that do occur in some exception words, it must be assumed that on such occasions the direct lexical route failed and *in addition the GPC route operated defectively*.

It is convenient to examine the evidence on surface dyslexia in two stages. We shall first review the argument that surface dyslexia consists in an inability to address a lexical entry directly by means of a visual or graphemic code; this seems to imply the negative corollary that the path from print to sound must be nonlexical in nature. Then we shall turn to the more specific argument that these patients are relying on a grapheme–phoneme correspondence strategy, which purportedly exists as a viable option for the normal reader.

One characteristic that we might expect of patients whose injury deprived them of a lexical route to pronunciation is that that should not exhibit word-frequency effects, since these are usually held to result from the manner in which the lexicon is organized. A similar argument can be applied to effects of grammatical class upon word reading. (This seems to be the argument implied by Allport, 1979.) It is of interest therefore that both of the surface dyslexic patients described by Marshall and Newcombe (1973) exhibit word-frequency and grammatical-class effects in reading.

Allport (1979) has pointed out that if the lexical route is unavailable then the surface dyslexic should be wholly unable to decide whether a word which he cannot pronounce is a real word or a pseudoword. Unfortunately no evidence appears to exist on this point. Similarly, to the extent that the lexical route to word-specific phonology is impaired then oral reading should be insensitive to whether the item to be read is a real word. Moreover, the associative priming effects obtained with normal subjects should not occur. Time to read aloud NURSE should not be reduced by preceding it with DOCTOR. Unfortunately, none of these tests seems to have been performed.

Another line of argument against the availability of a direct lexical access path appeals to the fact that in the surface dyslexic syndrome reading errors often consist of approximations which are not real words (Marshall, 1976). However, this result seems to raise questions which have received insufficient attention. For example, why does the patient not recognize his neologistic productions as nonwords? This cannot be due to a deficit of visual access to the lexicon. Yet we are told that Marshall and Newcombe's (1973) patient J.C. produced neologisms as 25% of his errors. Furthermore, some of these responses sounded very similar to the correct form, for example: *hiss*→hish; *sound*→ shound; *broad*→brode; *route*→rote. The same holds for their patient S.T. for whom *describe*→describ; *resent*→rissend. These spoken approximations are surely sufficient for a normal person to recognize the lexical item referred to. Failure at such recognition cannot be ascribed to defective visual access to the lexicon. But the puzzle deepens; it appears that such patient *can* occasionally access their semantic lexicon by means of such approximations. J.C. produced the revealing confusion: *omit*→ommit . . . that's the name of the prophet of Islam. Evidently we cannot simply ascribe the reading difficulties of such patients to impaired visual access to the lexicon.

Turning to the more specific question of what this syndrome tells us about the psychological reality of GPC based reading, there are two possible sources of evidence that these patients are reading by means of GPCs. The weaker line is based on the assumptions that (*a*) they do not possess a direct lexical access route, and (*b*) the only possible alternative is the GPC route (see, for example, Marshall and Newcombe, 1973, p. 191). We have already seen that (*a*) is probably oversimplified. (*b*) is clearly false, since, as our discussion of possibilities indicated, pronunciations might be achieved by an analogy-based strategy. Therefore we can reject the weak argument without further ado.

The stronger argument is based on the nature of oral reading errors in surface dyslexia. In the words of Marshall and Newcombe (1973), "These errors show that both subjects have especial difficulty with the context-sensitive nature of grapheme–phoneme mappings."

A sample of errors is shown in Table 8 for three cases reported by Marshall and Newcombe (1973 and 1977). I have sorted the errors into two categories: those that might be attributable to the use of grapheme–phoneme correspondences with faulty application of contextual constraints, and those that could not be accounted for in this way. There seems little doubt that a substantial proportion of errors could be attributed to inappropriate use of GPCs. Several instances occur of faulty handling of the silent E marker (*guest*→just, *recent*→rikunt). There is difficulty with silent consonants (izland) and with the segmentation of vowel digraphs (*neice*→nice). Such errors receive extensive analysis by Marshall and Newcombe (1973). However, we must be cautious before accepting this principle. Clearly there are many errors which cannot be accounted for in this way. Moreover, there are so many possible correspondences in English that any error which resulted from a visual or phonological confusion would have a more than negligible chance of involving an alterative "legal" correspondence.[10]

Table 8 Examples of reading errors in surface dyslexia for three cases taken from Marshall and Newcombe (1973, 1977). The errors are classified according to whether they could be attributed to a GPC strategy with the application of faulty contextual constraints

	Case J.C.		Case S.T.		Case R.B.	
GPC BASED?	*disease*	decease	*recent*	rikunt	*mow*	mau
	of	off	*gauge*	jug	*oust*	ost
	guest	just	*phase*	face		
	island	izland	*describe*	describ		
	bike	bik	*lace*	lass		
	omit	ommit	*logic*	lugus		
	unite	unit				
	insect	insist				
NOT GPC BASED	*monarch*	monarutch	*pigsty*	pigisti	*greet*	green
	barge	bargain	*reign*	region	*elope*	envelope
	different	difference	*banishment*	banment	*factory*	facts
	applaud	appolo	*boil*	bowl	*lend*	leg
	broad	broke	*refresh*	refreshment	*abolish*	boil
					had	hat
					hat	pag
					led	leg

What then are my reasons for denying that these GPC-based errors constitute evidence for the "psychological reality" of the GPC route in normal processing? Actually, there are a considerable number of reasons. One which is sufficient by itself to counter the psychological reality argument is as follows. The difficulty with the GPC route has always been that it requires a vast array of contextual rules to support it (see Section 4.2). *It is therefore inadmissible to cite as evidence for the viability of the GPC route errors which result from the almost total failure to apply contextual rules.* One might as well use these errors to argue for the lack of viability of the GPC route. Furthermore, it is of no avail to protest that these patients have, as an additional part of their impairment, a deficiency in applying the context rules; first, because this argument is entirely circular, and secondly, for the more general reason that the processing model of the syndrome becomes increasingly *ad hoc* with each additional posited impairment. Thus we would already have had to appeal to impaired direct lexical access and impaired GPC rules, and there remain other reading errors and other language deficits in surface dyslexia to be explained. The crucial point is this. The appropriate evidence in support of a role for GPC rules in fluent reading would be the existence of a condition in which direct lexical access to word-specific phonology was blocked, but reading, at least of regular words, was unimpaired and fluent. Yet the evidence that exists suggests, contrariwise, that lexical factors do influence these patients' reading, that regular words may be misread and even irregularized, and that even when reading is successful it is abnormally slow and sometimes accompanied by symptoms of abnormal strategies. (For example, the patient S.T., described as a surface dyslexic by Marshall and Newcombe, 1973, used the serial letter-naming strategy held to typify word-form dyslexia. It is worth pointing out, in this context, that if a patient is attempting to synthesize a pronunciation from letter-names then some errors will resemble faulty application of GPC rules. These might include soft G (gee) and C (cee).) The letter-naming behaviour suggests that this patient is following a strategy which bears no relationship to those typical of normal reading. To the extent that analysis proceeds letter by letter, it may do so for highly peculiar reasons which have no bearing upon the viability of the GPC route in normal reading.

Even in cases where there is no report of letter-naming strategies, word naming is extraordinarily slow and shows an exaggerated dependence on word length. The patient R.O.G., described by Shallice and Warrington (1980), took an average of 5·6 seconds to read orthographically regular words. Reading rate was a positively accelerated function of number of syllables.

In summary, the extremely laboured reading characteristic of surface dyslexia, being in some cases an order of magnitude slower than normal reading, in others characterized by attempts mediated by letter-naming, and generally being unusually dependent on word length, does not suggest at all that a mechanism serving normal reading has been revealed as a consequence of selective damage to alternative pathways. Whatever strategy the surface dyslexic is attempting to use, there is no compelling reason to suppose that it serves normal reading. To suggest that this surviving strategy is revealed in an impaired form because annihilatation of the lexical path is invariably accompanied by partial damage to the GPC path is possible but tortuous and *ad hoc*. (We shall return to the surface dyslexic syndrome when we consider effects of orthographic regularity in (*iii*) below.)

Before leaving Table 8 behind, it may be worth making an anecdotal remark about the availability of the set of legal GPCs. It turns out to be quite a difficult task to sort errors into two classes depending on whether or not they are legitimate in terms of GPC. This is rather like the task of recognizing the "legitimacy" of Shaw's spelling of *fish* as GHOTI. It simply isn't at all easy to recognize possible correspondences divorced from context. The standard way of dealing with such a difficulty is to claim that the knowledge involved is implicit, unavailable for conscious inspection. Whether this response is wholly satisfactory seems open to doubt.

Pronounceability of pseudowords

It is clear that we are able to assign a pronunciation quite rapidly to letter strings that possess no lexical representation. This has usually been taken as incontrovertible evidence of the existence of a nonlexical route from print to sound. Where the GPC procedure has been taken to be the only viable nonlexical route, this would imply that the ability to pronounce pseudowords constitutes evidence of the reality of the GPC route.

Once again we can distinguish two questions: the general one of whether nonword pronunciation is evidence for the possibility of nonlexical translation, and the particular one of whether the GPC procedure is the only viable form that such translation could take. In this case it will be convenient to discuss the two questions together.

As we have already observed, it is possible that a phonological lexicon exists independent of the semantic lexicon. Direct access to such a phonological lexicon (listing whole-word pronunciations) would actually be "nonlexical" in the usual sense of that term since what is normally intended is something like "without contact with the semantic lexicon". However, it is just as unreasonable to suppose that nonwords are listed in the phonological lexicon as in the semantic lexicon, so the possible existence of an independent pathway through a phonological lexicon is irrelevant to the nonword issue.

In our discussion of the argument from surface dyslexia we considered the line of reasoning that any evidence for a nonlexical route must be evidence for the GPC procedure. This was open to the fatal objection that pronunciation might equally be achieved by a strategy based upon analogies. This is of course as true for nonwords as it is for words, and in fact treatments of the analogy strategy have generally occurred in the context of the nonword pronunciation task. The analogy strategy has been recently examined by Baron and Strawson (1976), Baron (1977), Brooks (1977) and, most conclusively, by Glushko (1979), and we shall discuss evidence for the reality of such a strategy shortly. For the moment, its existence as a logical possibility is sufficient to disarm the argument that evidence for a nonlexical route must amount to evidence for the GPC procedure. The counter-argument can actually be pressed in two ways. It can be claimed that an analogy strategy is an alternative to the GPC strategy as a nonlexical route. In this formulation it is "nonlexical" by virtue of the fact that it applies to nonwords and is capable of treating parts of a word smaller than the whole lexical item. But it can also be argued that the analogy strategy constitutes a possible lexical route for deriving the pronunciation of nonwords. It is "lexical" in this formulation by virtue of being based upon the listings in a phonological lexicon of the words to which analogy is made. Notice that there is no contradiction between these two arguments, and either will suffice as counters to the GPC monopoly. The seeming contradiction depends on different ways of assigning the property "nonlexical". We have already seen that the motivation for distinguishing routes on the basis of whether or not they involve lexical contact usually involved a lexicon considered as the instrument for access to a semantic system. The reasons for this are historical and have to do with the aforementioned fact that interest in the translation of print into sound was until recently a by-product of the question of how the reader gained access to the meaning of printed language. Much of this work was based on the lexical decision task in which the subject is asked to decide whether a letter string is a real word. Accordingly, the definition of "lexical" in this context meant something like "involving consultation of memory in the depth required to decide whether a stimulus consists of a real word".

Another line of evidence that has been taken to imply the existence of a nonlexical path from print to sound consists of what I shall call "bar mitzvah performance". It is often held that oral reading is possible in the absence of any contact with the comprehension system. An apparent example of this which is frequently remarked upon occurs at the bar mitzvah of a Jewish child, when he is required to read a lengthy passage of Hebrew which he may well not understand. It is debatable whether the performer is conducting a continuous translation of print into sound or whether the script is merely providing occasional orthographic retrieval cues for a rote-learned stream of sounds, but Baron (1977) and others have cited this performance as evidence of a nonlexical path for oral reading. Similarly, it is often asserted that some children have learned simply to "bark at print", that is, to decode print into sound without making contact with meaning. However, it is not clear what is being denied here, and in particular it would be dangerous to equate "without comprehension" with "nonlexical". This point is expressed well in Rozin and Gleitman's description of the comprehension problem:

> Observation reveals that very early decoding acts sometimes do not lead the child to the meaning on the page. Until decoding skills become highly automated, at least, children of ten appear to expend so much effort and attention on decoding that they have trouble attending to the outcome . . . the young learner may report that he was "too busy reading" to understand what he just saw and uttered (Rozin and Gleitman, 1977, p. 102).

In such cases as bar mitzvah performance, the child's "barking at print", and related cases in which patients with acquired dyslexia appear to read without comprehension, little is added to our understanding of nonlexical strategies for reading. The comparison between such performance and the process of reading pseudowords may not be apposite. "Barking at print" might be achieved by a

GPC procedure guided by low-level (sublexical) constraints; it might be achieved by orthographic analogies; it might be achieved by a GPC procedure guided by lexical constraints, where the lexical knowledge used fell short of comprehension, or even what is required by the lexical decision task. For example, William James writes of the use of syntax by the uncomprehending reader:

> And this foreboding of the coming grammatical scheme combined with each successive uttered word is so practically accurate that a reader incapable of understanding four ideas of the book he is reading aloud can nevertheless read it with the most delicately modulated expression of intelligence (James, 1908, p. 253).

Finally, the existence of an independent phonological lexicon could support reading without contact with the semantic system (e.g. Schwartz *et al.*, 1980).

Effects of orthographic regularity

The argument from orthographic regularity is summarized by one of the most committed advocates of the GPC procedure as follows:

> Current work suggests that the classification of words as regular or exceptions actually has "psychological reality"; subjects behave differently with the two types of word. This is strong evidence in favour of the view that nonlexical phonological encoding uses a GPC procedure, since other methods for such encoding do not distinguish between regular words and exceptions, and hence cannot explain why this distinction is reflected in behaviour (Coltheart, 1978).

In contrast to this claim and in anticipation of the material that follows, we can summarize the effects of orthographic regularity on word-naming latency as follows. At a purely empirical level there is some evidence that regular words are associated with faster naming than exception words, but the effects are small and not entirely consistent. Moreover, most of the studies are methodologically flawed. Even if we accept the existence of the relationship, we are not obliged to go on to accept an explanation of the regularity effect as the product of a GPC-based strategy.

Perhaps the simplest way to perform an experiment on the regularity effect is to construct lists either of regular or of exception words and to determine the time it takes to complete oral reading of each type of list. Baron and Strawson (1976) did this in their pioneering experiment and obtained a regularity effect that was an order of magnitude larger than that of subsequent investigators. Unfortunately, the time taken to read a word list may be influenced by at least three processes: (*i*) the time taken to access a phonological representation of a word; (*ii*) the time to assemble and initiate a motor program for articulation; and (*iii*) the time taken up by the actual production of the vocalization. Any or all of these stages might plausibly be influenced by regularity, but only the first stage is relevant to the question of strategies for translating print into sound. This same criticism applies to the list-reading study by Coltheart *et al.* (1979), in which a regularity effect was also reported.

Serious doubt about Baron and Strawson's interpretation of their regularity effect is created by a subsequent study using the same words in a single-word-naming task. Mason (1978) has reported two such experiments on good and poor readers. In neither experiment and neither ability group was there any evidence of a regularity effect upon the latency to initiate vocalization. Most effects were in the opposite direction. (The sole exception was in Experiment I where a condition was included in which the words were printed in mixed-case.) An important word property which is not controlled in the Baron and Strawson (1976) and Mason (1978) studies has been pointed out by Coltheart *et al.* (1979), who note that the irregular words had a slightly higher frequency. Because naming latency is inversely related to frequency, a frequency effect and a regularity effect might have cancelled each other out to produce Mason's null effect. (This renders the massive effect obtained by Baron and Strawson even more inexplicable.)

Some of these factors were controlled in a study of naming latencies for single words, conducted by Gough and Cosky (1977). They obtained a small but reliable regularity effect of about 27 ms. In a further development, Stanovich and Bauer (1978) tested word-naming latencies for a subset of Baron and Strawson's stimuli, matched for length, frequency and visual appearance. They obtained a reliable 18 ms regularity effect. Furthermore, they were able to show that this effect was abolished in a task in which production latencies were measured without inclusion of orthographic decoding times. In this simple reaction time (RT) task, the words were presented for inspection and after a variable delay a signal was given to emit the word. Such RTs presumably reflect motor preparation times. The absence of a regularity effect in this task provides some assurance that the previous effect is truly related to orthographic decoding.

Before concluding this review of the empirical evidence on regularity effects it is worth briefly returning to surface dyslexia, for Shallice and Warrington (1980) have employed the word sets of Coltheart *et al.* (1979) in the study of two surface dyslexics. Unlike previous studies the data here consist of actual failures to read a word.

In the case of patient R.D.G. they found 92% performance on regular words and 64% on exceptions. A more substantial regularity effect is reported in the case of E.M. with 72% correct on regular words but only 13% on exceptions. It appears, however, that in an earlier phase of her illness E.M. was able to read more successfully, scoring 78% on the most difficult words in the Schonell Test and scarcely exhibiting any regularity effect. The critical point here is that at this time the patient's access to her semantic system was severely impaired. If

Shallice and Warrington are correct in their assumption that this incapacity for semantic access (measured by the Peabody test) indicates blockage of direct visual access to the lexicon, then the performance of E.M. is incompatible with Coltheart's conclusion that translation by GPC rule is the sole alternative strategy to retrieval of word-specific phonology by direct lexical access. At a time when E.M. is supposed to lack direct access her reading is relatively good and shows a negligible effect of regularity. Yet in GPC theory she should have been wholly unable to read exception words.

Even supposing that we accept the empirical case for regularity effects, does this commit us to accepting the nonlexical GPC strategy as the sole possible agent of this effect? The answer to this must be firmly negative, since there are two alternative interpretations in which regularity effects are attributed to lexical processes.

The more important alternative account is the lexical analogy theory proposed by Glushko (1979). This theory explains the tendency for exception words to take longer to name as due to their tendency to have visually similar neighbours that are sounded differently. For example, in analogy theories the difficulty in the exception word BREAST is that it has a large number of inconsistent neighbours, such as BEAST, FEAST, LEAST, and the pronunciations of these neighbouring words influences the decision about BREAST. We go on to examine this theory in detail later, suffice it to observe here these three points. (*a*) Analogy theory does not contain a strictly nonlexical mechanism. (*b*) The letter units that matter in analogy theory are those that determine similarity with neighbours, and these are large clusters of graphemes such as -EAST rather than the single graphemic units of GPC theory. (*c*) Regularity is not the true causal agent of the latency effects according to analogy theory, rather it is the fortuitous correlation of regularity with consistency of pronunciation among a group of visually similar words that is responsible for the effect.

The other logical alternative to the GPC account of regularity effects asserts that the effect does not depend upon the translatability of segments of the word at all. Instead, it is argued that whole-word pronunciation is stored differently for regular and exception words. This might be reflected in the organization of the semantic lexicon or the organization of a separate phonological lexicon. These differences in organization might arise through the history of our dealings with written words. Presumably our initial acquisition of exceptions was more tentative, and this may have a lasting effect on the accessibility of their phonological representation. Other evidence for lasting effects of acquisition history has recently come to light, albeit in a quite different context. Caroll and White (1973) have reported that the age at which a word is acquired affects its accessibility in picture naming. In this view, then, the GPC procedure has a purely historical reality which is preserved in the archaeology of the phonological lexicon.

An independent phonological lexicon

On several previous occasions we have entertained the possibility that there might exist a store of word pronunciations separate from the semantic lexicon. We have called this possibility the "phonological lexicon" but have noted that since it is by definition independent of the semantic lexicon, direct visual access to this store would have to be classed as a nonlexical route. This is because current usage of "nonlexical" denotes only independence from the semantic lexicon.

This possibility has received little attention until recently. Coltheart (1978), in arguing that the GPC route is the only viable nonlexical one, dismisses the notion of a phonological lexicon on the grounds that it is incapable of mediating all nonlexical reading. It seems clear that such a store cannot contain entries for nonwords that we can read. "Thus at best," Coltheart concludes, "this kind of theory is incomplete." However, there is no compelling reason to accept the ontological condition that this route has to carry all nonlexical traffic. Furthermore, it is not hard to make out a plausible case for the system to possess a phonological lexicon that is located toward the output side, containing articulatory commands for speaking words. Allport (1979) reviews a number of arguments for the existence of such an articulatory store with the property of being addressable in a graphemic code.

5.3 EVIDENCE FOR A DIRECT LEXICAL ROUTE TO WHOLE-WORD PHONOLOGY

A variety of reasons have been advanced for believing that subjects can arrive at a pronunciation by using the visual information in a direct search of the internal lexicon. When the entry corresponding to the visual form of the word is located, it gives direct access to the whole-word pronunciation. Usually this interpretation of the lexicon is one in which each entry serves as the nexus of the visual, phonological and semantic representations of a word, rather like a dictionary that incorporated parallel indexes for spelling, sound and meaning. This sort of lexicon is the one hitherto referred to as a "semantic lexicon". This rather arbitrary nomenclature was adopted for two reasons: (*i*) to distinguish it from an independent phonological lexicon in which the pronunciations of entire words can be accessed without making contact with semantic or syntactic information, and (*ii*) to emphasize the ability of such a semantic lexicon to serve as the basis for decisions about meaningfulness such as are involved in the lexical decision task. However, it must be admitted that most of the evidence adduced for the existence of a direct lexical route to pronunciation does not possitively require that contact be made with semantic or syntactic information. We shall begin with a review of this evidence.

Effects of lexical status

Under this heading we shall consider a primary line of evidence, consisting in faster pronunciation of words than pseudowords, and a theoretically related secondary line, faster pronunciation of common than rare words.

Forster and Chambers (1973) appear to have been the first to report an effect of lexical status on naming latency. They found that high-frequency words were named faster than either low-frequency words or pseudowords and they concluded that the naming of words can be accomplished by a "dictionary look-up". The more rapidly the entry for a word is located, the more rapidly naming can be initiated. Along with others, they assume that the lexicon is so organized that common words can be located most quickly. Hence there arises the word-frequency effect. Nonwords lack a lexical entry and so must depend upon another, parallel route which Forster and Chambers assume must be the GPC procedure. This they assume to be a slower route, hence the disadvantage of nonwords.

Forster and Chambers present a model of how the two processing routes yield pronunciations for the various types of stimulus. Their model sets out the basic characteristics of a dual process theory that has been widely adopted by subsequent writers. It is assumed that subjects always begin to compute GPCs at the same time as they initiate a lexical search. Whichever process is completed first controls pronunciation. Forster and Chambers appear to assume that, for words, the lexical search process is invariably completed first. However, as subsequent theorists have noted, as long as the lexical search is sometimes completed first, words will on average be named faster.

Frederiksen and Kroll (1976) also measured naming latencies for words and nonwords. The effects of lexical status and of word frequency were similar to those obtained by Forster and Chambers (1973). Latencies varied inversely with word frequency but even rare words (less than one occurrence per million) were named slightly faster than nonwords. It has been shown that word frequency is correlated with the orthographic and phonological characteristics of words (Landauer and Streeter, 1973), so it is possible that a word-frequency effect could be mediated by the difficulties encountered in orthographic translation (e.g. by the GPC procedure) rather than being evidence for the operation of a lexical route. However, Frederiksen and Kroll controlled for this possibility by matching their nonwords on orthographic structure with their words, for each word-frequency class. Since there was no difference amongst the groups of nonwords, it can be assumed that the frequency effect for the real words was truly a lexical effect and not simply due to structural differences.

Frederiksen and Kroll also report on two other sets of factors which influence naming times. One set consisted in a comparison between blocking and randomizing of the word/nonword variable. The systematic effects of this design feature are probably due to changes in the subject's strategies. We shall discuss this in Chapter 6 when considering the ways in which the various processing options can be combined in actual performance. The other set of factors shown to be influential was structural and included the number of letters in the stimulus and the orthographic complexity of the string from the viewpoint of translatability. We shall defer discussion of these factors until we consider the preparation of pronunciations in detail in Chapter 7.

There seems, then, to be agreement that lexical status confers an advantage on a letter string in the naming RT paradigm. Further confirmation of this fact comes from the study by Glushko (1979, Exp. 1). This probably constitutes sufficient grounds for the acceptance of the hypothesis that the lexical entry for a word gives access to its pronunciation. This entry might be contained in a single lexicon that relates semantic, phonological and orthographic features, or it might be in an independent phonological lexicon. Furthermore, the lexical entry might take the form of an articulatory program for speech or it might consist in an abstract phonological representation that requires further processing in order to yield speech. At any rate, this lexical route must either be faster on some occasions than the nonlexical alternatives, or else the lexically based information about pronunciation must add some weight to a process that accumulates evidence on pronunciations.

Logographs and homophones

A quite different argument for the existence of a lexical route to pronunciation is based on our ability to read logographs and homophones. We have already noted that English is not purely alphabetic and phonographic. Common logographic signs in English include arabic numerals, arithmetic signs, punctuation marks and the signs for a large range of units of measurement, such as £ and lb. The relationship between the structure of these signs and the structure of their spoken name is wholly arbitrary, so it would appear that the name must be derived by retrieval of the pronunciation as a whole via its lexical representation. Our ability to name pictured objects bears witness to the efficiency of the pathway from visual information through a semantic lexical entry to a phonological lexical entry. However, logographic forms are not pictures. Their structural relationship to the extra-linguistic world of things is as arbitrary as their relationship to the sound pattern. Now, if there exists a phonological lexicon that is independent of the semantic system, there seems to be no reason why a familiar logographic sign might not be used to access a whole-word pronunciation prior to retrieval of its meaning. Thus although we might hold that from the point of view of descriptive linguistics the logograph is best regarded as referring directly to morphology, this does not deny the possibility that the reader's mental processes involve direct translation of the logograph into a prelexical speech code. In terms of this analysis, Gelb's (1963) classification of the logograph as a phonographic sign, subject to translation at the "word-syllabic" level, turns out to be a *psychological hypothesis* about the forms of lexical representation addressed by logographic signs. (More recently, Gelb (1974) has adopted the term "logo-syllabic". In his classification such a script is still regarded as "phonographic" but is acknowledged to consist of a combination of morphemic and phonetic elements.)

The argument from homophones is rather less direct because it appeals to the comprehension of the word. If we consider the pronunciation of the written forms WEEK and WEAK, it might seem that no direct access to the lexicon is required. Whether by GPCs or by analogy the appropriate spoken form can be arrived at by a regular translation. However, in the case of a homophone the derived speech form will be lexically ambiguous. To resolve this semantic ambiguity there would have to exist a mechanism for checking the spelling of the written form. Theorists who deny the possibility of direct lexical access have therefore been obliged to postulate a spelling check for homophones (e.g. Rubinstein *et al.*, 1971). However, this postulate, while allowing the semantic interpretation of a homophone printed in isolation, also creates a serious puzzle, for if the lexicon contains a representation of spellings in order to check homophones, why can the correspondence between the written stimulus and this spelling representation not be used to locate the lexical entry in the first place (direct lexical route)? This is only a puzzle and not a refutation. We may feel that the spelling check mechanism is no more than an *ad hoc* invention to enable the theorist to continue to deny the existence of direct lexical access. Yet it is conceivable that the lexicon might contain visual representations of words that are adequate to check the spelling of an item already located by phonographic translation but are not adequate as a basis for lexical search. Another way of making this point is to say that the lexical entries might contain spelling information but that the lexicon is not indexed (organized) for spellings, just as most real dictionaries are not organized specifically for sound.

The argument from logographs is therefore compelling in a way that the argument from homophones is not.

Irregular words

Another reason that is sometimes given for accepting the possibility of direct lexical access is the very fact that we can read irregular words. However, the most that can be logically established by this argument is that the pronunciation of written words must at some stage involve consultation of the lexicon. This, of course, does not amount to a demonstration that the lexicon can be addressed directly using the visual form. The argument goes as follows. There are words so irregular in their orthographic translation that there is no determinate procedure, whether by GPC frequency or by analogy, for correctly deciding their pronunciation. The only way to assign their pronunciation is by a lexical check. If this cannot, *ex hypothesi*, by achieved by direct access, there would have to exist a mental listing of all correspondences that occur in the language. This would have to be used to generate the set of possible pronunciations (possible, but implausible). These phonological forms would then be used to search the lexicon. Finally, any phonological form that was located in the lexicon would have to initiate a spelling check as for the case of the homophone.

There are two reasons why the argument from irregular words is rather uninteresting. First, as we have just shown, the argument amounts to a way of tormenting the theorist who denies direct lexical access, rather than conclusively refuting him. Secondly the logographic sign can be regarded as the *ultimate case of orthographic irregularity*, and so the argument is best formulated in terms of our ability to assign spoken forms to logographs.

Lack of nonlexical routes in deep dyslexia

Neuropsychological investigations of patients with dyslexia acquired as a consequence of brain damage have recently focused on a dramatic pattern of impairments that has come to be known as *deep dyslexia* (Marshall and Newcombe, 1973). The convergence of clinical and theoretical interest upon this syndrome is largely due to a series of papers by Marshall and Newcombe (1966, 1973, 1977; Marshall, 1976) in which the authors attempt to interpret the pattern of impairments in terms of damage to information-processing routes of the sort discussed here. The evidence is complex, in that it concerns a whole pattern of tests, together with inferences about the nature of the processes underlying performance on these tasks, and it poses special problems of evaluation, being based on a small number of patients whose pattern of impairment differs subtly from one to another, whose abilities are unstable over time in ways that are not well charted, and who present their specific reading difficulties in a context of general language difficulties from which the reading difficulties are not easily segregated. We shall return to the interpretation of deep dyslexia on several later occasions, and for the moment I shall merely outline the general form of the interpretation as it bears on direct lexical access of pronunciations. (For an excellent, up-to-date collection of papers, see *Deep Dyslexia*, edited by Coltheart, Patterson and Marshall.)

The salient characteristics of deep dyslexia set out by Marshall (1976) are:

(*a*) Inability to read nonsense syllables aloud;
(*b*) Incidence of reading errors that resemble the stimulus semantically but not orthographically (e.g. *little*→small);
(*c*) Errors that almost always consist of real words;

(*d*) Incidence of reading errors that are semantically related to a word that looks like the stimulus word (e.g. *sympathy* (symphony?)→orchestra).

To this list we may add as potentially relevant to the present argument:

(*e*) Ability to identify as nonwords (in the lexical decision task) stimuli to which they were unable to assign a pronunciation (Patterson and Marcel, 1977);
(*f*) Severe difficulty with the identification of the word referred to by a homophonic misspelling such as *hoam* or *jayle* (Saffran and Marin, 1977).

These attributes are interpreted by means of a simple primary assumption together with some supplementary elaborations. The primary assumption is that these patients possess intact only the direct lexical route to pronunciations. From this it follows as an immediate consequence that they are unable to pronounce nonsense syllables, (*a*), since such items have no lexical representation from which a whole-word pronunciation can be derived. It seems unlikely that their difficulty with the nonwords is purely articulatory since they can repeat a nonsense syllable that is presented auditorily (Patterson and Marcel, 1977) and can read it aloud when it forms part of a word (e.g. the *wid* in *widow*; Saffran and Marin, 1977). Since they are able to classify these items correctly as nonwords, (*e*), it would seem that they are able to use the written form directly in a search of the lexicon. Furthermore, if their only available route to pronunciation is via a visually addressed lexical entry, then any pronunciation retrieved should be that of a real word, even when incorrect, (*c*).

Marshall (1976) accommodates points (*b*) and (*d*) by means of the supplementary assumption that the deep dyslexic suffers additional minor impairments of the "ability to analyse the visual configuration" and the "ability to select specific items within restricted domains of semantic memory". An alternative to this postulation of further impairments consists simply in the assumption that the direct access route is quite fallible, even in normal subjects. That is to say, the visual index for the lexicon is rather sloppy, and without further checking it commonly happens that the item located in the lexicon will be a neighbour of the one signified. Selection of neighbours in visual space will yield visually related errors (which are quite common).[12] Selection of a neighbouring item in semantic space will result in the curious semantic substitution described in (*b*). The occasional fortuitous combination of these near-misses will yield the infrequent, twice-removed errors of type (*d*).

Finally, an extension of the sloppy visual addressing assumption helps us to understand (*f*). Minor misspellings can be coped with. Presented with *kar* or *paynt* the patient can often select the correct spoken form becuase of the tolerance of the system to sloppy addressing, though *wurd* may produce the response *curd*. (These examples are taken from Saffran and Marin (1977). Actually, in a strict interpretation of the theory, it shouldn't help that the misspelling is homophonous with the desired response. Only visual similarity should matter. However, if that were so, then Saffran and Marin's patient should have been able to respond to many nonsense syllables with a visually similar real word. She did not do this, which is puzzling.) As the number of letters shared by the stimulus and desired response-word decreases, so does the likelihood of a correct response. Indeed, the chance of obtaining any response—whether vocal or written—diminishes markedly. We might expect performance to be dictated by two factors in this situation. First is the visual lexical density in the neighbourhood of the region designated by the stimulus; that is to say, how many visually similar words there are to the stimulus. Second is the tolerance of the system for accepting an approximation.

If the direct visual access system is inherently sloppy, why do we not find more evidence of confusions in the performance of unimpaired subjects? One reason is suggested by Saffran *et al.* (1976), who argue that the nonlexical means of orthographic translation at the disposal of normal readers may be used to generate a phonological representation that can be compared with the spoken form retrieved by direct lexical access. That is, the nonlexical route typically converges with the lexical.

To sum up, the syndrome known as deep dyslexia offers some support to the notion of a direct visual access route to the lexicon. The assumption that deep dyslexics possess this pathway and no other can be used to provide a reasonably satisfactory account of a whole pattern of impaired performance. Moreover, it is difficult to conceive of an alternative explanation of their marked inability to assign a pronunciation to a written pseudoword. However, one difficulty with the use of the direct access assumption to account for the entire pattern of difficulties is that there are patients who apparently cannot read nonwords but who lack the other symptoms (so-called "phonological dyslexia", see Patterson, 1981). This suggests that the parsimony of the direct access account has been overstated. Furthermore, there is always the general danger inherent in arguments from the clinical to the normal that the patient may have evolved special strategies to cope with his impairment. It is open to a sceptic to concede that these patients use direct lexical access but to deny any role for such a procedure in normal oral reading. After all, we have had to assume that the patient's direct access is very fallible. For these reasons it is fortunate that the direct access case does not have to rest upon the nature of reading errors in deep dyslexia.[13]

5.4 PRONUNCIATION BY LEXICAL ANALOGY

Venezky (1970) concluded his analysis of orthographic regularities with the cautious observation that the relationship between the GPC rules he described in his linguistic model and the processes actually mediating reading performance was unknown. Elsewhere he appears to make the assumption that *in practice* pronunciation is achieved by analogy with word prototypes. Thus Venezky and Calfee (1970, p. 280) write: "We are assuming that all letter-sound generalizations are realized as higher order organizations of real words which contain the related patterns, with special facilities for access during reading."

The first systematic attempts to investigate the derivation of pronunciation by analogy were intended as tests of the psychological reality of phonological theories, especially that of Chomsky and Halle (1968). In these studies (e.g. Ohala, 1974; Steinberg and Krohn, 1975; Baker and Smith, 1976; Smith and Baker, 1976; Smith, 1980) it is purely incidental that the material is presented visually, since the linguistic rules are not specifically intended for orthographic translation but, instead, for a generation of sound from an abstract lexical base. The general method of such investigations is to present the subject with pseudowords so constructed that rule-derived pronunciations conflict with those that might be suggested by analogy with visually similar words. Steinberg and Krohn's work centred on the vowel-alternation rules (e.g. prof*a*ne–prof*a*nity; ser*e*ne–ser*e*nity). Smith and Baker, on the other hand, were concerned with stress assignment.

How these tests work can be illustrated by an example drawn from Baker and Smith (1976). Consider the pseudoword *cinempa*. If it is pronounced in accordance with Chomsky and Halle's phonological rules, the stress should fall upon the second syllable (because it is a three-syllable word, with the penultimate syllable ending in more than one consonant and the final syllable containing a lax vowel). If, however, *cinempa* is pronounced by analogy with a visually similar word, that word will probably be *cinema* and the stress will therefore fall upon the first syllable.

The Baker and Smith experiments are appealing; they ask a well-structured question by means of what appears to be a crucial experimental test. However, as often happens in psychological research, the outcome of the experiment is equivocal and forces the authors to reconsider the nature of their task. From their research we may tentatively conclude that "when subjects are asked to pronounce a nonsense word, they do something more than search for a similar English word to act as a model, but neither do they apply a series of rules in a straightforward and consistent manner" (Baker and Smith, 1976, p. 23). In general their subjects were influenced by the structure of the final syllable and by form class, which are the determining variables in the Chomsky and Halle rules. However, these variables sometimes influenced performance in ways not predicted by the rules, and furthermore other, and supposedly irrelevant variables, such as the penultimate syllable, also appeared to influence stress assignment.

These experiments reveal some of the difficulties which would seem to face any investigation in this area. The more important of these difficulties are as follows. (*i*) The method requires the use of pseudowords. This means, as the authors concede, that the results can only show what the reader does when he is forced to and do not necessarily tell us what he does in reading normal English. However, Baker and Smith argue that it would be odd if the reader did not employ these complex skills in normal speech. This seems a surprising claim. I would prefer to argue in support of the pseudoword task that it would be odd if in normal speech and reading the speaker did not by-pass the whole analogy v. rules issue, by utilizing lexically stored whole-word pronunciations. The issue would *only* arise, in this view, when an unfamiliar form was encountered, and this is the situation mimicked by the pseudowords. (*ii*) To restrict the possible analogies, the pseudowords used were often rather bizarre in structure, e.g. *cinempa, zeranda, ollanteam, tupaivend*. It might be dangerous to generalize from performance on such items. (*iii*) The identity of the word used as an analogy has to be inferred. To direct that inference as clearly as possible, Baker and Smith (Exp. 1) chose pseudowords that resembled very closely one and only one real word, and this may make the subject's task highly unrepresentative. Conversely, when they wished to study the variables governing rule-based behaviour they choose pseudowords that did not resemble any real word (e.g. *tupaivend*). Such words are unusual almost by definition, and they only allow us to study rule-based behaviour in circumstances where we have arranged that analogies be hard to come by. Moreover, where Baker and Smith do set up a particular analogy, this is based on the assumption that analogies are made at the level of whole words. This might seem the simplest strategy for deciding stress assignment but that is no reason for assuming that it is what subjects are in fact doing.

Baker and Smith discuss several of these difficulties, and I have reviewed them in the context of their study only because it is a particularly detailed and interesting foray with these methods. It would seem, however, that these difficulties are likely to hold for any study of these questions.

A different approach to the investigation of the analogy strategy was taken by Baron (1977a, b). He divides rule-based strategies into three classes. His *component correspondences* are more or less equivalent to our GPC procedure. From this GPC class Baron distinguishes *analogies* on two grounds. First, the analogy strategy "makes use of larger units of known correspondences, whole words instead of letter or letter groups". Secondly, it "places greater reliance on strategies brought to bear at the time a word is pronounced, as opposed to the time the rules are learned" (Baron, 1977a, p. 181). Baron's final class of strategy he calls a *similarity* mechanism. This mechanism relies on the tendency for words that look similar to sound similar.

As an *a priori* classification of strategies Baron's scheme is open to criticism.

There seem to be at least two sorts of difficulty: the distinction between the analogy and similarity strategies is unclear, and the characteristics assigned to the analogy strategy to distinguish it from the GPC strategy are arbitrary and inessential. When we enquire into Baron's conception of the similarity strategy we find that it appears to refer to the possibility of accessing a whole-word pronunciation by means of an *approximate* phonological translation. Thus we are told that this mechanism copes with misspellings (Baron, 1977a, p. 181) and that it is only useful when we encounter for the first time spellings of words of which we already know the spoken form (p. 205). In our discussion of the GPC procedure we have already acknowledged this possibility, but it does not have the status of a possible mechanism at the same level as GPCs and analogies. The fact that approximate translations may be successfully recognized can be reconciled with any of a number of theories about the route by which the translation is achieved. Accordingly, we shall not consider the similarity mechanism as an alternative to GPCs, analogies, and the like.

We turn now to Baron's characterization of the analogy strategy. My principal objection here is to the arbitrary assumption that this strategy must depend on a deliberate pursuit of relationships that is only instigated by the presentation of the printed form, rather than an automatic process that makes use of relationships already represented in memory. Glushko (1979) has drawn attention to this unnecessary qualification that the use of analogy be a conscious strategy. However, it is not difficult to understand how Baron came to make the assumption of deliberateness. There may be two reasons.

Baron's first line of evidence for the use of analogies came from a pseudoword-naming task in which the subjects were given unlimited time to respond (Baron, 1977b). He found that his subjects sometimes pronounced pseudowords such as *yeart* so as to rhyme with real words which were visually similar but irregular in terms of GPCs (*heart*). Clearly, the lack of time pressure may have encouraged the subject to use deliberate (and unnatural strategies).

A second line of evidence that may have led Baron to assume deliberateness in the use of analogy comes from an experiment in which he showed that instructions to the subjects "to use words they already knew to help figure out the new ones" (Baron, 1977a, p. 211) had the effect of improving performance from 91% to 96% correct. Subjects were asked to produce all of the responses that they thought could be correct. (The stimuli were again pseudowords, and "correctness" was defined as conformity to GPC rules.) Whatever this study might tell us, it certainly seems unlikely to cast light upon automatic or spontaneous mechanisms governing the translation of print to sound. Furthermore, it is difficult to be sure that these instructions have a specific effect on analogy making, as distinct from the strategy of attending to GPC frequencies or merely double-checking candidate responses.

Baron's studies may cast little light upon the possibility of an automatic analogy strategy but they do contribute to a conceptual clarification of the relationship between GPC rules and analogies. This arises out of the insight that a primary difference between GPCs and analogies lies in the size of the unit used in translation. Consider the task of assigning a pronunciation to the pseudo-word *slood*. From the GPC viewpoint the most common correspondent of the vowel digraph is [u] as in *broom*. The GPC units are maximally analytic, and so segmentation (Venezky, 1970) yields up the irreducible OO as the unit of translation. However, if we take a larger unit, the frequency data can point in a different direction. Let us say we adopt a general procedure of locating the largest unit that is contained in another word. This might be the LOOD that occurs in *blood* and *flood*. In these the vowel digraph is sounded as [ə], so, in terms of the maximal unit, what is "regular" (i.e. most frequent) differs from what is "regular" at the minimal unit (GPC) level. This example shows that *it is possible to define versions of the GPC and analogy strategies in such a way that they only differ in the size of the unit of translation.*[14] Of course it is possible that the strategies may in fact differ in other ways as well.

In examining the effect of unit size upon the search for a pronunciation of *slood* we made the working assumption that the alternative to the maximal analyticity of the GPC analysis was to choose the largest unit that could be found in a real word. That seemed quite a plausible way for the analogy strategy to work but it was not a necessary assumption. An alternative way of viewing the status of translation units has been advanced by Brooks (1978). He distinguishes between *analytic* and *non-analytic correspondences.* Analytic correspondences are roughly equivalent to what we have called GPCs. However, we have called GPCs maximally analytic because they involve irreducible segments. This is the same sense of analyticity as used by linguists to characterize the phonographic properties of scripts. Brooks, on the other hand, means by *analytic* "that particular segments of the stimulus are associated by the learner with particular segments of the response". In this definition, translation is analytic if it relies upon a particular type of segment, regardless of whether this segment is of minimal size like the GPC. Brooks goes on to give an example of a strategy which is not analytic and which can be regarded as a type of analogy strategy. (He refers to this as the use of *indirect component correspondence.*)

Brooks makes the interesting claim for his analogy mechanism that it yields a word pronunciation without requiring any explicit analysis of the written or spoken forms into functional units. Nor does the mechanism require that a representation of either the written or spoken form exist in memory. When the unknown written form is presented, it activates the phonological representations of a set of words that it closely resembles visually. Then, in Brooks' (1978) words, "by some process of summation, the common components of the neighbouring responses could cue the components of the desired response without directly using any relation between components of the stimulus and components of the response." Brooks does not elaborate on the summation process, but it is not difficult to see how the mechanism could include the refinement of weighting the contribution to the sum according to the amount of orthographic similarity that a stored word has with the test word. Furthermore, such a device is, in a sense, responsive to frequencies, because the number of words entering the summation process reflects a sort of type count across an orthographic neighbourhood. However, it is not correspondence frequencies at a pre-ordained unit size that matters. To see this, we can return to our example of *slood*. Presentation of *slood* may activate a variety of fairly dissimilar words that contain the "regular" GPC correspondence OO→[u] (*boot*, *broom*, *proof*, etc.), but, in view of their dissimilarity from *slood* these will have little weight in the decision. The mildly irregular *good* and *look*, where OO→[U], are more similar and will carry greater weight. Maximum weight will be carried by the highly similar *blood* and *flood*, which contain the highly irregular GPC, OO→[ə]. It can readily be seen that the outcome of the summation process will depend jointly upon the number of exemplars of a correspondence and their similarity weighting. (No doubt there is scope here for one of those marvellously arbitrary mathematical models.)

Brooks (1978) reports an attempt to demonstrate orthographic learning that is non-analytic. In previous experiments Brooks (1977) and Baron (1977a) had designed a set of artificial symbols. These symbols were used to construct two kinds of script: one was constructed according to a regular GPC principle; in the other, the relationship between the graphemes of the script and the spoken sounds was arbitrary, and the script had to be associated with the spoken forms by means of rote, paired-associate learning. They found that after the associations had been learned, the GPC-based script could be translated into sound faster than the whole-word paired-associate script. Furthermore, this advantage in translation speed survived after hundreds of trials. Brooks' (1978) experiment was designed to investigate whether this advantage depends upon explicit knowledge of the alphabetic convention as distinct from an implicit (non-analytic) apprehension of overall shape–sound correlations. Accordingly, Brooks attempted to disguise the nature of the rules underlying the GPC script by not informing the subjects that either script had a functional alphabet and by reversing the spelling order in the GPC script (so that, for example, *nape* and *naps* differed in the leftmost symbol).

Brooks found that after an initial study period the GPC-based script was pronounced slightly but reliably faster and with fewer errors than the arbitrary script. Furthermore, even when subjects reported finding the GPC-based words easier, they claimed not to know why. Unfortunately, as Brooks admits, the possibility remains open that the subjects had unconsciously arrived at knowledge of the translation rules for the GPC script, though he denies the plausibility of such an account.

The most persuasive evidence for the use of analogies comes from an elegant study by Glushko (1979). He adopted the pseudoword pronunciation task, but in contrast to previous studies he designed a test that could be applied to reaction times. This provides some reassurance that the findings bear upon automatic mechanisms that might be used in normal oral reading. Central to Glushko's method is the concept of "regular" and "exception" pseudowords. His "exception" pseudowords differed by only the one letter from a real word containing an exceptional vowel correspondence (e.g. *haid–said*). His "regular" pseudowords lacked this attribute. Now, if existing words are used as analogies during the pronunciation of pseudowords, we would expect that the "exception" pseudowords would occasionally be pronounced using the exceptional GPC. That is what happened. Subjects produced 6·2% exceptional pronunciations for the "regular" psueodwords but 21·7% exceptional pronunciations for the "exception" pseudowords. Furthermore, 80% of the latter pronunciations conformed to the correspondence used in the visually similar (analogy) word. So far, these results confirm that when analogies are pitted against rules, pronunciations are often seen to be assigned by analogy. The fact that this has been shown in a RT paradigm adds force to previous reports of such a result. However, Glushko also obtained a regularity effect in the *latency* data for his pseudowords. Those that resembled an exceptional real word, even when pronounced regularly, tended to be named significantly more slowly (29 ms). This latency effect cannot be accounted for in terms of the general GPC procedure. These two types of pseudoword differ only in whether there are irregular words that resemble them. However, as we shall see later, such a latency effect is consistent with at least one class of analogy mechanism.

According to Glushko, previous advocates of the analogy strategy conceived it as applying to the pronunciation of pseudowords only. In essence it was nothing but a mechanism for dealing with novel written forms. He therefore set out to show that analogies were also employed in the pronunciation of familiar real words (Glushko, 1979, Experiment 3). He did this by comparing performance on (*i*) regular words which bore no resemblance to an exception word and (*ii*) regular words which did closely resemble an exception word. For example *haze* and *wave* are both regular in terms of GPCs but *wave* resembles *have*, which is an exception. ("Resemblance" was defined in terms of shared endings.)

The results supported Glushko's proposal that analogies are also used in the treatment of familiar words. Even when a word is strictly regular in GPCs, the existence of a misleading analogy slows the decision on pronunciation and increases the chances of mispronunciation. Indeed, the latency of pronouncing regular words when they are susceptible to a misleading (exception) analogy is similar to the latency for exception words themselves. This suggests that the distinction between regular and exception words is, from a psychological viewpoint, spurious. Conformity to abstract GPC rules cannot be the significant attribute. Yet a distinction between regular and exception words has played a fundamental role in arguments for the psychological reality of GPCs (Baron, 1977a; Coltheart, 1978). Disagreement about the existence of a regularity effect across the studies of Bauer and Stanovich (1980), Gough and Cosky (1977), Mason (1978) and Stanovich and Bauer (1978) man be due to the fact that regularity is not the true causal agent. The demonstration of an apparent regularity effect might depend upon the absence of misleading analogies for the regular words. For example, the regular word set used by Baron and Strawson (1976, Exp. 2) and by Mason (1978) and modified by Stanovich and Bauer (1978) contains a large number of words that meet Glushko's criterion of possessing misleading analogies. These include *goes* and *toes* (*does*: the verb, not the plural noun), *tone* and *bone* (*none*), *foul* (*soul*), *treat* (*great*) and *hand* (*wand*).

Other, less rigorous evidence for the employment of lexical analogies in oral reading exists. Marsh *et al.* (1977) have shown that fifth grade children call upon analogies when deciding how to pronounce new words. Meyer *et al.* (1975) showed that reading latencies could be influenced by prior presentation of an orthographic neighbour and that naming was slowed when the neighbour was inconsistent (COUCH–TOUCH). Glushko (1979) has demonstrated that such priming involves larger segments than the GPC. Kay and Marcel (1981) have used associative priming to show that the pronunciation of a pseudoword can be biased by priming its orthographic neighbours.

Up to this point we have established the credibility of the analogy strategy. As a mechanism that supplements the direct retrieval of whole word phonology there is a substantial body of evidence for its psychological reality, but a number of unanswered questions about the detailed workings of the strategy remain. The primary problems concern (*i*) the definition of resemblance, (*ii*) the mechanism for pooling or summing the evidence from analogous forms, and (*iii*) the way in which the analogy strategy combines with other strategies to produce a final decision on pronunciation. We examine these questions in the next chapter.

It must be clear that the concept of "resemblance" is crucial to the analogy formulation. Nevertheless, the experimental manipulation of resemblance has had to rest on an intuitive base. For Baker and Smith (1976) it was necessary to ensure a unique analogy and so the real word that served as the analogy required, itself, to be distinctive, and therefore usually polysyllabic (e.g. *cinema–cinempa*). This option was not open to Glushko, since he needed to have three classes of word that were fairly well matched on general graphemic pattern: exception words (*have*), regular words with exception analogies (*wave*), and regular words without exception analogies (*haze*, *wade*). Now, *haze* and *wave* both differ from *have* by a single consonant only, but *wave* is held to resemble *have* more because of "the psychological saliency and developmental primacy of rhyme". This is a plausible assumption, but it would be useful to have some independent way of determining resemblance in order to be able to make unequivocal and quantitative predictions about pronunciation.

Summary of evidence on routes from print to sound

It seems clear that information from direct access to whole-word phonology and from lexical analogies can be brought to bear on the decoding of written forms. The evidence on analogies is strong, and that on direct access to lexical phonology is apparently overwhelming. It is not yet clear whether this lexical information is retrieved from a general purpose semantic lexicon, an independent phonological/articulatory lexicon, or both of these. Ironically the avenue which has received most attention from linguists and from psychologists, that of the GPC-based translation by abstract rule, lacks any firm support. We have been unable to find any compelling reason to believe that abstract GPC rules play a role in normal reading aloud.

The method employed to establish the use of one or other of these sources of information has often involved pitting one "route" against another. This sort of experimental contrast, together with the terminology of "routes", "pathways" and the like, could easily be taken as implying that each source of information serves a self-sufficient mechanism and that these mechanisms operate in a parallel and independent manner. As it happens, this sort of assumption has tended to dominate recent thinking. This, however, seems due rather more to a failure to consider alternatives than to an overwhelming weight of positive support. Accordingly, we turn now to consider the question of how the various sources of information are combined in deciding on the pronunciation of a word.

Chapter 6

Towards a Working Model

Whatever the merits of the GPC hypothesis, it seems clear that it cannot offer a sufficient account of word naming. There is a large body of evidence to the effect that naming latencies are influenced by lexical factors to which a prelexical translation process should be indifferent. Thus, words can be named faster than pseudowords. Similarly, common words can be read aloud faster than rare words. Furthermore, it seems that the speed and accuracy of reading aloud are affected by the pronunciation of words that visually resemble the stimulus. One might add that stress assignment requires lexical information.

A pure, word-specific hypothesis based upon retrieval of whole-word phonology from the lexicon is also inadequate, standing on its own. One argument often deployed against the sufficiency of the word-specific mechanism is that we are capable of pronouncing pseudowords that are presumably not stored in our mental lexicon (see, for example, Coltheart, 1978, 1980). This argument will not serve our purpose because the question is how we read *words*. There might have to be a supplementary procedure for decoding new words and pseudowords, but once a pronunciation had been assigned retrieval of this from the lexicon might be the invariable means of reading the word aloud. Perhaps the strongest reason for denying the sufficiency of the pure, word-specific mechanism is the evidence of the use of lexical analogies. The key finding here is Glushko's (1979) demonstration that, even for a familiar, orthographically regular word, pronunciation is slowed if it has neighbours that are sounded differently. This implies that word-specific information is automatically pooled with analogies from neighbouring words.

With the rejection of pure GPC and pure word-specific accounts we are left with two principal candidates. First, we shall consider the dual process theory, which is based upon the assertion of two parallel and independent channels, one lexical and word specific, the other nonlexical and GPC-based. Then we shall consider analogy theory as a sufficient account that contains no strictly nonlexical mechanism. In a brief closing section we shall consider some developmental issues.

6.1 DUAL PROCESS THEORY

Discussion of the possible mechanisms for assigning pronunciations has tended to be formulated in dichotomous terms. A major influence here has undoubtedly been work on the lexical decision task which has been haunted by the question of whether access to the semantic lexicon is direct and visual or indirect and phonological. Consider, for instance, the following passage from the concluding section of Baron's (1977a) treatment of mechanisms for the translation of print into sound:

> representations of letters or visual features may be connected with representations of sounds or articulations either through direct, word-specific pathways or through pathways based on smaller units, that is, spelling–sound correspondences. Or for another example, meanings may be connected with print directly or through phonemic representations (Baron, 1977a, pp. 213–214).

This passage illustrates a number of points common to many such discussions. First there is the theoretical association of the word-naming task with the lexical decision task. Then there is the distinction between two "pathways", a direct connection between vision and the lexicon and an indirect path that utilizes spelling–sound correspondences as a nonlexical preliminary either to lexical access or to articulation. Finally, there is the implication that the two pathways are independent. Other advocates of this general view include Allport (1977, 1979), Coltheart (1978, 1980), Forster and Chambers (1973), Frederiksen and Kroll (1976), Marcel and Patterson (1978), Marshall (1976), and Morton and Patterson (1980).

In addition, most writers have gone further in specifying the nature of the pathways and have identified the nonlexical pathway with the GPC procedure. In these formulations, too, not only are alternative pathways distinguished but their independence is also asserted.

There is an important but often ignored difference between establishing that the system has access to distinct sources of information and establishing that these sources lead to fully formed candidate responses by means of independent pathways. What we must beware of in the present context is that the independence hypothesis does not gain admittance dressed up as the separate-sources hypothesis.

Double-dissociation and separate sources

By accepting the cases for both a direct lexical (word-specific) source and a lexical analogy source we have already committed ourselves to the principle of separate sources. In addition, it costs nothing to concede the possibility that GPC information, even if it cannot be called upon automatically to assist fluent word naming, can probably influence the painstaking deliberations of surface dyslexics and linguists. Several writers have recently attempted to develop this thesis of the separation of sources of information on which pronunciation depends. Interestingly, their methods have tended to have in common the study of individual differences, either as they occur in the contrasting patterns of dyslexic impairment or in the comparison of types of normal reader.

The first assertion that concerns us I have taken from the immensely influential discussion of acquired dyslexia by Marshall and Newcombe (1973). In contrasting the patterns of impairment, particularly in surface and deep dyslexia, they make the following claim.

> Dyslexic data reveal very clearly that these linguistically distinct aspects of words are involved in *functionally* separable performance systems. Accordingly, "threshold" models of normal word recognition . . . are required, envisaging differential access to the two forms (phonological and syntactico-semantic) of recoding of visually presented words (Marshall and Newcombe, 1973, pp. 193–194).

What we have to decide here is whether "functionally separable" and "differential access" mean anything more than the assertion of separate sources. The claim is echoed by Allport (1979), who writes:

> the single most important contribution to our knowledge of the separable subsystems involved in word recognition has come in my view from neuropsychological studies of dyslexic patients (Allport, 1979, p. 228).

Allport goes on to speak of a "sharp functional separation between mechanisms" which seems to imply that dyslexic conditions reveal that, underlying normal performance, there exist independent and self-sufficient processes of a lexical and non-lexical nature. There are, I think, several reasons why we need not accept this view.

First, there are reasons for not accepting the unqualified argument from dyslexic to normal behaviour. I have already reviewed some of the relevant points in the discussions of surface and deep dyslexia above. The most important points were the lack of assurance that the laborious and sometimes irrelevant strategies adopted in surface dyslexia bear any direct relation to pathways used in normal reading, and the fact that in deep dyslexia many problems are left unexplained by the assumption that these patients lack a nonlexical means of translating orthography. More particularly, in deep dyslexia there is clearly present a range of phonological difficulties that have nothing to do with orthography. There is also a more general difficulty in treating syndromes that arise as a consequence of brain damage (often extremely extensive) as if they consisted in the deletion of a single functional pathway with no rearrangement of the rest of the system. It would be ironic if, at a time when the subtractive method of analysing processing stages has been abandoned for the analysis of simple laboratory tasks (Sternberg, 1969), it were to be assumed that pure subtraction without rearrangement could result from massive brain damage. The question has been well expressed by Marcel and Patterson (1978), who ask whether:

> one can view the syndrome (deep dyslexia) analytically in terms of additive impairments to subsystems of normal reading and speech functioning or whether one has to treat the pathological state as a new integrated system.... Given that many patients are aware that they have a language problem, their observed communication probably results in part from strategies for use of an impaired system. This may well be true also of their performance in experimental situations.

Even if we accept the subtractive method as a working hypothesis, it is difficult to see why that hypothesis need go beyond the assertion of separate sources to the postulation of parallel and independent pathways. The fact that sources of linguistic information are sufficiently separated anatomically to sustain independent impairment in no way entails the conclusion that each source serves an independent and self-sufficient mechanism. An alternative (and purely rhetorical) way to put matters is to enquire: if we could somehow put the brains of a surface and a deep dyslexic together in committee, would we end up with a normal reader?

An alternative to the parallel-and-independent mechanisms view would seem to be one that appealed to the severity of impairment in both of these forms of acquired dyslexia as evidence that the separate sources of linguistic information are normally employed in mutual support.

Another, and more powerful, line of attack on the double-dissociation argument for the lexical v. nonlexical dichotomy is that analogy theory contains no nonlexical route yet is no less consistent with the symptom pattern of deep dyslexia than is GPC theory. There are various components of the analogy mechanism which, in failing, could yield an inability, for example, to name pseudowords. The large number of visual confusion errors in deep dyslexia suggests that the activation of orthographic neighbours is accomplished, perhaps even in exaggerated form. Possibly the most likely locus of impairment is the mechanism for synthesizing phonology from the stored pronunciations of orthographic neighbours. This amounts to a breakdown in a special aspect of post-lexical phonology. Some admittedly slender evidence of such a deficit can be found in reports that deep dyslexic patients are unable to match visually presented words on the basis of rhyme. (They tend to say "yes" erroneously to visually similar items like BEAR–FEAR but "no" to true cases like COME–SUM: cf. Morton and Patterson, 1980.) This is rather puzzling in the dual process view, since rhyme judgements do not require GPC translation and indeed are frequently not feasible using GPC translation. (How could a prelexical GPC mechanism be used to determine that BEAR and FEAR do not rhyme?)

A quite different basis for distinguishing between processing mechanisms by means of the study of differences between types of individual has been proposed by Baron (1977a; Baron and Strawson, 1976; Baron *et al.*, 1980). The "mechanisms" which Baron wishes to distinguish are a "word-specific" means of accessing pronunciation and an "orthographic" one. By "word-specific" Baron refers to the use of a visually addressable lexicon, whether it be a general-purpose semantic lexicon or an independent phonological lexicon. By "orthographic" Baron refers to translation by means of smaller units than the whole word, using either analogies or GPCs. His two extreme groups he calls "Chinese" and "Phoenicians". Chinese are supposed to be better at using the word-specific mechanism and Phoenicians better at the orthographic mechanism. Baron's general method involves using one set of tests for selecting his groups and then attempting to show that the groups differ in their performance on other tasks. The selection tasks and the subsequent performance tasks are held to converge upon the two hypothetical mechanisms.

The selection task for word-specific abilities involved measurement of the improvement between scores on a free-response spelling test and a forced-choice recognition test of spelling. The idea behind this is that the improvement must be achieved by accessing word-specific knowledge in the recognition test. This is the "looks-right" test. It is not difficult to conceive of objections to the logic of this measure: it depends on the assumption that the instructions not to revise the spellings in the free-response test prevented the use of the "looks-right" strategy in this test; it ignores the fact that the amount of improvement possible between tests depends on the number of errors on the first (free-response) test; it assumes that word-specific mechanisms available for selecting pronunciation are equally available for selecting spellings.

To measure ability with the orthographic strategy the subjects were required to detect pseudohomophones, i.e. members of a list of pseudowords that sounded like real words (*caik–cake*).

In the post-selection task, subjects were required to read aloud as rapidly as possible lists of "regular" and "exception" words. The main finding was an interaction between subject groups and list regularity. One way of describing this effect is to say that the groups did not differ on speed of reading the regular words, but the Chinese were faster than the Phoenicians on the exception words. Baron (1977a) concludes from this outcome that: (*i*) "different mechanisms" exist, (*ii*) readers differ in the extent to which they "rely on" one mechanism or the other, and (*iii*) exception words make relatively more use of one of the mechanisms.

I shall confine myself to two evaluative comments. First, the fact that a difference on the post-selection task was obtained should not blind us to the doubtful logic underlying the selection tasks; the former cannot be held to vindicate the latter. Secondly, the Chinese were actually faster overall on *both* sorts of list, though the difference was negligible on the regular words and substantial on the exception words. In the absence of a cross-over effect the results cannot be used to argue for a two-mechanism theory. (It is patently *ad hoc* to argue that some additional and unknown factor makes the Chinese faster at everything.) This lack of support for a two-factor theory can be illustrated by the following speculation. Suppose that an orthographic mechanism alone is used in this task. Moreover, let us provisionally accept the possibility that Baron himself states, that "exceptions might just use more complicated rules". If the Chinese turn out to be faster at using the rules, their advantage over the Phoenicians is most likely to be detectable with exception words, since these use complicated rules. As this is what Baron found, it seems that the data are logically incapable of supporting a two-mechanism explanation. Of course, one may choose to doubt the possibility that exceptions just use more complicated rules, but then one needn't have done the experiment in the first place, for Baron's reason was precisely to *test* the two-mechanism view of the difference between regular and exception words.

Horse-race models

As I have implied, many theorists have gone beyond the "separate sources" position to the assumption that there exist parallel, independent and self-sufficient mechanisms based upon these sources. In most formulations two mechanisms are contrasted in this way. For some, these are lexical search and GPC-based translation (Forster and Chambers, 1973; Frederiksen and Kroll, 1976; Coltheart, 1978). For others the contrast is between word-specific procedures and orthographic ones (Baron, 1977a). For present purposes I want to ignore the precise nature of the contrast and examine instead the general structure of the models of how the system as a whole arrives at a final pronunciation. Here we find that the most popular approach involves the horse-race model, named from the assumption that the alternative mechanisms start simultaneously and race to a solution, with the response executive choosing the first solution to appear at the finishing line and inhibiting subsequent solutions that arrive by slower routes.

Horse-race models have been widely adopted in recent attempts to explain the relative speed of various mental processes. Part of their charm no doubt lies in their drastically simple, first-past-the-post, method of combining information from diverse sources. Another interesting property of the horse race is that a speed advantage for *X* over *Y* can be explained in either of two ways. Obviously, *X* may be faster than *Y* if *X* and *Y* are processed by different routes with *X* having the faster route. But *X* may also be faster than *Y* even if they both use the faster route as long as *X* also has access to the slower route. As long as the slower route is *occasionally* faster, that is to say, this second route has finishing times that overlap distributionally with those of the fast route while having a larger mean latency, then *X* will be faster than *Y* on those very occasions and therefore *X* will have a lower average latency than *Y*. The horse-race model is, therefore, an efficient way of exploiting a small advantage.

Two general properties of horse-race models have generally received less attention than they deserve. The first is their implication for the distribution of reaction-times, for the decision which can call upon the faster of two underlying pathways will usually have a reduced variance and negative skew to its reaction-time distribution when compared with the distribution of RTs derived from a single underlying pathway. The second is that it requires an executive mechanism for selecting the first solution to arrive and rejecting subsequent (and possibly conflicting) solutions.

Now, we are already in a position to anticipate how various assumptions about the pathways available for naming different sorts of printed stimuli can be combined in a horse-race to yield a model of the expected final, pronunciation latencies. The earliest and simplest of these was advanced by Forster and Chambers (1973). They assumed that there were two available pathways leading to word-names, one via lexical search and another via GPC translation rules. Words can be successfully processed through either pathway, but nonwords can only be handled by the GPC route. Figure 8 is a summary diagram of this model.

Although Forster and Chambers do not discuss the question, clearly when the subject does not know in advance the lexical status of a stimulus, the lexical pathway must accept nonword inputs as it does words. It is not until lexical search has been completed that the lexical status of the item can be determined and, in the case of nonwords, the attempt to use the lexical route abandoned.

Forster and Chambers assume that the lexical route is always the faster of the two pathways. However, it seems plausible that as word frequency is decreased, with a consequent increase in the duration of lexical search, the likelihood of the GPC route winning the race would increase. Furthermore, it is clear from Forster and Chambers' data that the distributions of naming latencies for words and pseudowords *overlap*. This overlap is substantial for low-frequency words. This must imply that word-naming is accomplished by a mixture of strategies and that a means must be available for selecting the first speech program to become available.

Another matter which Forster and Chambers discuss is the form of speech representation that is yielded both by lexical search and by GPC translation. For either or both of these stages the product might be an abstract phonological code which requires further translation to become an acceptable program for articulation.

One major difficulty which Forster and Chambers do not discuss concerns the fate of "exception" words. Subsequent theorists have acknowledged the problem of exception words by specifying that the GPC procedure works only for regular words, but this is an entirely circular attempt at dealing with the difficulty. The crucial question is this: if the GPC procedure is wholly independent of the lexicon, how do we find out that a word is an exception? That is,

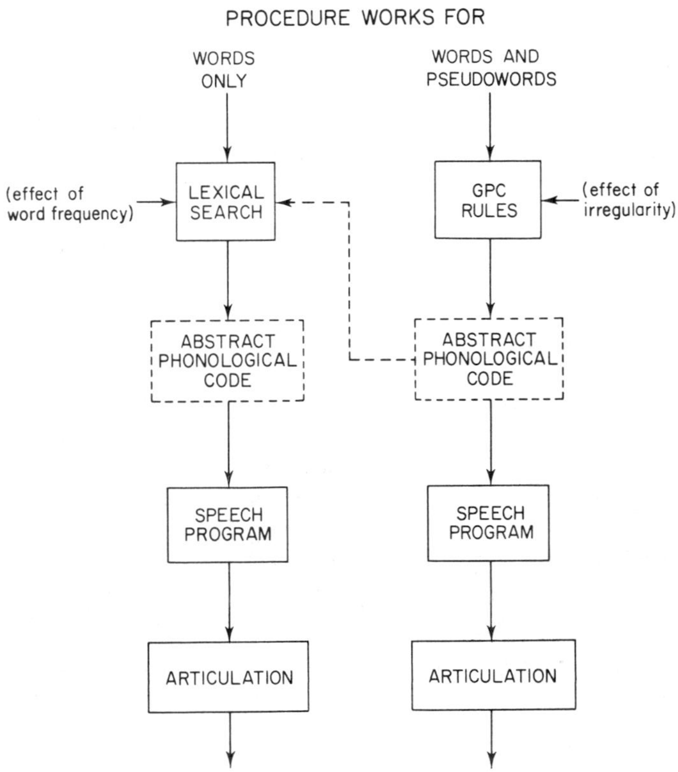

Fig. 8 A schematic diagram of the horse-race model of conversion of print to sound, freely interpreted after Forster and Chambers (1973).

why do we not mistranslate it as if it were orthographically regular? As soon as we admit some sort of lexical check on the products of translation, it seems we violate the independence of the pathways. In fact, as soon as we examine the problem of exception words, the defects of the horse-race model quickly become evident.

One way of resolving the pronunciation of exception words is by means of a search-and-test procedure in which the rules are applied in diminishing order of generality and at each application the resultant pronunciation is checked. Such a check constitutes a clear violation of the principle of informational independence of the pathways. Furthermore, as we have already seen, such a checking would have to consider the spelling as well as the sound. (If we simply checked the sound, then for *bread* we would accept the regular translation of the vowel digraph, since the lexicon contains *breed*. Even if we tried the correct translation, its acceptability cannot be determined by sound alone, since the sound-check might refer to the lexical item *bred*.) As soon as we accept the notion of a lexical check of spelling and sound, there would seem to be nothing to distinguish such a process from the lexical route itself.

If we are to preserve the essential characteristics of the horse-race model, we must abandon the notion of a lexical check and instead use the first-past-the-post property of the model to discriminate between alternative pronunciations of exception words. This enables us to maintain the ballistic property of the GPC procedure (its lack of lexical feedback). Table 9 shows two ways to achieve this, based on slightly different assumptions about the relative speed of the independent routes.

Table 9 Two horse-race models, based upon slightly different assumptions about the relative speed of the lexical and non-lexical pathways

SHARED ASSUMPTIONS

All stimuli are input to both channels. Nonwords fail at the lexical search stage and so can only be fully processed by the nonlexical channel. Words are processed through to an articulatory representation by both channels. The first channel to complete processing inhibits the output of the other channel.

DIFFERENTIAL ASSUMPTIONS

Model A	*Model B*
A The lexical channel is invariably faster	B The lexical channel is faster on average, but the distributions of completion-times for the two channels overlap

PREDICTIONS

A1 Words faster than nonwords	B1 Words faster than nonwords
A2 No effect of word regularity	B2 Correct responses to exception words faster than to regular words
A3 Exceptions pronounced correctly	B3 Some regularized pronunciations of exception words
A4 Nonwords always regular in pronunciation	B4 Nonwords always regular in pronunciation
	B5 Errors slower than correct responses on exception words

Given the complex properties of the models and the extreme difficulty of juggling the latency assumptions so as to enable prediction of even the basic effects of lexicality, word frequency and regularity, it is slightly startling to find that proponents of dual process theory have not given any heed to the detailed workings of the horse-race.

It is not difficult to illustrate these problems. Consider, for example, the consequences of assuming that the lexical route is always the faster. This would mean that word responses were always delivered via the lexical route, and it would follow that the naming latencies of words and pseudowords should not have overlapping distributions. Moreover, since only the GPC route is supposedly sensitive to regularity, words should not exhibit a regularity effect. Both these predictions are contradicted by the available evidence, so we cannot permit the assumption that the lexical route is always faster. The rejection of this assumption is not entirely trivial, however, because it is precisely this assumption that Coltheart *et al.* (1979) make in applying dual process theory to the lexical decision task.

Consider now the opposite assumption: that the GPC route is always faster. If this were so, we should have no lexicality effect and no word-frequency effect. Moreover, exception words would invariably be pronounced incorrectly, unless we assume that the GPC method is applied iteratively until a lexically acceptable soulution is found. If this were so, the response would have to await a lexical check, and so the original assumption that the GPC route is faster than the lexical route would be void. Furthermore, even if we assume iterative attempts at GPC translation with lexically checked solutions, we cannot account for nonword-naming latencies. Since no lexical check would ever work for them, they would have to be produced by a "deadline" mechanism and thus have longer latencies than exception words. This they do not appear to have.

It might seem that these difficulties can be avoided by the simple expedient of retreating to the position that the routes have overlapping latency distributions, so that sometimes one route is faster, sometimes the other. This certainly makes the theory more difficult to evaluate but does not necessarily avoid all the problems. One such problem has its origin in the way the horse-race model copes with the regularity effect. To the extent that regular words are faster than exception words, this must be due to regular words having the extra advantage of access to the GPC route. Correct pronunciations of exception words can only be derived from the lexical route. Similarly, pronunciations of pseudowords can only be derived from GPC translation. But exception words and pseudowords have very similar latencies (Glushko, 1979), so the mean latencies of the lexical and GPC routes must be roughly equal. Therefore, all the advantage that regular words enjoy over exception words, on one hand, and pseudowords, on the other hand, must be due to regular words being able to use on any occasion the faster of two routes whose mean latencies are equal. Variance alone is responsible for the advantage. This strange, though admittedly not impossible, conclusion is forced on us.

Bias of channel selection

The source of the difficulty which the horse-race model encountered with exception words was the impossibility of selecting the appropriate processing channel *a priori*. This is presumably a problem that is characteristic of the task normally facing the reader, since the regularity of words in prose is unpredictable. However, in some of the experiments in which regularity has been manipulated, regular and exception words have been segregated in different blocks of trials (Baron and Strawson, 1976; Mason, 1978). This design decision has passed without comment, but it is clear from the discussion above that signalling the orthographic regularity of stimuli in advance could have important implications. In fact, the most likely consequence of such forewarning should be for the subject not to attempt GPC-based translation of exception words. With this channel "switched off" for exception words, Model B will produce faster responses for regular than exception words. It seems unlikely that this design factor does have these predicted consequences, for Stanovich and Bauer (1978) and Glushko (1979) randomized regularity and yet obtained regularity effects. Moreover, Mason (1978), who blocked regularity, failed to get the effect. This question of the possibility of preselecting the appropriate channel is touched upon by Baron (1977a), who suggests that if the channels are automatic, as he assumes (i.e. do not require processing capacity), then there is little that the subject can do to avoid using the inappropriate channel, even when he is expecting exception words.

The available data on the manipulation of orthographic regularity clearly do not permit us to decide about the possibility of preselection of channels. We turn, therefore, to the manipulation of the word–nonword variable where some data relevant to the question do exist. Frederiksen and Kroll (1976) compared a randomized condition in which words and nonwords were presented for naming mixed in random order with a condition in which each stimulus type was segregated in a block of trials the nature of which was intimated to the subject in advance. The effect of foreknowledge of the lexical status of the stimulus material was to speed word naming by about 20 ms, while leaving the latency of nonword naming unchanged. (This may be an underestimate of the effect because, as Kroll has pointed out to me in a personal communication, the blocked condition for words may have seemed, in effect, slightly mixed to the subject. This is because it contained some low-frequency words that were actually treated as nonwords in a parallel lexical decision experiment.) From this effect Frederiksen and Kroll (1976, p. 366) conclude that "the degree of lexical involvement is greater when words are presented alone than when words mixed with nonwords." They do not commit themselves to any particular view of the relationship between the lexical and nonlexical strategies (e.g. independence), so it is unclear how this bias to a lexical strategy is controlled.

An ingeniously constructed alternative to this explanation has been presented by Coltheart (1978). He begins by considering the possibility that the superior performance with words in the blocked condition is due to the allocation of more central processing capacity to the lexical strategy in circumstances where it is a reliable means of deriving a pronunciation. This possibility he rejects on the grounds that nonwords should also benefit by being blocked. In this case, processing capacity should be able to be diverted toward the nonlexical mechanisms. Instead, Coltheart suggests, the word–nonword effect is greater in the blocked condition because the nonlexical strategy is used less there. The reason for this is that the orthographic translation mechanism produces errors on exception words, so when it is not required by the presence of nonwords mingled in the series it is switched off or, at least, attenuated in some way.

This hypothesis appears to contain implications for the horse-race model. It implies that the principle of capacity independence of the channels holds, since concentration on a single strategy is not itself the reason for the effect of blocking. However, the principle of informational independence must be abandoned, because there is a time cost to operating the orthographic channel, that is, in the mixed condition word naming is slower than in the blocked condition. If this slowing is due to the fact that the orthographic mechanism is being used and it is fallible (exception words), then this implies that *some checking of orthographically derived pronunciations is required.* Such checking violates the first-past-the-post principle of the model, of course, but it is also difficult to see what the check could consist of *other than a lexical consultation.*

Here we have reached an important juncture in the attempt to describe the relationship between channels in the production of a final response. With this last blow to a fundamental assumption of the independent-channels hypothesis, it is time to abandon the whole attempt to formulate the problem in such terms, and we therefore consider the possibility that information from the various sources is pooled prior to reaching a decision about pronunciation.

6.2 LEXICAL POOLING MODELS

At a general theoretical level in cognitive psychology there has recently been considerable interest in the formulation of an alternative to models in which processing activities are separated into discrete channels and stages. This alternative is symbolized by the metaphor of the *blackboard,* which was originally inspired by work on speech recognition (cf. Reddy, 1975) in which the problem is to assemble and integrate the information derived from various levels of analysis of the speech signal. The method of assembling this diverse information is symbolized by a blackboard, a representational device of limited capacity by means of which information from various sources and levels of analysis can be continuously accumulated. Information on the blackboard is continually being erased and up-dated, and this up-dating includes the current state of decisions in which several details on the blackboard are integrated into a higher-level interpretation. The limitation of the metaphor is that it does not tell us how decisions are reached.

A model for the pooling of information in order to assign pronunciation has been advanced by Glushko (1979). Although, like the simple blackboard metaphor, Glushko's model is informative about the pooling process but reticent about the decision-making process, the model is sufficiently explicit to allow the pooling hypothesis to be tested against the independent channels hypothesis. The outcome of this test clearly favours pooling.

The pooling hypothesis can be translated into the assertion that information from the various sources is entered into a common decision process (which Glushko calls "synthesis"). Glushko begins from certain plausible assumptions about this decision process. He assumes that decisions take longer to arrive at when they depend upon the integration of information about portions of the word and also when the various sources provide inconsistent information. The most interesting prediction that can be derived from these assumptions is that exception words will be slower than regular words because of conflicting sources of information. The lexically stored pronunciation conflicts with the conventional product of orthographic translation. This is a not uninteresting prediction because, as we have seen, it is difficult to derive it from a horse-race model, but of even greater interest is Glushko's extension of the prediction to regular and exception *pseudowords*. In our discussion of the analogy strategy we observed that *heaf* could be defined as an exception pseudoword by virtue of its close similarity to *deaf*, an exception real word. The fact that such exception pseudowords were much more subject to exceptional pronunciation than comparable regular pseudowords offered strong support to the idea that lexical analogy has reality as a source of information on pronunciation. However, the analogy hypothesis itself only predicts the nature of pronunciations. The existence, in addition, of a latency effect favouring regular pseudowords requires that the analogy hypothesis be elaborated. This elaboration is provided by the pooling hypothesis together with the assumption that inconsistent pointers slow the decision process.

The notion of pooling taken together with the assumption about the effect of consistency within the pool enables Glushko to make a completely new prediction which cannot be derived from any other existing model. One way of describing this prediction is to say that it involves a redefinition of orthographic regularity. From the traditional GPC viewpoint an exception word was such because it violated a GPC "rule", that is, a frequency-based generalization about how its graphemic constituents should be sounded. The definition of exceptionality there made implicit reference to the entire corpus of words that contained a given grapheme or functional graphemic pattern. Once the commonest correspondent is determined, the remaining, exceptional correspondences have no further significance. In Glushko's model it is also true that exception words suffer a disadvantage, but it arises for a different reason. Exception words (in the GPC sense) are inconsistent words (in the analogy sense), that is, they tend to have words which resemble them visually but in which a shared letter-pattern is sounded differently. Now, this change in definition of exceptionality has several implications.

The inconsistency view differs from GPC-defined exceptionality in not being dichotomous. In the pooling model the *degree* of inconsistency matters. In my introduction of the analogy hypothesis I suggested that inconsistency is likely to have an increasingly inhibitory effect as the visual similarity of the inconsistent words with the test word increases and also as the familiarity of the inconsistent analogy-words increases. It follows that a (GPC-defined) exception word might suffer from only minor inconsistency if none of the words using the regular GPC (i.e. words inconsistent with the test word) resembled it closely visually. However, at this juncture a new prediction arises, because a (GPC-defined) *regular word may also be inconsistent*. For example, *have* is an exception whereas *wave* is regular. Nevertheless both are inconsistent because of their close mutual resemblance and therefore the tendency of each to act as a misleading analogy for the other. Turning to Glushko's test of this prediction, we find that it is indeed inconsistency and not simply exceptionality that affects pronunciation latency. (Nevertheless, *have* suffers more from inconsistency: *have* is the only inconsistent close neighbour of *wave*, but *wave*, *cave*, *gave*, *nave*, *pave*, *rave*, *save* are all inconsistent with *have*.)

Is there a truly nonlexical source of information?

So far we have established that sources of information seem to be pooled rather than serving as the basis for independent and self-sufficient processing channels. Let us reconsider the extent to which even the sources of information can be said to be separate. I shall argue here that we can distinguish between information about whole-word pronunciations and information (based on analogy) about pronunciation of parts of a word but that it is probably invalid to characterize these alternatives as lexical and nonlexical, respectively. In short, I shall argue against the existence of a truly nonlexical source of information. The outline of the argument is that the analogy source of information is essentially lexical, therefore if we can reject abstract GPC rules, we are left only with a whole-word source which is lexical by definition and an analogy source which is lexical by argument.

We have already reviewed the case for abstract GPCs in Section 5.2. Our reasons for doubting their psychological reality were that they involved postulation of a system that is at once immensely complex and yet highly unreliable. Also, all the evidence adduced in their favour could be dismissed either as inapplicable (e.g. surface dyslexia) or as explicable in terms of the analogy mechanism (e.g. regularity effects, pronunciation of pseudowords). Glushko (1979) adds a further item of negative evidence. He found that although most exception words, when mispronounced, were regularized (e.g. *tomb* as in *bomb*), some were mispronounced in accord with an even more irregular analogy (e.g. *tomb* as in *comb*). The significance of this example is that the correspondent of -OMB in *comb* is unique. So if it influences decisions about *tomb*, it must do so by means of a lexical mechanism rather than an abstract rule. Another way to express this is to say that a rule governing only a single instance is logically indistinguishable from a lexical analogy. Generalizing from this example, it is not unreasonable to conclude, as Glushko suggests, that abstract representations of orthographic correspondences simply do not exist as the basis for automatic processing. The -OMB "rule" only exists in so far as it is embodied in the regional activation centred on entries for words like *bomb*, *tomb* and *comb*.

We are left, then, with a purely lexical mechanism in which a visual pattern, when presented for naming, activates an orthographic neighbourhood of closely resembling words. It is probably reasonable to assume that the strength of activation is proportional to the similarity to the presented pattern. When the stimulus is a familiar word, the lexical entries activated will include that for the word itself, as well as various analogies which may be either consistent or inconsistent. When the stimulus is a pseudoword, only (real word) analogies will be activated. These in turn may be consistent with each other, or inconsistent.

The decision process

Glushko has no more to say about the decision process which operates upon the pooled (lexical) information than is contained in the two assumptions used to predict the effects of lexical status (word–nonword) and regularity upon pronunciation latencies. We shall therefore consider these assumptions and I shall attempt to modify and extend them in order to offer a more complete model of the decision process.

It will be remembered that Glushko explains the faster naming of real words by means of the assumption that construction of a pronunciation takes longer when it has to rely on a number of sources of information, as is the case for pseudowords, but it is unclear what precisely is being assumed here. The only clarification which Glushko offers is to add that "the difference between the pronunciation of words and pseudowords is only quantitative; words are generally pronounced using larger units (up to the entire letter string) than pseudowords", Glushko (1979).

The problem here is a familiar one. We cannot assume that the subject knows in advance whether he is dealing with a word or a pseudoword. He must therefore proceed in the same way for each, and we must assume that as a result of the visual analysis of the display an orthographic neighbourhood in the lexicon becomes activated. The only difference is that when the stimulus is a familiar word the neighbourhood will contain that word itself as well as similar words. However, we know that in this case the system is not able to concentrate reliably on that lexical entry which is an exact match and ignore the neighbouring analogies. This conclusion follows from the evidence confirming the consistency principle. Even when a precisely matching lexical entry exists, the latency of pronunciation is influenced by the consistency with neighbouring entries. How then can we formulate the basis of a real-word advantage?

Predicting the real-word advantage

There are at least four possibilities. (*a*) When an exactly matching entry in the lexicon is activated, it tends to be the first entry to be activated. (*b*) When a matching lexical entry exists, it may lend more *weight* to the decision process. I have already suggested that analogies might be weighted in the decision process proportionally to their visual resemblance to the input. A perfectly matching lexical entry would constitute the upper limit of that weighting, and this in turn might permit a more rapid decision on the eventual pronunciation. Possibility (*c*) appears to be the one invoked by Glushko. Pseudowords have no lexical entry from which whole-word phonology can be retrieved, so they are entirely reliant on synthesis of their pronunciation from lexical analogies. Pseudoword pronunciations have to be assembled from segments, so the units involved are smaller than in words and there is more reassembly work to be done. It is this reassembly work (called synthesis by Glushko but not described further) which consumes the extra time taken for pseudowords. In the last possibility, (*d*), it is assumed that lexical activation levels rise more rapidly for words than nonwords. (Obviously for nonwords the activation is restricted to analogies.)

There is one strand of evidence which speaks against the first two possibilities. If the advantage of real words in naming speed were due to a factor which effectively increased the signal-to-noise ratio in the pool, as earlier activation of a word's specific lexical address or greater weighting of that lexical entry would do, then the inconsistency effect should be smaller for words than for nonwords. It appears that this is not the case. The critical interaction in Glushko's (1979) first experiment failed to approach significance. Moreover, if we compare across his Experiments 2 and 3, which involved, respectively, pseudowords alone and words alone, we find that regularity had a facilitatory effect of 22 ms for pseudowords and 21 ms for words.

Consider now possibility (*c*), that pseudowords are slower because their pronunciation has to be assembled from segments. We must take care over how we formulate this possibility if it is to be viable. The problem is that we know from the existence of the inconsistency effect that even when a word has available a lexical entry specifying whole-word pronunciation, performance is slowed by the existence of analogies that are inconsistent. Analogy information, based on shared segments, must therefore be automatically brought to bear before a pronunciation decision is reached. For this reason, it cannot be the necessity of awaiting analogy information that slows the response to pseudowords. Thus it must be assumed that it is the time taken to *assemble* the segments of the pseudoword (after decisions have been made about the sound of each segment) that is of consequence. However, all this leads to another difficulty, because it implies that the lexicality effect has a quite different basis from the word-frequency effect.

So far we have tended to discuss the decision process as though activation of lexical entries were instantaneous. It is now time to acknowledge that activation is extended in time. In addition to the likelihood of some random variability in activation rise times and to the possibility that rise times are inversely related to visual similarity, it is generally assumed that word frequency is a major determinant of activation latency. This is sometimes referred to as the "encoding bias" theory of word-frequency effects (e.g. Frederiksen and Kroll, 1976). Now, as soon as we have had to invoke activation rise times to explain faster naming of familiar words, we might as well extend it to cover the pseudoword disadvantage as the limiting case of unfamiliarity. Obviously when we do this, we refer to activation of lexical analogies just as much as to a stimulus's own lexical entry, if it possesses one.

Having acknowledged, for these reasons, that the activation process extends over time, we have to admit a situation in which the decision process operates upon a dynamically changing information pool. In particular, the early state of the pool will be largely determined by the orthographic translations of high-frequency words. (Interestingly it is the high-frequency words that tend to contain exceptional GPCs.) At this point we can derive an important prediction from the theory, for under time pressure subjects should tend to model their response after high-frequency analogies, even when these involve irregular GPCs. This tendency should be most clearly detectable for pseudowords, since their pronunciation is entirely reliant on analogy. However, predictions from the frequency and activation-speed assumption can also be derived for words. For example, low-frequency words should tend to yield more errors, under time pressures, in the direction of high-frequency inconsistent analogies.

Now comes the most difficult question. What form must the pooled information take for the decision process to operate on it? Clearly, excitation of orthographic entries in the lexicon must induce proportional activation of the corresponding phonological entries. If a pronunciation is to be computed from the pattern of activation, the phonological outputs must be specified as positionally tagged segments. Moreover, for lexical analogies there must be some way of signifying what orthographic segments are relevant. Hence, for example, when deciding how to pronounce SEW, the analogy DEW is marked at the orthographic stage so that the initial consonant is not considered by the phonological decision process. Thus, D__ can be excluded as orthographically irrelevant to the decision. In contrast, the /ju/ sound of _EW has to be considered, though it turns out to mislead.

Hermits and heretics in the lexicon

We now consider some classes of word that might be expected to have special properties in lexical pooling theory due to the nature of their orthographic neighbourhood. These classes we call *hermits* and *heretics* (in the traditional spirit of elephantine scholarly playfulness).

A lexical hermit is a letter string with no close orthographic neighbours. The word *lynx* is a hermit, as is the pseudoword *nerp*, since we cannot change one letter in either example to transform it into a familiar new word. There are two possible stages of lexical pooling models at which hermits suffer a disadvantage. First is the activation stage. It takes longer for activation to spread to remote analogies (*manx*, *minx*, *lymph*, etc. in the case of *lynx*). Second is the assembly stage, which Glushko held to be the locus of the lexicality effect. If a word has no close neighbours, the analogy mechanism depends upon the assembly of pronunciations from many small segments. In the limiting case, these segments, shared between the word and its activated analogies, will be as analytical as those postulated in the GPC procedure. However, even in this boundary case the theories differ, since the analogy theory does not require that the frequency of various correspondences have been codified in advance and stored as a "rule".

In unpublished experiments in my own laboratory I have found quite large effects of being a lexical hermit. Moreover, these effects are larger for pseudowords than real words. Presumably this is because pseudowords depend entirely upon analogies, so their remoteness matters more. Unfortunately there are difficulties in generating lexical hermits without incorporating in them other properties. For example, hermits are more often polysyllabic and they tend to have low positional and sequential frequencies in their letter arrangements. Our own experiments were contaminated with the latter problem.

Lexical heretics are words like *comb*, *sword*, and *have* which are maximally inconsistent. These are at odds with almost all their orthographic neighbours. Some, like *have*, possess many close neighbours who are united in a hostile orthodoxy (*cave*, *save*, *rave*, etc.); in others, like *comb*, neighbours are few and disparate (*tomb*, *bomb*, etc.).

Independent representation of letter-clusters

One way of coping with lexical hermits is by entering in the lexicon certain common letter-clusters with their sounds. Thus, in assigning a pronunciation to the hermit pseudoword TUPALIVENT we might look up segments of roughly syllabic size in this expanded phonological lexicon rather than wait for excitation to spread to very remote analogies.

The notion of translation at the letter-cluster level might seem to lie intermediate between lexical analogy theory and GPC theory, but this is not so. As soon as we expand the phonological listing in the lexicon to include non-lexical segments, such as syllables, we lose the parsimony of the purely lexical model. Moreover, if such segments are listed independently, the entries must either be implausibly prolific or else entries must be restricted to the "regular" pronunciation, i.e. that of highest frequency of occurrence. In the latter case we have abstract frequency-based rules, precisely as in GPC theory, but greatly expanded in order to take account of graphemic context.

From time to time authors have suggested such an expansion of the GPC model, but the idea has not been explicitly developed. Baron (1977a) speaks of orthographic translation at a variety of segmental levels. Shallice and Warrington (1980) state a similar opinion in their discussion of the occasional ability of deep dyslexic patients to read exception words with fair success. In a more radical model, Marcel (1980) postulates an Aural–Oral Lexicon in which all known segments are listed in a frequency-codified manner. This very expensive assumption seems to be made as a way of coping with our ability to pronounce pseudowords like *kwib* which contain clusters (KW) unknown in English.[15] This is but the lexical hermit in other guise, and in principle there is no need to go beyond a truly lexical account in which remote analogies like *krill* and *crib* are used. To be sure, this should result in slower responding.

Structural marking of lexical entries

So far, we have discussed visual activation of the lexicon as if the orthographic entries in the lexicon consisted of unstructured grapheme-strings corresponding to the input words. In this view, analogies are drawn on the sole basis of shared graphemes (in a given word-position). This appears to be the position taken in Glushko's (1979) seminal formulation.

Such a simple mechanism works reasonably well for the short monosyllabic words studied by Glushko but it becomes increasingly inefficient with longer words. Accordingly, I want to suggest that lexical entries are intelligently structured, as they are in linguistic models of generative phonology. One useful property of the orthographic entry to mark would be the consonant/vowel class of the graphemes. In this way the tendency for, say, *ace* and *act* to activate each other as analogies would be reduced. Another problem that could be reduced by the marking of structure is illustrated in the pair *react–reach*. In a lexical space determined simply by letter overlap these would be close neighbours, misleadingly so from a phonological point of view. It seems to me that introspection is of some help here because it actually comes as a surprise to realize that these items only differ by a single letter (I found myself double-checking this on the page). As long as the lexical entry contains morphological or syllabic marking, the inappropriate spread of activation between *react* and *reach* will be attenuated.

Blocking v. *randomizing lexicality and the single-route model*

There remains one major effect to be explained by the lexical pooling theory: the facilitatory effect on word-naming latencies of grouping the words in a homogeneous block of trials without the random admixture of nonword trials. This effect seems clearly demonstrated in Frederiksen and Kroll's (1976) experiment, and if we allow comparison across experiments and stimulus lists, we can find confirmation of the effect by comparing Glushko's (1979) Experiment 1 (randomized words and nonwords) with his Experiment 2 (nonwords only) and Experiment 3 (words only). In these comparisons, blocking confers a 66 ms advantage on words but only a 11·5 ms advantage on nonwords. Attempts to explain this effect in terms of a horse-race model have appealed to a biasing of strategies. Frederiksen and Kroll (1976) argued that subjects use the lexical route more when words are blocked. Coltheart (1978) pointed out difficulties with this view and argued instead that the effect arises because the subjects use the nonlexical route less when words are blocked. We have seen that this argument, too, is not without its difficulties. If we tried to adapt the strategy argument to the "single channel" lexical pooling model, we would have to assume that when words were presented in blocks there was a tendency either for analogies not to be activated, or for them to carry less weight in the decision process, thereby simplifying the decision. I find the former view uncongenial because I assume spreading activation to be automatic. However, there is a test of both arguments: if analogy information can be inhibited by either means, it follows that the interference effect caused by the presence of inconsistent analogies should be diminished in the blocked-word condition. The only relevant data involves us in a comparison once again across experiments. We find that in Glushko's Experiment 1 with mixed words and nonwords, the consistency effect for words is 20 ms. In Experiment 3 with words alone, the effect is 21 ms, despite the fact that the words are overall 66 ms faster in this experiment. This suggests that the use of analogy is not inhibited by presentation of words alone and that we must look elsewhere for an explanation of the overall advantage in this condition.

What I suggest is that the blocking effect exists at the initial activation stage. I have already advanced the assumption that word stimuli produce faster lexical activation than pseudowords and that this, rather than any strictly phonological process, underlies the lexicality and word-frequency effects. It is necessary now to extend this assumption to cover the interaction between the lexicality effect (word v. pseudoword RT) and the design factor (blocked v. randomized lexicality).

I do not have a proposal to make about the source of the increase in the lexicality effect with blocking, but I can offer circumstantial evidence for the activation interpretation, or at least for a non-phonological interpretation. This evidence rests on the fact that a parallel interaction between blocking and lexicality is to be found in tachistoscopic recognition and visual comparison tasks where there is no requirement to assign pronunciation (see, for example, Manelis, 1974). In a recent discussion of this effect in comparison and identification tasks (Henderson, 1980b), I have suggested that the familiarity of common words is obscured when they are embedded in a context of pseudowords.

The decision rule

We have said little about the decision rule itself, other than to imply that the various candidate pronunciations that are activated will carry a weighting in the decision process, according to the number of items activated with that pronunciation, the visual similarity to the stimulus, and possibly the word frequency of the activated items. The candidate that is most heavily weighted will be chosen.

Clearly the value of weightings must be such that heretics like *have* are generally correctly pronounced despite the weight of inconsistent analogies. This suggests that amount of visual overlap weighs heavily so that activation of the lexical entry for *have* itself (maximal overlap) outweighs the inconsistent activations of *cave*, *save*, etc. Nevertheless, the weight from a word's own entry can be overridden by priming inconsistent analogies, as in the *MacHenry–machinery* or *mown–down* effects (e.g. Bradshaw and Nettleton, 1974).

Summary

All theories that give an account of the process of orthographic translation start from a distinction between two or more separate sources of information. One of these is agreed to be lexical, consisting in a word-specific association between spelling and sound. Concerning the other there is less agreement. Some hold it to consist of grapheme–phoneme correspondence rules; others hold it to consist of analogies, involving larger graphemic clusters and lacking the systematization implied by the concept of an abstract rule. The GPC source is invariably defined as nonlexical, but the analogy source can be regarded either as lexical or nonlexical.

Turning to the applicability of each source to the various types of possible stimuli, we find obvious agreement that nonwords do not have access to the word-specific source. Where a GPC source is postulated it is generally assumed that all types of stimuli have access to it, though the extent to which they depend upon it can only be determined from a model of the organization of the combined processing system. In the same way, all stimuli are held to have access to the analogy source. The GPC and the analogy sources differ somewhat in their applicability to the pronunciation of exception words. Exception words must have *access* to the GPC source since their exceptionality cannot be determined other than by lexical means. However, correct pronunciations of exception words cannot *depend* upon the GPC source, by definition (unless, we assume an iterative lexical checking procedure, in which case the GPC procedure becomes a mere subroutine of the lexical, word-specific procedure). This problem which exception words encounter with the hypothetical GPC procedure needs to be examined in the context of theories of the way in which information from the sources is combined or decided between in the choice of a final response.

Theories of the organization of the combined processing system tend to group themselves according to their assumptions about the nature of the sources of information. Thus the traditional models are based upon a lexical (word-specific) source and a GPC source. The sources are assumed each to serve an independent processing pathway. The problem of deciding between the products of either pathway is usually dealt with by postulating a "horse-race" in which the first product to become available is executed. This model comfortably predicts faster pronunciation of regular words than pseudowords, for, as long as the processing latency distributions for the two pathways overlap, words benefit by being based on whichever pathway delivers its product first. However, the horse-race model has great difficulty in accommodating performance with exception words. The central difficulty is as follows. The majority of exception words are pronounced correctly, even in speeded responding. Since this cannot be done by an independent GPC channel, it must be either that the lexical channel almost always completes first or that the GPC product is subjected to a lexical check (of both spelling and sound entries in the lexicon).

The addition to the horse-race theory of a lexical check postulate seems to render it incoherent. In particular, since such a lexical check would have to be mandatory when we do not know in advance the status of a stimulus item, its postulation completely removes the independence of the lexical and GPC channels which was the defining feature of the model. Furthermore, the horse-race model with a supplementary lexical check requires elaboration if it is to predict a latency advantage for regular words as compared to exception words. This might be achieved, however, by assuming that on some trials lexical search is sufficiently slow that the GPC channel is the faster despite the addition of the lexical check stage. This would give an edge on those trials to regular words. With some such elaboration the lexical check, dual-process model can perhaps be made viable. However, the appealing simplicity of the independent channels assumption is lost without achieving the flexibility of the single-channel, pooling models.

Before turning to the pooling models we must consider the other alternative, in which an attempt is made to accommodate correct pronunciation of exception words by assuming that lexical search is always faster than the GPC procedure. To the extent that exception words are correctly pronounced, this would mean that words always depend for their pronunciation on the lexical channel and nonwords on GPCs. This possibility can probably be safely rejected, if only because it is clear that the distributions of pronunciation latancies for words and nonwords have considerable overlap. Moreover, some new principle would have to be introduced to account for the faster naming of regular than exception words in most studies, such as the assumption that regularity is reflected in the organization of the lexicon.

In view of the difficulties encountered with the dual-process, independent-channels models we examined an alternative, single-channel conception. This model can be considered as using two sources of information: word-specific associations and lexical analogies. Words generally draw upon both sources and nonwords are confined to the use of the lexical analogy source, but there is no great distinction to be made between the two sources. Both are lexical and are activated automatically when pronunciation is attempted. Some of the reasons for preferring this model are reducible to reasons for preferring an analogy hypothesis to a GPC hypothesis. This argument has been summarized in the previous section. However, the analogy source might serve either a single-channel or a multiple, independent-channels system, and here we are concerned with the single-channel conception. The lexical pooling model proposed is based on Glushko's (1979) activation and synthesis model. The major assumptions are as follows.

Activation

(*i*) Any written word-like form that is presented for pronunciation will directly excite entries in a visually addressable lexicon. This leads to the activation of the pronunciations listed for those entries.

(*ii*) Stimuli activate a region of visually related forms. Amount of resemblance determines the probability of activation, or perhaps the weighting of that entry in the decision process. The appropriate metric of resemblance is not yet fully determined but it relates to the size of shared letter-clusters and is greatest for shared final clusters (the visual equivalent of rhyme).

(*iii*) Activation of a region develops more rapidly for words than nonwords.
(*iv*) Activation for words generally includes the particular lexical entry for that word.
(*v*) Activation latency for a particular entry is inversely related to the frequency of the word represented by that entry.

Pooling and decision

(*vi*) For each activated lexical entry its corresponding pronunciation is entered into a pool of "suggestions" which are examined by the decision process. Where an activated entry resembles but is not identical with the item presented, we speak of an "analogy".
(*vii*) The greater the consensus obtained for each phonetic segment the faster the pronunciation decision can be made. Where the "suggestions" are not unanimous, we speak of "inconsistency".

The particular strengths of the lexical pooling model are partly those of the analogy assumption that it incorporates, but the pooling assumption permits certain interesting additional predictions. One major prediction includes the reinterpretation of "exceptionality" as a particular case of "inconsistency". This prediction has been born out by Glushko's (1979) Experiment 3. Further detailed predictions can be derived from the resemblance clause of assumption (*ii*) and from word frequency assumption (*v*). These have yet to be tested.

Certain possible difficulties for the lexical pooling model were examined. One concerns the basis for the prediction of faster naming of words than nonwords. Glushko's activation-plus-synthesis model gives a plausible alternative explanation to the horse-race assumption, in asserting that assembly of a nonword pronunciation from analogies takes longer, even when these are mutually consistent, than use of a whole-word specification. The lexical pooling model abandons this assumption in favour of the assumption of faster activation induced by words. This assumption was preferred because of its possibility of extension to cover the blocked v. mixed effect on words. This it was assumed that when words are blocked they can be named faster because blocking exaggerates their tendency to provoke faster lexical activation. Despite a feeble attempt to show external support for this assumption, this solution to the blocking problem remains rather *ad hoc*. The only viable alternative explanation was Coltheart's suggestion that blocking was facilitatory by virtue of allowing attenuation of the GPC channel. This seemed to imply that the products of the GPC channel had to be subjected to a lexical check, and this in turn was fatal for the independent-channels model.

We discussed the notion that the contrasting forms of acquired dyslexia constitute evidence in favour of dual processing models. If this amounts to no more than the claim that separate sources of information are available to the decision machinery, then it is unremarkable. All current theories make some distinction between the information serving word pronunciation and that serving nonwords. The further the claim goes beyond that assertion, the less it is warranted. In particular, we saw that the limits of translation competence in deep dyslexia were not coincident with the word–nonword boundary. Many words, from abstract nouns to grammatical functors, could not be translated in speech. The evidence suggests that such word-translating abilities as remain to the deep dyslexic depend upon unusual processing pathways, probably originating in an exclusively right hemisphere lexicon. At a more general level, we were reminded of the dangers of assuming "pure subtraction", that is, of assuming that in brain injury a certain processing pathway can be blocked with no consequent rearrangement of the rest of the cognitive system.

6.3 LEARNING TO READ

The child's first attempts at acquiring a sight vocabulary of words often resemble paired-associate learning. This is especially true of the spontaneous learning that occurs for brand names or the names of television personalities. It has often been assumed that, in some sense or other, these associations are global: the word is treated as a unitary symbol without attention to its constituent elements. This is the view urged on us by proponents of "look–say" methods of teaching reading. It is also the view taken of the direct lexical route in some formulations of dual process theory. For example, Allport (1977, p. 527) contrasts the nonlexical GPC route with a direct lexical route involving "whole-word pattern analysis", a process he likens to that underlying the association of a logograph with its meaning.

There are several difficulties with this view, and with the teaching methods based upon it. First, as a method of learning it is ineffective. Such evidence as exists in favour or one or other teaching method has tended to suggest that look–say methods lead to an early acquisition of a small sight vocabulary and then little progress beyond this. Even contemporary advocates of eclectic approaches tend only to advocate wholistic strategies for an initial vocabulary of about 50 words. (See Chall, 1967, for an introduction to work in this area.)

Traditionally, the debate between proponents of look–say and phonic methods has purported to hinge upon the difference between emphasis of vision–meaning associations and vision–sound associations. However, this formulation may omit mention of differences in the methods which are actually much more important than these conceptual abstractions. We shall turn to these shortly.

Before leaving the logographic interpretation of look–say strategies it is worth observing that logographic methods of teaching alphabetic languages seem to lead to a much slower rate of acquisition of sight vocabulary than is true with truly logographic languages. This is mischevious speculation on my part and certainly a rigorous comparison is not possible. Moreover, logographies such as Chinese are taught in a very different manner from look–say methods. However, it is worth giving some thought to the visual design characteristics that might set alphabetic script at a disadvantage when presented to the child as a logography.

It is, in any case, unwise to assume that the global paired-associate method induces an association between the response and the total stimulus configuration. Gough and Hillinger (1980) have astutely pointed out that this picture does not even correspond to what we know about the nature of paired-associate and discrimination learning. What is more likely to take place is that the child attempts to weld the association to an isolated visual feature of the stimulus. These authors cite the apposite findings on pre-school children who are trained either on lists of visually similar or dissimilar words (cf. Otto and Pizillo, 1970). It is easier to find minimal cues to distinguish dissimilar words and the children learn these lists faster, although training on dissimilar lists transfers less well to new words, presumably, precisely because of their fragmentary and partial representation in visual memory.

This brings me to a related point about alternative methods which I have made before in discussing phonics (Henderson, 1977). Such methods emphasize grapheme–phoneme correspondences (or correspondences of larger segments), but in so doing they also draw attention to the visual constituents of words. This concentration upon the graphemic composition of words may be important irrespective of the letter–sound associations.

What is required by the sort of lexical pooling model advanced here, and perhaps also required in certain versions of the direct route in dual process theories, is the construction of a well-defined orthographic entry in the lexicon. This is particularly necessary for the synthesis of pronunciation by analogy as in the case of a new word. Whereas a partial visual specification of a word may occasionally be adequate to activate a lexical entry if one exists, the assembly of pronunciation for a word that is not part of the reader's sight vocabulary requires a detailed orthographic specification.

The evidence on skilled visual identification of words which we examine in detail in Part III suggests that identification depends upon a preliminary graphemic specification of the word. This evidence converges on the thesis that the lexicon requires a graphemic index.

Another aspect of phonic methods that is of more general interest because of its implication for the compilation of visual addresses in the lexicon and perhaps also for the mapping of orthographic neighbourhoods is the use of selected words sets. Phonic programmes have generally emphasized training sets such as *pin*, *pen*, *pan*, high in visual similarity. Given the irregularity of correspondence of English vowels, these sets have often been constructed round a fixed vowel (*red*, *hen*, *pet*, etc.). Some programmes, following the advice of linguists such as Bloomfield, concentrate initially on regular vowel sets, eschewing early contact with common but exception words like *come* and *go*. All these programs are based on a GPC-based *description* of the difficulty of reading English. Moreover, in many of them the child is explicitly drilled in grapheme–phoneme translation. Finally, children who fail to learn to read can usually be shown to have failed to acquire a knowledge of GPCs. Expressed in this way, it is easy to see the frailty of the connection between the successes or failures of phonic methods and the purported reality of the GPC route. Furthermore, there is a general difficulty in seeing how exercise of the GPC route would lead to the construction of visual entries in the lexicon to mediate direct access for familiar words. Once again it is the assumed independence of the routes that creates theoretical problems.

As Marcel (1980) has acutely observed, many of the misreading errors made by children (and also by surface dyslexic patients) consist in the substitution of visually similar real words, substitutions which could not arise from GPC mistranslation, e.g. *gone*→"grown". It would be wrong to leap to the alternative conclusion that these error indicate the use of lexical analogies, for they are as likely to result from partial analysis of the printed form, but it is interesting that so many reading errors are real words. Such errors are scarcely likely to be the product of a nonlexical route.

Although so far we have concentrated on the necessity of building accurate graphemic entries in the lexicon, it must be acknowledged that this is unlikely to be the major source of difficulty in reading. Backward reading is particularly well predicted by an inability to read aloud pseudowords (e.g. Firth, 1972). Moreover, poor readers are at a greater disadvantage on low-frequency words and pseudowords in naming latency tasks (Frederiksen, 1976). This suggests that poor readers have particular difficulty with synthesizing a pronunciation when no listing of whole-word phonology is to be found in the lexicon. Rather indirect support for this notion is to be found in the deleterious effect of syllabic length on the poor reader's naming latency, especially for pseudowords (Mason, 1978), although this interpretation depends on the insecure assumption that syllabic length effects have to do with the synthesis of pronunciation from segments (see Chapter 7).

In effect, this deficit in the synthesis of pronunciation disables the poor reader in the acquisition of new words. Once again, it is difficult to understand this in terms of a dual process theory in which the route for synthesizing pronunciation of unfamiliar words is wholly independent of the lexical route. The only learning of which the GPC route is capable is learning of abstract rules based on correspondence frequencies. Word-specific knowledge can only be accrued in the lexicon, so exercise of the GPC route on new words cannot readily yield word-specific knowledge. However, the lexical pooling model can be developed so as to give an account of the interaction between synthesis of pronunciations for new words and growth of word-specific knowledge. Since this model synthesizes pronunciation by means of the lexicon, it is easy to create new lexical entries on the basis of this activity. Obviously a deficit which is most marked in the synthesis of pronunciation for new words has to be attributed to some aspect of the analogy mechanism. Because it seems intuitively unlikely that poor readers suffer from a defective spread of activation in the lexicon, we can focus instead upon two other possibilities. Either poor readers may fail to develop properly structured lexical entries and thus appropriately organized orthographic neighbourhoods, or the process responsible for assembling a pronunciation from the activated analogies may be defective. Whichever of these processes underlies the disability of the backward reader it is not difficult to understand the generality of the impairment resulting from a deficit of pronunciation synthesis in lexical pooling theory. Even in the reading of highly familiar words by skilled adults the operation of the analogy-synthesis mechanism was evident (the inconsistency effect reported by Glushko, 1979, for "regular" words). This seems to suggest that retrieval of whole-word phonology and synthesis from analogy are interactive, reinforcing processes.

Turning to the teaching of reading, I shall add one final speculation to this already swollen collection. In GPC theory it seems clear that we should teach those very correspondence rules which lie at the heart of the phonics approach, although, to be sure, there are various ways in which such tuition may fail. Lexical pooling theory gives a less clear prescription for teaching. Certainly attention to the graphemic construction of the word is important. Presumably the use of training sets drawn from an orthographic neighbourhood is another aspect of standard practice which is helpful. However, the depressing implication of lexical pooling theory is that the analogy process itself, not being rule-like, is largely incapable of formal and explicit tuition. Analogizing is pragmatic and tacit, and if it is to be taught, it will have to be implicitly rather than explicitly.

Chapter 7

Preparation for Articulation

Our discussion of the translation of print into sound has hitherto centred on general conceptions of the means whereby an appropriate pronunciation is decided upon. We now consider a miscellany of other questions which have to do with reading aloud and which can be divided roughly into issues related to the organization of oral reading as a serial activity and issues pertaining to the pronunciation of individual words. In Section 1 we examine the serial organization of fluent oral reading, beginning with a review of some recent work on the preparation of speech. Although this work has to do with the organization of utterances that have already been formulated rather than with the derivation of speech from printed text, it does provide a useful baseline for our discussion and should help us to distinguish between effects peculiar to reading and those to do with speaking, whatever the source of the utterance. We then consider how the processes of perception, translation and speech production are linked together, taking the eye–voice span as the focal point for our enquiry. In Section 2 we return to a more microscopic concern with the determinants of pronunciation latencies for individual words, in particular effects due to word structure, such as number of letters and number of syllables in the word to be named. We examine these effects in the context of theoretical claims about the distinction between abstract phonological codes and articulatory programs, and claims about the extent to which articulation is preprogrammed before production commences.

7.1 READING ALOUD CONSIDERED AS A CONTINUOUS ACTIVITY

Since at least the time of Lashley (1951) it has been clear that sensory delays do not allow feedback to intervene between each element in a rapid sequence of responses. In playing a cadenza or reciting a poem, whole "phrases" must be planned or programmed in advance. A feature of such plans for action is that they seem to possess a hierarchical organization, and this is nowhere more evident than in language behaviour. Indeed, it was the hierarchical structure of language (as expressed in the Chomskyan, generative conception of grammar) that Miller Galanter and Pribram (1960) took as a paradigm for hierarchically organized behaviour. Speech appears to be organized in a hierarchy which stems from pre-linguistic conceptualizations, but even if we confine our attention to speech as a phonetic or articulatory continuum, we find ourselves confronted with a hierarchy of units, from the phone through the syllable up to larger structures such as the intonation contour and the prosodic structures (patterns of stress).

The process of formulating utterances is rather inaccessible to experimental investigation, but certain gross relationships can be detected through the analysis of natural speech. A good example of this is to be found in Goldman-Eisler's (1961) work in which pauses in continuous speech are shown to bear a systematic relationship to the information content of the material that follows.

Linguists have commonly distinguished between two sorts of pauses (see, for example, Clark, 1971). *Conventional pauses* occur at syntactic boundaries in order to permit breathing and are part of the overall intonation pattern. A person reading aloud, for whom the utterance is already formulated in the text, generally manifests only conventional, breathing pauses (Henderson *et al.*, 1965). The person engaged in spontaneous speech also produces *idiosyncratic pauses.* These are related to the need to compose the utterance, to select terms, and are more common before high-information content words than function words.

If we want to examine in more detail the preparation of articulatory sequences, as yet we can do no better than examine a somewhat artificial situation in which it is possible to investigate the preparation for the articulation of already formulated utterances, that is, speech which amounts to mere recitation.

Preparation and production of already formulated utterances

Consider the following simple task. We give a subject a short list of words to commit to memory. Immediately the items have been encoded in short term memory (STM) we present a "start" command. The subject's task thereupon is to recite the series of words rapidly with the object of completing the utterances as quickly as possible. We measure how long this takes to completion, but we can also covertly measure the delay between the "start" command and the onset of the subject's vocalization. We are now in a position to ask this question: what is the subject's state of articulatory preparedness on the arrival of the "start" command?

Let us examine some possible states of affairs.

Theory (*i*). Speech program fully constructed: "start" leads to immediate production.

Theory (*ii*). Speech program constructed as a disorderly queue: "start" leads to search for the first sub-program to be executed.

Theory (iii). Speech program not constructed: "start" leads to preprogramming of complete utterance before production.

Theory (iv). Speech program not constructed: "start" leads to overlapping construction and execution.

These theories differ with respect to at least two major principles. Theories *(i–iii)* posit *preprogramming*, that is, for sufficiently brief utterances the entire speech program is held to be constructed before execution (although Theory *(ii)* places some limits on the extent to which programming is finalized). In contrast, Theory *(iv)* posits overlapping construction and execution of the program. The first unit is programmed and while it is being executed, further programming is achieved in parallel. However, of the three preprogramming theories, only Theories *(i)* and *(ii)* assert that programming actually precedes the "start" command.

We can narrow this range of candidates by examining the preparation-time data, which reflect the delay between the "start" command and the commencement of vocalization. Here we find agreement between a number of recent studies that preparation-time increases in a more or less linear manner as a function of utterance length (Sternberg *et al.*, 1978; Henderson *et al.*, 1981). This function is predicted by Theories *(ii)* and *(iii)*. The sub-program search theory, Theory *(ii)*, predicts a rising preparation time function because before speaking can commence, memory must be searched for the sub-program representing the first word to be spoken. This search time is assumed to increase with the number of sub-programs to be searched through (i.e. the length of the utterance). The program construction theory, Theory *(iii)*, predicts the relationship between utterance length and preparation time, because it is assumed that the time to construct or activate a speech program is a function of the number of units to be programmed (utterance length).

The slope and intercept values depend upon the subject's state of practice, but for the highly practised reciters studied by Sternberg and Monsell, preparation times increase in a roughly linear manner with a slope of about 10 ms per word in the utterance. Completion times, measured from the onset of speech to the completion of the entire utterance, indicate a rate of speech of about 5 monosyllabic words per second for very short utterances. However, the completion times increase in a quadratic manner, indicating a diminution in the rate of speech with increased length of the utterance.

At least two independent lines of argument favour the sub-program search theory. The first was advanced by Sternberg *et al.* (1978) in their original formulation of the theory. They showed how the sub-program search theory could be made to link together the linear preparation-time functions with the quadratically curved completion time functions in a single account. Their argument can be briefly summarized as follows. If before the execution of each word its sub-program has to be searched for amongst the collection of sub-programs and if as the utterance progresses sub-programs get no easier to find (perhaps because those already executed are tagged but remain in the store), then the articulation of successive words in the utterance will be separated by a pause during which search for the next sub-program takes place. The duration of that pause will increase with the slope (over number of words) that is observed in preparation time. The accumulation of these brief pauses in longer utterances will give completion times their quadratic curvature. This account fits the data rather well, and in particular the preparation-time slope and the inter-response pause slope are very similar.

The second line of evidence comes from our own laboratory. We (Henderson *et al.*, 1979) were able to show that when the "start" command indicated in an unpredictable manner either whole-report or report of the first item only, preparation-times in the part report condition depended on the length of the series originally presented rather than on the length of the utterance cued (one word only). That is, preparation time in part-report did not differ from that obtained when the entire series had to be spoken. This finding is perhaps counter-intuitive, but it is predicted by the sub-program search theory and not by the program construction theory. Undiminished preparation-times are predicted for part-report in the following way. Because the subject does not know in advance what sort of report will be required, he must construct a program for full-report anyhow. If the part-report command occurs, his initial task is identical to that which the theory asserts prefaces full-report, namely, he searches through the ensemble of word sub-programs for the first to be executed. This search time depends on the size of the ensemble, as previously described. Part-report is distinguished merely by terminating after production of the first word rather than this initiating search for the sub-program for the second word.

The picture which emerges from this discussion of recitation tasks is one in which short utterances are preprogrammed before production commences. In the program construction theory this preprogramming cannot be achieved, or at least finalized, until the decision to start speaking has been taken. On the other hand, in the sub-program search theory, which is favoured by the tests reviewed above, preprogramming can be effected in advance of the decision to start speaking but the sequencing of the sub-programs is not achieved in advance. Instead, this sequencing is done piecemeal as each unit is ready to be executed.

Before closing this account of speech preparation in recitation it must be acknowledged that most of the research reviewed has utilized utterances of random words. However, in a crucial experiment Sternberg *et al.* (1978) have shown that preparation-time slopes are unaffected by the insertion of unstressed connectives (*and*, *or*, etc.) between each noun in an utterance. This strongly implies that at the level of programming that is revealed in this task the critical units are not simply words but *stress groups*, i.e., units of prosody.

Evidence of advanced planning in natural speech comes from the study of speech errors. "Slips of the tongue" have attracted considerable attention recently as indications of phonological advanced planning, and many authors have attempted to classify types of errors in accordance with a theory of the level of planning involved. Thus word exchange errors (e.g. you have hissed all my mystery lectures) frequently occur across clause boundaries. This has been taken to indicate a high level of planning at which underlying grammatical relations (Garrett, 1975) or the "meaning" of an utterance (Johnson-Laird, 1977) are represented. At a lower level, there occur the more common phonemic errors, which are generally confined within a clause or *tone group* (Fodor *et al.*, 1974). It has been reported by Nooteboom and Cohen (1975) that the frequency of anticipatory phonemic errors (e.g. kice ream cone) decreases with increased separation of the confused phonemes, up to a maximum of about eight syllables. Some authors have argued that errors involving even the smallest speech segments occur at a phonemic rather than a phonetic level (Fromkin, 1973; Ellis, 1979). Their primary reason is that the transpositions obey contextual constraints such as coarticulation rules. This argument might be extended to imply that the speech code that is available for words in the lexicon consists of a fairly abstract phonological representation rather than final articulatory program.

Preparation and production of utterances in reading aloud

We can now consider a small but highly significant modification to the task just reviewed. This modification transforms it from a recitation to a reading task. Suppose that the presentation of the stimulus material and the "start" command coincide. That is, the arrival of the printed text starts the timing process. The time taken to translate the printed words into speech is now included in our performance measure. This change in the nature of the task confronts the subject with some new decisions. He can continue to preprogram the entire utterance before initiating articulation, although in this situation the preprogramming will cost preparation-time, or he can overlap programming with execution. If programming time is negligible compared to execution time, the subject can fill preparation time with preprogramming of the first response unit only, programming further units while this first unit is being executed. Lastly, at the other extreme from complete preprogramming, the subject might operate as a "singular translator", attending to the identification, translation, and execution of one word at a time.

Another feature of this oral reading task is that it forces us to consider the depth to which processing might be conducted preparatory to embarking on the utterance. For example, in complete preprogramming, speech planning is in maximum "depth"; in another view, some preliminary processing might be conducted on the entire array short of articulatory programming, and this would be the case, for example, if the display were encoded into a perceptual buffer store where it could be operated upon by an overlapping process of program construction and execution.

An idealized description of the data from several experiments of this sort is shown in Fig. 9. Preparation times once again increase with the number of words presented. The slope of this increase is greater than in the recitation task, and the curve is negatively accelerated.

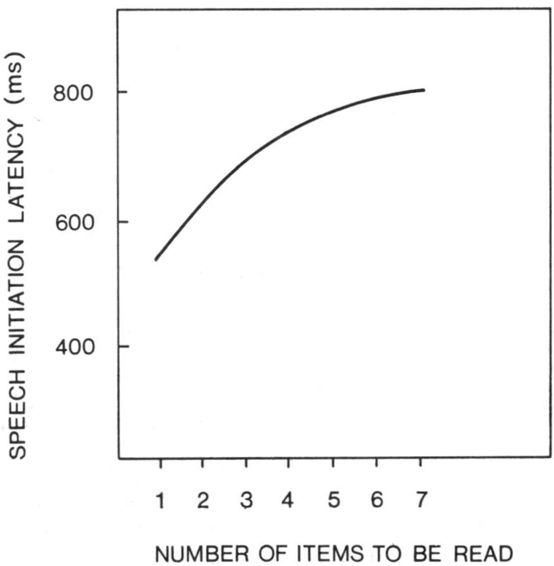

Fig. 9 Idealized graph showing the relationship between preparation time and the number of letter names to be read. After Henderson *et al.*, 1981.

This increase in preparation time with the number of words to be read allows us to rule out the rather uninteresting singular processor. Clearly subjects do not take a single word at a time and process it from visual to articulated form. What about the hypothesis lying at the other extreme of advanced planning? Could it be that the reader processes the input right through to the level of a speech program for the entire utterance before commencing articulation? Our primary reason for rejecting that possibility is that the completion time function appears quite different from that in the recitation task. In the reading task the completion times are linear rather than quadratic, and when its slope is compared to the linear component of the recitation task it appears that the underlying rate of speech in reading aloud is considerably lower than in recitation. This suggests that the level to which the advanced planning of the utterance is carried is lower, or less final, in the reading task (and by implication that the pauses between words caused by sub-program retrieval are absent, as the lack of a quadratic component to the function attests).

These observations suggest that preparation in the reading task consists in encoding the material into an intermediate level of code. Such a procedure has several advantages. The accumulation of material in some sort of input buffer allows the process of motor programming to be freed from the necessity to wait upon the vagaries of input coding for individual stimuli. Moreover, as Shaffer and Hardwick (1970) have pointed out, the operation of the response process upon a queue of items allows the input to be treated in terms of larger groupings. Considerations of intonation and prosody suggest in any case that speech programming must normally involve output groupings at least as large as the phrase (see Lehiste, 1977).

If preparation time in the reading task is largely taken up with the translation of the text into an intermediate level code, we must assume that speech programming occurs in a piecemeal way. The fact that the rate of speech that can be achieved is much lower in the reading task than it was in the recitation task can be attributed to various properties of speech programming. What seems clear is that it is not possible to overlap preprogramming and execution so that no time-cost is incurred.

Although speech rate may suffer because such piecemeal preprogramming is not conducted on sufficient large response groupings to be efficient, it seems more likely, since the rate difference is detectable in short utterances, that there is competition between the processes involved in programming and execution. Either they cannot coexist and must be interleaved, or if they coexist, execution is slowed by concurrent programming of future speech.

The eye–voice span in continuous reading

What we have observed of the preparation to read aloud a brief utterance is equivalent to the eye–voice span (EVS) in continuous reading. When we read aloud there is a lag between the point fixated by the eye and the word being articulated. At the instant that a word is articulated the eye is typically looking about four words ahead.

The EVS was first systematically investigated by Quantz (1897). His method was to slip a card over the page of a subject engaged in reading aloud and to record the number of words spoken after the text was obscured. This number he treated as an index of the amount by which the reader was looking ahead. This simple technique enabled Quantz to make several discoveries about the EVS: he found that the span was larger at the beginning of the line of text, it contracted with difficult text and it was influenced by punctuation. Quantz also found the EVS to be larger in rapid readers. Most of these findings have been confirmed by later workers. Thus the EVS has been shown to increase with age (Buswell,

1920) and with reading speed (Morton, 1964). There is agreement that the span is shorter for difficult material (Buswell, 1920; Anderson, 1937). However, more recently attention has shifted from gross variables such as "difficulty" of the text to more differentiated concepts such as grammatical structure. Levin and his associates (Levin and Kaplan, 1970, 1971; see also Gibson and Levin, 1975, for a review) have shown that the EVS in children varied from about two words for random word lists to about four words for sentences. The span was highly elastic and tended to extend to the end of a phrase boundary. Span also increased with the predictability of grammatical forms in comparisons of active and passive sentences and of left and right embedding.

While the correlates of the eye–voice span are fairly well catalogued, the function of the span has been the subject of less penetrating analysis. The seeds of one possible account are contained in early speculations about the consequences of the layout of meaning over time in speech. Thus in a characteristic passage from his *Psychology*, Williams James (1908) enquires: "How comes it about that a man reading something aloud for the first time is able immediately to emphasise all his words aright, unless from the very first he have a sense of at least the form of the sentence yet to come?" For Quantz, similarly, the EVS was a condition for proper phrasing. He wrote: "a certain considerable distance between eye and voice is a condition of intelligent and intelligible reading" (Quantz, 1897). However, the requirements of organizing intonation and stress across phrase groups in speech cannot be a necessary condition for the EVS: a similar lag between intake and output occurs in typing, and when this lag is prevented by depriving the typist of preview of the text ahead, typing speed falls markedly (Shaffer and Hardwick, 1968). It seems, then, that an input–output lag is characteristic of many, indeed probably all, transcription tasks such as reading, typing and sight-reading music, irrespective of the response mode. A fundamental requirement for any such lag to occur is that a buffer store must exist in which the input can be queued until the output process can operate upon it. The question then arises: to what extent can the variations in the size of the EVS be attributed to the properties of this buffer store?

Before we can satisfactorily enquire into this question we must dispose of some interpretative problems. First, it would be naïve to accept without question that the point to which the reader can continue after occlusion of the text is identical with the point of fixation. Assumptions about fixations are best anchored in techniques whereby eye-movements and speech are the subject of continuous, synchronized measurement (e.g. Morton, 1964). Nevertheless, it seems evident that span effects measured in the occlusion paradigms are not artifacts of guessing (Gibson and Levin, 1975).

A more serious difficulty arises in the assumption that the span is a direct measure of what is "seen" in advance of speech. Some of the difficulties with this view have been discussed by Kolers (1971), but the central problem appears to have passed almost without notice. The problem can best be explicated by re-examining the outward behavioural aspect of the EVS. Once it is established that the eye moves in swift, discrete saccades which may traverse two or three words, that fact by itself entails the existence of an eye–voice span. The question of the extent of the span then becomes allied with the question of what determines the magnitude of a saccade. Saccadic movements are ballistic. Their direction and distance must be fully programmed in advance, and this programming appears to take more than a negligible amount of time. In simple non-linguistic fixation-tracking tasks, the time taken to program and initiate a saccade is about a fifth of a second (Alpern, 1971). It appears to follow, if these results can be generalized to reading, that the magnitude of a saccade, and thus the EVS at the instant of its completion, must be determined by the apprehension of the material in *previous* fixations. Therefore to talk of the EVS, as Gibson and Levin (1975) appear to do, as if its extent were determined by the precise nature of the material extending between vocalization and fixation must be misleading. The saccade must be programmed on the basis of an extrapolation or prediction about the nature of future material, based largely on the immediate past. Given that fixations generally last about 250 ms, then fixation $n + 1$ must begin to be programmed almost at the instant that the eye has settled on fixation n. For this reason Kolers (1970) has been able to remark upon the lack of consistent relationship between the precise locus fixated and the linguistic nature of the information at that locus (see also Rayner, 1975).[16]

7.2 PREPARATION FOR THE ARTICULATION OF INDIVIDUAL WORDS

Earlier in this chapter and throughout Chapter 5 we managed to discuss the representation of a word's pronunciation in the lexicon without theoretical commitment to the form of that representation. Where this question has been discussed by other authors it has generally been in terms of the distinction between an abstract phonological representation and an articulatory program (e.g. Forster and Chambers, 1973). Strictly speaking this dichotomy is oversimplified. To the extent that speech programs are hierarchical, their highest level of specification may be close to an abstract phonological code. However, we shall continue to employ this simple dichotomy as a shorthand way of referring to the level of phonological specification.

There are various persuasive but perhaps inconclusive arguments in favour of the proposition that articulatory programs are not immediately available in the lexicon. One possible argument is the rather general one that it would be highly uneconomical of storage for the lexicon to contain detailed programs for word pronunciation, because once an abstract phonological description is provided for a lexical item, most of the articulatory details can be derived by the application of general rules. (This is one of the central principles of Chomsky and Halle's generative theory of phonology.) Moreover, even if articulatory programs were immediately available in the lexicon, some final programming would still have to be done to link lexical units together to form an utterance. Coarticulation constraints would have to be applied at word boundaries, and intonation and stress would have to be assigned to phrase groups. For example, as Cutler (1980) and others have pointed out, lexical stress varies with the prosodic context. We tend to say "I counted fourtéen" but "I've fóurteen books".

If the previous speculations are correct, there should be a stage after word phonology is retrieved from the lexicon at which it is translated into an articulatory program. However, when we turn to look for tasks which might permit the investigation of this programming we are confronted with a dilemma. Where subjects are required to recite a previously specified utterance, it appears that programming is achieved in advance of the signal to commence speaking. According to the sub-program search theory, all that is detectable in the hesitation before vocalization is the retrieval (and possibly the "unpacking") of the sub-program for each unit of the assembled program. On the other hand, when we do not allow advanced preparation but instead present the text and the start command simultaneously, as we do in the single-frame rapid reading task, articulatory programming must contribute to the timing measures although there are at least two complications which prevent its isolation. First, in the choice RT task it is difficult to disentangle response planning from stimulus analysis and also from other response effects such as S–R compatability. This problem is discussed in detail by Sternberg *et al.* (1978). Secondly, if, as I suggested in our discussion of the rapid reading task, programming overlaps with execution, then preparation time will only include the programming time for the first item or items. Programming time for the remaining items will have its effect on the speech rate.

Although we have discussed articulatory programming as though even when it is piecemeal and overlaps with execution it always involves preprogramming of individual words, some authors have asserted that even single words are not invariably completely preprogrammed. Klapp and Wyatt (1976) have argued that in longer words programming and execution overlap within individual words. Frederiksen and Kroll (1976) argued that, at least in cases where an entire pronunciation is not retrieved from the lexicon, orthographic translation and articulatory programming are part of the same process, which is conducted in a left-to-right manner across the word, with articulation commencing before translation/programming is completed. Both these arguments rest on the effects of structural characteristics of words upon their naming latencies, and accordingly we shall now review these effects.

Phonotactic complexity and naming latency

The issue here rests entirely on the *post hoc* analysis of some data by Frederiksen and Kroll (1976). It is worth considering in some detail because the questions raised by their claims are central to our present concern.

Frederiksen and Kroll begin from the denial that orthographic translation involves the derivation of an abstract phonological representation of the entire word before articulation commences. Instead, they assume that "articulation begins as soon as the initial element in the array has been translated" (Frederiksen and Kroll, 1976, p. 376). They advance three reasons for holding this proposition. Their first is based on the common finding that the duration of spoken consonants is greater at the beginning than at the end of words. They argue that this is because at the beginning of a word there is competition between the construction and execution of the motor program whereas by the end construction has been completed before execution. This competition at the initial portion slows the execution process. This argument rests on a number of arbitrary and implausible assumptions, and I shall mention only the plausible alternative explanation that consonant duration varies in this way as one of several ways of phonetically marking syllabic boundaries. (See Christie (1974) for a discussion of the effects of duration on perceived boundaries; see Massaro (1975) for a discussion of the linguistic relevance of syllabic boundaries.)

Frederiksen and Kroll's second argument stems from their failure to obtain an effect of number of syllables on word-naming latency. This, they argue, is because translation of the second syllable does not take place until articulation of the first syllable is initiated. We shall defer a discussion of syllabic effects until p. 181, noting here only that failure to find a syllabic effect is presumably compatible with a rather large number of possibilities. It could be said to be consistent with their theory but not to offer particular support for it.

The third argument is the most interesting and is based on the finding that phonotactic complexity slows naming latency when it occurs at the beginning but not at the end of words. Obviously this might be expected if only the beginning was programmed before articulation commenced.

One possibility is that Frederiksen and Kroll's phonotactic complexity variable is correlated with some other variable which is active at an earlier stage of processing than motor programming. (What I have called "phonotactic complexity" they call "orthographic structure", though in their theory its supposed effect on motor programming has no relevance to orthography.) There is some basis for denying a locus prior to articulatory coding because they failed to obtain the phonotactic effect when the same words were used in the lexical decision task.

Frederiksen and Kroll's position is best examined in terms of two distinct propositions: that a complete *phonological* representation is not constructed before articulation commences and that a complete *motor program* is not constructed in advance. The former claim can be rejected on other grounds (Henderson and Chard, 1980). First, as Frederiksen and Kroll themselves show, naming latency is affected by number of letters in the word, *so something must be done to the entire word before articulation commences.* They concede that array length affects the time taken to achieve a phonological representation, and therefore the array length effect is inconsistent with their claim that phonological translation is not completed prior to articulation. Secondly, this claim can be rejected on linguistic grounds. In words such as *chase* (v. *chasm*) the pronunciation of the initial portion cannot be assigned until the entire word has been translated. In words such as *ember* (v. *embed*) the stress cannot be assigned until the entire word has been translated. In fact stress assignment in English crucially depends on an analysis of the later syllables of polysyllabic words (Baker and Smith, 1976). For these reasons it seems that phonological translation cannot be accomplished in a serial, left to right manner so as to overlap with articulation. The second proposition is more difficult to decide (i.e. overlapping articulatory programming and execution) and we return to it below.

Syllabic effects

It is ironical that Frederiksen and Kroll should give the absence of a syllabic effect in word naming as a reason for believing in overlapping program construction and execution, whereas Klapp and Wyatt (1976) use its presence in support of the same argument. The logical aspect of this paradox can readily be resolved. Frederiksen and Kroll believe preprogramming to extend less than a syllable ahead, so later syllables in a word are not expected to exert effects on latencies; Klapp and Wyatt believe preprogramming to extend about three to five syllables ahead and therefore predict large differences over increases in syllabic length from one to three syllables, with the effect of further increase tapering off thereafter. The empirical paradox, however, is not so easily resolved, for syllabic effects in naming tasks are highly elusive.

In early word-naming studies manipulations of the number of syllables were so confounded with other variables as to yield uninterpretable effects (see Henderson *et al.*, 1973). One difficulty is that with alphabetic script we can control either word length or orthographic pattern but not both at the same time. For example, we can compare *cot* with *cotton* (syllables confounded with array size) or *coasts* with *cotton* (syllables confounded with orthographic pattern). The digit set seems to offer a way round this but introduces other artifacts (Henderson *et al.*, 1973).

Klapp and Wyatt (1976, Table 1) list five published papers in support of their claim that number of syllables has a negatively accelerated effect upon naming latency. Of these, all but that of Klapp *et al.* (1973) can be disregarded on the basis of the criticisms made by Henderson *et al.* (1973). The remaining paper reports a significant difference of 14 ms in the time taken to initiate naming of a one- or two-syllable word or pictured object. Subsequent failures to detect syllabic effects in word naming have been reported by Forster and Chambers (1973), Frederiksen and Kroll (1976), Mason (1978), and Cosky (1980). In several of these studies an effect was obtained which lay within the range of magnitudes reported by Klapp and Wyatt (1976) but which failed to attain significance: Forster and Chambers reported an increase in latency of 10 ms between one- and two-syllable words of four letters; Mason reported a 16 ms increase for words of four and six letters; on the other hand, in Frederiksen and Kroll's study the difference was in the wrong direction. It is difficult to avoid the conclusion overall that there is as yet no reliable evidence of a syllabic effect in naming latencies. However, those effects which have been reported have invariably amounted to less than 20 ms, and it may be that the effect is so small as to be difficult to detect.

Table 10 Increase in pronunciation latency (ms) between one- and two-syllable stimuli as a function of reader ability and lexical status of the stimulus[a]

	Reader ability	High-frequency words	Pseudowords
MASON STUDY	Good	9	67
	Poor	22	121
FREDERIKSEN STUDY	Good	10	32
	Poor	28	65

[a] Data from Mason (1978, table 5) and Frederiksen (1976, fig. 7). In the latter case the numbers are estimates based on measurements of graphs. Classification of reader ability was by a comprehension test in both studies and has no absolute significance. The Mason groups had more extreme test scores.

Studies of individual differences offer a way to resolve the inconsistencies in report of syllabic effects. In two studies which have investigated reader ability, syllabic effects have been obtained for poor or slow readers. Frederiksen (1976) used the Nelson-Denny Reading Test to classify his subjects, who were high-school students. Naming latency was inversely related to reading ability, and as others have found, this relationship was stronger for nonwords than words. A syllabic effect was obtained (1 v. 2 syllables) and this effect was larger for poor readers and for nonwords. Similar results have been reported by Mason (1978). She found a syllabic effect which was negligible for skilled readers naming real words; however, the effect showed a large increase with nonwords and with poorer readers (Nelson-Denny Test), though only the lexicality effect was significant in this *post hoc* analysis. Frederiksen's (1976) and Mason's (1978) syllabic effects are summarized in Table 10. Since there is no particular reason to suspect that poor readers have more difficulty with motor programming or that nonwords are more complex to program, the most appropriate conclusion to draw is that syllabic effects in reading–naming tasks involve orthographic translation rather than motor programming. When a skilled reader arrives at the phonological representation of a familiar word, this process may be unaffected by the number of syllables that it contains. On the other hand if the stimulus is a pseudoword, so that a pronunciation has to be constructed from various consistuents (whether these be lexical analogies or GPCs), then syllabic length begins to be a factor. Poor readers are often thought to be particularly deficient at synthesizing a pronunciation, and so it is to be expected that they will exhibit larger syllabic effects, especially on nonwords.

This interpretation of syllabic effects can be combined with another theory to yield a further prediction. Coltheart *et al.* (1979), have recently constructed a persuasive argument to the effect that "no" responses in the lexical decision task (i.e. the decision that an item is not a real word) are influenced by phonological recoding. If their argument is correct, and if it is also correct to claim, as I do above, that syllabic effects occur at a stage of translation into a phonological code rather than a stage of articulatory programming, then we should find a syllabic effect for poor readers in the negative lexical decision times. In this case the response is a keypress or a spoken "no" so there is no reason to expect that any syllabic effect that is detected should be due to motor programming.

Several of the naming latency studies mentioned above used a control condition which was essentially a single-word version of the recitation task. A word was presented and encoded. After a brief delay a "start" command was given, and the latency for initiating vocalization of the word was determined. Generally this task has been conceived of as providing no more than a control baseline in order to ensure that the device for detecting vocalization was not differentially sensitive to certain initial sounds. Several authors (see Klapp, 1976) had reported that such recitation latencies for single words were unaffected by the number of syllables that they contained. A possible unremarked exception to this failure to find a syllabic effect occurs in the study by Forster and Chambers (1973), where their Appendix allows the calculation of the difference between one- and two-syllable, four-letter words, in the recitation control condition. This shows a 17 ms advantage for one-syllable words.

Recently, however, Sternberg *et al.* (1978) have reported an extremely small but reliable syllabic effect in their studies of the rapid recitation of multi-word utterances. They contrasted pairs of lists such as *bay*, *rum*, *track* v. *baby*, *rumble*, *tractor*, so that each matched pair of words either consisted of or started with the same stressed syllable. They collected a very large amount of data from highly practised subjects, which allowed them to detect tiny effects.

When the preparation times (latency of onset of vocalization) were plotted over number of words in the utterance, the slopes did not differ for utterances consisting of one syllable and of two-syllable words. The intercept values did differ, however. The mean preparation time for two-syllable words was a significant 4·5 ms longer than for one-syllable words.

Sternberg *et al.* suggest the following explanation for the syllabic effect in the recitation task (1978, p. 136). Suppose that in addition to the search for the first sub-program to be executed, preparation time included the time to "unpack", that unit into constituents at a lower level, such as syllables. If the duration of this unpacking process increased with the number of components to be unpacked from the unit, there would be a syllabic effect on preparation times that would depend exclusively on the syllabic structure of the first word (or stress group) of the series.

In conclusion, we have accepted the existence of two independent mechanisms for syllabic effects. One of these applies only to recitation tasks and depends upon the number of syllables (or even more elementary articulatory units) of the first word or stress group in an utterance. In practised subjects there is an effect of about 5 ms per syllable on preparation latencies. Sternberg *et al.* interpret this effect as due to unpacking of the hierarchical speech programme into a lower level (less abstract) code, immediately prior to execution of the response.

The other mechanism which yields syllabic effects is restricted to reading–naming tasks. The effect is due to orthographic translation, and it is most likely to be manifest when orthographic translation is most difficult, as when the reader is unskilled or the stimulus is a nonword. Under these circumstances the effect may be substantial, perhaps an order of magnitude larger than the effect arising from unpacking of the speech-motor program.

Number of letters

Certainly the most prevalent of the structural effects on naming latencies is that of number of letters in the stimulus word. Table 11 lists eight studies in which an array size (number of letters) effect was found in the reading–naming task. This effect ranges in magnitude from an increase of 6 to 63 ms per letter. In the three studies which have contained varying levels of reader-ability, the array-size effect has been shown to increase as reader ability diminishes. Two studies which included a recitation control condition show that when the encoding of the word takes place off-line an array size effect is undetectable.

The effect of array-size on naming latency has attracted most theoretical comment in the study by Frederiksen and Kroll (1976) and consequent discussion by Coltheart (1978). Frederiksen and Kroll were concerned with the array-size effect as a product of orthographic translation and found that words and non-words in a naming-latency task yielded an array-length effect, as well as the previously mentioned effect of phonotactic complexity. When the same stimuli were used in a lexical decision task, neither of these structural features appeared to influence performance. Accordingly, they argued that lexical decisions could not have required prior translation of the stimulus into phonological form.

Table 11 Studies in which word-naming latencies investigated as a function of number of letters in the stimulus word

	Reading-naming	Other findings
	ms/letter	
Cosky (1980)	15	No effect of number of phonemes
Cosky (1976)	22	
Glushko (1979)[a]	50	
Frederiksen and Kroll (1978)	28	
Mason (1978)	23	Larger effect for poor readers; No effect in word recitation control
Forster and Chambers (1973)[b]	29	No effect in word recitation control
Frederiksen (1976)	6	Larger effect for poor readers
Seymour and Porpodas (1980)	63	Larger effect for poor readers
	$\bar{x}$ 29·5	

[a] Data processed from Appendix to Glushko (1979).
[b] Data processed from Appendix to Forster and Chambers (1973).

Coltheart (1978) has drawn attention to an apparent inconsistency in Frederiksen and Kroll's argument. If the array-size effect on naming latency is due to phonological recoding, the slope of the function relating latency to number of letters in the array should be reduced for words. This follows because Frederiksen and Kroll accept the GPC theory in which lexical and nonlexical routes to pronunciation are sharply distinguished. In this view, faster responding to words is due to the use of the lexical route. However, on the basis of their lexical decision data they argue that this route is insensitive to array-size. To the extent, then, that word naming depends upon the lexical route, the array-size effect for words should be diluted. There is no evidence of such an effect in their data (but there is in other studies, e.g. Frederiksen, 1976). Coltheart (1978) suggests the counter-argument that the array-size effect may be due to motor-programming as distinct from phonological recoding. (It will be recalled that a central feature of Frederiksen and Kroll's interpretation was their rejection of a distinction between phonological and articulatory coding.)

I would like now to discuss my reasons for rejecting both of these views, commencing with the one I take to be the more vulnerable. For this analysis it will be necessary to consider the various effects of word structure together. Accordingly, the following material should also serve as a summary of the present section.

Frederiksen and Kroll's model

This model asserts the unity of phonological recoding and articulatory programming. This single process overlaps with the execution of vocalization. It is affected by both array-size and phonotactic complexity but not by syllabic length.

My reasons for rejecting this model can be summarized as follows. First, on general grounds, as we saw when discussing the effects of phonotactic complexity, it is necessary to postulate orthographic translation of the complete array into some form of phonological code prior to articulation. Thus, either phonological coding requires to be distinguished from articulatory coding, or, if the unity of the two processes is maintained, they must be completed before articulation is initiated.

Secondly, it makes no sense to assert that array-size and phonotactic complexity affect the same stage, since phonotactic complexity has been shown to matter only at the beginning of a word whereas array-size is by definition a characteristic of the entire word.

The most consistent interpretation of Frederiksen and Kroll's own data is therefore that apparently there are at least two distinct underlying processes. The first requires us to consider the entire word and results in an abstract phonological code. This operation is affected by array size. The second process transforms the phonological code in a serial manner into an articulatory program. This process overlaps in time with the actual execution of the program and it is affected by phonotactic complexity.

Coltheart's suggestion

Coltheart (1978) is in agreement with the need to partition phonological from articulatory coding, but in contrast to the reinterpretation that I have just offered, he suggests that array-size affects the articulatory coding stage. Since phonotactic complexity must also be presumed to affect this stage, this seems to lead to the same sort of difficulty as Frederiksen and Kroll's theory, namely that a whole-word effect (array-size) and a part-word effect (initial phonotactic complexity) are located at the same stage.

I believe that there are other difficulties as well for any theory that locates the array-size effect at an articulatory programming stage, though these difficulties are perhaps less clear cut. First is the question of an array-size effect in lexical decisions. I take it that any such effect would be compatible with the location of the effect at the phonological coding but not the motor programming stage. Frederiksen and Kroll found no array-size effect in lexical decisions though there was a non-significant tendency for negative (nonword) latencies to increase with array size. This effect was about 14 ms per letter, and Frederiksen and Kroll (1976, p. 377) note that it may indicate that phonological recoding can occur on a proportion of nonword trials. Other investigators have obtained reliable effects of array-size on lexical decisions (Forster and Chambers, 1973; Whaley, 1978; Richards and Doggett, 1976), although there is little consistency in the way these effects are distributed over words and nonwords. Where a theory distinguishes phonological from articulatory effects, these array-size effects in lexical decisions would seem to belong more naturally to the non-articulatory class.

Another way of examining this issue is to enquire why an articulatory coding process should be sensitive to a visual quantity like *number of letters*. It would seem more likely that the *number of phonemes* (or articulatory gestures) should be the true determinant of performance, on the articulatory position. Such evidence as exists, offers no support for this position. In Whaley's (1978) regression analysis, number of letters was a marginally better predictor of lexical decision latencies than number of phonemes. Moreover, I have reanalysed the data of Glushko's (1979 Exp. 1) study of word and nonword naming. When the four-letter strings are divided into those of three v. four phonemes the effect of number of phonemes is trivial and in the wrong direction for both words and nonwords. The most persuasive negative evidence comes from the study by Cosky (1980), who found a 15 ms letter length effect whereas in an equivalent experiment the effect of phoneme length was −2 ms.

Finally, as with the syllabic effect, the tendency for the array-size effect to be much greater in poor readers (see Table 11) favours phonological recoding over articulatory programming as the locus for the effect.

The model I have arrived at is summarized in Fig. 10. Clearly there are many details of the underlying processes that are not represented in this crude summary, but for our limited purpose here the model contains the crucial distinction of orthographic translation (phonological recoding) from articulatory programming. Orthographic translation is conducted upon the entire string prior to articulatory programming, but articulatory programming may overlap with execution of speech. This is symbolized by overlapping the components of the diagram in the left-to-right flow. The various effects of word structure, lexical status and reader ability are shown in relation to the processing stage on which they may act. Syllabic length is shown parenthetically, to mark the fact that its action may only be detected at certain levels of other factors such as reader ability.

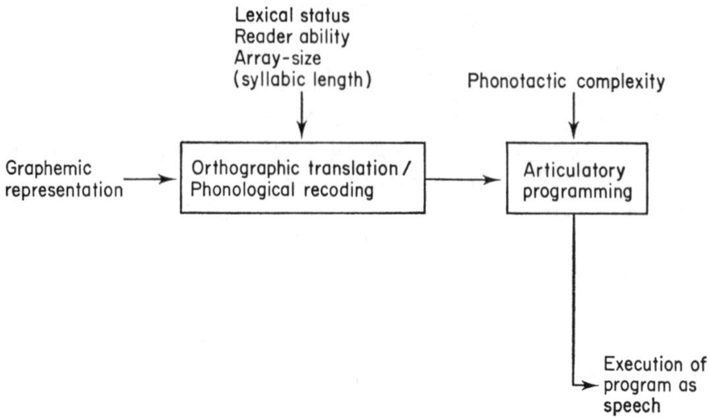

Fig. 10 A diagram summarizing the conclusions concerning the effects of various aspects of word structure on the processing stages underlying word-naming latencies. (See text for explication.)

Effects of word length and the lexical analogy model

With respect to the structural effects that I hold to act upon orthographic translation, namely array-size and syllabic length, we have not yet enquired how it is that they exercise their effects. In the GPC theory, array-size reflects the number of graphemic units to be segmented and translated, so any effect is unsurprising. It is less clear why syllabic length should affect the GPC procedure, at least for poor readers, but it would probably not be difficult to construct an explanation. Since I have preferred theories based upon lexical analogy to those based upon the GPC procedure, it is worth briefly indicating how the lexical analogy procedure might be sensitive to word structure.

I suspect that there exist a number of ways to reconcile the lexical analogy mechanism with array-size and syllabic length effects. Rather than produce an arbitrary catalogue of these I wish to draw attention to one particularly interesting possibility in which word structure has its effect because of its correlation with *visual lexicon density*, that is, longer words, in terms of letters or syllables, have fewer orthographic neighbours. There exist fewer words of high visual similarity with which analogy can be made. This relationship between structure and lexicon density is probably intuitively obvious for array-size but less so for syllabic length. There is, however, some empirical evidence for both these relationships in a study by Kroll (1976). She used a behavioural measure of effective visual lexicon density, requiring subjects to generate as many words as possible by changing a single letter in a base word, and found that the number of words that could be generated declined with increases in array-size and syllabic length. Furthermore, these factors interacted such that the array-size effect was much larger for one syllable base words.

If visual lexicon density is the critical variable underlying array-size and syllabic length effects, it might affect the analogy procedure by increasing the time taken to arrive at sufficient evidence to allow construction of a pronunciation. Alternatively, construction of a phonological representation may be delayed because it requires to be assembled from analogies with small portions of the word. In either case the effect of length should be greater for pseudowords, which are wholly reliant upon analogy. (In this context it is worth noting that Frederiksen and Kroll's failure to find an increased array-size for nonwords is difficult to reconcile with any orthographic translation interpretation of the effect of array-size. Mason, however (1978), did find such an interaction, as did Frederiksen (1976.)

Chapter 8

Performance Depending upon Script

In Part 1 we devoted a considerable amount of attention to the formal distinctions between types of script. We also noted that these distinctions were not necessarily informative about how the reader actually treats a particular form of script. In the same way we noted that formal conceptions of the "efficiency" of a type of script required to be kept apart from psychological conceptions of "efficiency". In this chapter we turn to some of the psychological evidence of how performance depends upon type of script.

Section 1 deals largely with comparisons that can be made within a language and within an individual, but across types of script. This is probably the most rigorous of the various comparisons that we shall discuss. The most illuminating contrast between scripts has tended to be that between logographic characters, by which lexical reference is made "directly", and phonographic characters, which refer most immediately to the sound segments of spoken forms. Accordingly, our discussion will centre upon the most celebrated of these contrasts, that between Kanji logographs and the Kana syllabary in Japanese, but we shall also consider similar contrasts within Chinese. Within the English language we shall be able to examine comparisons between the usual alphabetic script and the logographic system of Arabic numerals, as well as forms that have uncertain status, such as the letter–name compounds (e.g. FBI).

In Section 2, we remain with intra-language comparisons but transfer our attention to individual differences, in particular those involving a selective impairment of the handling of one form of script consequent upon brain damage. This sort of evidence, as I have emphasized, tends to depend upon clinical reports which frequently omit important detail. Moreover, generalizations from abnormal to normal behaviour are always haunted by the possibility that abnormal performance is based on the development of novel strategies to cope with the impairment. This possibility must ever be weighted against the more optimistic neuropsychological assumption that these syndromes involve the excision of certain processing mechanisms, as it were, so as to reveal the design of the normal system. Nevertheless, the findings obtained are broadly consistent with those in Section 1.

By far the most insecure comparison we can make is that which confounds type of script with spoken language and also with culture. This is exactly what we do when we compare the ease with which, say, Japanese children and English children acquire reading skills with their respective written languages, and this perilous enterprise is considered in Section 3.

8.1 COMPARISONS OF DIFFERENT SCRIPTS WITHIN LANGUAGES AND INDIVIDUALS

Discrimination and recall of characters

A number of experimenters have recently addressed themselves to the confusability of characters in discrimination and in immediate recall. Many of these studies carry on the tradition in which letters are used as semantically empty material for the study of rote learning processes. There is no reason to accept that findings drawn from such tasks are relevant to the study of how written characters are treated in reading. After all, the way in which we regard a letter to be rote learned need have little in common with the way in which we regard it as part of a word to be read. I shall therefore not dwell extensively on the points that emerge from this literature.

It has long been established for English that visually presented letters tend to be phonetically recoded for retention in short term memory (e.g. Conrad, 1964). This has usually been taken to be informative about the nature of STM rather than providing any penetrating insight into our handling of English script. However, attempts have been made to see whether such phonetic coding also holds for characters drawn from other types of script. In one of the first investigations of this sort, Erickson *et al* (1973) used Kanji characters in a probed recall task. Performance was much more impaired by phonetic confusability in the character list than by visual or semantic confusability.

There are a number of difficulties in interpreting Erickson *et al.*'s experiment, especially as it bears upon reading. For example, the central question in reading is what, from a psychological point of view, is the immediate referent of a logographic character. However, it is by no means clear that confusability effects result from this first encoding operation. This can be understood from an analogy with picture memory, for it is at least conceivable that memory for pictured objects might be influenced by the phonetic confusability of the objects names. Surely we would not want to conclude from this that pictures refer directly to the names of objects? In sum, there is no reason at all to accept the equivalence of memory code with lexical access code.

A second difficulty arises through Erickson *et al.*'s assertion that the Kanji characters might be used to access a phonological code and then this code used to access meaning. The problem here is that Japanese contains a very large number of homophones, and these cannot be semantically interpreted in the absence of context. To convert the visual information into phonological information would therefore be to discard the information necessary for semantic identification.

A third difficulty concerns the control of amount of confusability in the Erickson *et al.* experiment. Kanji characters are reputedly very visually distinctive, and even when subjects use a visual code there may be little evidence of visual confusion.

Other investigators have reported evidence of phonetic recoding in memory for logographs. Mae (1976) measured recognition memory for Chinese characters and found that errors tended to be phonetic confusions. Yik (1978) also used Chinese characters and found evidence of both visual and phonetic confusions.

A direct counter to the notion that logographs evoke a prelexical phonological code is to be found in a study by Steinberg and Yamada (1978). They compared the ability of Japanese pre-school children to learn Kanji and Kana symbols. The Kanji had to be associated with the word they referred to and the Kana with the meaningless syllable to which they referred. This, too, is a memory experiment, but at least it mimics what Japanese children are taught when they learn to read. Learning rate for the Kanji was greatly superior, and moreover the authors were able to show that this was because the response associated with Kanji symbols was meaningful.

A more ingenious comparison in which scripts can be compared for memorability without allowing the nature of the response term to covary was made in Park and Arbuckle's (1977) study of recall of Korean graphemes. Rather than attempting to show that confusional errors for logographs resembled in nature those for alphabetic letters, they directly compared recall of words represented by logographs with recall of those *same* words presented in alphabetic letters, (It will be recalled from Chapter 1 that written Korean represents many levels, from the articulatory feature, through the phoneme and syllable, up to the word. The more analytic graphemes are those of the Korean alphabet, *Hangul*, but whole lexical units may be represented by logographic characters borrowed from Chinese.) Park and Arbuckle found that the words were recognized and recalled more successfully when represented by logographs than when presented in Hangul alphabetic script. Unlike other workers, Park and Arbuckle do not discuss their findings in terms of simple oppositions such as visual v. verbal coding. Instead, they utilize the notion of a single dimension of richness of encoding (Craik and Tulving, 1975) and go on to identify this dimension with a continuum of stimuli running from pictures through logographs to alphabetic words. Thus they regard the superior recall of logographs when compared to alphabetic words as a weaker action of the same mechanism that gives rise to the well-established superiority of pictures over words. "Ideograms," they write, "thus may be in some sense 'weak' pictures" (p. 641).

Park and Arbuckle's study is an ingenious one. The comparison of scripts is achieved within an individual subject, and the lexical referent is the same whatever the type of script employed. Can we therefore conclude that any differences in performance between the logographic and alphabetic scripts are due to differences in the processes linking the visual signs to their lexical addresses? As it turns out, despite the ingenuity of the design an alarming number of theoretical interpretations of the script effect remain possible, ranging from the artifactual to the fundamental.

On the artifactual side we must consider that the logographic representation of the word may have been simply a more familiar way of representing the word. An alternative source of confusion has been discussed by Taylor (1980). This arises from the fact that in Korean, as in Japanese and Chinese, the spoken language is high in lexical ambiguity. Homophones abound and so alphabetic script is lexically ambiguous: whereas the logograph for *peace* refers only to that concept, the alphabetic rendering of the word can also mean various other unrelated things.

Despite these reservations it is useful to consider some more interesting interpretations in which the memory advantage is attributed to fundamental differences in the way that either form of script is encoded. Let us start from the analogy between logographs and pictures that recurs throughout this literature. It is well established that a concept is more likely to be remembered when expressed by a picture than a word. Now, there are various ways in which the perception of a pictured object might differ from perception of the alphabetically written name of the object. (*i*) Pictures are generally more visually complex than words. (*ii*) Pictures exercise the mechanisms concerned with seeing the world and acting on it, whereas linguistic signs are artificial. (*iii*) Pictures are concrete and particular; they instantiate concepts rather than represent them. Even an idealized picture of a chair takes a particular physical form. (*iv*) Pictures probably evoke a different and richer pattern of associations than do names. A picture of a chair may remind us of a function of chairs or an episode involving a chair. (*v*) Pictures may refer less directly to spoken language than do words. (*vi*) The manner of learning to read pictures may differ considerably from that of learning to read words. And so on. The list is not exhaustive.

There is no doubt that generally logographic signs are visually more complex than alphabetic ones. For example, Tanaka (1977) has reported that Kanji characters are more discriminable than Kana. However, it is probably misleading to consider the visual complexity of a logograph as if it were a semantically empty spatial pattern. Nelson *et al.* (1976) have suggested that in the case of pictures their advantage in memorability over (alphabetic) words is due to greater configurational distinctiveness rather than a greater amount of semantic content. By extension, it might be asked whether the advantage of logographs in memory tasks is located at a visual or semantic stage of processing, but I doubt whether that question is interpretable, since it is no more possible for the fluent reader to regard a logograph as a purely visual pattern than for a Structuralist's subject to perceive a book simply as a red rectangle.

At this point it may be instructive to consider the following hypothetical test of the generality of the logograph's advantage in memorability. In English we can write the numbers logographically, using arabic numerals, or alphabetically (7 v. seven). I am prepared to hazard the guess that memory tasks are insensitive to the difference between these scripts. One factor that might be important here is the visual simplicity of numerals as compared to most other logographic signs. But in addition to this, I think most of us have the intuition that the test is unfair because of the nature of the semantic referent of numerals. Numbers are abstract and they are semantically meagre fare. Abstraction should not matter to the test (Park and Arbuckle found no interaction between the script effect and the abstractness of the word), but the connotative meagreness of a number may disable the comparison with logographs for common nouns. One particular feature of the Far Eastern logograph that distinguishes it from our numerals is the semantic radical, that component of many signs which serves to classify it semantically. For example, the Kanji for *tree* is a component of the signs for *desk*, *board*, *cane*, *pine*, etc. (Moreover, this particular radical has preserved a vaguely pictographic form.) Chinese, Japanese and Korean dictionaries organize their logographic entries according to the radicals. For these reasons it is unwise to assume that because two written forms in different script refer to the same ostensible lexical form, they access the same semantic system.

The analogy between logograph reading and picture identification has been pursued further in a recent comparison of Stroop Test performance using logographic and alphabetic script. The Stroop Test is based upon the difficulty one encounters in naming the colour of ink when that ink is used to spell the name of a conflicting colour. Biederman and Tsao (1979) compared the magnitude of the Stroop effect obtained for Chinese subjects presented with alphabetic words. Stroop interference was greater for the logographs. Biederman and Tsao interpret this finding within the following conception. Chinese characters permit more direct access to meaning than alphabetic script. This direct access procedure is similar to the process involved in colour naming. Thus reading Chinese and naming colours compete for "the same perceptual capacities". The interference produced by this competition is added to the response competition that is also assumed to hold generally for this task.

Biederman and Tsao's discussion gathers together many of the arguments that have been brought to bear upon the comparison of logographic and alphabetic processing. Furthermore, it does so in the context of an experiment which has, on the face of it, much more to do with reading than the STM tasks. For these reasons, it is worth examining their account more fully.

Central to Biederman and Tsao's account is the notion that logographs permit a more direct access to meaning than does alphabetic script. The question is how we are to interpret "direct", in this context. The answer, for Biederman and Tsao, centres round the analogy with picture perception. They give some justification of this analogy by citing an elegant experiment by So *et al.* (1977), who showed that whereas in English the word "pineapple" takes longer to classify as fruit than a picture of a pineapple, the Chinese logograph can be classified as fast as the picture. Of course, this does not tell us that a logograph is processed like a picture, but it does anchor the claim about "more direct" access to meaning in an operational test.

Biederman and Tsao are careful to concede that logographs do not *look like* their referents, but they argue that they do induce "configurational" processing. This key concept is explicated in two ways: by analogy with such "seeing as" experiences as occur when we look at clouds or Rorschach cards, and by contrast with the abstract rule system that the English reader is held to bring to a word. Unfortunately neither of these lines of argument is very helpful. It is difficult to know how literally we are to take the analogy with "seeing as" or whether this analogy amounts to more than Park and Arbuckle's (1977) "weak picture" view of logographs. On the other hand the contrast with a rule-based approach to alphabetic script is not clear. One difficulty arises from the authors' consistent failure to distinguish explicitly between access to semantics and to phonology. Thus it is unclear whether the rules referred to are rules for deriving phonology. Assuming that this is so, we must turn for further enlightenment to theories of the translation of alphabetic script into sound. When we do (see Chapter 5), it seems that "abstract rule" based theories are those that employ a GPC procedure. But, as we have seen, this is usually embodied in a dual process theory which also contains a direct lexical route to phonology. The question then becomes how to distinguish the direct lexical route for alphabetic script from the direct access to meaning via logographs.

To sum up so far, what we have reviewed consists of the argument that reading Kanji, picture perception and colour-patch naming have something in common which sets them apart from the reading of words in alphabetic script (or syllabic script, see Park and Arbuckle, 1977, footnote 2). This is used as a basis for the prediction that these similar activities will compete with one another, producing interference. However, even this prediction does not set Kanji categorically apart from English. Brooks (1967) has argued that reading English is a sufficiently "visual" activity to interfere selectively with a visualization task.

Let us examine the nature of the Stroop interference more closely. A general difficulty exists for "perceptual conflict" theories of the Stroop effect (e.g. Hock and Egeth, 1970): they provide no account of why congruent stimuli (word/colour) actually *facilitate* performance when compared to irrelevant-word controls. According to Biederman and Tsao the extra interference caused by the use of Kanji script arises out of competition for similar pattern-recognition capacities. From this assumption we might expect that response-congruence (or incongruence) would be wholly irrelevant. Therefore we can certainly predict that as far as the extra interference caused by logographic script is concerned, congruent words/colours should produce as much interference as incongruent. Indeed, it is difficult to see why the words even require to be colour names. If the interference that is specific to logographs is caused by their "configurational" mode of processing then it is unclear what role the particular referent of the logograph should have. Since Biederman and Tsao (1979, p. 130) specifically dissociate the logographic effect from "semantic and response interference", we might reasonably expect them to predict that ink-colour naming would be interfered with by any Kanji as compared to alphabetic word.

It can be understood from the foregoing that little more has been achieved than the insight that reading logographic script has more in common with picture perception than does reading alphabetic script. I have dwelt at length on the Biederman and Tsao study, not because I believe that it provides a penetrating insight into the essential differences between the processes underlying logographic and alphabetic reading but because it illustrates how the picture-processing simile might be pursued. I think this approach is more likely to provide some definition of the processes underlying reading than will the contrast of visual and phonetic errors in the free recall of words. Moreover, even the limitations of the Biederman and Tsao account are instructive.[17] These reveal how easy it is to arrive at conclusions such as that logographic processing involves "direct" access to meaning, is "configurational", resembles picture-processing and colour-processing, etc., and how difficult it is to move beyond them. Given the difficulty of refining this description of the nature of the processes, it is easy to see how seductive it might be to suspend the attempt to analyse the underlying processes and instead to treat similarities and differences in "geographical" terms, that is, in terms of cerebral localization. It is with this approach that Biederman and Isao close their paper. We turn to it next.

Script and cerebral lateralization

It has been suggested that there are two kinds of people in this world: those who believe that there are two kinds of people in the world, and those who do not. Certainly, dichotomies have always been popular in psychology, and by investing us with bilateral symmetry Nature has given the psychologist much sport with two-ness, whether it be binaural, binocular or due to the separation of the brain into two hemispheres.

Since Broca first noted in the mid-nineteenth century that speech pathology was associated with damage to the left cerebral hemisphere, attempts have been made to specify the aspects of linguistic performance that depend upon the left hemisphere. Reading, in its various senses, has not escaped this attention. It is not my intention, however, to review the vast, Ozymandias-like literature on laterality and reading; instead it is to focus only on the relationship between laterality and types of script.

First we must mention the traditional and extreme doctrine in which it is held that all reading competence is restricted exclusively to the left hemisphere, at least in right-handed individuals. This view has been advanced by Benson and Geschwind (1969) amongst others. If this were so, and if the "word-blindness" of the right hemisphere held for all scripts, there would, happily, be nothing further to review in this section. It is now understood, however, that the extreme position has been based on a false but prevalent equation of *reading* with *reading aloud.* Studies such as that of Smith (1966), who described the abilities of a patient after surgical removal of the left cerebral hemisphere, have revealed that a fair amount of *comprehension* of written language can be mediated by the right hemisphere. What the right hemisphere apparently cannot readily do is to derive sound from print (see, for example, Moscovitch, 1976). For some theorists this incapacity of the right hemisphere arises through the lack of speech production machinery in that hemisphere. This cannot be correct, because patients after removal of the left hemisphere show some preservation of speech (Smith, 1966). Furthermore, in some patients with aphasia occasioned by left hemisphere damage, blockading of the right hemisphere with drugs removes their residual speech abilities (Kinsbourne, 1971).

It seems likely, however, that the right hemisphere normally lacks the means for converting print to sound. For example, Zaidel (1978) has shown in a split-brain patient that the right hemisphere possesses the phonological competence to match pictured objects on the basis of their rhyming names but is unable to match words to pictures by rhyme. Such evidence has led many to accept the null hypothesis, as it were, that the right hemisphere cannot derive speech from print (see Coltheart, 1980, for a review). Certainly it seems safe to conclude that any such capacity on the part of the right hemisphere is very slight.

Given that the left hemisphere is specialized for processing the phonological reference of script and that logographs seem not to make immediate reference to phonology, it is of some interest to enquire into the existence of cerebral specialization for various forms of script. This question has usually been pursued by the use of the tachistocopic recognition task, which results in a measure of the duration of presentation that is required in order for a word to be correctly reported. Presentation of the word can then be made to either visual hemifield. The choice of hemifield is assumed to determine the cerebral hemisphere at which the information first arrives.

A general difficulty which attends the interpretation of such studies is the decision as to which components of the task were responsible for any laterality effect that is obtained. For this reason the naming–latency task is an inappropriate measure, because any effect obtained might have been due to hemispheric differences in the speed of access to articulatory production. On the other hand, a same–different word-matching task is inappropriate, because it allows the logical possibility that words be treated as non-linguistic shapes. Here it must be conceded that the usual tachistoscopic word recognition task, though extremely ancient, is not especially well understood, and to a certain extent laterality effects obtained with this task share the opacity of the task itself.

With alphabetic script it is fairly well established that a left hemisphere advantage obtains[18] (White, 1969). There are some failures to find a laterality effect, however, and it is not yet clear whether these can satisfactorily be explained away by the choice of task or procedure (see, e.g., Hardyck *et al.*, 1977).

Superior performance when presentation is to the left cerebral hemisphere has also been reliably obtained with the Japanese syllabic script, Kana (Hirata and Osaka, 1967; Sasanuma *et al.*, 1977; Endo *et al.*, 1978). This is to be expected, since Kana is entirely phonographic in its reference.

In contrast, the Japanese logographic script, Kanji, is generally more accurately recognized with presentation to the right hemisphere (Hatta, 1977) though a tendency in this direction failed to reach statistical significance in the study of Sasanuma *et al.* (1977). In the latter study, however, the logographic stimuli consisted of a pair of Kanji forming a nonsense word. The use of multiple characters appears to lead to unexpected effects, since Hatta (1978) found that multiple Kanji produced a left hemisphere advantage. A similar pattern of results has been obtained with Chinese readers. Tzeng *et al.* (1978) reported a right hemisphere advantage both for single Chinese characters that contained a phonetic component and those of purely pictographic origin. Similarly, Tzeng *et al* (1979) found a right hemisphere advantage for single Chinese characters, but this changed to a left hemisphere advantage when pairs of vertically arranged characters were used. A similar left hemisphere advantage for pairs of characters was obtained by Kershner and Gwan-Rong Jeng (1972).

These findings confront us with several theoretical choices between which we cannot yet adjudicate with assuredness. Probably the simplest view is one in which it is held that the difference in lateralization between logographs and phonographs is due to lateralization of the appropriate visual pattern-recognition machinery. The obvious difficulty for this view consists of the reversal of the logograph effect with multiple characters. One might attempt to deal with this difficulty by assuming that the right hemisphere system for processing logographs has a severe capacity limitation. We can then distinguish a number of theories which develop that assumption. An important question which divides these theoretical possibilities is whether multiple Kanji are analysed by the same (right hemisphere) system as single Kanji. To illustrate this division, let us consider two candidates chosen so as to exhibit the contrast.

What I shall call the "conservative" theory holds that initial pattern analysis favours phonographs presented to the left hemisphere and logographs presented to the right hemisphere, irrespective of the number of characters displayed. The right hemisphere system suffers capacity limitations and this limitation is subsequent to pattern analysis. Therefore, as the number of logographs presented is enlarged, the amount of information loss between pattern analysis and eventual report increases. (This might be because *report* is a left hemisphere function.) A pathological form of this sort of limitation has been postulated by Marshall (1976) to account for the greater impairment of Kanji reading in conduction aphasia. Marshall argued that the one-to-one mapping of characters on to response units in Kana serves to minimize the problem created by defective output organization. Kanji reading is more vulnerable to this disabiltiy, since the S–R mapping is less systematic. In accordance with this view, Yamadori and Ikumura (1975) found in a patient with conduction aphasia that Kanji reading was several impaired by increases in the syllabic length of the response, whereas Kana reading was not.

Our alternative to the conservative theory asserts that when more than one logograph is presented, pattern analysis is based on left hemisphere function. In this theory, which we shall call the "radical" theory, it is assumed that it is not the nature of the script but the nature of the entire task that determines hemispheric advantage. This appears to be the hypothesis guiding Tzeng *et al.* (1979) when they argue that recognition of a single Kanji is a "holistic" task, hence a right hemisphere speciality, whereas decipherment of a multiple-Kanji combination is an "analytical" task for which the left hemisphere is better suited.

A disadvantage of the comparison of performance on items presented to one or other visual hemifield is that there is no reason to accept a hemifield/hemisphere advantage as indicating that the ability to process that item is a *monopoly* of that hemisphere (though students of laterality seem frequently to be attracted to that inference). In principle, the clinical cases in which there is a total inability to perform certain simple tasks seem capable of supporting stronger inferences, but these pose a new set of interpretative problems of their own. We shall discuss these cases in the next section but we may anticipate somewhat by admitting to the present discussion a relatively simple clinical case. Sugishita *et al.* (1978) have reported the recognition performance for Kana and Kanji in three patients who had undergone surgical section of the splenium of the corpus callosum, thus partially isolating the two hemispheres. With left hemisphere presentation, reading of single Kanji and Kana was almost perfect, and this offers circumstantial support to the thesis that the right hemisphere does not have a monopoly on Kanji processing. When presentation was to the right hemisphere oral reading of both scripts was impaired, but that for Kana was more so. (Comprehension impairment was less severe but followed a similar pattern.)

One important feature of these results is that the normal right hemisphere advantage for single Kanji is not replicated. Indeed, for Patient 2 there is a marked left hemisphere advantage even with the comprehension test (word–picture matching). The authors interpret this as showing that whereas the right hemisphere is specialized for "configurational" processing (better Kanji than Kana performance by right hemisphere), the left hemisphere is at least as capable of such processing (better Kanji performance with left than right hemisphere presentation). However, it is also possible that a true superiority of the right hemisphere at Kanji detection is disguised by the fact that left hemisphere pattern analysis has access to a superior system of phonological recoding and that this confers some advantage even on the word–picture matching task used to assess comprehension.

Arabic numerals are the main logographic system used in English, but unlike Kanji they are not particularly visually distinct from the phonographic elements of the language. (For this reason it would be interesting to know whether those who characterize Kanji processing as "configurational" are prepared to extend this description to numbers. Certainly the picture processing simile used by Biederman and Tsao concerning Chinese logographs has its parallel in the work of Besner and Coltheart (1979) on arabic numerals.)

In a study of normals using numerals, Hirata and Osaka (1967) reported superior performance with right hemisphere tachistoscopic presentation. This finding is supported by the evidence on split-brain patients (Teng and Sperry, 1973), but a contrary result on normals has recently been reported by Besner *et al.* (in press).

One last form of script worth mentioning is the use of alphabetic script to form "words" from initial letters (e.g. FBI). Some of these words are in common usage and they have recently been adopted for a variety of experimental purposes (see Henderson, 1974). Those of particular interest are not the acronyms like NASA (nasah) in which normal phonographic translation is preserved, but the letter–name strings like FBI (eff bee eye) in which normal translation is eschewed. Despite the abnormality of the grapheme–phoneme mappings, it is arguable that such words remain phonographic and so perhaps it is not surprising to find reports of a left hemisphere advantage (Besner, personal communication). Besner found an interaction between the laterality effect and familiarity (e.g. FBI v. IBF). Familiarity had a negligible effect in right hemisphere presentations but a reliable effect in left hemisphere presentations. Even for unfamiliar letter strings, however, there was a marked left hemisphere advantage.

Let us attempt now to summarize what has been learned from experiments using presentation to either visual hemifield. The data can best be organized by assessing them against the general hypothesis that the left hemisphere is specialized for the processing of phonographic script and the right hemisphere for logographic script, and that these differences are due neither to superficial aspects of the visual design of the script nor to the semantic reference of the stimuli but instead to the nature of the script as a code (cf. Coltheart, 1980).

The findings of a left hemisphere advantage for phonographic script, whether alphabetic or syllabic, is reasonably secure. It is a less simple matter to decide at what depth of processing the left hemisphere advantage is located. There is some evidence that the magnitude of the left hemisphere advantage is determined by quite superficial aspects of the spatial design of the stimuli. Young *et al.* (1980) have claimed that very large stimuli show no asymmetry of report accuracy, a claim disputed by Besner *et al.* (in press). Bryden and Allard (1976) have reported a reversal of the left hemisphere advantage when a difficult typeface is used.

There is some evidence that laterality is also dependent on semantics. In quite a large number of studies of tachistoscopic report (e.g. Ellis and Shepherd, 1974; Marcel and Patterson, 1978) and lexical decision RT (e.g. Day, 1977) the left hemisphere advantage has been abolished for high imageability words.

Even when there is reason to suppose that the left hemisphere advantage is due to the phonological reference of alphabetic script, it is not always clear that it is the translation of script into speech that gives rise to the advantage rather than, say, the process of retrieving or synthesizing phonology. It is notable that the left hemisphere advantage is generally larger for pseudowords (Young *et al.*, 1980). For such reasons, it may be wiser to conclude that it is the nature of the task rather than the linguistic characteristics of the alphabet that determine hemisphere asymmetry of performance.

The evidence for a reversed (right hemisphere) advantage for logographic scripts is even less secure. The major difficulty that we have noted is that multiple logographs seem to yield a left-hemisphere advantage, and this holds even for pairs of logographs that constitute a word (thus diminishing the attractiveness of the argument that multiple symbols introduce an extraneous memory component to the task). Moreover, there is little relevant evidence on arabic numerals. This is especially unfortunate because a right hemisphere advatage for numerals in alphabetic readers would, if obtained, greatly strengthen the argument that it is the nature of the script that induces hemispheric advantages.

Before closing this account of laterality effects as a function of type of script, it is worth considering two general points about the nature of the arguments. The first is that the mechanism relating hemispheric specialization and presentation locus (visual hemifield) effects is not at all well understood. Some authors appear to accept the inference linking one to the other as not requiring justification. However, in normal subjects when there is unimpaired communication between the hemispheres it is generally assumed that presentation locus effects are caused by loss of information during transfer. (Reaction time effects may either by explicable in terms of information loss or in terms of transmission time.) A curious feature of the extensive literature of laterality effects is the general lack of hesitancy at assuming so gross an inefficiency in the design of brains.

The second point can be summarized in the following question. What is added to our understanding of the way in which scripts are processed by the demonstration of hemifield-of-presentation effects? I think the answer must be: so far, very little. It could be argued that hemifield effects provide further support for the supposition that certain processes are similar, say, picture perception and Kanji recognition. But against this claim should be set the fact that we do not yet know what aspect of Kanji recognition gives rise to the right hemisphere advantage. In this context, the reversal of the effect with multiple Kanji cannot be ignored. Furthermore, it is worth distinguishing between the assertion that two activities are favoured by the same hemisphere and the assertion that they share important processing characteristics. Although we can only distinguish between two hemispheres, it is to be hoped that rather finer distinctions between types of process can be arrived at. Again, even if we granted that the "similarity" has been established between the processing of pictures and logographs, how would this help? We don't understand picture perception either. On the whole, it seems to me that the greatest import of the laterality effects lies in two directions. One points to the mundane fact that we may understand a further source of variance in our data. The other indicates the objective of a fruitful convergence between studies of normal and brain-injured reading.

On the other hand, there are difficulties with the approach based on laterality effects. Perhaps the most general is the insidious presumption that the tangible twoness of the hemispheres confers an extra solidity upon the theoretical dichotomies that have become associated with that silent, anatomical fact. This tacit assumption is the more obviously false when we have regard to the extreme vagueness which typifies information-processing descriptions of the specialization of the hemisphere, replete as they often are with ill-defined contrasts such as "analytical" v. "holistic" and "sequential" v. "intuitive".

8.2 SCRIPT-SPECIFIC IMPAIRMENTS IN BRAIN DAMAGE

The contrast between Kanji logographs and the Kana syllabary in Japanese has been used to study reading disorders consequent upon brain damage. Many aphasic patients show major impairment in handling either script. However, recently there has accumulated evidence of reading difficulties in which one script suffers much less than the other. In these cases of selective impairment, Kanji sparing (i.e. much greater impairment of performance with Kana) occurs more commonly than Kana sparing.

It is unfortunate that so much of the literature on script-specific impairment is restricted to the Japanese example. Although Japanese presents the clearest contrast between logographic and phonographic elements within a single language, the comparison is complicated by other factors. Kana is learned first by the child. Also, in adult reading the Hiragana syllabary is largely restricted to the writing of grammatical function words, the Katakana syllabary to foreign borrowings and Kanji to content words. Attempts have been made to control for some of these factors but such controls must remain imperfect.

To a limited extent other script comparisons have been made. The earliest is undoubtedly the observation of number sparing (arabic numerals) in patients whose reading of alphabetic script is highly impaired. Unfortunately, the significance of this finding with respect to the study of scripts generally escaped early workers, and many of the observations are unsystematic.

Another possible basis for comparison is present in bilingual subjects whose competence extends across more than one form of script. This comparison is of course complicated by other factors that have to do with bilingualism, but it is free from the confounding of script type with semantic and syntactic factors that generally occurs in within-language comparisons.

Logograph sparing

Déjerine, one of the most influential of the nineteenth-century students of dyslexia, distinguished a syndrome which he called "pure alexia" and which he held to involve a divorce of "the centre for visual images of letters" from the centre serving their verbal interpretation (Déjerine, 1891). He remarked that in such cases the ability to read numerals generally survived despite severe impairment of other reading. This he held to be due to the fact that number reading was a symbolic rather than a verbal matter.

These observations were extended by Hinshelwood (1899), who described five cases in which some word naming was preserved. These patients could not name the individual letters, either singly or in a word that they have read, yet they were able to read numbers quite successfully. Hinshelwood's interpretation of the partial independence of performance with words, letters and numbers was that each of these abilities depended on a separate brain centre.

Subsequent reports of number sparing in cases where reading of alphabetic material is severely impaired have been quite common (see, for example, Benson and Geschwind, 1969; Hécaen and Kremin, 1976), but these reports often lack sufficient detail to permit a scientific evaluation, and the number sparing coexists with a bewilderingly variable pattern of other disabilities. The most detailed results are probably those presented by Hécaen and Kremin (1976, pp. 305–308) for six "alexic" patients. One patient (C.L.I.) was virtually unable to perform any of the reading tests, either of oral reading or visual recognition. His only successes were at reading aloud arabic numerals and at recognizing, but not naming, single letters. In the four remaining patients for whom the comparison can be made, naming of arabic numbers was much more successful than of alphabetically written numbers. This observation is potentially interesting because it allows the comparison of scripts with semantic and syntactic factors controlled. Furthermore, the patients were French and therefore the alphabetic numbers lacked the orthographic irregularity which bedevils this comparison in English (e.g. *one*, *two*, *four*). However, the force of the comparison is greatly weakened by the fact that reading of isolated letters was almost as good as that of arabic numerals, so that we cannot distinguish between the graphemic and the logographic attributes of the numerals.

Turning to Kanji sparing in cases where the reading of Kana is greatly impaired, we find an early report by Asayama (1914, cited in Lyman *et al.*, 1938). A single case is described in which all oral reading is severely impaired. Comprehension of Kanji is, however, much superior to that of Kana. A similar superiority is manifest in the writing of Kanji. Asayama's interpretation is that Kanji comprehension, unlike Kana, does not depend upon phonological recoding and therefore survives damage to this recoding system. This view has endured to the present day without substantial revision.

More recently, Kanji sparing has been reported by Sasanuma and her associates in a number of papers (Sasanuma and Fujimura, 1971; Sasanuma, 1975, 1980) and by Yamadori (1975). In surveying test results for 378 aphasic patients, Sasanuma (1975) distinguishes between two types of patient who exhibit Kanji sparing. One type displays the symptoms of Broca's aphasia, having very hesitant speech. There is evidence in both their speech and writing of an inability to produce the grammatic functors for which Kana script is reserved in adult writing. The second type of patient possesses fluent speech and usually displays symptoms of Wernicke's aphasia. Such patients are less numerous and the script effect is less consistent.

Yamadori (1975) presents a detailed description of a single case. When presented with conventional mixed script the patient would read aloud only those words rendered in Kanji. Kana characters presented alone could rarely be read and the patient was uncertain even of the infrequent correct response. In contrast, Kanji characters presented alone were often named confidently and accurately. Number reading was very poor, however, suggesting that there was no general sparing of logographs. No Kana could be written and only "Japan" and the patient's name could be written in Kanji.

Phonograph sparing

According to Sasanuma's (1975) survey, cases of selective impairment of Kanji reading are much rarer than the converse impairment. Sasanuma reports but a single case, noting its similarity to what Imura (1963) had called "semantic-form aphasia". The patient could write 100% of Kana characters to dictation but only 20% of Kanji. There is some evidence that where Kanji could be written, they were treated as phonographic signs and phonetic confusions were often made.

Some idea of this strategy can be gathered in the English example: "be-4 he 8 dinner". An important feature of the Kana sparing was that it only involved translation between print and sound. There was no *comprehension* of Kana script. In a fuller report of this case, Sasanuma and Monoi (1975) point out that some comprehension of arabic numerals was present. More recently Sasanuma (1980) has reported on a further patient (K.K.) who could read aloud almost all Kana words but less than half Kanji words.

A different sort of evidence is presented in a classic report by Lyman *et al.* (1938) in which the scripts concerned belonged to different languages. Their patient was a Chinese who had been fluent in Chinese and English. On admission to hospital he was found to have fluent speech and comprehension in both languages. Presented with simple reading material in Chinese script he could only read two characters, but he could cope well with non-Chinese logographs such as numerals and £ signs. He could read 19 out of 20 English words, though sometimes a successful reading was based on an abnormal "spelling-out" strategy of the sort found in surface or spelling dyslexia. After operation for the removal of a massive occipitoparietal tumour in the left hemisphere, the patient's reading was retested. Both Chinese and English had improved, Chinese rather more so, but oral reading and comprehension were both still very much better in English. When having difficulty, the patient's strategy with English was to spell out the word and in Chinese to trace out the outline of the character.

The Grand Dichotomy

In Chapters 5 and 6 we saw that theorizing about the translation of print into sound in English has been dominated by a dichotomy. As expressed in the dual process theory, this dichotomy was between two methods of assigning pronunciations and meanings. One of these methods was held to involve direct, visual access to the lexicon and the other was held to involve reference to a corpus of rules in order to translate graphemes into phonemes, with the resultant pronunciation used to gain access to lexical meanings. Both these methods were held to be applicable to the oral reading of orthographically regular English words. In advocating this dual process view, theorists often appealed to two further dichotomies: that between orthographically regular and irregular words, and that between the two syndromes of acquired dyslexia known as surface dyslexia and deep dyslexia. In Chapter 6, I gave my reasons for declining to accept the dichotomous view of the underlying processing options and we shall not dwell on these further.

In this chapter we have concentrated on a similar-sounding dichotomy formulated at another level, that between scripts which are, broadly speaking, phonographic (alphabets and syllabaries) and those that are logographic (or pictographic). A notable feature of the way in which this dichotomy has been advanced is that it has generally ignored the finer distinction in alphabetic script between regular and irregular words. This is at least partly due to a concentration of attention on the relatively clear dichotomy between logographs and syllabographs in Japanese. So far, it does not seem to have occurred to a dual process theorist to compare, say, the lateralization of reading for regular and irregular English words. This raises the question of how far the notion of a quasi-logographic processing option for English can be pushed.

We shall consider now three successive approximations to a Dichotomizing Principle. The first dichotomy is based on the linguistic classification of scripts. The second dichotomy is based upon a process distinction, that between direct lexical access and the "phonological route". The third dichotomy is embodied in the two hemispheres of the brain.

Table 12 shows the dichotomy based on the classification of scripts into two types: pleremic scripts, in which the individual grapheme expresses an element of meaning, and cenemic scripts, in which the graphemes are semantically empty but generally make some sort of reference to speech sounds (see Chapter 1 for a fuller discussion).

Table 12 A linguistically grounded dichotomy, based on whether the graphemes of a script are semantically informed (pleremic) or empty (cenemic)

	Pleremic	Cenemic
Types of script	Logographic and pictographic	Syllabic and alphabetic
Examples	Kanji Arabic numerals Chinese	Kana Hangul English
Selective impairment	Surface dyslexia?	Deep dyslexia?
Locus of presentation effect	Right-hemisphere superiority	Left-hemisphere superiority
Processing mode	"Configurational" "Pictorial" "Visual"	"Rule-based" "Phonological"

As an organizing principle, the classification of scripts is, by itself, inadequate. Consider, for example, the relationship between type of script and hemispheric specialization. We have seen that the evidence here is equivocal and that lateralization depends on visual and semantic features of written language as well as the type of script. Moreover, it is probable that the nature of the experimental task matters at least as much as the linguistic classification of the script.

There are other difficulties, too. English may be treated in various ways and it is certainly clear that the reading of some sorts of English words is fairly well-preserved in deep dyslexia.

Let us turn, then, to a dichotomy that is motivated by information processing considerations. The dichotomy illustrated in Table 13 is an extension of that proposed in dual process theory and as such is vulnerable to the criticisms of

Table 13 A dichotomy of information-processing routes, generalizing the dual process theory of English reading

	Direct lexical route	Phonological route
Applicable to	Irregular English Regular English Arabic numerals Kanji	Pseudowords Regular English Kana
Selective impairment	Surface dyslexia?	Deep dyslexia?
Locus of presentation effect	Right-hemisphere superiority	Left-hemisphere superiority

dual process theory considered in Chapters 5 and 6. On the other hand, the distinction between English read by direct and by phonological routes gives a somewhat better fit than the linguistic classification to the disability manifest in deep dyslexia and, more especially, phonological dyslexia, emphasizing, as it does, the difficulty with reading of pseudowords. Moreover, the restriction of pseudowords to the phonological route coheres with the findings of a larger left hemisphere advantage for these items.

However, the left column hangs together less well. Is reading of English words by the direct route like reading of numerals and Kanji? As we shall see in Chapters 9 and 10, there are good reasons for believing that the identification of English words is mediated by an abstract graphemic code. Moreover, in deep dyslexia patients can read words in which the graphemes are presented in unfamiliar arrangements (vertical listing; mixed letter-case), thereby refuting the notion that their alphabetic reading treats the entire word as an integral sign (Saffran, 1980).

Irregular words have access to the direct route only. Does this mean that they should exhibit a right hemisphere advantage? Should they also behave more like logographs? These implications are not, I think, congenial.

In Table 14 we can see the dichotomy taking a form that begins to resemble some current theories of deep dyslexia (e.g. Coltheart, 1980; Saffran *et al.*, 1980). This dichotomy is the more seductive because its base is physical, tangible, so clearly located in the design of the contents of the skull.

As a story about deep dyslexia it reads well. Deep dyslexia is invariably associated with extensive damage to the left hemisphere. The oral reading which

Table 14 A tangible dichotomy, based on the specialization of the two cerebral hemispheres

	Left hemisphere	Right hemisphere
Specialized for	All English words English pseudowords	Concrete English words
		Arabic numerals
	Kana	Kanji
Selective impairment	Deep dyslexia	?
Processing mode	?	Direct (nonphonological) access

survives is largely restricted to concrete words. Number sparing is common. It has been suggested that in Japanese patients the equivalent syndrome involves Kanji sparing with a severe disability in handling Kana. Moreover, oral reading appears to involve direct access to the lexicon accompanied by retrieval of whole-word phonology, if only because of the almost total inability to read pseudowords. For these reasons Coltheart (1980) has argued that reading in deep dyslexia involves direct access to a right hemisphere lexicon which contains entries for concrete contentives. (Coltheart further assumes that semantic information retrieved from this lexicon is transmitted to the damaged left hemisphere where it is used to access whole-word phonology in the left-hemisphere lexicon.)

However, this scheme is not without attendant difficulties. Once again we are faced with the unreliability of the evidence for a right hemisphere advantage in logograph reading. Moreover, there is little evidence that different types of logographic script suffer impairment in a correlated fashion. We find a report by Yamadori (1975) of a Japanese patient who showed a dissociation of Kanji and Kana reading with Kana selectively impaired. However, the ability to read numerals was also very poor. Conversely, in the case reported by Sasanuma and Monoi (1975), selective impairment of Kanji is accompanied by good performance at reading numerals. Moreover, Lyman *et al.* (1938) in their report of the bilingual patient whose reading of Chinese was so much worse than English, state that he would often read strings of numbers and fractions with ease. None of these studies offers much encouragement to the view that selective impairment of scripts adheres consistently to the pleremic–cenemic dichotomy.

Concerning the putative association between the right-hemisphere and Kanji processing there are also difficulties. For instance, it is not easy to explain why in the patients M.U. (Sasanuma and Monoi, 1975) and K.K. (Sasanuma, 1980) *left* hemisphere damage should result in selective impairment of Kanji. Nor is it easy to see why there are not reports (as far as I know) of Japanese patients with dyslexia consequent upon right hemisphere brain damage.

Conclusion

There are almost certainly more functional distinctions to be made between types of script than are dreamt of in the Grand Dichotomy and predicted by dual process theory. Digits resemble Kana and alphabetic graphemes in being simple forms composed of a few strokes. Kanji, and the Chinese characters from which they derive, consist of complex and distinctive shapes. One consequence of this is that Oriental logographs have their status as script defined at first glance in a way that is probably not true of arabic numerals (but see Jonides and Gleitman, 1972).

A different sort of distinction concerns the manner in which the apprentice reader is taught to regard a script. Chinese children are taught to regard the logographic characters as pictures. Another feature of the teaching of Chinese script is that the tasks of learning to read and to write seem to be brought together much more closely than they are in learning to read alphabetic languages. This accords with the prevalence of character-sketching gestures in Chinese conversation and in Chinese dyslexics when struggling with a word. In an often quoted passage, the Chinese linguist Wang (1973) has observed that: "To a Chinese the character for 'horse' means *horse* with no mediation through the sound /ma/. The image is so vivid that one can almost sense an abstract figure galloping across the page." The pictographic attitude to logographs is illustrated by the fondness of the Japanese for visual puns based on the Kanji characters. Martin (1972) provides a delightful example of a Japanese whose family name could also mean "branchless" and who therefore took to writing it using the Kanji for "tree" without the branching downstrokes on either side of the character.

Neither the pictorial coding of the graphemes nor the close association between recognition and production applies to the teaching of arabic numerals, at least in English. However, the teaching of reading in English does involve a notorious division between look–say methods and phonics. Marcel (1978) has cited some unpublished data by Alegria to the effect that the method of teaching alphabetic reading may have short term consequences for the child's phonological awareness; however, it is very doubtful whether the difference between methods has any long term consequences for the reader's manner of treating the script. Moreover, the look–say method, despite its disregarding the phonographic analyticity of alphabetic script, does not really seem to resemble the teaching of reading in Chinese. It is unclear, therefore, to what extent differences in the reader's treatment of scripts is due to the formal properties of the script as a system of representation or due to the way in which competence with a script is acquired and supported. "Reading," as Marcel (1978) has observed, "is essentially an epistemological matter."

8.3 SCRIPTS AND LITERACY

A major cause of recent interest in the ease of acquisition of the various types of script has been a series of claims that in Japanese the incidence of reading difficulty is exceptionally low and that this is due to the ease of acquisition of the syllabary early in the child's schooling (Makita, 1968; Muraishi, 1972; Sakamoto and Makita, 1973; Muraishi, 1976). Indeed, Sakamoto and Makita have reported that many Japanese children teach themselves the syllabary before entering school.

The other syllabary which has attracted most comment in the context of literacy is the one invented by Sequoya for the Cherokee Indian language. Walker (1969) makes a number of informal observations about the strikingly high literacy level prevalent among Cherokee in the early nineteenth century. However, the influence of cultural factors is evident in their recent severe decline in literacy (Halle, 1972).

A different sort of claim on behalf of syllabic script has been made by Gleitman and Rozin (1973; Rozin and Gleitman, 1977). They have reported that first grade children in a deprived area can acquire a limited syllabary for English with little difficulty. The implications of this demonstration are, however, difficult to evaluate in the absence of a large number of necessary controls. Their Syllabary Curriculum is probably highly motivating, independent of the formal structure of the scripts employed. As they observe: "a primary emphasis of the syllabic stage of training is the fun of reading" (Rozin and Gleitman, 1977, p. 119). Rozin and Gleitman also present a number of other reasons for caution in interpreting this study (Rozin and Gleitman, 1977, pp. 124–130). Certainly there seems to be no reason to accept that it is the formal nature of the script which confers any advantage to the program. As Glushko (1980) and Marcel (1978) have observed, the major insight embodied in the Rozin and Gleitman program is that learning to read involves the acquisition of a more general understanding of script-as-representation. To this end, the orthographic eclecticism of the program together within its evolutionary sequencing (pictograph → logograph → syllabary → alphabet) may be more important than the nature of the representation used at a particular stage.

It is unfortunate that the evidence in favour of the syllabary rests so much on Japanese Kana. Makita (1968), in first drawing attention to the high rate of literacy in Japan, mentioned many cultural factors that might be operative in addition to scriptal factors. Another factor generally ignored is the extremely simple syllabic structure of spoken Japanese (see Chapter 1). Not only does this allow an economical representation of the spoken language, it may also lead to earlier development of an explicit knowledge of phonological segments (see, Muraishi, 1976). In contrast to Japanese, Korean has a more complex syllabic structure with V, CV, VC, CVC, and CVCC syllables. The syllabary copes with this complexity by being analytical: each syllabic sign is constructed out of alphabet elements. Given this alphabetic base, Korean would seem to require a more analytic insight into phonological segmentation. It would therefore be interesting to compare its ease of acquisition with Kana, but apart from the statement by Taylor (1980) that there are virtually no disabled readers in the "normal" population in Korea, I have been unable to discover any discussion of Korean literacy.

One question which does not seem to have been asked, but to which the answer is in any case obscured by the usual cross-cultural complications, is whether the introduction to reading via Kana influences the rate of acquisition of Kanji logographs when compared to reading acquisition in Chinese. Certainly the Chinese curriculum seems to demand a more rapid acquisition of logographs in the first few years of schooling.

It is generally conceded that the memory demands made by an arbitrary logography such as Chinese and its Japanese and Korean derivatives lead to great difficulty of acquisition. However, a moment's reflection reveals the emptiness of any attempt at a direct comparison of the ease of acquisition of logographic and phonographic scripts. In simplified terms, the problem with a logography is the acquisition of a visual "vocabulary", whereas the problem with a phonography is better understood as one of understanding a principle of representation. It is this transparency of the representational principle in logography, and *a fortiori* in pictography, which induced Gleitman and Rozin to use it to introduce the concept of reading.

It is notoriously difficult to evaluate the early competence which can develop in the use of a logography. These difficulties are encapsulated in the example of chimpanzees, such as Sarah, who have learned to communicate by means of logographic tokens (Premack, 1976). Whatever underlies such performance, it is not generally suggested that Sarah is engaged in "reading". Velletri-Glass *et al.* (1973) and Baker *et al.* (1975) have extended this type of communication to severely aphasic patients who lack almost all conventional linguistic competence. There seems no more reason to describe their performance as "reading" than that of the chimpanzees. On the other hand Rozin *et al.* (1971) boldly describe their backward readers who have learned to use a limited set of logographs to represent English words as "reading".

It is unfortunate that the most carefully controlled cross-language comparisons of reading acquisition have usually been restricted to alphabetic script (Thorndike, 1973; Downing, 1973; Gibson and Levin, 1975). Interest in the nature of the writing system has been concentrated on the "regularity" of grapheme–phoneme correspondences. The results of these comparisons are, however, highly inconclusive. As Gibson and Levin (1975, p. 531) sum up the state of knowledge:

It is not clear to what extent the orthographies of languages affect the acquisition or level of reading achievement. The lack of standardized reading tests in most countries, the variations in the total time spent on reading, and the variety of instructional methods used make valid comparisons difficult. However, it is clear that reading failures do occur even in countries with regular orthographies. It is also apparent that there is little connection between the phonetic regularity of correspondence in a language's orthography and the method by which reading is taught.

Part Three

Visual Word Recognition

Introduction

The decision as to the overall organization of this part of the book has not been easy. A superficial survey of the literature on word recognition reveals at least two sorts of classifications that exist at a fairly atheoretical level. Probably the most boring of these is that based on a division into experimental tasks. The classic task in this area has always been the tachistoscopic recognition threshold task, or one of its threshold-yielding variants. With the popularization of reaction-time (RT) measures of performance in the 1960s, due to the work of Neisser, Sternberg, Posner and others, binary classification RT came to be of interest in a range of word-processing tasks, such as the search of word lists for a word-target, the search of a word for a letter-target and, most notably, the same–different comparison of words.

At first there was probably no clearly discernible division between the issues to which these different measures were addressed. Students of the threshold tasks may have been encouraged by a belief that they were investigating the basic limits on the capacity of the system for the uptake of information. Adherents of the RT paradigms, on the other hand, were more impressed by the tractability of chronometric data.

At this level of discourse, the 1970s were distinguished by at least two developments. One was the appearance of certain new tasks, such as the lexical decision task. In this case, invention consisted in the discovery of another sort of question which the subject could be asked about a stimulus word. Such discoveries can generate enormous amounts of research. This happens because of the acceptance, often implicit, of theories that link the task to some general set of conceptual issues. Thus, measurement of the speed with which subjects could verify such properties as the yellowness of canaries became an exceedingly popular enterprise as soon as it came to be supposed that such measures allowed us to make inferences about the structure of our knowledge of the world. In much the same way, measuring the speed with which subjects could decide that *mantiness* is not a word owed its popularity to the belief that such measures could be brought to bear on the question of how our mental dictionary is organized.

Despite the development of some new tasks, it has often seemed to me that the attribute of contemporary experimentation that would most astonish the nineteenth-century cognitive psychologist is that the basic experimental tasks remain much the same. It might have been supposed, by analogy with other sciences, that new and more penetrating insights would depend upon the development of totally new instruments of measurement, a sort of cognitive psychology equivalent of single-cell recording. Such expectations are doomed to disappointment. The prevalent experimental tasks that support the study of word recognition remain ones like asking the subject what he saw in a brief glimpse at the stimulus.

I am inclined to believe that the most significant historical development is in the formulation of theoretical possibilities. It is more than a trivial assertion that contemporary information-processing theories are formulated in a language which is capable of expressing finer distinctions, as well as more complicated states of affairs. An important consequence of this is that the inferences linking task performance to theory have become less straightforward. Experiments consist less in demonstrations and more in *arguments*. This leads me to the second development at the experimental level, one of more import than the development of new paradigms: the development of a finer control over the experimental tasks. A particularly striking illustration of this is to be found in the investigation of the word superiority effect (see Section 9.2 for a fuller discussion). It has become fashionable to present this effect as if it were an argument made first by Cattell in 1886 and then rediscovered in essentially the same form by Reicher and Wheeler at the end of the 1960s (see, for example Theois and Muise, 1976). This is a sloppy misconception. Cattell's original experiments permitted, at best, the rejection of one, rather uninteresting theory, that of serial letter processing as a basis for word identification. The lack of experimental controls and selective manipulations in his classic studies meant that the results placed few constraints upon the possible interpretations of the underlying mental processes. Cattell's own particular interpretation is vague, unjustified, and almost certainly false. What has happened between then and now, however, should not be conceived of as a purely methodological advance, amounting to the addition of a few experimental controls. Instead, the new development is better understood as a consequence of the capacity of the information-processing theoretical language to represent finer distinctions between possible mental operations. It is an important truism that methodological controls are preceded logically and psychologically by novel conceptions of the psychological processes that might be operating. In order, for example, to embark upon attempts to control for various sorts of guessing in a recognition task, one must have some conception of the sorts of cues that might be available to the subject in the situation. These may sometimes turn out to be extremely subtle, and to envisage their employment by the subject we must be able to conceive of the subjects' possession of highly organized and accessible knowledge about the structure of his world.

From the foregoing, it should be evident that in research on word perception the experimental task is a general purpose tool. A classification of tasks holds little information about the evolution of theory. Furthermore, there are other reasons for declining to organize our discussion around types of measurement. Not the least of these is the desire to avoid encouragement of that approach which Tulving and Madigan (1970) have called "the functional autonomy of methods". Another reason for not regarding the boundaries between types of task as marking out theoretical domains is that distinctions which from the procedural viewpoint seem unsubstantial may nevertheless be crucial for purposes of theoretical interpretation. A simple example of such a distinction is that between the word-naming RT task and the tachistoscopic word-recognition task. In the first, the time taken to initiate naming of a word is measured from its display onset. In the second, the duration of display necessary for a subject to be able to name the displayed word is measured. In a superficial examination these tasks might both appear to be straightforward measures of the detectability of a word. Certainly, early experimentalists, such as J. M. Cattell used the two tasks as if interchangeable for this purpose. Moreover, this line of thought is encouraged by the practice, perhaps most common in the clinical literature, of referring to both tasks indifferently as "word recognition" tasks. However, for the present purposes the word-naming RT task is discussed almost exclusively as it bears upon the process of translating print into sound. So this apparently minor procedural difference between the tasks results in their treatment in quite distinct (though overlapping) theoretical contexts.

A final reason for declining to organize our discussion in accordance with the boundaries between tasks is that an important recent development has been the reinterpretation of what I have elsewhere called "rules for mapping theory onto experimental paradigms" (Henderson, 1977, p. 63). Perhaps the most notable of these developments has been the shift from regarding "simple" detection tasks as indices of the rate of uptake of information in favour of regarding them as indices of the recoverability of the products of encoding stages. This distinction is brought out in Allport's (1979) discussion of the ambiguity of words like "recognition" and "perception", which refer both to the process of encoding information and to the sensory experience, or at least the ability to report it.

Closely allied to the task-based taxonomy is the principle of organization that centres round "effects". At the most atheoretical level these consist of what Estes (1979) has called "new systematic variables", such as orthographic regularity, letter positional frequency, and the like. In some cases these variables came to be investigated due to some quite specific theoretical prediction. The regularity of spelling–sound correspondences is such a variable. In other cases the existence of an effect provoked an interest independent of particular theory.

This held, perhaps, for the word frequency effect and for the effect of letter positional frequency.

In still other cases, effects that became the focus of interest could not be adequately summarized as the discovery of a new variable. Often these really constitute whole collections of phenomena, as is the case with word superiority effects or subliminal perception effects. In these particular cases a major source of interest was the challenge to some traditional, and often rather general, way of regarding cognition. The contrast between such effects and effects which consist in the discovery of new variables is clearly evident in the example of the word superiority effect, since the demonstration of that phenomenon provoked a volume of research addressed to the question of what exactly the operative variables were. One consequence of this has been that effects can be construed in quite different theoretical contexts from one time to another.

In dividing material between the following four chapters I have centred each chapter on a general theoretical idea. The central idea in Chapters 9 and 10 is one which in itself is rather uncontroversial: the idea of visual pattern analysis. Chapter 9 focuses on the idea that words are perceived "as a whole", and Chapter 10 pursues the alternative notion that word identification is contingent on a preliminary analysis at the graphemic level. Chapter 11 deals with a less easily defined collection of ideas about attention and conscious awareness in the perception of words. What is possibly controversial here is not the heading itself, though this has not been traditionally regarded as "an area of research on word recognition", but my allocation of studies to this domain. This allocation includes studies which certainly purport to be concerned with the substance of the earlier chapters. Finally, Chapter 12 centres upon the concept of a mental dictionary or lexicon. To some extent it might be true to say that the division between the topics of Chapters 10 and 12 correspond to distinctions between processing stages, and that Chapter 11 deals with later-coming or more central processes. But this distinction holds only loosely. It is equally the case that some of the approaches centring on the concept of a visual lexicon do so out of a preference for a fairly abstract level of treatment of word recognition. This is true, for instance, of approaches that make use of the "logogen" concept (Morton, 1979). It is also true of certain statistical approaches to perceptual theory, such as that of Broadbent (1971), in which the treatment of word recognition takes place under the heading "Perception of one out of many multi-dimensional stimuli".

Chapter 9

Words Considered as Visual Patterns

9.1 ELEMENTARY FEATURE ANALYSIS

Surprisingly little is known about the initial stages of analysis of letters or words; indeed the problem has attracted remarkably little attention. One possible reason is that many students of word recognition have tacitly accepted a distinctive feature theory for letter and word recognition in which the elementary features are fragments of contour. It is possible to suggest several grounds for this tacit commitment.

One line of reasoning stems from analogy with the successful application of critical feature theory to the analysis of speech sounds (Jacobson *et al.*,1961). Another stems from the amazingly widespread belief that neurophysiological investigations of single-cell analysers have "shown" that the basic constituents of perceptual analysis are lines and angles.

One of the difficulties here is that writers frequently seem to have mistaken the vague assertion that letters are recognized by "feature analysis" for a commitment to a particular theory. A typical instance can be found in Massaro and Schmuller's (1975) discussion of letter confusion data. Having reviewed evidence that letter similarity impairs discrimination and that errors resemble correct responses, Massaro and Schmuller conclude that these studies "demonstrate that visual features of letters are employed in letter recognition" (1975, p. 212). The trouble with this conclusion is not that it is wrong but that it appears to be saying more than it really does. To be sure, our intuitions about "similarity" amongst letters are given substance in these discrimination experiments. In a loose sense, we may therefore speak of letters as "sharing features". But this by no means entails the conclusion that there exists a fixed set of physical entities like portions of contour on which discrimination is based.

A rather subtle consideration which may have led theorists to favour the distinctive-features approach is mentioned by Estes (1979), who points out that the concept of critical features provides the basis for a relatively simple hierarchical model in which the same sort of filtering and combinatorial operations occur at each level—features, letter, word, and so on.

In conclusion, there has so far been little progress in our understanding of elementary feature analysis in letter and word recognition. Most research has been concentrated on distinctive feature theory, often with the limited objective of compiling a feature list to account for confusions obtained with a single typeface. Even in this limited exercise, the proposed lists have often been less predictive than subjects' intuitive judgements of similarity among letters (Holbrook, 1975). Alternatives to the traditional distinctive-features approaches exist; two of the more recent are the propositional description of form (Oden, 1979) and the spatial-frequency description of form (see, for example, Kinchla, 1977), but these alternative formulations have not yet been subjected to sufficiently detailed examination to allow an evaluation of their promise. Syntactic and spatial-frequency approaches are probably best interpreted as offering new proposals about the nature of the features used rather than about the way these features define perceptual objects. An alternative to the distinctive-features approach to the definition problem has been proposed by Posner (1969), who advanced the notion of *prototypes*. These are a theoretical device designed to deal with the problem of shape constancy. Possible forms that a letter might take are seen as giving rise to distributions of values along a set of featural dimensions. A prototype letter represents the means of these various distributions. Again, the theory is not adequately worked out in detail. Its interest lies not in any assertion it makes about the nature of the features used in letter recognition but lies instead in the view taken of the process of using the features for perceptual decision making.

The general neglect of the elementary level of pattern-analysis in word recognition has, one might speculate, at least two causes. One is the tacit acceptance of a distinctive features theory combined with an attitude that the description of a particular list of proposed features is a mere housekeeping exercise which need not detain us. This sort of indifference to the problem of embodying hypotheses in a working model has perhaps characterized psychological theorizing about perception. The other cause of neglect is the assumption that the first stage of word recognition consists in the use of feature analysis to assign letter identities to the perceptual array. The important point here is that if this assumption holds true, we can shelve the problem of elementary feature analysis and still make progress in understanding word recognition by dealing with later and more tractable stages. That is, the first "stage" can be subtracted in theoretical analysis without violating the nature of the entire perceptual process. The letter-mediation assumption is the one I shall make in what follows, but it is important to remember that it *is* an assumption and that it is neither universally conceded nor strongly substantiated.

Let me close this passage with an observation on the nature of letters as visual patterns. Written language is composed of invented patterns. This invests their design with an arbitrariness which does not hold even for spoken forms.

Although there is a sense in which we can speak of the speech signal as an invention, the nature of the signal is, as we have seen, highly constrained by the articulatory production machinery. This is not true of the production of print (though it may well be so for handwriting). Now, this difference between the production constraints upon the variance of speech sounds and of printed forms probably has important consequences for the pattern recognition problem. It is, for example, rather important to note that the influential application of distinctive-features theory to speech recognition deals in *articulatory* and not *acoustic* features (e.g. voiced–unvoiced, nasal–oral). These categorical differences of state in the production machinery for speech have no obvious equivalent in printed forms. (For this reason the positing of "allographs" that are analogous to "allophones" seems to me highly misleading.) The primary consequence of this difference in production constraints is that the problem of abstracting an invariant form from the various realizations of a letter is quite different from the equivalent problem with speech signals. For distinctive-features theory, this may lead to a different feature set for each typeface. This might turn out to be the sort of requirement facing any theory of letter recognition but the existence of this difficulty illustrates the superficiality of the analogy between speech and print in this respect. (Allard and Henderson, 1976, have discussed the status of this analogy in a slightly different context.)

9.2 PERCEPTUAL UNITS IN WORD RECOGNITION

Much of the traditional literature on the perception of words has centred around the question of what "perceptual units" are used by the reader. This preoccupation with units has arisen largely for the following reason. It has long been known that word recognition is performed more competently than it would be if words comprised random strings of letters. Word recognition is, to use an unfashionable word, intelligent. The subject possesses skills which enable him to capitalize on the structure that exists in word arrays. Until quite recently the most commonly adopted explanation of this skill was in terms of perceptual units. Thus it was held that the linguistic structure of the visual array allowed the use of larger perceptual units to mediate recognition (i.e. larger units than could be used to recognize random letter strings). These larger units were generally thought of as being the size of whole words, though in some accounts they were held to be of size intermediate between the letter and the word, that is, the syllable, letter cluster or "spelling pattern".

There are two fundamental questions about the operation of perceptual units which receive no answer in many of the theories that employ the concept. The first question is about the nature of these units. How do they function? In pursuit of this question we can ask, for example, whether a letter cluster that constitutes a hypothetical perceptual unit is served by a single, elementary feature analyser. This appears to be the view taken by Smith and Haviland (1972) when they write: "when S expects a word to be presented he segments the initial input into perceptual units, which are larger than single letters". However, an alternative interpretation denies that the units are primitive feature detectors and asserts instead that the units function as descriptions stored in pattern memory which are addressed by means of elementary features. Of course, this distinction itself depends upon a certain general view of the process of pattern recognition, but this dependency serves to make an important point, namely that the postulation of perceptual units can only be understood when presented in the context of a general view of the recognition process. (The danger is that because we have paradigms in other contexts for interpreting notions like "a unit of analysis", we shall accept the importation of the concept into the study of word recognition without questioning its status.)

The second unanswered question is, on the face of it, much simpler. Why should the use of larger perceptual units facilitate recognition? Perhaps because it is so easy to think of a number of possible answers many theorists have not felt it necessary to advance a specific candidate. However, here again we can quickly see that an answer to the question of why it helps to use larger (and hence fewer) perceptual units can only be construed in terms of a theory of the recognition process.

Before considering the theories in any more detail, it is helpful to look back on some of the findings which served as an inspiration for various perceptual unit theories. Most of these findings concern, at least in a loose sense, the superior "perceptibility" of words compared with nonwords or single letters. It is useful to have a name for this collection and I propose to borrow the name recently applied to one or two of the phenomena and generalize it to cover the whole collection. This should do no harm since the term is sufficiently vague in any case. Let us call this collection of effects "word superiority effects".

Early demonstrations of word superiority effects

The earliest demonstrations of word superiority effects are owed to J. M. Cattell, a pupil of Wundt. Cattell was intent on establishing the *perception time* required by a variety of stimuli. Using a naming RT task, he showed that it took less time to initiate the naming of a word than a single letter (Cattell, 1886). A problem with this naming task is that it conflates perception time with the time required to arrive at an articulatory representation. Another demonstration of Cattell's which also appears to bear more on response organization than on perception was that letters in words could be read aloud faster than random letters (cited in Huey, 1908, p. 73). What is interesting about this task is that, whatever the stimulus structure, the overt unit of response is the same—a letter name.

Perhaps the most influential demonstration of Cattell's involved the tachistoscopic full report task in which the amount of material that can be reported from a single fixation-glimpse is determined. He found that whereas only 3 or 4 random letters could be reported, when the material consisted of short words, 2–4 of these could be reported (Cattell, 1885). This finding was confirmed by Erdmann and Dodge (1898), who also progressed beyond it to an investigation of recognition threshold values in which they found that words could be identified at retinal eccentricities and at viewing distances which did not permit identification of their component letters when displayed in isolation. This comparison of threshold values is the direct precursor of most modern word superiority effects (e.g. Reicher, 1969; Wheeler, 1970).

These early studies did not confine their investigation of stimulus structure to real words. Zeitler (1900) used the full report paradigm to show that the number of consonants that could be reported in a single glimpse was increased by interspersing them with vowels so as to create a syllabic organization. This effect has been unwittingly rediscovered by Spoehr and Smith (1975).

One final effect must be mentioned because it illustrates how early theories centred on the description of perceptual *experience*. Cattell (1885) and Huey (1908) commented that even when report of a briefly displayed sentence was erroneous, it rarely consisted of fragments of words. Furthermore, it does not appear that this tendency toward whole-word responses is due to a conscious bias in report, since erroneous words are often experienced as compelling percepts. This phenomenon was further explored by Pillsbury (1897), using mutilated and misspelled words. He found that with brief displays of such stimuli the words were reported as normal in appearance. More recently, the compelling nature of mistaken word-percepts has been remarked upon by Wheeler (1970) and Adams (1979).

Early interpretations of word superiority effects

The "perceptual units" interpretation of word superiority is clearly instanced in the theoretical approach taken by Cattell. It is difficult to grasp these early conceptions without understanding something of the theoretical vocabulary of nineteenth-century psychology. One crucial aspect of this is the definition of "perception" itself. I have elsewhere pointed out (Henderson, 1977, p. 45) that we have a long epistemological tradition in which perception has been defined as *that which eventuates in conscious experience of the world*. It was this view that led to the dismissal of subliminal perception as inherently paradoxical. This confusion arises out of a failure to distinguish between "perception" as experience and "perception" as the extraction of information from the world. Cattell's attempts to measure the "perception time" for various sorts of stimuli were therefore essentially intended as measures of the time required for an experience to be formed. A consequence of the definition of perception in terms of awareness was that perception seemed to be unmediated and without temporal extension. Another way of expressing this is by way of the observation that their theoretical language for discussing information-processing operations was extremely impoverished.

At least two attempts had been made to analyse perception into underlying states or processes. One consisted in the Structuralists' attempt to analyse experience into elementary sensations and had been largely discredited; it was, in any case, a purely phenomenological program. The other attempt, which was much more significant but in fact scarcely more influential, was Helmholtz's postulation of *unconscious inference*. This mechanism provided a way for our knowledge of the world to influence perception. As such, it offered an account of perceptual skill and also of certain sorts of illusory perception in which inference overrides the stimulus data. However, Helmholtz tended to argue for the process in a very limited domain of visual effects, such as colour contrast, and apart from a brief flirtation with the concept by Wundt it never achieved wide currency.

A primary consequence of this lack of theoretical vocabulary for distinguishing underlying processes is that Cattell does not attempt to separate out the function of *units* in the analysis of the stimulus from their function in the attentional awareness of the products of that analysis. (As we shall see, a failure to make this distinction also characterizes much contemporary work.) One way of illustrating this ambiguity which I have used before (Henderson, 1980a) is to contrast Cattell's interpretation of word superiority with that of a modern student of the effect. Thus, whereas Wheeler (1970) couches his conclusion in information-processing terms "word recognition cannot be analysed into a set of independent letter recognition processes", Cattell's (1886) claim that "we do not therefore perceive separately the letters of which a word is composed" brings out perfectly the ambiguity of the word "perceive". Cattell might equally be discussing perception as experience or as information processing. Notice, however, how much more natural it seems to move to proposals about perceptual units from Cattell's "not perceive separately the letters" than from Wheeler's "not process independently".

Some further clues as to the status of perceptual units are given in Huey's (1908) discussion of the concept. In one passage Huey makes explicit the conceptual link between these hypothetical units and the span of attention, which was a central preoccupation of nineteenth-century psychology, usually defined as the number of objects which could be apprehended in a single glimpse. (See, for example, Jevons, 1871, on immediate judgements of numerosity.) This number was generally thought to be four or five. "To attempt to distribute the attention over more than about this number," Huey writes, "is only successful when we can in some way *unitize* them" (Huey, 1908, p. 69; my italics). To a modern ear this conception of unitization is reminiscent of Miller's (1956) classic discussion of chunking and the span of immediate memory. What is being described is apparently not an early stage in the uptake of stimulus information but a property of the synthesis of a representation of this information in consciousness. However, this does not seem to have been the interpretation arrived at by Cattell, who preferred instead the notion that unitization took place in the uptake of information by the use of global features to identify a word.

Erdmann and Dodge were also adherents of the perceptual-units account of word superiority, and Huey discusses their use of a rather cute metaphor. In this, the relationship between a word and its constituents is compared to that of a tree and its branches and leaves. "Why should not a familiar word-form be recognised on sight," it is asked, as with the tree in which "the total form is the main thing . . . one may always analyse the whole into its parts. . . . But we do not do this in actual reading any more than in regarding a landscape" (Huey, 1908, p. 75). The remarkable thing about this metaphor is how perfectly it preserves the ambiguity of the perceptual-units position, but this should not distract us from the fact that the analogy is a thoroughly bad one. Trees are not composed out of an alphabet.

Early demonstrations of word superiority effects seem then, to be ambiguous, but Cattell, and Erdmann and Dodge, interpreted them as evidence for perceptual unitization occurring at a stage that we might call feature analysis. More particularly they assumed that the overall outline of the word acted as a unitary, global feature for the purpose of recognition. This view was by no means unanimous at the time, however, and in the criticisms made then are to be found the seeds of modern reappraisals of the word superiority effects.

Goldscheider and Müller (1893) were impressed by the way in which an incomplete word might be "filled out" in perceptual experience. From this they formed a theory of "determining letters" which constituted a sufficient basis for word perception. This was one of the first of the *inferential* models of word recognition, though the principle of inference was certainly not clearly developed by the authors. A more explicit statement of the inference position had to await the work of Zeitler (1900), who argued that the perceptual experience of whole words was the result of a secondary stage of the recognition process. The primary stage consisted in the detection of dominant features. These features might be letters or letter-clusters. Phenomenal experience, in his view, generally arose out of the combination of the detection of crucial features with inference from past associations.

Zeitler specifically argued against the importance of the overall outline of the word. He showed that erroneous responses frequently did not conserve word-length and sometimes even changed the word envelope created by ascenders and descenders. He also distinguished between information about the position and the identity of letters in a word. Here he takes the astonishingly modern position, recently echoed by Estes (1975) and Adams (1979), that knowledge of word structure is brought to bear to reconstitute letter position information that is lost in perceptual analysis.

Let us attempt to reconstruct the fundamental argument in information-processing language. On one hand is the school of Cattell and Erdmann & Dodge who attribute the skill in word identification to the use of a larger unit of perceptual analysis, where this unit is often the "total word-form". On the other hand is the position adopted by Goldscheider & Müller and Zeitler in which only certain dominant letters are the focus of analysis and past associations are used to flesh out the percept. While Zeitler's account, in particular, is strikingly similar in outline to modern inferential views of word perception, this comparison should not be pushed too far. He had the fundamental insight that the unitary quality of the word-percept might conceal more analytical detection processes which occurred as a preliminary to the synthesis of a representation. However, Zeitler was unable to abandon the introspective criterion and seems to have believed that by attending carefully enough to perceptual experience this two-stage process of detection and synthesis could be discerned. Moreover, the notion of dominant features was ambiguous. Sometimes it was phenomenologically grounded, as in the most clearly perceived letters of a word; at other times, usually when the reading of phrases is being discussed, the dominant features are spoken of as syllables and words which are critical to the *sense* of the phrase.

Perhaps the clearest statement of the view that the unitary quality of perceptual experience is due to attentional processes subsequent to feature analysis comes from Huey, who writes: "There is a hierarchy of recognition habits, the exercise of the higher drafting away the consciousness that would otherwise serve for completing the recognition of the particular letters" (Huey, 1908, p. 112). In another passage (p. 151), he urges the distinction of feature analysis and memory associations functioning as "automatic" and "silent" workers from the 'stage effects" which these processes arouse in consciousness.

The major difficulties for these early theorists were three. First, they were distracted by the ambiguity of terms like "see" and "recognize". Even such a careful discussant as Huey equivocates between the senses of perception as information processing and as awareness. Curiously enough he tends to reserve "seeing" for the uptake of stimulus information. For example, he urges the distinction "between what is actually 'seen' . . . and what is mentally supplied" (1908, p. 63). But it is clear that both of these are held to influence awareness. Frequently, though not consistently, Huey uses the term "recognition" to describe the actual state of awareness. A consequence of this is that when he asserts that "It is perfectly certain that words are not perceived by a successive recognition of letter after letter, or even by any simultaneous recognition of all the letters as such" (Huey, 1908, p. 111), we should understand that he is describing our perceptual awareness of a word rather than the analytic processes upon which that awareness depends. This is clear from the continuation: "*by whatever cues the recognition may be set off*, it is certainly a recognition of word-wholes".

This leads to the second difficulty, which was the lack of a language for discussing perception as information processing. There is little evidence that the nineteenth-century students of word recognition understood what it was that had to be explained in pattern recognition. In this context, it is worth noting that Neisser (1967) begins his seminal book on cognition with the rejection of the ancient theory of *eidola*, in which it is supposed that faint replicas of objects can enter awareness directly. For our early theorists *identification* was reduced to *looking at* (often referred to as *apperception* following the usage of Leibniz and Wundt). This amounts to a weak version of the Representative Theory of perception, a philosophical view in which it is asserted that perception is achieved by the formation of "pictures in the mind". The most succinct criticism of this theory that I know of is reproduced in Fig. 11.

A final difficulty with nineteenth-century work was the nature of the experimental evidence that was adduced. It is significant that Cattell, Erdmann and Dodge on one hand and Zeitler, Goldscheider and Müller on the other came to such different conclusions on the basis of much the same sort of experimental demonstrations. This in itself is not unusual; what is remarkable is the apparent lack of any attempt to do the adjudicating experiments. Furthermore, it is evident from the discussion of the role of perceptual inference in the word superiority effect that conscious and deliberate guessing might be used by the subject to augment the superiority of words over nonwords, in addition to, or instead of any unconscious inferences from partial cues that served to "fill-out" the percept. Despite this possibility, no attempt was made to estimate the tendency to guess, or to control it. We can summarize these weaknesses in the early experiments in terms of three classes of possible artifact in the demonstration of word superiority. First is the set of possibilities that we shall loosely term "guessing". (The investigation of this set has been a major preoccupation of modern research.) A second set of problems centres upon Cattell's various RT experiments in which the advantage of word stimuli may be due to processes of response retrieval or response organization rather than perceptual processes. Lastly, the studies of full report may reflect superior memory for word stimuli rather than superiority at any earlier stage of processing. None of these possible artifacts is uninteresting, but they must be excluded as a preliminary to the sort of debate that we have just considered.

Towards a clarification of the issues

Whilst granting the possibility of various nonperceptual factors contributing to

Fig. 11 An epistemological joke. From the cover of G. Vesey's *Perception*, Open University Press (1973).

the word superiority effects, it does seem reasonable to conclude from the recognition threshold studies, at least, that word identification is not mediated by the sequential process of letter identification. Such a serial letter identification mechanism was the traditional doctrine against which Cattell and his successors reacted (see, for example, Huey, 1908, pp. 71–72). Having succeeded in casting doubt upon it, their limitation consisted in the restricted view that they were able to take of the alternatives.

In alphabetic script, words are composed of a rather small set of basic visual elements, or graphemes, so it is a natural starting point to enquire whether word recognition is not based, in some sense, upon letter recognition. An obvious advantage to such an arrangement is that a graphemic description of a word (considered as a visual pattern) is a fairly economical one. The main alternative to this letter-mediated theory is based on the assumption that elementary features are used to address a store of word units directly.

A factor which has tended to obscure the question of whether word perception is mediated by letter identification is that theories in which such mediation is denied have often been referred to as "wholistic" (or holistic). In previous work (Henderson, 1980a) I have argued that in the absence of certain qualifications the assertion that a perceptual process is "wholistic" is almost uninterpretable. Let me summarize the distinctions that are required.

Word recognition can be said to be wholistic in at least four distinct senses. One sense of wholism has to do with the translation of written forms into speech, that is, the subject matter of Chapters 5 and 6. Thus scripts which are not phonographically analytical, such as, in their different ways, the logographies and the syllabaries, might be said to be translated into sound wholistically. Moreover, we can contrast procedures for the phonographic translation of English on the same basis. This is most clearly seen in the dual process theory, in which the lexical procedure involves translation at a whole-word level and the GPC procedure involves translation at the alphabetic level.

It might be thought that the question of wholism at the phonographic translation level has little to do with the visual perception of words. In opposition to this view, however, there exist theories such as that of Spoehr and Smith (1973) in which the same mechanism is proposed to serve visual recognition and translation into speech.

The remaining forms of wholism following the lines of the distinction between the two senses of "perception", that is, they refer either to the quality of perceptual experience or to the manner of uptake of stimulus information. What I shall call the *attentional* form of wholism emphasizes the unitary quality of awareness. This would include the tendency remarked upon by Cattell (1885) and Huey (1908) for erroneous percepts under impoverished viewing conditions to consist of whole words rather than fragments, and also the tendency described by Pillsbury (1897) for stimulus words with missing letters to have these lacunae filled in perceptually.

In contrast to the attentional version of wholism stand those versions in which the very uptake of stimulus information is characterized as wholistic. We shall shortly consider two slightly different forms of this *feature analytic* wholism, but first let us savour the gross distinction between attentional and feature analytic wholism.

We can now see that this distinction offers a way to describe what was at issue between Cattell and Zeitler. Cattell believed the word superiority effects to be revealing feature-analytic wholism. Words possessed certain global features, the detection of which allowed the direct discovery of word identity. On the other hand, for Zeitler the word superiority effects were due to unconscious inferences by which word identity was established on the basis of partial information. But these inferences were truly unconscious (as distinct from deliberate guesses), and what enters perceptual awareness is generally an inferred whole word. Zeitler therefore espoused attentional wholism in so far as he held that we tend consciously to experience only the end-product of our inferences. His attentional wholism is tempered, however, by the belief that we can be induced to attend more analytically, that is, to a more literal level of description of words.

So strongly do I wish to insist on the distinction of feature analytic wholism from attentional wholism that further discussion of attentional wholism is deferred to Chapter 11.

Let us turn now to a closer examination of wholism at the feature-analytic stage. Within this domain I want to introduce two further distinctions, one major and one minor. The major distinction is between theories of feature analysis that assert wholism at the stage of feature *extraction* and theories that assert wholism at the stage of *interpretation* of the extracted features. Cattell's was an extraction theory, because he believed that the stimulus contained features that straddled the individual letters, features that were directly detectable. All the early wholistic feature analysis theories were extraction theories. For our last class of theory, the wholistic feature-interpretation theories, we must turn to much more recent writers. This is because the process which I call feature interpretation, that is, the stage at which the features that have been extracted are compared with the descriptions of visual objects that are stored in memory, is a hypothetical one which reflects a particular information-processing analysis of perception. Wholistic extraction and wholistic interpretation theories have in common the denial that word identification depends upon letter identification. This is the most explicit ground for calling them "wholistic". The extraction theories assert that word identification and letter identification are based on different sets of features. Interpretation theories do not require this assumption. In an interpretation theory the postulated features may be very elementary. Letter identification is by-passed on the way to word recognition, not because the features cannot be applied to letter identification but simply because *they are not applied.* Thus the extracted features are used to address directly the stored pattern-descriptions for individual words.

We turn now to the minor distinction, which I have chosen not to regard as relevant to the main classification of types of wholism because it bears only upon the size of the postulated "wholes". So far, in discussing *perceptual units* we have identified wholism with a whole-word level of analysis but it must be acknowledged now that perceptual units have also been proposed for letter clusters of various sorts. Since these units, too, are postulated as alternatives to the individual letter, it is convenient to regard letter-cluster-based theories of feature analysis as "wholistic".

9.3 WHOLE-WORD UNITS IN FEATURE EXTRACTION

We can distinguish at least two sorts of global features that might be extracted from word displays to aid identification. The simplest possibility is that the *word envelope*, that is, the overall outline of the word, is used as a cue. This cue, upon which Cattell and later Erdmann and Dodge focused their attention, can be described more elegantly in terms of the spatial-frequency analysis of form (see Broadbent, 1977). Such an analysis can be understood in terms of a progressive blurring of a word display. As the degree of blur increases, so the high-frequency spatial information is filtered out. That is, the information about sudden brightness changes along a spatial dimension. Eventually we are left with a gross image, lacking detail and corresponding roughly to the word envelope. There is a case to be made for the role of such information in the early stages of the processing of real world scenes, and some authors have recently suggested a considerable extension of the idea that low-frequency spatial information has precedence in perception, by applying the notion to alphabetic forms (Navon, 1977; Kinchla, 1977).

The second sort of feature consists of patterns that straddle groups of letters. These might involve quite fine detail, but the pattern is wholistic by virtue of its inclusion of information from several letters. Such internal word-features were first considered by Wheeler (1970) as a basis for word superiority effects. Following Henderson (1977), I shall call these *transgraphemic features.*

Before entering into an evaluation of the role of such features it is worth considering certain potentially misleading arguments. These take the form of unwarranted claims to have demonstrated a rôle for global features in word identification, and we shall encounter an alarming number of these siren songs. Perhaps the most blatant is the confusion of evidence for some form of parallel processing of letters with evidence for the operation of global features. As I have previously pointed out, Cattell believed that in rejecting a serial-exhaustive letter-processing model he could reject any model in which word recognition was mediated by assignment of individual letter identities (Henderson, 1980a). A second mistake occurs in the supposition that evidence that subjects can be induced to attend to global features necessarily implies that such features are used as discriminative cues in word identification. (Stated baldly, this faulty logic is readily detected, but so often it passes unnoticed when it is implicit in an extended experimental report.) Thirdly, we must examine arguments from confusability data with care. For example, if *list* is confused more with *lint* than with *lilt*, this might indicate that envelope cues are operative, but it might instead simply indicate that *s* is more like *n* than it is like *l*. Finally, we must distinguish between cues that may be used in the subject's brief struggles with artificial stimuli in the laboratory and those used in his natural encounters with real words.

In what follows, I shall attempt to show that most of the arguments in *favour* of global word-features are based on one or more of these confusions. Furthermore, reasonably compelling evidence *against* the importance of such features exists.

Word envelope cues

The earliest tests for the use of word envelope cues were based on the nature of recognition errors. Huey (1908) reviews the evidence from studies by Zeitler and by Messmer which showed that erroneous responses often differed greatly in length from the stimulus word. Messmer claimed that this was particularly true for children, and Zeitler added that the pattern of ascenders and descenders was also often lost in the response.

In modern research confusional errors have also been studied. Havens and Foote, in a number of papers (e.g. 1963), have claimed that words with distinctive envelopes are more easily recognized than other equally common words. Moreover, contrary to Zeitler, they claim that envelopes are generally preserved in erroneous responses. I have already indicated the reason for dismissing this sort of result as evidence for envelope cues. The letters possessing ascenders or descenders are likely to be most confusable with other letters of the same type. (This is supported by the confusion matrix analysis of Bouma, 1971, and others). It follows that the results of Havens and Foote are perfectly compatible with a model based on individual letter identification.

Another group of studies is based upon similarity judgements among words. In a typical experiment the subject makes a four alternative forced-choice judgement about which word a test word most closely resembles. This technique has been used by Marchbanks and Levin (1965), Rayner (1976) and Dunn-Ranklin (1978) among others. Most studies agree on the importance of the initial letter for similarity judgements but evidence on the influence of word envelope is inconsistent. The results may be highly sensitive to the nature of the response alternatives and to the subject's interpretation of what is intended by "similarity".

A fatal difficulty with this task is that there is no reason to accept that the features used to choose amongst a few experimental alternatives are the same ones used to discriminate a word's identity in normal reading. Confronted with the strange task of deciding whether *cig* is more like *aiy* or *lik*, the subject may well hope to learn from the alternatives what his experimenter has in mind by his question. Moreover, these studies, too, seem to suffer from an inability to discriminate between similarity of envelopes and similarity of individual letters.

A more ingenious study, by Posnansky and Rayner (1977), provides an implicit measure of similarity, by using a variant of the Stroop task. Subjects were given a pictured object to name as quickly as possible. This form contained a word or nonsense word. When the word was the name of the object, i.e. the required response, the naming latency was reduced. This is not surprising. What is more interesting is the effect on RT of the nonwords: in this case, word envelope and letter-sharing were varied independently, and, for example, if the object to be named were an *apple*, the stimulus for the similar word envelope but low letter-sharing condition would be *oqqtc*. The results showed that both kinds of similarity to the object name were effective in facilitating RT. This task has the considerable virtue of avoiding explicit judgements of similarity, and it does mimic some of the automatic processing that characterizes reading. Unfortunately it does nothing to consolidate the status of word envelopes, for, as the above example makes clear, envelope similarity is once again highly correlated with individual letter similarity.

In summary, studies specifically directed towards the question of the role of envelope cues have totally failed to provide relevant evidence. It is very difficult to isolate the envelope factor, yet an adequate test of the question requires the independent manipulation of individual letter confusability and envelope confusability. One possible direction which research might take involves the redefinition of word envelopes in terms of low spatial frequency components. It might then be possible to use selective adaptation and masking techniques to investigate the salience of low frequency cues that are peculiar to the word pattern. A rather more indirect attack on the question has recently been explored by Broadbent and Broadbent (1977), who compare letter deletion and word-blurring as methods of degrading legibility.

A different and less direct approach to the question of envelope cues has consisted in the examination of properties of lower-case print, to which these cues are largely confined. The generally superior legibility of words in lower-case print is often attributed to the presence of a distinctive envelope (e.g. Tinker, 1965), and this in turn is often given as the reason for starting children off with lower-case reading material. However, there are a great many factors besides word envelopes which distinguish upper- and lower-case forms. Moreover, lower-case superiority is not invariably found. McClelland (1976), for example, found no difference in report accuracy between upper- and lower-case forms in the recognition of single words. Most modern demonstrations of word superiority effects have been achieved using upper-case stimuli, and McClelland's results reveal that the magnitude of his word superiority effect was actually slightly greater for upper-case stimuli.

Even where gross envelope cues are available, it has been shown that they are poor discriminators of word identity. Gross (1975) analysed the most common words in children's readers and found that the envelope allowed identification in less than one-quarter of the words. This sort of evidence, however, is not conclusive, since in a hierarchical discrimination net a cue that was rapidly extracted, even if not a powerful discriminator, might nevertheless place useful constraints upon the possible identification decisions.

A rather more persuasive rebuttal is that provided by F. Smith (1969), who found no increase in oral reading time for a passage in which the word envelope was a spurious one created by increasing the size of alternate letters in upper-case print. There is reason to believe that this test is insensitive, so some impairment may have gone undetected. Nevertheless, Smith was able to show with the same test reliable impairment when size alternation was applied to lower-case print. In this case not only is the envelope disrupted but so are the size cues for the identity of *individual* letters, since ascenders and descenders cannot be reliably detected. (We shall consider further evidence from print-mutilation studies below.)

Transgraphemic features

Another possible global cue is the transgraphemic feature, a pattern made up from portions of the contour of an adjacent set of letters. Unlike the envelope these transgraphemic features may be internal to the word array. Such features have been discussed by Wheeler (1970) in his treatment of the hypothesis that words may possess more features than letters, and by Henderson (1977), though neither source adequately distinguishes their role in feature extraction (our present concern) from feature interpretation.

In this passage we shall consider evidence from studies of type-fount familiarity, as it bears on the reality of transgraphemic features. Our primary concern is with a study by McClelland (1977). He taught subjects to attach a meaning to pseudowords like *bardel* and after considerable training measured the speed with which those associative responses could be given to the words. The use of upper-case versus cursive script was varied independently in training and test trials, so that the test presentations could be either in the same fount or different fount from the training. When the fount used in the test phase was familiar from training, subjects were able to respond about 50 ms faster. However, the disadvantage of the unfamiliar fount was quickly reduced. For example, two test exposures were sufficient to remove the disadvantage, after 40 training trials with the other fount.

McClelland regards the fount-familiarity effect as somewhat indirect evidence for the role of global visual features in word learning. However, there are a number of fairly straightforward reasons for declining to accept this argument. Let us consider first the representativeness of the type-fount manipulation. Transgraphemic features, if they are to be useful, must discriminate between words. Type fount does not do this. Moreover, in this experiment fount was the sole variable and it could only assume two states. Apart from anything else, this makes the manipulation highly *noticeable*. We may doubt, therefore, whether a very transitory effect gained with a single two-state transgraphemic feature which is irrelevant to word identification is likely to be informative about real-life word perception.

A more complex, but perhaps more penetrating, criticism of McClelland's argument is that what he has measured is an aspect of *episodic* memory for words; that is, memory not for the abstract identity of the word but for the circumstances of a particular occurrence of a word. (This distinction loosely follows that of Tulving (1972), between "semantic" and "episodic" memory.) This comment can best be understood by considering a group of very similar experiments which are certainly not intended to bear upon the mechanisms of pattern recognition. These experiments have been concerned with showing that in classic short term memory paradigms the physical circumstances attending the presentation of a word may influence its recognizability after a substantial delay. These physical circumstances have included the presentation modality, speaker's voice and type-case. In the last instance, for example, Kirsner (1973) showed that a change of type-case in a continuous recognition memory task diminished the speed and accuracy with which a word could be recognized as having already been presented. Now, these experiments have utilized highly familiar words, and it is unreasonable to suppose that variables such as speaker's voice or type-case play a *general* role in the recognition of such words as patterns. What these experiments show is that such variables play a role in the tagging of particular episodic occurrences of a word within the frame of the experiment. Consider the following *reductio ad absurdum*. If McClelland had presented *bardel* on a green background in training and shown that it was less recognizable when the background was red in the test trial, would we have considered for a moment that this told us something about the role of wholistic cues in word detection?

We could invest McClelland's type-fount manipulation with more ecological validity if we could find a group of words which occur in a particular type-face in the real world. As it happens, there is a limited set of word-like forms for which this is true. These are the lexically represented abbreviations like FBI, BBC and NATO. Somewhat to my embarrassment in the present context, I must admit to having shown that the familiarity of these stimuli is case-specific. Henderson and Chard (1976) reported that the facilitatory effect of meaningfulness on visual comparison RT was case-specific. FBI could be matched faster than IBF but the same was not true of fbi v. ibf. This effect has subsequently been confirmed by Seymour and Jack (1978) and by Besner *et al.* (1979). Does this constitute evidence for the role of global feature extraction? Certainly it does suggest that in these unusual instances the lexical access code is case-specific. Nevertheless, I believe that it is misleading to draw any general conclusion about visual feature extraction from these examples. Case is a peculiarly abstract sort of feature. Indeed, it is not even transgraphemic. Finally, the effect does not generalize to lower-case abbreviations such as *etc.* (Seymour and Jack, 1978).

Disruption of global features

So far we have concentrated on the failure of attempts to demonstrate a role for global feature extraction. We turn now to a set of experiments having the opposite purpose. These experiments are based on the following premises. If envelope or other transgraphemic features play a role in word identification, they should contribute to the word superiority effects. That is, they should form an extra source of information allowing us to discriminate the identity of familiar words, as compared to nonwords. Moreover, changing the type-case or type-fount *within* a word should disrupt the processing of transgraphemic features, because this manipulation renders the envelope and the conjunction of contours across letters totally unfamiliar. Therefore, such disruption would be expected to reduce or to abolish word superiority effects if global features have the role proposed for them.

This logic was explored by McClelland (1976), who presented words, pseudowords and random strings for recognition in upper-case, lower-case and alternating case. He was able to show that the word superiority effect was not reliant upon the use of transgraphemic features. Even with alternating-case stimuli, words were more accurately recognized than pseudowords, and pseudowords than random strings. Moreover, the magnitude of the word v. pseudoword effect was undiminished with case alternation. So much is clear. However, there is a difficulty with another aspect of McClelland's results. Case alternation reduced performance with words and pseudowords (this, of course, has many possible explanations that are irrelevant to the question of global features) but had no effect on random strings. The superiority of words and pseudowords over random strings, though reliable with alternating case, was nevertheless reduced over that obtained with normal type. So some contribution might be made by global features to the nonlexical effect (redundant v. random strings). On the other hand the level of performance with random strings was very low in McClelland's experiment, and it may be that a basement effect rendered the case-alternation effect undetectable.

This conclusion is drawn by Adams (1979), who ran a similar study in which, however, basement effects were precluded by the use of a wide range of performance values. Adams also used a more radical form of pattern disruption in which the case, size and fount of every letter varied. She showed that disruption affected words, pseudowords and random strings equally, with the word superiority effects undiminished.

The use of case-changes within stimuli to disrupt their visual appearance has also been used in the same–different RT task. The pattern of results is inconsistent from experiment to experiment, but results have generally been interpreted as favouring a role for transgraphemic units of processing.

Let us consider first the word v. pseudoword effect, for this comparison is the one most likely to be germane to the role of whole-word features. Taylor *et al.* (1977) have reported a diminution of the RT advantage of words over pseudowords when case-changes are introduced. However, his effect was obtained only for one out of two experiments (Exp. 3) and only for *same* responses. Moreover, even at the maximum level of visual disruption a substantial word superiority effect remained, as it also did in the study by Bruder (1978, Exp. 3).

Taylor *et al.* also consider another argument for the existence of global features that are disrupted by case-changes. This is based on the reasoning that a whole-word level of analysis would be disrupted by a single case-transition (e.g. WORd) whereas smaller "perceptual units" are likely to require more case transitions (e.g. WoRd) before they are disrupted. Now, it appears that the time required to match a word does increase with the number of case transitions that it contains (Pollatsek *et al.*, 1975, Exp. 2; Taylor *et al.*, 1977); moreover, this slowing is greatest for the introduction of the first case transition in most of these experiments. Taylor *et al.*, conclude from this that "units" of various size are used in the task, the major decrement produced by a single case-transition indicating the operation of whole-word units and the increased slowing with further transitions indicating smaller "spelling pattern" units being disrupted.

These arguments are very weak. Almost any theory that predicted a deleterious effect of case-changing within a word would predict that the effect would increase with the number of case-transitions. This would be so even for the extreme case of a theory in which letters were processed separately and serially. As to the tendency for the greatest effect to be occasioned by the difference between zero and one transition, if this were a symptom of the dropping out of whole-word detector units then it should not occur for pseudowords, as it does in Taylor *et al.*'s Exp. 3, and for nonwords, as it does in Pollatsek *et al.*'s Exps 1 and 2. There appears to be nothing, then, in the literature on same–different judgements that adds to the case for the operation of whole-word features.

Turning to the visual comparison of nonwords (i.e. random letter strings, as opposed to pseudowords), we find one of the more consistent effects of case-transitions: they disabled judgements about nonwords much less than those about words and pseudowords (Pollatsek *et al.*, 1975; Taylor *et al.*, 1977; Bruder, 1978, Exps 2 and 3). This finding agrees with that of McClelland (1976) using tachistoscopic thresholds, but not with that of Adams (1979).

It would be unwise to leave this discussion of visual comparisons without considering certain difficulties that attend the interpretation of such tasks. Perhaps the greatest of these is the uncertainty about the level of code involved in the comparison. Words might be compared as nonlinguistic spatial patterns, as graphemic codes, as abstract lexical codes and as phonological codes, among other possibilities. The task requirements can be arranged so as to place some constraints upon the utility of particular codes (e.g. the exclusion of phonologically based comparisons by Pollatsek *et al.*, 1975; Besner and Jackson, 1975), but it is extremely difficult to be sure at what level effects are operative. Furthermore, the effects which obtain in *same* judgements are often absent in *different* judgements (e.g. Besner and Jackson, 1975). Finally, the task is exceptionally sensitive to strategies adopted by the subject, and design decisions such as whether the word condition is blocked may exercise a substantial influence on the outcome (Henderson, 1974; Carr *et al.*, 1979).

In summary, mutilations of visual configuration which would be expected to disrupt any global features that helped to define whole words generally affect words and pseudowords equally and almost invariably leave the word superiority effect unimpaired. This fact seems to be fatal for wholistic feature extraction theories that postulate word-defining units. However, there is some evidence that random letter strings are less impaired by mutilation than either words or pseudowords. This evidence is inconsistent in the threshold task. It is a little clearer in the same–different task, but this task presents other difficulties of interpretation. Nevertheless, it would be wise to consider that the superior perceptibility of pseudowords over random nonwords may be reduced, if not abolished, by mutilation. If so, this could be construed as evidence for the operation of perceptual units at a level intermediate between letters and words. Such hypothetical units have been called "letter-clusters" and "spelling patterns" and have usually been conceived of as operating at the feature extraction stage. This conception is shared by Gibson and her associates (e.g. Gibson and Levin, 1975) and by E. E. Smith (e.g. Smith and Haviland, 1972), and we close our discussion of wholistic feature extraction with an examination of these theories.

9.4 LETTER-CLUSTER UNITS IN WHOLISTIC MODELS

Letter-cluster units, like whole-word units, can be formulated at either the feature extraction or the feature interpretation stage. We shall focus our discussion on one instance of either type of theory. Whereas the two theories differ in the stage at which they postulate a role for these perceptual units, they are in accord on the negative proposition of wholism: the denial of an account of word recognition in which letter identification occurs as an intermediate stage. That this need not be true of all letter cluster theories, however, is evident from

Taylor *et al.* (1977), who merely refer to such units as consisting of "interdependently processed letters" (p. 385). As a complication, there also exist theories like that of Healy (1976) which refer to something like letter cluster units. However, I have chosen to regard this as a theory of a quite different sort, since it posits a role for units in the conscious monitoring of the products of encoding operations rather than making any claim about the layout of the encoding operations at either an extraction or an interpretation stage. Such attentional theories are reserved for discussion in the next chapter.

Gibson's spelling pattern theory

One of the earliest of modern perceptual unit theories to be developed was that of Gibson (Gibson *et al.* 1962, 1970; Gibson, 1965; Gibson and Levin, 1975). Gibson's theory is primarily intended to give an account of the pseudoword superiority effect, that is, the superior recognition performance on regular-looking, pronounceable stimuli as compared to random letter strings. The theory is somewhat difficult to classify in information-processing terms because attention is focused on the attempt to specify the type of structure that facilitates stimulus processing rather than describe the way in which that structure is used to facilitate processing. However, since Gibson speaks of sensitivity to larger perceptual units (Gibson *et al.*, 1962) and the "efficient extraction of units larger than the letter" (Gibson and Levin, 1975, p. 200), it appears reasonable to regard the theory as a wholistic feature extraction theory.

In the first study of this series, Gibson *et al.* (1962) compared two types of stimuli in a tachistoscopic full report task. One type of stimulus was held to be "orthographically legal" and pronounceable and consisted of pseudowords like *sland*. The other type was generated by exchanging the consonant clusters at either end of the word (e.g. *ndasl*) to yield a string that was held to be unpronounceable and orthographically illegal. (We shall examine these descriptions of the stimuli below; see also Chapter 4, Section 4.)

Gibson *et al.* found that the percentage of stimuli reported correctly was substantially greater for the pseudowords than the nonwords. Performance improved with increased exposure duration, but the magnitude of the pseudoword advantage did not change. They decided that pronounceability facilitated perception and did so because pronounceable sequences consisted of "spelling patterns" that could be detected as a unit. A spelling pattern was defined by Gibson (1965) as "a cluster of graphemes in a given environment which has an invariant pronunciation according to the rules of English".

The interpretation of this experiment raises at least three sorts of problem: (*i*) do the results really reflect greater "perceptibility" of the pseudowords, as distinct from retention in memory or even guessability? (*ii*) is the operative form of linguistic structure correctly described as pronounceability? (*iii*) is the way that structure is used by the perceptual system correctly described in the definition of spelling patterns?

Massaro (1975c) has pointed out that the constancy of the pseudoword advantage over the range of exposure durations suggests that the advantage is not perceptual in nature. However, although this is a fatal difficulty in this and other early experiments, more recent work, using improved controls for memory and for guessing, has confirmed the existence of a pseudoword advantage under such conditions.

In a later experiment, Gibson *et al.* (1970) reported evidence against their previous identification of the operative form of structure as pronounceability. Their main finding was that a pseudoword advantage obtained equally for congenitally deaf as for hearing subjects. This suggested to them that it was not the relationship of spelling to sound that mattered but the orthographic pattern itself. This rejection of a role for phonology on the basis of results on the deaf is unwarranted, as Coltheart (1977) has pointed out. A number of recent studies support the conclusion that the deaf are able to abstract a phonological code from lip-reading (Dodd, 1976, 1980; Dodd and Hermelin, 1977). A pseudoword advantage with deaf subjects therefore presents no compelling reason to abandon the idea that what matters is some aspect of pronounceability.

With the rejection of the pronounceability factor, the position to which Gibson comes is that the basis for the efficient recognition of words is the intra-word sequential constraints that exist in the corpus of English spellings. This conclusion, taken by itself, is not so different from that reached by several authors (e.g. Massaro, 1975c; Baron and Thurston, 1973) who nevertheless eschew wholism, so it is worth enquiring why Gibson has chosen to express her view of the process for utilizing such redundancy in terms of perceptual units larger than the individual letter.

One factor which seems to have influenced Gibson is a general characterizing of skill as involving transactions with ever larger "chunks" of the environment. This is of course a way of speaking of skill which has a long history. Gibson and Levin (1975, p. 475) quote Goldscheider and Müller and Huey with approval in this context. Now, this characterization does indeed seem to capture some of the flavour of skilled reading. In much the same way, students of attention remark upon the fact that, with skill in driving, changing gear and steering no longer seem to be two independent and competing, concurrent tasks and, in playing the piano, there is a level of skill at which the left hand and right hand parts become integrated into a single "whole". The limitation of this language is that it is based on implicit metaphors and tells us nothing about underlying processes. Unfortunately the appeal to rather vague metaphors may be accepted as if it were a process description.

Another, more technical ground can be given for Gibson's advocacy of perceptual units. At the heart of her attempts to describe the operative form of intraword redundancy lies a distinction between two forms of structure: probabilistic patterns amongst letters and rule-based patterns. Gibson *et al.* (1970), having decided from their results with the deaf that pronounceability was not the effective ingredient in pseudoword superiority, examined instead the transitional probabilities of the letters in the strings. We shall consider this sort of evidence in detail below; suffice it to say that they found no evidence that the probability of correct recognition was predictable from the transitional probabilities of the letter sequence. This negative result led them to assert that, from a psychological point of view, structure was created not by high-frequency combinations of letters but rather by "orthographic rules". Orthographic rules, Gibson and Levin (1975, pp. 172–173) tell us, "govern what sequence of letters and groups of letters may be put together to form words". Spelling is therefore supposed to possess a sort of syntax which specifies what sequences of letters are legal in the language.

It seems clear that in Gibson's theory the notion that spelling patterns form perceptual units affecting the efficiency with which information is extracted from a word is inspired, as a concept, by the view of intraword redundancy as the product of a system of rules. However, it is extremely unclear what there is about rule-based structure which requires multi-letter spelling patterns for efficient information extraction. Furthermore neither the rules nor the spelling patterns are ever specified. What, one might enquire, are the spelling patterns in *word*?

The fundamental problem arises through the abandonment of the criterion of pronunciation. When spelling patterns were defined as units of phonographic translation, there was the possibility of a phonological criterion for what constituted a unit. With the retreat to a purely graphotactic basis for orthographic rules, the constituents of all "legal" strings have the same status. In fact, with this view the concept of a unit only becomes useful for describing the structure of illegal strings. So *sland* comprises a single unit and *ndasl* comprises three units *n-das-l*. Curiously, Gibson does not pursue these implications. Development of this approach, with a detailed specification of units, is left to a theory that is explicitly grounded in pronounceability, and to which we now turn our attention.

Spoehr and Smith's syllabification theory

Spoehr and Smith's theory is much more explicit about the sequence of information-processing stages that it postulates, and one product of this is that the commitment to a perceptual unit account comes out unequivocally. This aspect of the theory is the subject of one of the first papers in the series over which the theory developed. Smith and Haviland (1972) attempted to adjudicate between alternative mechanisms serving the advantage of words and pseudowords in recognition tasks. These they called "inference" and "unitization". The inference mechanism arrives at word identification by combining letter detection with the utilization of redundancy in the letter string so as to effect economies in processing. In contrast, the unitization mechanism operates as follows. "When S expects a word to be presented he segments the initial input into perceptual units, which are larger than single letters and correspond to pronounceable English sequences, and then analyses these units" (Smith and Haviland, 1972, p. 59).

What Smith and Haviland actually showed, though not uninteresting, certainly has no necessary bearing on unitization. They compared recognition thresholds for two types of trigram, CVC words and CCC nonwords. The nonwords were derived from the words by a rule that prescribed replacement of the medial vowel by an equivalent consonant. Thus *rag* became *rsg*. Performance was measured by the probed forced-choice method. For example, one of the items above might be followed by a pointer indicating that the identity of the initial letter was to be reported, together with the response alternatives *r* and *b*. Accuracy of report was found to be greater for the letters in a word. Furthermore, this word superiority did not decline even when the equal predictability of the letters within the nonwords was brought out by explicit training in the rules for generating the stimuli; nor did the word superiority decline over several days of practice.

What are we to conclude from this demonstration? Unfortunately the stimulus classification confounds meaningfulness and pronounceability, so either might have formed the basis of the word advantage. What the persistence of the word advantage over sessions of practice tells us, together with the survival of the advantage after the subject's attention is drawn to the equal predictability of both types of stimuli, is that this word superiority effect is not dependent on deliberate and sophisticated guessing. In this case, the word advantage is, to use a glib term, *automatic*. If the advantage is based on an inferential process, it is a preconscious one. Such an inferential process would nevertheless be mediated by letter identification, even though only its final product becomes available in awareness. In view of these possibilities the only general conclusion that we can draw from this experiment is that it is naïve to imagine that a few practice trials, or the teaching of some artificial predictive tricks, can simulate an aspect of natural language learning. (Some further, technical criticisms of the interpretation of Smith and Haviland's study are suggested in Massaro, 1975d, pp. 394–398.)

The first full statement of what Spoehr and Smith mean by "unitization" is to be found in Spoehr and Smith (1973) and Smith and Spoehr (1974). In the latter work they specifically reject an extraction locus for the operation of letter-cluster units, noting that the same evidence that argues against word-shape features also argues against global letter-cluster features. Instead they prefer a feature-interpretation locus for the operation of their perceptual units. However, their theory is unique amongst interpretation-stage wholistic models because it does not deny a mediating role for a letter code in word recognition. Letter identities are not by-passed by the route from primitive features to cluster units. But in some curious fashion the stage at which letter-by-letter analysis is conducted cannot serve as the basis for responding in the recognition task. This can only be understood in the context of the full model, to which we now turn.

Spoehr and Smith make the following assumptions. (*a*) When a word is presented, primitive features are extracted and used to assign letter identities to each position in the array. This categorical information is consigned to a buffer store, pending the operation of the next process. As already noted, this letter information cannot serve as direct instructions to the response process. (The relationship of this buffer store to the classic notion of *iconic memory* is not clear.) Then, (*b*), the stored letter identities are operated upon by a "parsing" process, which segments the array into higher-order units in a different code. These units are held to resemble syllables. (More specifically they are the VCG units that Hansen and Rogers (1973) postulate as units for speech production.) This parsing process is referred to as "unitization". Finally, (*c*), the VCG units are translated into a phonological/articulatory code. The code resulting from this translation is then stored in active short term memory.

Before examining this model in detail, it is worth attempting to put some of its general features in perspective. First, it is clear that the model is intended to explain the effect of orthographic structure (or pronounceability), that is, the advantage of pseudowords over random strings. It is not intended to predict superiority of real words over pseudowords, or of real words over single letters. Smith and Spoehr (1974) doubt the evidence for such effects. (This was probably easier to do then than now.)

A second general feature is that it treats the pseudoword advantage as a true pronounceability effect rather than as a purely graphotactic effect. Furthermore, the theory takes a strong and explicit line on pronounceability: pronounceability effects occur because the results of the preliminary letter identification stage are unavailable for response decisions. "It is not until the translation process is completed that perceptual processing is assumed to be over" (Smith and Spoehr, 1974). This assumption means that the problems of visual identification and of translation into speech are not viewed separately. For this reason, the theory is unique in that it cannot be assigned exclusively to a single class of wholistic theory (see pp. 229–231 and Henderson, 1980a).

The third general feature of the theory worth noting is the way in which pronounceability influences performance on visual recognition tasks. It appears that it may do so at two stages, that of parsing into syllable-like groupings and that of translating these groupings into a speech code. In early papers (e.g.

Spoehr and Smith, 1973) attention was focused on effects arising during parsing. The main prediction here was that recognition accuracy should be an inverse function of syllabic length, since syllabic length determined the number of perceptual units into which the array had to be parsed, and the more there are of these units the more difficult the parsing (or the subsequent translation; Spoehr and Smith (1973) are highly equivocal on the exact reason for an effect of the number of units). In later papers (Spoehr and Smith, 1975; Spoehr, 1978), the focus of attention is transferred to the details of the translation stage, wherein the syllable-like VCG units created by parsing are translated into phonemes, following a procedure described by MacKay (1972).

The reason for this shift of attention is straightforward. The early studies were directed to the prediction of effects within words, primarily of syllabic length: hence the concern with the number of units created by parsing. The later studies were concerned with pseudoword–nonword contrasts. As it turned out, nonwords were not wholly accountable in terms of the number of units required, and so the theory was extended in order to explain these effects in terms of the procedure for assigning a phonemic code to the units (i.e. translation).

We can now assess the theory by considering each hypothetical processing stage in turn, concluding with a general evaluation of the predictive success of the model.

Letter analysis

Parsing into syllabic units depends upon a preliminary stage of letter identification. This postulate raises two problems. First, how can parsing be achieved when letter identification is incomplete, as it must sometimes be with tachistoscopic presentation? Second, why can this letter code not be used directly for responding in recognition tasks? Spoehr and Smith (1973) seem to acknowledge these difficulties but offer no solution. A possible solution to the first problem is that parsing need not depend upon a full analysis of letter identities. Although the testing of a parsing against lexical entries depends upon full letter identification, the parsing process itself merely requires classification of the string into vowels and consonants. Posner (1970) presented evidence that such classification did not precede letter identification, but his task required explicit classification and thus is irrelevant to the present question. However, Henderson and Chard (1978) have advanced tentative evidence of the existence of early vowel detection in visual analysis. Thus it might be possible to maintain the parsing procedure with incomplete letter identification.

Concerning the unavailability for report of the letter identities assigned at this stage, little more can be said than that this is indeed a logical possibility. Elsewhere, I have belaboured the distinction between positing the role for an encoding operation, and asserting the accessibility of that code for conscious scrutiny and intentional responding (Henderson, 1977, 1978; see also Chapter 11).

Despite the possibility of a solution to these two problems, a general question remains for the theory in its account of erroneous or missing responses. Difficulties at the parsing and the translation stages are used to account for various effects of letter-array structure. However, the relatively massive effects of tachistoscopic exposure duration itself must presumably affect the first, letter-analysis stage. Yet, given that any performance depends upon the running through of the entire sequence of operations, it is left unclear how exactly exposure duration exercises its influence on the final report of letters.

Parsing

Probably the best-analysed problems with the model lie at the parsing stage. The first problem is the subject of a cogent discussion by Coltheart (1978), who argues that the parsing procedure cannot be made to work for many English words.

Coltheart was concerned with Hansen and Rodgers' parsing procedure as a method of arriving at a phonological code with which to address the mental lexicon. His criticisms centre on two questions, one concerned with parsing and the other with translation. First he shows that the parsing rules are either incorrect or incomplete. A common example of this inadequacy occurs with CVCCVC words like *dagger* and *fungus*. The first parse yields DAG/GER and the second attempt yields DA/GGER. Neither alternative serves as an appropriate preliminary to grapheme–phoneme translation. Of course one could simply add to the rules so that eventually a more appropriate parsing solution would be tried, in this case DAGG/ER. But consider a case like *fungus*. Correct translation of the medial NG requires a parsing solution which would look something like FUNG/GUS. No process that translates syllables independently can cope with this sort of situation, because the context rule that determines NG→/ŋg/ straddles the syllabic boundary (see Coltheart, 1978, for further details). The general point at issue is this: the primary problem for prelexical translation of print into a speech code is to resolve the ambiguity in grapheme–phoneme correspondences; early segmentation of the graphemic array into syllables is largely irrelevant to this problem, and, as Coltheart shows for cases like *fungus*, segmentation with independent translation of the segments may actually obscure the contextual constraints that lead to a resolution of the ambiguity.

A different problem with the parsing procedure is brought out by Massaro (1975c). He takes up the recursive, trial-and-error nature of the parsing process, pointing out that the number of parses required would increase considerably with word length, even with the inadequate set of rules proposed. Performance on the recognition task should therefore be highly sensitive to the number of parses required. This effect might be expected to be much larger than any effect of the eventual number of segments arrived at. After all, the parsing process is operating on the contents of a sensory buffer store. Yet Spoehr and Smith nowhere present a test of this effect. Indeed, they make the curious assumption (Spoehr and Smith, 1973, discussion of Exp. 2) that the best predictor of recognition performance is the first attempted parsing, whether correct or not.

Translation

The crucial difficulty for the theory with the translation stage is one facing all prelexical orthographic translation procedures: when a phonological representation (the product of translation) is used to address the lexicon, it may fail to resolve ambiguities that were resolved in the original graphemic array. This is true of homophones such as *board/bored*. But it is also true of mistranslations which may match an incorrect lexical entry, e.g. the translation of *loves* may lead to a spurious match with the entry for *loaves*. Coltheart (1978) points out that the syllabification procedure may actually increase the incidence of such mis-identifications.

Another way to look at this question is to conduct a direct test of the notion that visual identification performance exhibits the errors that would be expected if spelling information were discarded in translation. This has been done by Baron and Thurston (1973) and by Hawkins *et al.* (1976). They found that the advantage of pronounceable stimuli in recognition was maintained even when the stimuli consisted of homophones. This finding serves to confirm that response decisions are not made on the basis of an exclusively phonological representation of the stimulus.

Predictions from the theory

Already we have been able to show that Spoehr and Smith's theory is not viable, without having regard to the particular predictions claimed for it. Turning now to these predictions, we find further difficulties.

As we have remarked, early statements of the theory concentrated on the parsing process and hence on syllabic effects. Subsequent research has presented a very inconsistent picture of syllabic effects. In the same–different task, effects are generally absent (Barron and Pittinger, 1974; Chambers and Forster, 1975; Johnson, 1975). In one case, an effect obtained for syllabic length disappeared when the analysis was based on the VCG unit (Taylor *et al.*, 1977). The only attempt to replicate the syllabic length effect using the threshold task appears to be that of Spoehr (1978). She found that effects of syllabic (and phonemic) length only emerged when the stimulus word was followed by a masking stimulus, and there was also a delay before the response alternatives became available to the subject. This suggests that whatever process is responsible for syllabic effects plays an ancillary role in recognition and only becomes evident when conditions present a danger of loss of the information derived from early encoding stages.

It is difficult to avoid the conclusion that the parsing stage of the model creates formidable logical difficulties while generating few novel predictions. Syllabic effects in recognition are rather elusive, and when they occur it is not in circumstances which encourage the view that early syllabification is fundamental to the perception of words. Such syllabic effects may be due to processing stages that are both "late" and optional. The predictions derived from assumptions about the translation stage in the later papers (Spoehr and Smith, 1975; Spoehr, 1978) are perhaps the more interesting. The insight here is a development of Zeitler's (1900) discovery that a random consonant string could be reported more successfully when vowels were inserted in the sequence so as to give it a pronounceable structure. Spoehr and Smith formalize this proposal using McKay's (1972) procedure for phoneme assignment. The procedure is generalized to nonwords by assuming that phonotactically illegal consonant clusters are "regularized" by the insertion of an unstressed vowel. An example of the procedure is shown in Table 15. It can be seen that unpronounceable strings require a greater number of operations to achieve a translation, a fact which can be used to predict poorer recognition performance for these strings. (Incidentally the model provides no guidance as to how such strings could be parsed before translation, since they lack the vowels from which VCG analysis commences.)

Table 15 also shows various other measures of the regularity of strings. It is notable that they all tend to provide a similar view of the regularity of the items. (The pronounceability scores relate inversely to regularity, whereas the visual regularity scores relate positively.) The mere fact of a successful prediction of the ordering of these items in recognition performance therefore cannot be taken as supportive of any particular theory.

One last aspect of the predictive power of the Spoehr and Smith theory is worth mentioning: the restriction of its predictions to the pseudoword effect. As it stands, the theory is incapable of explaining either the lexicality effect (superior recognition of real words than pseudowords) or the word–letter effect (superior recognition of words than single letters). The word–letter effect may lie beyond the scope of any pronounceability theory but the lexicality effect need not do so. After all, in Chapter 5 we found a lot of evidence that lexical membership could diminish naming latency. The point to note here is that the Spoehr and Smith model, by positing prelexical translation into the speech code, contains no mechanism whereby lexicality can influence translation and thus recognition performance.

Table 15 A comparison of measures of string regularity for three stimulus items used as examples by Spoehr and Smith (1975). The procedure for decomposition of the string and phoneme assignment follows Spoehr and Smith. Six measures of regularity are given: the first two are the ones proposed by Spoehr and Smith and derived from their translation procedure; the third is the number of vowels that require to be inserted in order to avoid phonotactically illegal consonant clusters; the fourth and fifth are summed single letter and bigram positional frequencies. Direct comparison of measures applied to strings of different length should be interpreted with caution. The sixth measure shows the number of immediate orthographic neighbours in the lexicon.

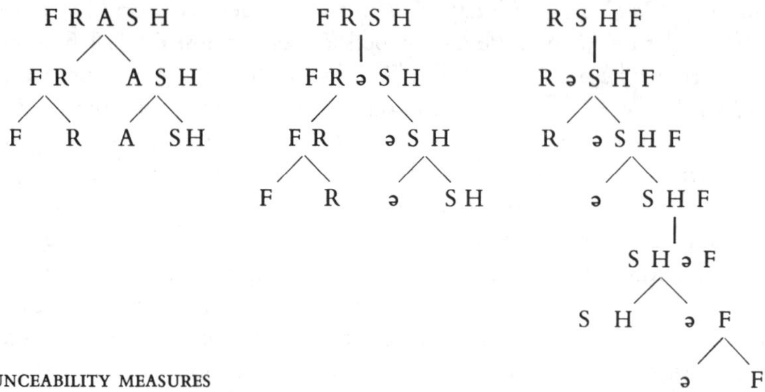

ITEM	FRASH	FRSH	RSHF
PRONOUNCEABILITY MEASURES			
1 Tree depth	2	3	6
2 Number of nodes	6	7	10
3 Vowel insertions	0	1	2
VISUAL REDUNDANCY MEASURES			
4 Summed SLPF	1432	1284	162
5 Summed BPF	127	151	0
LEXICAL NEIGHBOUR MEASURE			
6 Neighbours	5	2	0

9.5 WHOLE-WORD UNITS IN FEATURE INTERPRETATION

We return now to theories that postulate whole-word perceptual units but this time to a class of theory that exhibits a weaker form of wholism than is involved in the wholistic feature extraction models. The interpretation-stage models which we shall discuss share the assumption that the extracted features are not transgraphemic but rather are components of letters. The features used to address word units are of exactly the same species as those that serve letter identification. However, the models also share the assumption that less features are required to specify a word-unit than are required to specify that same array considered as a string of independent letters. The redundancy of a letter string that forms a word allows its definition as a unit by an economical selection of features.

We shall consider four models that share this general approach. The first is that of F. Smith (1971). His model is primarily addressed to the prediction of the lexicality effect, the superiority of words over pseudowords and nonwords, but it can also, at least in principle, accommodate the word v. single letter effect. A second model, that of Johnson (1975), is in effect a minor variant of Smith's model, but it contains a new assumption intended to provide a specific account of superior performance on words than on single letters within words. Third, we shall examine the model proposed by Rumelhart and Siple (1974). This is the most powerful of the wholistic feature interpretation models and it is capable of accommodating word frequency effects as well as word v. pseudoword and pseudoword v. nonword effects. Rumelhart and Siple's model shares with our fourth model, that of Henderson (1977), the attribute of drawing upon two sources of structural information. Knowledge of sequential redundancies amongst letters is used to confer an advantage on pseudowords as compared to random strings, but in addition to this, knowledge of lexical spellings can be used, when a word is expected, to place greater constraints upon the possibilities and to confer an advantage upon real words as compared to pseudowords. These two models differ critically, however, in the way this knowledge is used. In the Rumelhart and Siple model structural knowledge is used to limit the set of responses to the expected class of stimuli. This response bias is set before stimulus arrival and thus the model is essentially a passive one. In contrast, the Henderson (1977) model is an active one in which there is feedback from the knowledge in pattern memory to the process of feature analysis itself. The feature analysis machinery is regarded as having a limited capacity, and the expectation that the stimulus is a word, or at least a pseudoword, can be used to select those feature tests that are most appropriate to adjudicate between possible responses.

All these interpretation models are sensitive to the subject's expectations about the class of stimulus item to be presented. The strategy of treating a stimulus word as a string of independent letters is available to them, but where a word is expected (or even a pseudoword in the Henderson and Rumelhart and Siple models), the interpretation of the extracted features can be based on that hypothesis. As a consequence, fewer features need to be extracted to reach a response decision and the description of the stimulus as a string of letter identities is by-passed.

F. Smith's immediate word identification model

The starting point for Smith's theorizing was the nineteenth-century demonstrations of word advantages in recognition. In contrast to the view taken earlier in this chapter, Smith accepts the evidence advanced by Cattell as incontrovertible proof that word recognition is not mediated by letter identification. However, Smith proceeds to consider and to reject the alternative view that the reader possesses a unitary template for each of the 50,000 or so words that he is able to recognize and that recognition involves sorting through these templates in search of a match to the stimulus. This view is an extreme form of what we have called wholistic extraction theory. Smith's point is that whatever the nature of our mental representations of printed words they do not exist in a dimensionless "space"; they are organized. A little visual information can serve to limit the zone in which the stimulus lies, and so a successful theory must not only account for the fact that word perception is analytical and based on a coherent system of underlying dimension or features, it also must accommodate the fact that particular combinations of these features, when they constitute familiar words, are more readily identified. Smith's solution to this dilemma is to locate the role of a whole-word mechanism at the interpretation stage, where the elementary extracted features are compared with feature lists stored in pattern memory.

The extracted features are the same, whatever the nature of the stimulus. In this the model differs from those of Johnson (1975) and Henderson (1977). As Smith describes it (1971, p. 128): "the only difference between the manner in which letters and words are identified lies in the categories, and associated feature lists, that the perceiver employs in his analysis of featural information." If the analysis is into letter identities, the feature lists associated with the 26 letter categories are consulted. If the analysis is of words, the feature lists are consulted which are associated with those words that the reader can "identify on sight". In this case, word identification is said to be "immediate", inasmuch as it is not mediated by an autonomous stage of letter identification.

The immediate word identification works as follows. The array is segmented into letter positions, and each of these positions functions in feature analysis rather like an independent channel so that extracted feature information is tagged for the position at which it occurred. No particular assumptions are made about the nature of the features, though in illustrative examples Smith treats these as binary distinctive features. At each letter position the full repertoire of feature tests is conducted. For a given type-fount some subset of these tests is sufficient to specify the identity of a particular letter. This is known as the "criterial set".

For any letter-array, including a word, we can therefore construct a matrix in which the rows are the feature tests in the perceiver's repertoire and the columns are the letter positions in the stimulus array. Consider such a matrix for the stimulus HORSE. To perform an exhaustive analysis of the array at the letter identification level we require the featural information that comprises the criterial set for each of these five letters. Thus in letter-position four we require the outcome of the feature tests sufficient to discriminate S from the other 25 letters. But, Smith argues, if we are bent on word recognition, this is more than we need to know about that letter position. At this point Smith introduces two arguments. The general argument goes as follows. The average reader knows about 20,000 five-letter words. But if the 26 letters could occur independently of each position of a five-letter array, there would be 26^5 possible arrays, almost 12 million. Now, if we had an ideally powerful set of binary feature tests we would require five tests at each letter position to achieve letter identification ($2^5 = 32$, and there are only 26 letters). On the other hand, to chose amongst 20,000 words would require 15 of these ideal feature tests ($2^{15} = 32{,}768$, and we only postulated 20,000 five-letter words). So that leaves us with an average of three tests per letter position.

All this general argument does is to illustrate the fact that words are redundant, that to identify a word we do not require as much information as is required to adjudicate amongst the 26 possible letters at each letter position. Smith makes this point by means of the idealized case treated in "information theory". It is difficult to know the precise status to attach to this line of argument. Perhaps it is intended to do no more than illustrate the concept of redundancy and to bring out the principle that a criterial set of features, sufficient for the identification of a word, might contain inadequate information to adjudicate between the 26 possible letters at each position, when positions are analysed independently. However, if the argument is intended to suggest the form of psychological processes that must be operating, it would be necessary to examine in much more detail than Smith does the demands that such processes would make on the capacities of the processing system.

Smith also advances a more specific argument, which takes the form of an example of contextual constraints on the letter sequence within a word. To see this, we return to our letter string HORSE. Consider the decision about the fourth letter position. If we have no contextual information, we are confronted with 26 possibilities. In the extreme case, in which the other four letter positions are successfully analysed, this context limits the possibilities to two, since only S and D can complete real words. By the same token, the second letter position does not require any feature extraction, given the availability of the other letter identities.

What we are examining here is once again the concept of visual lexicon density (or "orthographic neighbourhood"). An important implication of Smith's illustration is that a word that inhabits a sparsely populated zone of the visual lexicon—let us say a word that cannot be transformed into another word by changing a single letter—should be more readily identified in so far as it requires a smaller criterial set of features.

Notice, however, that the example of HORSE was discussed as if word identification were mediated by decisions about letter identities: for example, given HOR_E the decision about the fourth letter was between D and S. However, this level of decision-making is actually denied in Smith's model of the word advantage. It is the contextual constraint amongst features rather than letters that is supposedly used by the perceiver. Presumably Smith does not cast his examples in terms of the operation of featural constraints because he wishes to remain neutral on the question of what the features are. In addition, the example of letter constraints is easy to follow because our knowledge of words is explicitly organized around letters. On the other hand we cannot readily summon to mind four-letter words whose first and fourth letters contain closed curves.

There are in fact two ways in which the contextual constraint of feature possibilities can have an effect on performance, and Smith's account equivocates between them. The redundancy of word strings permits the use of an economical criterial set of features to define the word. As we have seen, this means that less information is required to identify a word than to identify its constituent letters when these are treated independently (i.e. without considering lexical constraints). It is this consequence of constraints with which Smith introduces his model. However, thereafter Smith discusses constraints as if they facilitated sequential decision-making. This is evident in the example using HORSE, which takes the form: "If we knew that, then this would follow". Now, whereas the use of redundancy to reduce the size of the criterial feature set suggests a purely passive model, the switch to a sequential decision-making view suggests an active model. This active model can take either of two distinct forms. One, sometimes called sophisticated guessing, is epitomized by the approach taken by Rumelhart and Siple (see below). In essence, this approach uses sequential decision-making to optimize guessing when necessary feature information is lacking. For example, given HOR_E, we can then choose our guess from the limited set S and D rather than from the full set of 26 letters. The other sequential decision-making mechanism consists in interactive feature analysis. This approach is the one that I have taken previously (Henderson, 1977). Given HOR_E, we can then concentrate our ongoing feature analysis on the crucial tests necessary to adjudicate between S and D, that is, we can use constraints to shape the course of feature testing. If my analysis is correct, Smith's equivocation is not just between forms of words for illustrating the constrainedness of written language but also between quite different underlying models.

Smith's criterial feature set model is in many ways more sophisticated than the wholistic feature extraction model, not least because it is based upon a richer characterization of the structure embodied in written words. However, it is subject to a number of damaging criticisms, most of which follow from its eschewal of a mediating stage of letter identification.

Smith's model is the only one of this type to contain specific proposals for dealing with the problem of how we recognize words despite the enormous variations of type-fount and type-case in which they appear. This is, of course, a special instance of the general problem of shape constancy. We shall refer to it as the problem of *graphemic invariance*, since a grapheme is the abstract category underlying particular letter-forms such as A, a and *a*. Smith's way of dealing with graphemic invariance is to assume that the same elementary features are extracted no matter what the type-fount. However, for each type-fount there will exist a different collection of criterial sets. That is, the subset of features that defines A may be unrelated to that which defines a.

The attempt to incorporate a solution to the problem of graphemic invariances into the model is both courageous and disastrous. The central problem can be outlined in the following way. If we have never seen the word *cat* in, say, upper-case print before, we have not had the opportunity to develop a criterial feature set for it and so we cannot employ an immediate word recognition strategy on the stimulus. This consequence seems absurd because of the general implication that becoming familiar with a type-style requires experience of each word in that style rather than merely experience with the way the 26 letters appear in that type-style. The point is that if graphemic invariance is not dealt with until the lexical (whole-word) level, then the perceiver is unable to derive generalizations about type-face.

Another aspect of the type-fount problem is that it seems desirable that some general information about the nature of a particular fount be extracted at an early stage and used to guide processing of material in that fount. Certainly when processing handwriting the reader probably develops some general predictive rules to transform the script into an invariant and abstract representation of the graphic information. However, in Smith's model there is no general way in which a type-style can be represented. It is simply that if a word has been encountered in a given type-style, the multiple defining feature sets stored for that word will include a set consisting of the criterial features for the word in that particular type. As several authors have pointed out (Massaro, 1975c; Rozin and Gleitman, 1977), a consequence of the inability of the Smith model to generalize type-style information is that it is necessary to postulate an indefinitely expandable number of feature sets for each word. This is, in effect, the "yellow Volkswagen detector" problem (Weisstein, 1973).

In addition to these general difficulties with the model there are a number of problems that can be described more succinctly. The model is incapable of predicting a pseudoword advantage, even though the superiority of pseudowords and nonwords is the most robust of the whole collection of word superiority effects. Moreover, the model requires accurate letter-position information because the interpretation of the extracted features depends on their being tagged for position (cf. Smith, 1971, pp. 129–130). This is difficult to reconcile with a variety of facts about recognition errors. These include the lack of conservation of letter length in erroneous responses (Zeitler, 1900) and the instability of letter-position information with brief exposures (Estes, 1975; McClelland, 1976; Adams, 1979). Another difficulty, already noted, is that a word cannot be processed *as a word* when its type-style has never before been encountered. This leaves the model vulnerable to that scourge of wholistic models—the demonstration that the lexicality effect (words superior to pseudo-words) survives case and type-fount alternation (McClelland, 1976; Adams, 1979). Finally, in so far as Smith wavers toward a sophisticated guessing model involving the use of lexical constraints, then his formulation is exposed to the attack by Johnston (1978) on such models. What is at issue here is whether the reader is aided by the constraint that HOR_E imposes on the possible fourth letters. We shall discuss the evidence against this mechanism in the context of Rumelhart and Siple's model.

N. F. Johnson's letter-concealment model

The model advanced by Johnson (1975) shares important attributes with that of F. Smith but is applied to a quite different set of predictions. In common with Smith, Johnson assumes that the elementary features extracted in letter recognition do not differ in class from those used in word recognition but that a word requires fewer defining features per letter than these same letters would require if processed outside of the word context. To this core, Johnson adds a number of further assumptions that are more or less peculiar to his theory.

Johnson makes a number of assumptions that centre round the notion of a fixed-capacity feature analysis. For any perceptual unit there is available a fixed number of feature analysers and all of these are employed in the analysis of that unit. If a unit contains constituent elements that in other circumstances might themselves function as units (for example, letters within a word), the choice of features used is independent for the larger unit from that used for the constituent element when it is treated as a unit. For example, the single letter W, when treated as a perceptual unit, will be allocated the same number of analysis channels as WORD when it is treated as a unit, but the defining features of W and WORD are chosen independently.

Johnson's remaining assumptions centre upon the decision about what is to be treated as a perceptual unit. Generally a letter in isolation and a familiar word will both be treated as units and therefore defined by the same number of features. When a display is presented, the first attempt is always to treat it as a single unit. If this fails, it is subdivided into several units and each of these units has available the fixed number of feature analysers. (No attempt is made to set out the principles governing this subdivision nor to explain how appropriate units can be chosen before feature analysis is accomplished.)

An important extension of the unitization assumption involves the difference between experimental tasks. The model is designed to accommodate findings with the visual comparison task. In this task it is held that there is sufficient display time to allow the pattern to be processed in terms of larger units. On the other hand, in the tachistoscopic threshold task where display duration is limited, the unit will generally be the individual letter.

It is convenient to make a fairly sharp division between the general characteristics of Johnson's model and the fate of those few specific predictions that have been derived from it. As we have seen, there are two major sets of assumptions about unitization and the allocation of a constant and fixed feature analysis capacity to each unit. A general consequence of the exclusion of the threshold task from the rule stating the tendency to use the largest available unit is that the model is incapable of giving any account of the various word superiority effects obtained with threshold tasks. This limitation sets Johnson's model apart from all other perceptual unit accounts. It is not necessarily fatal but it does mean that there is an imbalance between the strong assertions made in the model and the severely limited domain of its predictions. This inevitably leads to a particularly careful scrutiny of these predictions.

The assumption of fixed-capacity feature analysis is a curious one. One difficulty is that no explanation whatsoever is provided of how larger units are identified by means of the same number of features as smaller units, of how (to use Johnson's example) P and PERCEIVE are both identified on the basis of the same number of features (albeit an independently chosen set of features). This omission is the more remarkable since proposals about the precise form of redundancy used in the recognition of larger units have generally been taken to be central to the whole question of perceptual units.

Leaving aside this troublesome question of how the fixed capacity analyser copes with larger perceptual units, we can still enquire as to the *grounds* for the fixed capacity assumption. (It should be noted that it does not seem to be the capacity for feature extraction that Johnson holds to be limited but rather the capacity of some comparator that interfaces extraction to pattern memory. Therefore it is the interpretation process that is limited in this way.) The problem with this assumption is that it seems to be entirely *ad hoc*. Its whole purpose is to accommodate Johnson's findings with his visual comparison task.

Johnson's empirical case for his model has been the subject of a number of recent criticisms (Henderson, 1975; Massaro and Klitze, 1977; Henderson and Chard, 1980), and here I shall only summarize them. Johnson's first argument is that word-matching is not influenced by the number of letters in the pair of words and therefore that the words must have been processed "as a unit" (in the sense of the model's assumptions). To this there are two answers. First, the unitization account is not the only possible one: a parallel processing model operating at the individual-letter level might equally be advanced. Second, many authors *have* reported a deleterious effect of increased length (e.g. Eichelman, 1970; Henderson, 1974; Chambers and Forster, 1975; Bruder, 1978).

Johnson's second argument has attracted more interest. He has claimed that it takes longer to decide whether a target letter is present in a word than whether two letters are the same or whether two words are the same. From this he concludes the words are processed as whole units in such a way as to conceal the identity of the letters of which they are composed. We can decide that the pair *word–word* is the same by matching two whole-word units, but when asked whether *word* contains *w*, we analyse *word* as a unit and then (in some unspecified way) unpack that unit to gain access to its constituent letters.

Once again there are both empirical and theoretical difficulties with the argument. Procedural changes can apparently produce a reliable reversal of Johnson's effect: Massaro and Klitzke (1977), Marmurek (1977) and Henderson and Chard (1978) were able to obtain faster matching in the *w–word* condition than in the *word–word* condition. Probably the most interesting of the procedural variables that reverse the effect is the contrast of simultaneous and successive presentation of the stimulus pair. It turns out that successive presentation is a necessary condition for Johnson's effect (Marmurek, 1977; Henderson and Chard, 1978). This suggests that when a delay intervenes between the presentation of a word and a letter target, the subject tends to transfer his attention from a graphemic level of code to a deeper lexical code, with the consequence that it takes longer to retrieve graphemic information. This effect is not uninteresting, but it has no bearing whatsoever on the question of how words are identified on first presentation.

Johnson's theory asserts wholism at the interpretation stage, but his data suggest a quite different sort of theory which locates wholistic effects at an attentional stage which governs the ease of subsequent recovery of various levels of perceptual code. We return to this type of wholism in Chapter 11.

Rumelhart and Siple's sophisticated guessing theory

Before describing the model advanced by Rumelhart and Siple (1974; see also, Rumelhart, 1976), it is useful to set it in relationship to various other developments. Of the models so far described, Rumelhart and Siple's most resembles that of F. Smith in that the redundancy of highly structured stimuli is used at the feature interpretation stage to permit identification of these stimuli by means of fewer features than would otherwise be required to describe an array of independent letters. Rumelhart and Siple's model differs principally from Smith's in three ways. First, it utilizes orthographic as well as lexical knowledge so that pseudoword superiority can be predicted as well as true word superiority.

Secondly, no attempt is made to accommodate the problem of graphemic invariance; indeed, Rumelhart and Siple's experiments are conducted with a novel type-fount in order to simplify the problem of defining features. Third, the interpretation process is described in terms of explicit and quantitative decision rules, in contrast to Smith's approach which amounts to no more than a statement of the *principle* of redundancy utilization.

A different relationship exists between the Rumelhart and Siple model and a family of models that are associated with the word frequency effect. (The tendency of high-frequency words to be more readily reported in recognition tasks.) These models have become known as Sophisticated Guessing Theories, following Broadbent (1967). The general form of these models is that when a word is presented, a set of "fragments" or component features is detected. These are used to isolate a subset of candidate responses which are compatible with the extracted features. The subject then chooses intelligently from this subset (hence "sophisticated" guessing), according to his expectations of what stimulus was more likely to have occurred. What distinguishes these models is their description of how the information extracted from the stimulus is combined with knowledge about the structure of the world, in making a decision.

The term "guessing" is in fact undesirable in the present context, since it implies a conscious strategy, i.e. that the inferential process is a separate stage which follows and is contingent upon perceptual experience. Rumelhart and Siple, on the other hand, suggest that the decision process determines what the subject actually "sees". This question requires more attention because the experimental procedure employed by Rumelhart and Siple seems designed to encourage deliberate guessing. (A full report of all letters is required on each trial.)

A third set of relationships exists between this model and other inference models such as those of Thompson and Massaro (1973) and Estes (1975). These latter models, however, assume that inferences are conducted on a base of individual letter identities. That is to say, they are not wholistic. From the close resemblance between the members of this whole family of inference models it would appear that the lack of a letter mediation stage in the Rumelhart and Siple model is not a fundamental property of the model. This is true also of the interactive model that we shall attend to next. Neither is wholistic in the sense of a denial of mediation by letter identification, a strictly necessary attribute.

Rumelhart and Siple's model has the following structural features. Visual information is assumed to enter the system through a sensory buffer store. Feature analysis is conducted upon the contents of this store, resulting in a feature description. Then the main pattern recognition process operates on the feature description in order to classify it ("naming" in the author's parlance). The main part of the model is the decision rule whereby the featural information is combined with the perceiver's *a priori* expectation to assign a classification. The possible classifications are derived from a sensory–memory dictionary.

The decision assumptions state that only those response alternatives that are consistent with the extracted features can be considered. Furthermore, a dictionary unit will not be considered as a response if, while compatible with the extracted features, it contains more than a criterial number of features in excess of those extracted. If no dictionary units meet these conditions, the subject bases his response entirely on his *a priori* expectations. If, however, the extracted features do yield a set of response candidates, a Bayesian response rule is used to decide amongst the candidates. This rule takes into account both the strength of the *a priori* expectation of a given unit and the likelihood that this unit was presented given the set of extracted features.

The application of this model to word recognition is essentially dependent on the assumption that the subject's expectations can be assigned to three classes: words, pseudowords, and random strings. The subject's expectation of a particular word can then be understood as the product of the subjective probability of the word class and the probability of the particular word within that class as reflected in measure of word frequency. It can be seen from this that the *word frequency effect* is incorporated in the model as a natural prediction.

We can now see the general principle by which word superiority effects can be generated by the model. Usually a set of features extracted under imperfect viewing conditions will be compatible with a relatively large number of random letter arrays, but a much smaller set of pseudowords and an even more restricted set of real words. Provided that the subject attaches some likelihood to the string being a word, words will have more chance of successful recognition by virtue of comprising a smaller set of candidates.

Expectation within the set of word candidates is determined, other things being equal, by word frequency. Thus high-frequency words are more likely to have a recognition advantage over pseudowords. Expectations within the pseudowords set are less obviously arrived at, and Rumelhart and Siple make the tractable but otherwise arbitrary assumption that pseudoword expectations are determined by the transitional probabilities of the letter sequence as assessed by norms of bigram frequency.

Rumelhart and Siple's own attempt to assess the predictive success of their model is based on techniques peculiar to mathematical modelling. In particular, the values of the various free parameters are estimated retrospectively from the data. The most important of these parameters is the subjects' expectations about the various classes of stimuli. It is difficult to evaluate this sort of predictive enterprise, and one might prefer a direct test of the fundamental assumptions of the theory. Fortunately some of the appropriate tests exist elsewhere in the literature.

Tests of what we may call the inferential characteristic of the model exist in terms of the word and the pseudoword assumptions. Words that resemble few other words are members of more lexically constrained sets and should be identified more successfully. Johnston (1978) has shown that they are not. Moreover, since pseudoword expectations are based upon bigram frequency, such frequencies should correlate positively with recognition success. McClelland and Johnston (1977) have shown that they do not. (Rumelhart and Siple did find a positive correlation but their procedure encouraged post-perceptual guessing and no attempt was made to isolate bigram frequency from other aspects of word structure. Massaro *et al.* (1980) also found a cluster-frequency effect using *post hoc* regression analysis.)

Another obvious area of enquiry is the role of stimulus–class expectations, and here the evidence is equivocal. Performance on pseudowords appears to be improved by the expectation that pseudowords will be presented (Aderman and Smith, 1971; Carr *et al.*, 1978), but Carr *et al.* were unable to find any evidence of improved recognition of real words when these were expected.

The last assumption is the wholistic one, which asserts that word recognition is not mediated by letter identification but rather whole-word candidates are directly activated in the sensory memory dictionary by feature descriptions. We have already seen that this assumption is difficult to reconcile with at least two findings. First, the fact that the word v. pseudoword effect survives case and fount alternation which should greatly perturb descriptions at the elementary feature level (McClelland, 1976; Adams, 1979). Second, the fact that although dictionary activation and inference-making depend on fairly accurate tagging of extracted features with respect to their positional origins, Estes (1975) and Adams (1979) have found that a considerable amount of letter identity information may be extracted without precise positional information. For these reasons it is worth noting that the rejection of preliminary letter identification is not an essential element in this or the following model, whereas it certainly is in those of Smith and Johnston.

Henderson's interactive model

This model is based on a suggestion by Wheeler (1970) that feature extraction might be influenced by context. We may consider this mechanism as a more powerful development of the "sophisticated guessing" mechanism. Consider the final candidate set arrived at in sophisticated guessing theory. All the candidates are compatible with the extracted featural information, and so we have to utilize a decision rule that appeals to aprioristic considerations. But consider what might happen if a set of candidates could be specified *while feature extraction was still under way*: we might redistribute processing capacity to the letter positions that were still highly unresolved, but we might go beyond this and conduct our feature testing at those positions in the light of the possible candidates. Thus given HOR_E we would conduct those feature tests most likely to adjudicate between S and D in the fourth position. However, rather than regarding the establishment of a set of candidates as a single event, we can conceive of the candidate set as a dynamic list, continuously subject to deletions as more featural information becomes available.

It must be acknowledged that the power of such a system is dependent upon a number of strong assumptions. Feature extraction must be of limited capacity if directed feature testing is to be helpful. Moreover, it must be directable rather than fully automatic. Finally, access to the sensory memory dictionary and feedback from it must be very rapid compared to the process of feature extraction.

For all its vagueness about details this model is vulnerable to the same attacks upon its inferential and wholistic assumptions as that of Rumelhart and Siple. In particular the lack of facilitation by lexical constraint (Johnston, 1978) and the lack of interaction between mutilation and word superiority (McClelland, 1976; Adams, 1979) appear to be fatal.

Overall assessment of interpretative wholism models

One fundamental difficulty haunts the models that reject a letter-mediated stage in word recognition: the resistance of the word–pseudoword effect to case and fount alternations. Smith's model got into difficulties by assuming that all feature combinations that had ever been experienced in the presentations of a word were listed in the pattern memory for that word. To accommodate the case-alternation effect one would have to go beyond this and assume that *all possible feature combinations* are listed, an assumption which is clearly absurd.

As it happens, the extant wholistic interpretation models belong to the larger class of models that explain word superiority effects by appealing to inferential processes. Here we have been able to anticipate the severe difficulties that would appear to face members of that class. These are the absence of an effect of lexical constraint (orthographic neighbours) and the absence of an effect of bigram frequency.

In addition to these general difficulties, each of the four models reviewed suffered from certain other problems that were specific to its own assumptions.

Chapter 10

Visual Analysis of Words: Letter-Mediated Theories

In this chapter we conclude our discussion of the visual processing of words by examining letter-mediated theories. As a preliminary to the consideration of theory, I present in Section 1 a résumé of the main findings on word superiority. These are the findings that any successful theory would have to accommodate.

We consider first the comparison of recognition performance on words with that on single letters. It was a loose version of this comparison that yielded the word superiority effect remarked upon by Cattell and by Erdmann and Dodge. Modern interest in word superiority effects received its major impetus from the more controlled demonstrations of this effect by Reicher (1969) and by Wheeler (1970).

We continue our review with the examination of pseudoword superiority, that is, superior performance on pseudowords as compared to random letter strings. Pseudowords, in this context, should be understood to be wordlike forms that are meaningless but readily pronounceable and conform to the phonotactic and graphotactic patterns of the language. Attention was drawn to this effect first by Zeitler (1900) and more recently by Gibson *et al.* (1962). However, it was Baron and Thurston (1973) who proposed that this effect be regarded as the basis of word superiority. The comparison of performance on pseudowords and random strings has served as the forum for debate about the role of pronounceability and of letter positional and sequential redundancy.

Next we turn to the lexicality effect, which is based upon the comparison of performance on words and pseudowords. In the ideal version of this comparison, structuredness is equated and the only factor that varies is whether or not the string possesses an entry in the mental lexicon. The existence of this effect is perhaps the least agreed, and for proponents of general theories of word superiority the choice has either been to refuse to recognize the effect (e.g. Baron and Thurston, 1973; Smith and Spoehr, 1974; Carr *et al.*, 1979) or else to attempt to bring together the lexicality effect and the pseudoword effect in a common framework (e.g. Rumelhart and Siple, 1974; Henderson, 1977; McClelland and Johnston, 1977; Adams, 1979).

This résumé concludes with an examination of the word superiority effects obtained in supra-threshold reaction-time tasks such as letter search and same–different judgements. Many of these effects parallel those obtained in the threshold task, but there are also some differences which merit attention.

Section 2 is concerned with theory. I shall attempt to outline a broad distinction between inferential theories and noninferential theories. Inferential theories assert that word superiority effects depend upon the use of contextual constraint to assist feature interpretation. Perhaps the most straightforward of these is the descendant of sophisticated guessing theory. A consistent exponent of this type of theory has been Massaro (e.g. Massaro, 1973). In his theory, contextual constraints are used to limit the set of candidate letters. The mechanism resembles that proposed by Rumelhart and Siple (1974) save for the addition of a mediating stage of letter identification. This stage displaces the postulation of direct access of whole-word units by elementary features. A different sort of inference theory is that of Estes (1975) in which the principal source of the word advantage is the use of the lexical constraints upon letter sequencing to reduce the uncertainty arising from loss of letter-position information during feature analysis. Finally, the criterion-bias model (Adams, 1979) is another close relative of sophisticated guessing theory. In sophisticated guessing theories, the extracted feature information is used to arrive at a candidate set of possibilities and then a decision process that is guided by contextual constraints is used to chose from among the members of the set of candidates, but in criterion bias, featural information is used to derive a measure of the strength of evidence that an input corresponds to a particular letter category. This sensory measure sums with the criterion bias that is induced by contextual information. Recognition depends upon the letter category that receives the greatest summed value.

In contrast to this entire class of inferential theories stands the class of theory that asserts what I shall call "top-down stabilization" of graphemic information. In simple terms, we can say that these theories depend upon the assumption that graphemic representations are unstable, being vulnerable to information loss through masking, memory interference and the like. The availability of a higher-level code such as a phonological or abstract lexical representation serves to stabilize the lower-level (graphemic) specification. Versions of this type of theory have been advanced by McClelland and Johnston (1977), Seymour and Jack (1978) and Henderson and Chard (1980a).

Finally, in a brief third section, we shall discuss the more general implications of work on the visual analysis of words.

10.1 RÉSUMÉ OF WORD SUPERIORITY EFFECTS

The word–letter effect

The nineteenth-century work on word superiority, including the claim to have shown that words could be recognized under conditions that did not allow recognition of any of their component letters, was discussed in Section 9.2. We noted that various guessing strategies might have given rise to this result. At the end of the 1960s an important and influential attempt was made to examine this phenomenon under better controlled conditions. Reicher (1969) presented brief exposures of single letters, nonwords, or words, which were immediately followed by a mask. Accompanying the mask was a recognition probe which consisted in an indication of a letter position concerning which a report had to be made, together with a pair of letters, one of which had occupied the probed position. The subject responded by making a forced choice between these letters. Since the subject did not know in advance which position would be probed, the experimenter could build up a picture over trials of the state of the subject's recognition competence for each type of stimulus. The principal finding was that performance on words was better than on either single letters or nonwords.

The significance of Reicher's findings lay in his use of two important controls, one for guessing and one for differential memory loss. The guessing control consisted in the selection of response alternatives so that for word displays either would complete a common word. Thus if the fourth position of WORD was probed then the alternatives could be D or K. Nothing in the WOR_ context seems to aid the choice between D and K. This same forced-choice probe also purported to minimize the role of memory, since no matter what the nature of the display was, only a single letter had to be reported. (However, in some recent interpretations—reviewed in the next section of this chapter—memory factors are still held to be crucial.)

Reicher's results were replicated by Wheeler (1970) with the addition of some further controls. Once again letter recognition with a word context was found to be about 10% more accurate than recognition of the same letters in isolation. Subsequent studies have provided further reassurance about the reliability of this effect (Johnston and McClelland, 1973; Mezrich, 1973; Thompson and Massaro, 1973; Juola *et al.*, 1974; Estes, 1975 exp. 2; Hawkins *et al.*, 1976; McClelland and Johnston, 1977). It has even been possible to obtain an advantage of words over single "letters" using the Japanese Kana syllabary (Miura, 1978).

Debate about the necessary conditions for a word–letter effect has centred upon two factors: the role of masking and the claim that the effect disappears when the response alternatives are known in advance of stimulus presentation.

Johnston and McClelland (1973) made the important claim that the word-letter effect depended on the use of patterned masking. They found that word superiority obtained when the stimuli were preceded and followed by a visual mask, but when no mask was used the difference in performance between words and letters was abolished. Juola *et al.* (1974) confirmed that no word–letter effect obtained in the absence of masking, and Bjork and Estes (1973) and Massaro and

Klitzke (1979) confirmed that single letters suffered more interference from masking than did words.

If words do indeed owe their advantage over single letters to a greater capacity to survive masking, this would appear to place important constraints upon the theoretical possibilities. Moreover, this finding suggests that the word–letter effect reported by Erdmann and Dodge and other early writers can be dismissed as due to sophisticated guessing, since they did not employ masking. In view of these implications it is curious to find that the role of masking has received little further theoretical or experimental attention. (The role of masking is pursued on pp. 307–309.)

The question of whether the word advantage depends upon a lack of foreknowledge of the response alternatives does not yet admit of a clear answer. Both Massaro and Estes have attempted to show, in a number of papers, that the effect is reversed when the response alternatives are provided in advance, converting the task into a sort of search or detection task (Bjork and Estes, 1973; Massaro, 1973; Thompson and Massaro, 1973; Estes *et al.* 1974; Estes, 1975). They reasoned that if intra-word constraints functioned by limiting the letter possibilities at the probed position, this effect would be removed by presenting alternatives in advance, because the alternatives would themselves constrain the possibilities. The general finding with the detection procedure was that words and nonwords yielded equal levels of performance with single letters superior to either.

There are several difficulties with these results, both methodological and theoretical. Perhaps the simplest and most general theoretical difficulty is that the obtained outcome does not seem to be prohibited by any of the main competing theories of word superiority.

It is clear that advanced presentation of alternatives is not in itself a sufficient condition for abolition of word superiority. Reicher (1969) and Johnston and McClelland (1973) obtained a word superiority effect with advanced presentation, but Estes (1975) has attributed this inconsistency to the presentation of the alternatives either in another modality or another format from the stimulus display. However, Estes' conditions are met by two other studies in which a word superiority effect was found: Carr *et al.* (1976) precued with four alternatives but no positional information; Matthews *et al.* (1976) precued letter-position and provided a five-alternative forced-choice. However, it might be argued that these alternatives were insufficiently restricted to abolish the word constraint effect. Evidence against this conclusion was found by Spector and Purcell (1977): using precued alternatives but no advanced specification of the critical letter position they found superiority of words over nonwords. The magnitude of this effect was independent of the size of the set of precued alternatives.

The studies by Massaro and those by Estes differed from each other in an important way: in Massaro's precue condition there was no positional uncertainty about the critical display letter. The word context was invariably A_E and the nonword context was V_H with the targets C, G, P or R inserted in the medial position. Apart from the artificiality of this manipulation and the difficulty of generalizing on the basis of a single example of each type of context, there is a serious danger that the subject may simply ignore the context, abandoning any word-processing strategy that is available. Such a possibility is rendered more credible as a consequence of an elegant demonstration by Johnston and McClelland (1974). They were able to show that when subjects were instructed to concentrate their attention on a precued critical letter position, the advantage of words over nonwords was reversed. The word advantage was restituted, however, when the subjects attended to the entire array.

Estes' experiments are not open to this form of objection, because in the precue condition the critical letter position was not indicated. However, it is still open to doubt whether the subject would use a word-processing strategy when exposed to 360 trials in each of which he must simply decide whether an R or L was present (Estes, 1975). This argument is taken further by Purcell *et al.* (1978), who pointed out that failures to obtain a word advantage generally occur when the display subtends a large visual angle. They reported that a word–nonword effect was abolished by increasing the size of the display and concluded that with large displays, such as that used by Estes, a word-processing strategy was not automatic and might have to be induced by means such as Johnston and McClelland (1974) employed.

In summary, it is clear that the superior recognition of letters in words as compared to isolated letters can be abolished under some circumstances. It is unclear whether these abolitions of the word advantage are due to neutralization of the constraints imposed by linguistic redundancy or to the deflection of the perceiver from a word-processing strategy. The evidence on the role of masking is more consistent, and it appears that single letters are more vulnerable than words to visual masking. This suggests that words may owe their advantage to a greater ability to survive masking. Such a dependence would appear to have stronger implications for theory than does the precuing effect.

Orthographic structure and the pseudoword advantage

Strings of letters that are meaningless but nevertheless look wordlike (*pseudowords*) are easier for the perceiver to deal with in a variety of recognition tasks than strings of letters that contain no positional or sequential organization and are not readily pronounceable. Pseudowords possess this advantage despite the fact that they lack meaning and there is no reason to assume that they are listed in our mental lexicons. One way to regard them is as infinitely low-frequency words: they possess all the attributes of word candidates but they have never actually been encountered. If their advantage is attributable to familiarity, it must be some general aspect of their construction that is familiar, since the particular sequence of letters bounded by spaces is, by definition, unfamiliar.

The advantage of such stimuli over random letter strings was demonstrated by Zeitler (1900) simply by inserting vowels into an array of random consonants to give it a crude syllabic structure. Recently this theme has been returned to by Gibson and her colleagues (Gibson *et al.*, 1962, 1970), followed by Aderman and Smith (1971). However, it was Baron and Thurston (1973) who first compared real words with pseudowords and showed that much of the advantage of real words over random strings was shared also by pseudowords. (In fact they claimed that all of the advantage was thus accountable, but we shall shortly dispute this claim.)

A pseudoword advantage has been confirmed in a large number of recent investigations using the Wheeler–Reicher paradigm, the same–different RT task and the letter search RT task. The only major exceptions have been the studies by Estes and by Massaro referred to above, in which presentation of the response alternatives prior to the stimulus display led to equal performance on words and nonwords. It is reasonable to assume that the pseudoword advantage would be as vulnerable to this operation as that for real words. (Pseudowords were not explicitly studied in these experiments but some of Estes' nonword stimuli turn out to have been pseudowords.)

We have already seen that early opinion on pseudoword superiority held it to be due to pronounceability. More recent writers have tended to prefer the view that it is the visual regularity of the spelling pattern that matters. We have considered and rejected Gibson *et al.*'s (1970) reasons for abandoning the pronounceability hypothesis (based on their demonstration of a pseudoword advantage in the prelingually deaf; cf. Chapter 9, Section 4). We shall turn to more recent arguments below.

If pseudowords owe their advantage to the possession of wordlike structure then this raises two questions. First, what structural attributes are essential to this effect? Second, how is it that these attributes are processed so as to yield the effect? The first question can be posed at a fairly atheoretical level. We could simply attempt to manipulate various structural factors independently, looking for the one (or ones) that served as a sufficient condition for a pseudoword advantage, and then, having identified the relevant stimulus attributes, we could proceed to the second question. Presumably knowledge of what attributes of wordlikeness were relevant would help to constrain our search for the type of mechanism responsible for the effect.

We shall roughly shape our discussion in accordance with the division between these two questions, restricting ourselves in this résumé to the empirical question of the relevant form of wordlikeness. It must be admitted that the division is to some extent artificial. The choice of structural attributes to be tested is determined by hypotheses about the underlying mechanism. Furthermore, it is often not practicable to manipulate orthographic factors independently. Frequently the introduction of one form of structure into a letter string creates other, correlated forms of structure. Because pseudowords generally have high letter-positional redundancy, letter sequence redundancy, pronounceability, and resemblance to an actual morpheme or word, demonstrations that the introduction of one form of structure improves performance are usually inconclusive. I have therefore placed far greater emphasis on negative demonstrations, that is, the elimination of attributes from consideration by showing that they can be manipulated without effects on recognition performance.

There is no doubt that as readers we possess powerful intuitions about the characteristic patterning of letters in the words of a language. As Gibson and Levin (1975) have pointed out, this holds even for foreign languages with which we may be superficially acquainted. Czech seems to be full of crackling consonant clusters (*strc*, *krk*), whereas Italian is characterized by "liquid" consonant-vowel alternations (*amabile*, *pomodoro*). The orthographic regularities that we infer in our own language may result from quite subtle intuitions. As Baker (1980) and Smith (1980) have shown (see also Chapter 4), these may include an appraisal of the likely etymological source of a word as well as hypotheses about its morphological structure. These estimates probably shape our conception of the plausibility of a pseudoword as well as suggesting what conventions govern the spelling or the pronunciation of an unfamiliar form (Albrow, 1972).

Given the complexity of these forms of inferred structure, it may be naïve to suppose that wordlikeness can be manipulated simply in terms of the positional or sequential redundancies of the letter array. Nevertheless, such measures have dominated attempts to characterize wordlikeness (see Section 4.4) and have also served as the base from which pseudowords have been generated and calibrated for experimental purposes. The main competitor of this method of constructing pseudowords has been the method of starting from a real word and substituting certain letters, usually vowels, to produce a nonlexical item. Medial vowels are subject to few orthographic constraints so this procedure is generally very successful at yielding word-like forms, but the procedure itself guarantees that *the pseudoword has at least one lexical item as a very close orthographic neighbour* and this may have implications for the way in which such pseudowords are processed (see Sections 5.4 and 6.2).

Attempts to reveal the structural attributes of pseudowords responsible for their recognition advantage have centred on three characteristics: positional redundancy (single letter positional frequencies), sequential redundancy (bigram or trigram frequencies), and pronounceability. These attributes have generally been investigated in one of two ways. In one method, letter strings have been constructed so as to maximize one of these factors, and performance on these stimuli is compared with that on unstructured letter strings. This method is open to the fundamental objection that the various structural attributes are highly intercorrelated and manipulation of one almost invariably leads to changes in the values of other attributes. Let us examine the string used as an example of positional redundancy by Mason (1975). If we arrange the letters A, B, D, E, I, R to maximize the summed positional frequencies of each letter, we get BARIED. However, this arrangement of the letters also comes close to maximizing the summed bigram and trigram positional frequencies according to the norms of Mayzner and Tresselt, 1975, and Mayzner *et al.*, 1975). Furthermore, the resultant string is pronounceable, by any reckoning, and has a marked resemblance to a common inflected morpheme structure. On the other hand, in the first attempt to subject measures of orthographic structure to regression analysis (Gibson *et al.*, 1970) several of the contending measures were neglected.

Mention of regression leads us to the second method of investigating orthographic structure. In this method, *post hoc* analyses have been conducted to investigate the relationship of performance to one of the structural factors, this analysis being performed within a single type of item, such as word, pseudoword, or random letter strings. Not the least problem with such *post hoc* analyses is that they may involve too small a range of values on the orthographic dimension (see Henderson and Chard, 1980).

Studies of the effect of positional redundancy allow a number of generalizations to be made without apparent contradiction. In studies comparing letter strings of high and low positional redundancy, positional redundancy has related to speed of letter search through nonwords (Mason, 1975; Massaro *et al.*, 1979), speed of word naming (Mason, 1978a), and accuracy of tachistoscopic word perception (Mason, 1978a; Massaro *et al.*, 1979). Moreover, the speed with which a nonword string can be rejected in the lexical decision task varies inversely with positional redundancy (Henderson and Chard, 1980). In another set of studies, positional redundancy was not explicitly manipulated but its effect on tachistoscopic report accuracy was evaluated by *post hoc* analysis. McClelland (1976) found that the accuracy with which a probed letter could be reported from a random letter array increased when it occupied a position in which it frequently occurred in words. In a more detailed analysis McClelland and Johnston (1977) found that for both words and pseudowords the accuracy of letter report was higher when the letters occupied positions in which they commonly occurred. This positional redundancy effect did not interact with the advantage of words over pseudowords.

From these studies it is probably safe to conclude that high single-letter positional frequency is associated with superior performance. It is not clear whether this relationship is causal or mediated by some concealed factor which tends to vary along with manipulations of positional redundancy. Two facts suggest indirectly that we can neglect the possibility of mediation by another factor. First, the most likely of the associated factors, sequential redundancy, appears to be ruled out by evidence that we shall shortly turn to. Secondly, positional redundancy effects have been demonstrated within words, within pseudowords, and within consonant arrays. So different are these contexts that it seems unlikely that a concealed factor could covary with positional redundancy across these types of array.

What remains to be seen is the manner in which positional redundancy facilitates performances. At least four possibilities suggest themselves. (*i*) The effect may be due to typical differences in the positions occupied by consonants and vowels. (Some theorists have speculated about a role for early vowel detection in the preliminary analysis of words e.g. Henderson and Chard (1980) and p. 160 above, but these speculations remain vague.) (*ii*) The effect may be due to constraints operating at the feature interpretation level, i.e. a version of what is sometimes called "sophisticated guessing". One result that is difficult to reconcile with this hypothesis is reported by McClelland (1976), who found an advantage of pseudoword context over a random context when subjects were required to report a cued letter, even though the positional frequency of this critical letter was equated across the pseudowords and random strings. (*iii*) The effect may be a by-product, due to positional constraints tending to keep apart letters that are visually confusable. Mason (1978b) has presented a rather circumstantial argument for this view. (*iv*) The summed positional frequency of the letters in a string seems to correlate with the number of orthographic neighbours possessed by the string. Local properties of orthographic space rather than abstract frequency information *per se* may be responsible for the effect on performance—an idea developed below.

Whatever turns out to be the case, positional redundancy is evidently not the cause of an advantage of real words over pseudowords. Whether it can adequately account for the advantage of pseudowords over random strings is an unresolved question, but it begins to appear more likely that the observed effect on performance is mediated by some other factor or factors which are fortuitously related to positional redundancy.

In contrast to the results for positional redundancy, there is very little evidence of an effect of sequential redundancy on recognition performance. The measure of sequential redundancy adopted most frequently is the frequency of a letter bigram at a given position in words of a given length. Using such a measure, Manelis (1974), McClelland and Johnston (1977) and Johnston (1978) failed to find a dependence of tachistoscopic report accuracy on sequential redundancy, and Chambers and Forster (1975) found no effect upon the speed of same–different judgements. The study of McClelland and Johnston is particularly crucial, since it involved a planned test of the bigram effect with many other aspects of orthographic structure controlled. Furthermore, these same experiments revealed a reliable effect of positional redundancy. Where an association between performance and a measure of sequential redundancy has been found, other confounding factors have been present (e.g. pronounceability: cf. Herrmann and McLaughlin, 1973; Massaro *et al.*, 1980). It may therefore be concluded that recognition performance is not directly influenced by the sequential redundancy of letter arrays.

It has generally been supposed that what remains of orthographic structure when positional and sequential redundancy have been accounted for is pronounceability. However, pronounceability has usually been invoked as an intuitive concept without much explication. It is possible to distinguish several quite different aspects of pronounceability. One aspect was covered in our discussion of E. E. Smith's syllabification theory. Another has to do with phonotactic constraints. It is possible to infer that certain sound sequences are avoided in English, especially within a syllable. For example, /abt/ and /krk/ could not be English syllables. This appears to be one of the factors lurking behind Gibson and Levin's (1975) rather elusive concept of orthographic rules. Unfortunately such phonotactic constraints have no determinate effect upon spelling. For example, in words like *subpoena* the conjunction of consonants differing only in the voicing feature (BP) is handled by not sounding the first one. Nevertheless, phonotactic constraints imply graphotactic constraints, at least probabilistically. To some extent these constraints are reflected in bigram frequencies such as are tabulated in the Mayzner and Tresselt (1965) norms. However, these norms do not adequately express the constraints since they deal with frequency as a continuum rather than with the difference between (ideally) zero and nonzero frequency. Furthermore, they depend upon word length, which is irrelevant to pronounceability, and ignore position within the syllable, which is highly relevant. The only extant attempt to investigate the effects of such constraints occurs in work by Massaro *et al.* (1979, 1980). They factorially manipulated positional redundancy and pronounceability, defining pronounceability according to the rules expressed in Venezky's (1970) treatise on English orthography (see Chapter 4). Both factors exerted an effect on speed of letter search and on accuracy of tachistoscopic report. It has been pointed out by Krueger (1979) and by Henderson and Chard (1980) that Massaro *et al.*'s pronounceability factor might equally well have been called sequential redundancy. Given other failures to obtain effects of bigram frequency, however, the positive finds of Massaro *et al.* using their measure of orthographic legality lend modest support to the pronounceability case.

Attempts to refute the pronounceability position have for some reason concentrated exclusively upon the assumption that if pronounceability has an effect upon visual recognition, it must do so because the subject actually transforms the visual information into a phonetic code. Gibson *et al.* (1970) make this assumption when they reject pronounceability on the basis of the pseudoword advantage shown by deaf subjects (see p. 240). This reasoning also lies behind the homophone test employed by Baron and Thurston (1973), Baron (1975) and

Hawkins *et al.* (1976). The logic of the homophone test is as follows. If the perceiver performs better on pronounceable items because he transforms them into a purely phonetic recoding, then his performance on such items will be selectively impaired if his performance is assessed by requiring him to choose between response alternatives that sound identical. Since these studies of the word superiority effect revealed that the advantage of words over nonwords was not diminished when homophonic response alternatives were used, the authors concluded that this aspect of word superiority could not have been due to the subject using a pronunciation strategy.

This line of argument has perhaps not received the critical attention it deserves. As an attack on the position in which a pseudoword advantage is attributed to pronounceability it has two weak links. First, it involves the assumption that for pronounceability to matter, the subject must actually engage in recoding of the stimulus into a phonetic form. Yet pronounceability might create visible structure that is not successfully captured by norms of sequential and positional letter frequencies. Secondly, the attack involves the further assumption that phonetic recoding of the stimulus must involve *discarding of the spelling information*, i.e. the orthographic information which would permit an informed choice between homophonic alternatives. Here we find an unhappy but rather general consequence of theorizing conducted in terms of a serial array of boxes and arrows. If we suppose that recoding consists in moving from a box containing orthographic information to a box in which the information has been wholly discarded in favour of a phonetic translation, then homophones would present a much greater problem for reading than they do. However, the general consequences of assuming that recoding is strictly serial with loss of earlier codes seem so absurd that there is no reason to accept this assumption when applied to translation into phonological codes.

In summary, two aspects of orthographic structure survive as candidates for a role in the pseudoword advantage: positional constraints on letter occurrences and pronounceability. Neither of these types of structure points unequivocally to a particular form of mechanism.

Concerning pronounceability, I have argued that attempted refutations have failed. This candidate therefore survives, but it must be conceded that there is little agreement as to how this attribute could be used to aid recognition. For Massaro *et al.* (1979, 1980) pronounceability operates visibly by creating a form of constraint on letter sequences. For Spoehr and Smith (1973; 1975) pronounceability has its effect because visual identification is assumed to involve translation into a speech code. A third position, adopted rather furtively by Henderson and Chard (1980), is that pronounceability permits a separate and later stage of processing to exert "top-down" facilitation upon the graphic domain. We return to these questions later in this chapter when we consider theories of word superiority.

Concerning positional constraints upon letter occurrence, the most straightforward mechanism for an effect is through a process of inference (or "sophisticated guessing"), a possibility that I have not favoured. My own preference—on frankly speculative grounds—is for a mechanism involving facilitative interaction amongst members of an orthographic neighbourhood. In this view, the positional frequency tabulations need not be internally represented at all. They only predict performance to the extent that they are reflected in the local structure of the lexicon when a region of the visual lexicon is stimulated by a letter-array. Thus we might expect a pseudoword to have a perceptual advantage over a random string to the extent that it has orthographic overlap with real words, perhaps especially, high-frequency words. What this implies is that, as in the lexical pooling theory of pronunciation-assignment, pseudowords do not draw upon a different mechanism from real words. The two types of stimuli differ merely in the fact that the region of orthographic space excited by their display contains, in the case of a real word, a representation of the word itself.[19]

Lexicality and the contrast of words v. pseudowords

Baron and Thurston (1973) were the first to suggest explicitly that words and pseudowords shared an equal advantage over random strings and that word superiority effects therefore depend on the presence of orthographic structure in a stimulus array but are uninfluenced by the lexical status of the stimulus. Clearly the comparison of performance on words and pseudowords is a crucial one for theory. Unfortunately it is difficult to arrive at any firm empirical conclusions.

We can with some confidence ignore the failure by Baron and Thurston to find a lexicality effect. Manelis (1974) has discussed various problems in the design of Baron and Thurston's study. The most serious of these, taken alone, is fatal: the words used were generally of low frequency, while the nonword category included items that were rare words as well as meaningful slang.

On the whole, adequately designed studies have tended to obtain an advantage for words over pseudowords, but this finding has not emerged absolutely consistently. Using various measures of tachistoscopic report accuracy, Juola *et al.* (1974), Manelis (1974), McClelland (1976), McClelland and Johnston (1977) and Adams (1979) have obtained reliable effects of lexicality.

Two factors must be controlled in such comparisons. Clearly, word frequency must be high if a word advantage is to be given a chance to materialize, and if a spurious advantage is to be avoided then pseudowords must be matched to words on orthographic structure.

It is well known that, at least under some circumstances, accuracy of report increases with word frequency. This effect of frequency might in itself be taken as evidence of a lexicality effect in perception. The frequency effect has often been ascribed to sophisticated guessing taking place between perception and response (see Chapter 12). However, McClelland and Johnston (1977) found an advantage of words over pseudowords and a frequency effect within the word stimuli in conditions where evidence of sophisticated guessing was absent. Failure to control word frequency is a likely source of the inconsistency of the word advantage across experiments in the study by Spoehr and Smith (1975) as well as the failure by Baron and Thurston to obtain any effect.

The injunction to equate structuredness between words and pseudowords is more problematic, because as we have seen, an adequate definition of orthographic structure is lacking. Generally this matching has been achieved by changing a single letter in the words to produce comparable pseudowords (e.g. Manelis, 1974) or by matching on positional and sequential redundancy (e.g. McClelland, 1976).

An intriguing complication in this literature is the study by Carr *et al.* (1978) in which a reliable lexicality effect could only be obtained when the subject had no expectation that pseudowords would be among the stimuli. Performance on words and random strings was unaffected by expectation that they would be presented, but performance on pseudowords was better than on random strings only when subjects knew that pseudowords could occur. Given the reliability of the lexicality effect in other studies, it seems safe to accept the working hypothesis that a word advantage exists even when pseudowords are expected. However, the interesting implication of the lexicality effect was, in any case, that words and pseudowords are processed by different mechanisms. This conclusion is reinforced by Carr *et al.*'s demonstration of a selective effect of expectation on the two types of stimuli. Furthermore, their results suggest the rather surprising conclusion that the lexical processing mechanism is automatically available whereas the mechanism responsible for the advantage of pseudowords over random strings depends upon attentional control.

An advantage of real words over pseudowords has also been generally obtained for the speed of same–different judgements. This appears to hold widely for "same" decisions (Barron and Pittinger, 1974; Baron, 1975; Chambers and Forster, 1975; Barron and Henderson, 1977; Taylor *et al.*, 1977; Bruder, 1978; but for an anomalous result see Carr *et al.*, 1979). The picture for "different" decisions is less clear. In most studies no reliable difference emerges (Barron and Pittinger, 1974; Baron, 1975; Chambers and Forster, 1975; Barron and Henderson, 1977; Bruder, 1978), but occasionally a word advantage or disadvantage may appear (Taylor *et al.*, 1977). Given the weight of evidence for a word advantage in "same" decisions and equal performance in "different" decisions, it seems reasonable to conclude that the same–different task provides evidence of a lexicality effect that is consistent with that obtained for tachistoscopic report accuracy. Further support for the suggestion that words may call upon a lexical mechanism comes from the demonstration by Chambers and Forster (1975) and by Bruder (1978) that the word advantage depends upon word frequency.

These conclusions have been challenged on two grounds by Baron (1975), Pollatsek and Carr (1979) and Carr *et al.* (1979). They argue first that the word advantage for "same" decisions is not reliably obtained and secondly that when such an advantage is obtained it is a consequence of a criterion bias whereby words preferentially elicit "same" decisions and nonwords "different" decisions. The first point is easily disposed of because those few studies that have failed to obtain a lexicality effect even for "same" decisions (Carr *et al.*, 1979; and perhaps Baron, 1975) have used stimuli for which the effect is least to be expected, i.e. words of few letters and uncontrolled frequency. Many authors have shown that word superiority effects diminish with decreases in string length (e.g. Bruder, 1978), yet the stimuli used by Carr *et al.* were only three letters in length. Even more crucial is the maximization of word frequency: although this is fundamental to the logic of a word–pseudoword comparison, Baron's (1975) pseudowords include some real words and both Baron's and Carr *et al.*'s words are often of very low frequency (e.g. SOT, VAT, DAF).

The criterion bias argument is less easily analysed. Clearly there is something to be explained in the interaction of lexicality with type of decision ("same" v. "different"). Nevertheless, criterion bias cannot amount to a sufficient cause for these results, since several of the studies show a reliable word advantage when types of response are combined, and even when "different" RTs favour pseudowords this effect is smaller than the "same" RT advantage for words.

Moreover, as with the tachistoscopic literature, the main thrust of the claimed word advantage consists in the suggestion that different (if overlapping) mechanisms serve the processing of words and pseudowords. Support for this suggestion is provided by the large body of evidence that lexicality alone, in the absence of orthographic structure, is a sufficient cause of a "word" advantage (Egeth and Blecker, 1971; Henderson, 1974; Henderson and Chard, 1976; Seymour and Jack, 1978; Besner *et al.*, in press). These experiments rely on the contrast of lexical stimuli like FBI with nonlexical controls like IBF.

In sum, I believe it is safe to conclude that under appropriate testing conditions a lexicality advantage emerges reliably. Elsewhere (Henderson, 1980b), I have provided a fuller review of the literature together with a discussion of what the "appropriate" testing conditions might be.

What cannot yet be decided is whether the underlying mechanisms serving the pseudoword advantage (over random arrays) and the real word advantage (over pseudowords) are totally distinct one from another. To the extent that the two classes of stimuli are differentially sensitive to expectation, the mechanisms must diverge at some stage but may nevertheless share a common principle of operation.

When it is assumed that the pseudoword advantage is attributable to inference based upon knowledge of positional or sequential letter redundancies, it is open to the theorist to assume that lexical knowledge carries with it more constraint of the same type. This is the approach favoured by Rumelhart and Siple (1974) but argued against in the above. Another single-principle approach is that of McClelland and Rumelhart (1980) in which all facilitatory effects of structure are due to feedback from the excitation of lexical items that share an orthographic neighbourhood. Yet another general approach is taken by Henderson and Chard (1980), who assume that words and pseudowords typically excite different types of higher-level code but that these have in common a greater robustness and accessibility than a stimulus description confined to the graphemic level.

10.2 THEORIES OF WORD SUPERIORITY

This section focuses on the main attempts to explain word superiority effects. Fortunately we have already examined many of the theories in some detail in the context of particular items of evidence, so we can concentrate on a review of certain broader issues as they bear on general types of theory. Accordingly, we shall pursue our discussion under five general headings: preliminary letter identification, uptake of information, inferential processes, criterion bias, and robustness of codes.

Preliminary letter identification

In Chapter 9 we considered and rejected various wholistic assertions about feature analysis in word recognition, so we began this chapter with the assumption that word recognition depends upon preliminary letter identification. Although we found various specific problems with each version of wholistic theory, it must be acknowledged that the general rejection of wholism in favour of preliminary letter identification rests on one main support: the difficulty of otherwise accounting for the fact that word superiority survives case alternation within the letter array. (But see also Evett and Humphreys, 1981.)

One question that follows from the assumption of preliminary letter identification is whether the representation at this stage is of physical letter forms or of abstract graphemes. The evidence on this point is not conclusive, and this is possibly a strategic option, under the subject's control and depending upon the sort of decision about the word that is required. McClelland (1976) has shown that in a threshold experiment for stimuli in which letter-case varied, the subject's ability to report word-case (upper, lower or mixed) is very poor (about 50%). He cites this as evidence that the preliminary code is an abstract graphemic one, and this position is also adopted by Allport (1979) and Henderson and Chard (1980), but it is not difficult to conceive of objections to this argument.

In McClelland's experiment, case information is irrelevant and distracting. This may have one of two consequences. Either the subject may opt not to synthesize a literal level of description of the array, or he may form such a representation but not attend to it, so that he is unable explicitly to recover the information. Support for this latter view comes from Kirsner's (1972) demonstration that case change influences the speed and accuracy with which the recurrence of a word can be identified in running recognition memory. In this instance, of course, case knowledge is not interrogated explicitly. Moreover, when physical information is required by the nature of the task a word advantage remains. Pollatsek *et al.* (1975) found that subjects could detect the difference between LEAF and LeAF faster than in equivalent random strings, so it appears that whether lexical access is mediated by a physical letter code or an abstract graphemic code, as here assumed, top-down enhancement of lower-level information can extend to physical codes.

We can build up some sort of picture of the preliminary letter representation from various other findings. Two sources of information are of particular importance in this respect: the subject's knowledge of the position of letters that he succeeds in identifying and the independence of letter processing for the various letters within a stimulus array.

Several authors have reported evidence of some independence between knowledge of the identity and the position of letters in an array. It seems clearly established that in random letter strings the tendency toward letter transpositions in full report is particularly strong (Estes, 1975; McClelland and Johnston, 1977; Johnston, 1978; Adams, 1979). The implication that appreciable uncertainty attaches to the location of a character that has been successfully identified is itself an interesting one. Estes (1975) has taken a particularly strong line on positional uncertainty, asserting that the reduction of such uncertainty by the use of redundancy is the sole cause of the superiority of words and pseudowords over random strings. In contradiction to this, Johnston (1978) and Adams (1979) have shown that random strings are reported less accurately than words, even when position report is ignored. Moreover, if orthographic constraints were used inferentially to reconstitute letter-position information, there should still be room for a considerable number of transpositions in pseudowords. Yet Adams (1979) found only 3 out of 611 in fully reported pseudowords.

An important discussion of the problem of assembling the information derived from specialized processors, such as those for position and identity, has been presented by Allport (1977). He points out that: "in any complex cognitive system in which specialised 'knowledge sources' contribute from within different domains of knowledge, the problem inevitably arises as to how these separate specialists are to communicate with each other" (Allport, 1977, p. 526).

The solution that Allport advances is adapted from the model of speech perception known as Hearsay II (see Reddy and Newell, 1975). In this system, processors operating at various levels (phonemic, syllabic, lexical, etc.) interact through the medium of a central "blackboard", a device on which can be entered hypotheses at any level concerning the input message. In Allport's formulation, the "blackboard" for word perception receives input from a visual code that carries nonlinguistic, spatial pattern information about the layout of an array. It also receives input from lexical and phonological processors. The visual code contains an uneconomical description of a letter array. Unless this description can be condensed by coordinating the visual code with the lexical or phonological code, detail, such as letter position, is likely to be lost.

As regards independence of letter processing within an array, independence seems to hold for random strings but not for words. McClelland and Johnston (1977) tested for independence in two ways. First, they showed that for words and pseudowords, but not for random strings, the probability of correctly reporting all the letters was greater than would be predicted, assuming that letters were processed independently with the efficiency estimated from the probed recognition performance on single letters. Secondly, they showed that for words and pseudowords there was a positive correlation between accuracy of report at different positions within the array. Moreover, this correlation increased the closer the two positions were within the word. These tendencies were absent in random letter strings. The first of these tests was also applied by Adams (1979), who found that for words correct report of the entire string was more frequent than would be expected from independent letter processing. This was not true for Adams's pseudowords. As Adams has pointed out, this test of nonindependence is a severe one, since a positive outcome is being worked against by the existence of a serial position effect. (Performance varies systematically as a function of array position.)

So far we have discussed this issue in terms of dependencies between processing operations on the letters of the array. Although this might be taken to imply that such dependencies must occur during the process of information extraction, it is equally possible that the dependencies between letters occur at the stage of information readoff or retrieval. This possibility is rendered the more likely because the primary form of dependency seems to consist in an exceptionally high incidence of perfect reports of all letters of a word. The contrast between effects arising at the uptake and at the recovery of information is developed in what follows.

Uptake of information

The main set of theories that have asserted superior uptake of visual information in words comprises the wholistic feature extraction theories reviewed and rejected in the previous chapter. These theories attributed superior uptake of information to the availability of more global features in words and pseudowords.

The interactive feature search theory (Henderson, 1977) is also essentially an uptake theory, since it asserts that feature testing is guided by hypotheses about the accumulating evidence at various levels. As we saw in the last chapter, this sort of theory is vulnerable to the general assault on inference theories mounted by McClelland and Johnston (1977) and Johnston (1978).

Another theory that can be reckoned as an uptake theory has been advanced by Mason (1978a) to explain the apparently facilitatory effect of positional redundancy amongst letters. Mason argues that the constraints upon the positioning of letters in English words tend to keep visually similar letters out of the same word or to maximize the distance between them in a word. This effect in turn might tend to minimize competition for feature detectors by similar letters (see, for example, Estes, 1972). What is interesting about this suggestion is that it provides a basis for the observed effects of single letter positional frequency without postulating an inference mechanism; moreover, it avoids the troublesome assumption that positional information itself requires to be encoded for an effect to be manifest. However, so far the evidence for Mason's theory is rather indirect and its application would appear to be limited to aspects of the pseudoword advantage.

An equally restricted uptake theory was mentioned in the previous section of this chapter where we discussed the poor resolution of the positions of letters that seemed to be responsible in part for the inferior performance on random letter strings. We considered the possibility that the less severe demands made by letter identification in words releases more processing capacity for the tagging of positional information in words.

In summary, it appears that no comprehensive explanation of word superiority effects is to be found in uptake theories. The surviving candidates in this class offer at best a partial account of the pseudoword advantage. Further experimental attacks against the class of uptake theories have recently been reported by Krueger and Shapiro (1979) and by Massaro (1979).

If we set aside uptake theories, we are left with the problem of how higher-level knowledge of the structure of written language can be brought to bear upon perceptual decisions about letters. There is also the question of what the nature of that knowledge is.

Inference theories

The answer to these questions offered by the broad class of inference theories is as follows. Knowledge of the positional or sequential constraints upon the occurrences of letters in the words of the language is brought to bear upon the perceptual decisions about the identity of letters. According to the particular form of knowledge brought to bear, the perceiver is able, when deciding about a particular letter, to exclude from consideration candidates which (*i*) seldom occur in that position in a word, (*ii*) seldom occur in that letter context, or (*iii*) could not complete an actual word in that context. Such theories are sometimes called sophisticated guessing theories in acknowledgement of the way in which the perceiver intelligently reduces the range of possibilities amongst which a choice has to be made. Although, as I have previously indicated, "guessing" carries the unnecessary implication of a deliberate strategy, such calculations might be conducted automatically by the perceptual system.

Inference theory has been persistently championed by Massaro (e.g. 1973, 1979) and a version of it was advanced by Rumelhart and Siple (1974). In addition, Estes' (1975) account of the superior recognition of letter positioning in words appears to involve inference.

How inference might operate was described by Thompson and Massaro (1973) as follows. Assume that a subject has correctly detected information indicating that a four letter word consisted of WOR_ plus a curved letter in the fourth position. The curved feature is consistent with D, O or Q. If the subject assumes that the letters spell a word, he decides D, and choses correctly when the alternatives D or K are presented, but if the curved feature could be held in memory until the arrival of the response alternative D or K, the decision could be made just as well for an isolated D as for the D in WORD. So it is necessary for Massaro to assume that elementary featural information can only be held long enough to guide a choice between the alternatives offered by the linguistic knowledge sources but *not* long enough to guide the choice between the alternatives specified by the experimenter in the forced-choice task. That is, a perceptual commitment is made in the light of any applicable knowledge about the structure of words, and then the featural information on which this decision was based is immediately discarded, so that it cannot be re-consulted if further information is provided in the form of forced-choice alternatives.

The workings of the hypothetical process of inference are usually illustrated for the simple case in which all the letters but the critical one are correctly identified, as in WOR_. Clearly, however, if inference is to operate throughout the performance band-width, the computations become very much more complex as fewer features are detected and therefore the sensory data is compatible with a large number of linguistically acceptable possibilities.

The primary evidence against inference theories consists in the evidence against the efficacy of sequential and lexical constraints (e.g. McClelland and Johnston, 1977; Johnston, 1978). Inference accounts hold that words owe their perceptual advantage to our knowledge of their internal structure as arrays of graphemes. The lack of evidence that such structural factors actually matter is therefore highly critical. There is perhaps some room for doubt on the question of whether weak effects of sequential constraint exist. However, the lack of any evidence that lexical constraint matters is particularly devastating to inference theory, given that the superiority of words over pseudowords requires to be explained.

Moreover, a unique prediction of inference theory that once appeared to be valid has since met disconfirmation. Both Massaro (e.g. Thompson and Massaro, 1973) and Estes (e.g. Estes, 1975) have argued that word superiority should be abolished by presenting the response alternatives in advance, since this limitation of the possibilities can then be used to guide the decisions made on the basis of feature detection. Thus, the information supplied in advance will override constraints derived from the subject's linguistic knowledge. While the original evidence appeared to favour this prediction, more recent studies have shown word superiority effects in such tasks provided that the display conditions are conducive to word perception (Purcell and Stanovich, in press).

It is also possible to argue that inference theories provide no ready account of some of the word superiority effects obtained in reaction-time tasks. This is particularly true of tasks in which letter identification is not a sufficient basis for responding, for example when a (case-specific) physical match is required so that a subject must respond "no" to BREAD–bread (Besner and Jackson, 1975) or LEAF–LeAF (Pollatsek *et al.*, 1975). The use of inference to speed grapheme identification in words cannot itself serve as the basis of word superiority in such matching tasks.

Criterion-bias theories

A traditional rival of inference theories as an account of perceptual decision-making consists in the class of criterion-bias theories, in which sensory evidence and linguistic knowledge combine together in the activation of detector units. The combination of sensory evidence with linguistic knowledge is often expressed in the metaphor of a vessel (detector unit) into which the sensory evidence flows. The detector becomes critically activated when the fluid reaches a criterial level. This criterion can be manipulated separately for each vessel by allowing the system of stored linguistic knowledge to prime each vessel with a specific resting-level of fluid. This, in effect, biases the criterion by controlling the amount of sensory evidence fluid that is required to fill the vessel to the critical level. (Freudian energy-based hydraulics is supplanted by information-bearing hydraulics, but the metaphorical plumbing survives the theory that it embodies!)

Traditional criterion-bias accounts only deal with bias at a word detector level (Broadbent, 1967; Morton, 1969; Allport, 1977). In this case a word detector's criterion is generally set according to the frequency of occurrence of the word. It can also vary transiently in response to the immediate context of preceding words. Because of their concentration on the word level of analysis these, theories have generally been very vague about the details of preliminary processing in word recognition. To the extent that they make assumptions about the manner in which sensory evidence is accumulated, these assumptions have tended to be wholistic.

A recent development has been the extension of the criterion-bias notion to cover letter detection as well as word detection and to admit letter-context as a source of knowledge through which detector criteria can be biased. In Adams's (1979) formulation, the critical value for a letter detector is determined by letter-context in such a way as to reflect the frequency of letter sequence occurrences in the language.

Formulated in these simple terms there is little to distinguish a criterion-bias account from an inference account in the realm of existing data, and it would appear that the ineffectiveness of sequential and lexical constraints is just as much an embarrassment to Adams's model as it was to Massaro's. Moreover, the criterion-bias account does not, in this form, explain why a word-context should facilitate decisions based on letter-case (the Besner and Jackson and the Pollatsek *et al.* findings). Finally, neither class of model, as considered so far, offers an explanation of the dependence of the word-letter effect upon masking.

Since the words above were written an important extension of the criterion-bias account has been advanced by McClelland and Rumelhart (1980). They proposed a model having at least three levels: features, letters, and words. Most of the interesting properties of the model are generated by interactive feedback between the word and letter levels of analysis. In this way linguistic knowledge is brought to bear upon perception of the letter array. Feedback between levels consists of excitatory and inhibitory connections between lexical and graphemic units. Feedback also occurs between the units within a level.

To the extent that a letter unit is activated by the feature-level, this unit in turn activates word units that contain the letter and inhibits other word units that do not contain it. As word units are activated they compete amongst themselves, and according to their state of activation they send inhibitory or excitatory feedback down to the letter units.

What set the model apart from other criterion-bias (e.g. Adams, 1979) or interactive (e.g. Henderson, 1977) notions are the complexity and the explictness of the assumptions that are made. In fact the model contains 18 parameters. Many of these describe either the resting levels of units or the strength of the excitatory and inhibitory action of units on other units, both within and between levels.

The strength of the model is that choice of the appropriate value of these parameters allows the prediction of many of the known effects in tachistoscopic word recognition. These successful predictions include the various word and pseudoword advantages over single letters and random letter strings, as well as the role of masking in these effects. Moreover, it is possible to choose parameter values such that no effects of letter-sequence frequency or lexical constraint are obtained. The difficulty of explaining word superiority effects without such unwanted constraint effects was the clear undoing of the models previously reviewed.

The weakness of the model is its arbitrary and *post hoc* character. Clearly with enough parameters to juggle with, we can predict almost anything at all, and this model requires rather a lot of parameters. Moreover, the values of these parameters must be chosen carefully to generate the required predictions. A few of the parameters are given zero values as a simplifying assumption, but most are assigned values in an *ad hoc* manner. That is to say, no independent test or justification is offered for the assumed value, which is apparently chosen to generate the prediction of already known effects. Such mathematical modelling is notoriously difficult to evaluate (see, for example, Coltheart and Coltheart, 1972). It is desirable to have some way of judging the plausibility of the fundamental assumptions (parameters and their values). Failing this, it is desirable at least to have an independent method for estimating parameter values. Furthermore, we must be assured that the model is not as complex as the set of successful predictions. The *reductio ad absurdum* consists in having to add further assumptions to make each new prediction. Finally, it is desirable that the model not only accommodates already known facts but also successfully generates new predictions.

Recoverability of information and the robustness of coding

The final class of model has been outlined by Seymour (1979) and Henderson and Chard (1980). Seymour assumes that when a lexical representation of a grapheme array has been accessed, it can be used to "improve the quality of a description being formed in the graphemic register" (Seymour, 1979, p. 133).

Seymour's formulation confronts us with two problems. First, it shares with all the foregoing accounts a concentration on the abstract graphemic level, yet the evidence of word superiority in physical-match tasks (Besner and Jackson, 1975; Pollatsek *et al.*, 1975) suggests that facilitation extends down to a level at which the physical form of letters is represented. The second problem is of a more general nature. The difficulty is that it is not clear how Seymour's formulation of the robust code position differs from a criterion-bias account such as that of McClelland and Rumelhart (1980).

The grounds for a distinction are sketched by Henderson and Chard (1980), who characterize the robust code position as having to do with the accessibility to conscious scrutiny of lower-level representation of the stimulus, in contrast to views based on the speed and accuracy with which lower-level descriptions can be formed.

The central tenet of the present view is that performance in tasks, even of the apparent simplicity of the masked tachistoscopic identification task or the various searching and matching reaction time tasks, is not a direct reflection of the speed or accuracy with which a description of the stimulus is initially formed. Such tasks are not transparent, affording a direct view of stimulus encoding stages. Instead, performance in these tasks depends upon the conscious manipulation of descriptions of the stimulus, involving the search, comparison and recovery of components of that description. In sum, this is a view of word superiority effects occurring at later stages of processing than those concerned with the initial formation of graphemic representations.

The present version of the position starts from the assumption that it is important for the perceptual system to form a robust and economical description of pattern information. This view of word recognition echoes a general view of perception that has been set out by Hochberg (1968) amongst others. In particular, I suggest, as Allport (1977) and Marcel (in press) have also done, that the ability to retain a stimulus description in working memory and to recover its detail in consciousness depends upon the formation of a robust description of the pattern. The availability of a lexical code, or even of a description of orthographic structure, serves as a robust frame for the information in a letter array.

It is obvious how a lexical code may provide such a framework but less obvious perhaps how the structure of a pseudoword can be entered into a stimulus description. I have assumed that these descriptions are formulated at the level of an abstract phonological code. This may serve as a general description of the structure of a pseudoword while lacking much of the specific detail necessary to achieve an articulatory specification. It is important to note that this code does not replace the visual information, as is assumed in the homophone test of phonetic recoding (see pp. 270–271). It is combined with the visual information in the perceptual description.

How, then, does the availability of a more robust description of the stimulus assist performance? In part, the answer to this will depend on the task, for I assume that robust codes are more memorable, more amenable to manipulation and comparison, and less susceptible to interference by "central" masking. Consider first the general situation. With brief presentation of a random string we assume that a robust description of the letter array cannot be formed and that therefore information loss is likely to ensue. It is this loss of conscious access that subjects in the span of apprehension task are trying to describe (cf. Sperling, 1960).

Several authors have speculated about information loss during the processing of letter arrays. Thus, Wheeler (1970) and Thompson and Massaro (1973) have suggested that the system must arrive at a perceptual decision about letter identities before the experimenter-defined response alternatives became available. For example, if only enough data is accumulated about a test letter to narrow down the possibilities to D, O, Q, the perceiver must choose randomly if it is an isolated letter. Given the context WOR_, however, the perceiver can choose D on the hypothesis that the string formed a word. Now, this is a statement of the inference position that we know to be falsified by the finding of no sequential redundancy effects. Nevertheless, what is of interest in the present context is the ancillary assumption of information loss. For, whatever the basis of the perceptual decision, both theorists assume that this decision is accompanied by loss of the original featural information. As a consequence, when the response alternatives arrive, the featural information is no longer available. If, in the single letter condition, the subject has not guessed correctly from the candidate set D, Q, O, then the arrival of the explicit response alternatives D or K do not help. By the time they become available the featural basis on which Q or O was guessed has been "forgotten".

The assumption that perceptual decisions leave a single surviving candidate and are accompanied by the loss of all featural information is, of course, a rather extreme version of the information loss position. A less radical suggestion has been made by Henderson (1977), who speculates that words and pseudowords allow more efficient retention of stimulus information while perceptual decisions are being made.

A weakness of the Wheeler and Thompson and Massaro accounts is that they are directed toward an explanation of the word v. single letter effect. Yet it appears that word superiority in this comparison depends on the use of a patterned mask (see Section 10.1). What this dependency suggests is that information loss is not an automatic consequence of perceptual decision making, as these theorists suggest, but instead it appears that perceptual alternatives that are held in a letter-level code are more vulnerable to disruption by masking than those in phonological or lexical codes.

In the comparison of words and pseudowords with random letter strings word superiority obtains even in the absence of masking (Juola *et al.*, 1974). In this case, I would argue that the information load of the random string is sufficient to result in greater information loss than occurs for words or pseudowords, even without the disruptive effect of masking.

Robust coding not only conveys resistance to information loss due to high load and to masking, it also conserves information during the manipulation of codes. This is attested by the word superiority effects in same–different judgements. Here perceptual codes have to be compared. We saw that the important finding in this task is that word superiority survives even when the lexical or phonological codes cannot themselves serve as the basis of comparison, for example when subjects are required to respond "different" to pairs such as WORD–word or WORd–WORD (Besner and Jackson, 1975; Pollatsek *et al.*, 1975). This result implies that the availability of a lexical or phonological framework serves to enhance visual information (see also Seymour and Jack,

1978). Visual letter information is more stable and accessible during comparison, when it is embodied in a robust code such as a word allows.

It follows also from this analysis that increasing load by increasing string length should magnify the word advantage, and this appears to be the case (see Henderson, 1980b, for a review). I would also predict that increasing the amount of manipulation required in the comparison should increase the word advantage, as when the two items of the pair were at different orientations one from the other.

A considerable extension of the robustness effect has been reported by Henderson *et al.* (1981). They found that subjects were faster at naming the letters in a word than in a nonword and that this effect obtained even when the letters were continuously displayed during performance.

In summary, this discussion serves both to clarify the sense in which a lexical or phonological code can be said to provide a robust framework for visual information and to illustrate the predictive power of this conception as applied to a diversity of tasks.

10.3 GENERAL IMPLICATIONS

In this chapter we have so far taken a fairly narrow view of a difficult and intricate literature. In this brief final section we shall stand back from the experimental details in order to review the issues in a wider perspective. First we shall consider the question of optional strategies in word perception. Then we shall turn to the general conception of perception that emerges from the earlier sections. Lastly, we shall have regard to other phenomena in perception bearing some resemblance to word superiority effects.

Strategies

In a recent collection of papers on the role of processing strategies in cognition, Coltheart (1978) predicted that the concept of "strategy" would dominate the immediate future as the concept of "code" had the immediate past. This may come to be, but it must be conceded that at present theoretical attention to strategies in word recognition is largely limited to their nuisance value. The prevailing approach to strategy variation stems from a long tradition in which the Good Experiment is held to be one that tears aside the idiosyncrasies of strategy in order to allow us to gaze upon the underlying mental structures (cf. Henderson, 1977). This is probably why theorists have tended to resort to the concept of strategic options only when it is necessary to resolve some inconsistency in the outcome of experiments directed toward the identification of the code used in a particular task. This is in fact true of Coltheart's own concern with strategy, bearing as it does on the question of whether subjects' employ a visual or a phonological code in order to address the mental lexicon during reading.

One major expectation we might have about a comprehensive theory of strategy variation in word perception is that it might enable us to relate more closely the study of skilled word recognition to teaching practice in the pedagogy of reading. As Marcel (1978) has pointed out in a valuable polemic, our present inability to relate these two domains has to do with the lack of a model of intervention. This in turn follows from our inability to treat the way in which information-processing strategies can be modified by the conscious level of communication employed in explicit pedagogy. Somehow, notwithstanding the conventional way of setting psychology apart from linguistics, it seems that the cognitive psychologist's theory of word recognition centres more on competence than on performance.

In contrast to what we need to know to arrive at a systematic theory of word recognition strategies, present findings are tentative and highly limited in application. Nevertheless it is worth mentioning some of the issues that emerge.

One pervasive issue concerns the possibility that the findings on which we based our earlier discussion themselves result from atypical strategies adopted to cope with highly artificial tasks. The general form of this criticism is not new but it can be given fresh life in a variety of ways. For example, it might be argued that a tendency toward wholistic feature extraction is obscured by the use of the probed letter recognition technique. At a more general level, Broadbent (1979) has dismissed much of the experimental material reviewed in this chapter as only relevant to the recognition of letters in words rather than the recognition of words themselves. Now, a difficulty with this comment is that it may seem to imply more than it does, namely a preference for one sort of response test of recognition over another. Nevertheless, it is easy to agree in principle with the idea that the response requirements of a task may influence the features which the subject extracts from the stimulus, or at least the level of code to which he attends. It is therefore reassuring that many of the findings that we have taken as crucial in the foregoing can be obtained equally with full report as with forced-choice recognition of individually sampled letters. Yet even here there are possible problems, since in those studies in which various response measures are obtained on a given word (e.g. the careful series of studies by Johnston and McClelland) the general adoption of, say, a letter-processing strategy could in principle be determined by the inclusion of a letter-probe measure.

Consider, for example, the main grounds for rejecting feature analytic wholism. These consisted of the demonstrations of word superiority effects for "case alternation" stimuli. Since these effects were manifest even in the absence of probed letter recognition (e.g. Adams, 1979) it seems safe to conclude that wholistic encoding is not involved. However, this is not to say that the level of codes to which the perceiver attends is incapable of being influenced by task demands in any situation. Two factors which do appear to influence the level of processing are the subject's expectations about the sort of stimuli that might be presented (e.g. words or random strings) and, more subtly, the extent of his attention to letter context.

The primary evidence for the effect of breadth of attention comes from the important demonstration by Johnston and McClelland (1974) that a word advantage in recognition depended upon the perceiver including the whole word in his attentional compass rather than just a predesignated critical letter. I have read into this the general moral that it is easy to set up a task in such a way that *word* processing will not take place. This is what I have taken Estes and Massaro to be doing when they have failed to obtain a word advantage with precued letter alternatives. Indeed, inconsistencies in word superiority findings even with precuing (cf. Henderson, 1978) suggest that it is not precuing itself that matters but rather its influence on the subject's strategy selection.

A different source of strategy variation arises in factors that influence the subject's expectation about the type of stimulus that will be presented (e.g. Carr *et al.*, 1978) or whether a block of trials is homogeneous with respect to type of stimuli (Manelis, 1974). Such manipulations are relevant to the question of whether words, pseudowords and random strings recruit different processing mechanisms and whether these mechanisms are automatically engaged by stimulus presentation.

Another and even less explored possibility of strategy variation occurs in the realm of consistent individual differences in performance. For instance, Manelis (1974) reported a tendency for word superiority to be bimodally distributed across subjects. Such reports have tended to be *post hoc*, not surprisingly, and have seldom been followed up systematically.

One feature of most word perception experiments that has possible implications for the subject's choice of processing strategies arises from the simple fact that the stimulus words are presented for recognition alone and out of context. Unfortunately, the implications of this procedure, while potentially important, are at present very unclear. There is no doubt that in word recognition context matters. The question is whether it merely biases mechanisms that exist in the service of recognition of isolated words or whether isolated words induce some quite special strategy. It would certainly be unwise to dismiss the experimental literature on word recognition on the vague grounds that isolated words are "artificial" stimuli. In a very real sense all printed language is "artificial". Moreover, the child's first attempts at reading are usually directed toward isolated words. We do not generally think of this experience as inducing strategies that are wholly inappropriate for reading of connected text.

Nevertheless, there are some possible consequences of restricting consideration to the recognition of isolated words. One accidental property of such stimuli is that they have almost always been foveal. However, an aspect of the presentation of isolated words that interests me more is that the situation may limit the possibility of "top-down" processing. Thus we have been led to reject the possibility of directive feedback from lexical or phonological levels to the level of letter analysis. (In this, I suspect that recognition of printed words differs from speech and handwriting.) However, it seems likely that top-down processing plays a major role in reading text, and there is even some evidence that it plays a role in visual search through lists of nouns (Henderson and Chard, 1977). Interactive feedback from semantic and syntactic levels to the lexical (or morphological) level therefore remains a possibility that cannot readily be explored by means of single word displays.

The concept of "perception"

The problem of perception was at one time construed as that of giving a causal account of the source of perceptual experiences. The percept or mental image of the stimulus was regarded as marking the successful terminus of the act of perceiving. In more recent information-processing accounts, perception has been construed in terms of the uptake of information in feature analysis. Nevertheless, aspects of the phenomenological view seem to survive in many modern accounts, in so far as perception is regarded as an early stage in cognition having a clearly marked terminus that enables the distinction of perception from subsequent processes such as memory, comparison and the like.

This restricted concept of perception is manifest in a more specific form in research on reading, where it is often assumed that the only interesting limitations on reading performance are those of information uptake. An implication of this assumption is that for an experimental effect to have relevance to the real-world practice of reading the effect must be shown to be truly "perceptual", i.e. located at uptake. It is in this spirit that much of the debate about the word superiority effect has been conducted.

In contrast to this view, I have argued that most word superiority effects are due, not to the process of information uptake and the speed with which codes can be arrived at, but instead to the nature of the codes and their stability and accessability to deliberation. Yet I would also want to argue that this does not set performance in these word recognition experiments apart as the unnatural product of laboratory artifice. I prefer the conclusion that the robustness and recoverability of codes are major limiting factors in perception as it functions in real life.

In very rough terms, we can summarize the distinctive aspects of our characterization of perception as follows.

(*i*) The immediate product of feature analysis is a collection of *aspects* of the stimulus. These aspects are at this stage independent. For example, the position and the identity of a feature may be separate aspects. Aspects may also differ as to the level of knowledge represented. A word may be represented simultaneously as a string of grapheme identities and as an address in the lexicon.

(*ii*) These representations are preconscious. Further processing is required for this information to enter awareness and to serve as a basis for intentional response decisions.

(*iii*) For the information about aspects to be admitted to awareness, the aspects generally have to be integrated into a composite description of the stimulus object. We can attend to the redness of a book, but we cannot generally have a pure experience of disembodied redness anymore than we can have a position-free awareness of the identity of a letter in a word or indeed have a selective awareness of disembodied colour in the Stroop test. (A more general implication of this is that the system is designed so as to militate against the sort of "non-epistemic seeing" that is crucial to certain philosophical accounts of perception (cf. Dretske, 1969). In practice, seeing involves beliefs about stimulus objects.)

(*iv*) The prohibition on conscious access to aspects that have not been integrated into a composite object description is part of a more general requirement for entry of information into consciousness. This consists in the need to form a robust description of the stimulus object. Robust descriptions are generally those of higher level, such as a lexical address for a string of letters or a three-dimensional solid for an assembly of intersecting lines.

Analogies to word superiority

Throughout the 1970s a number of reports on different visual tasks have accumulated which exhibit the general property that an element is more readily detected when embedded in a familiar context than when presented alone. Biederman (1972) found that an object can more readily be located in a picture of a real-world scene when the scene is coherent than when the objects are scrambled. In a closer analogy, Weisstein and Harris (1974) have reported an "object superiority effect" wherein a line segment could be more readily recognized when part of a coherent three-dimensional drawing than when part of a less coherent flat design. Furthermore, the analogy with word recognition is made more explicit in a study by Schendel and Shaw (1976). They showed that a line segment could be recognized more readily when part of a letter than when presented alone.

The analogy can be pursued further since the line-in-context v. line-alone effect can be likened to the letter-in-word v. letter-alone effect, while the coherent v. incoherent context effect can be likened to the word v. random string effect. Moreover, as in word superiority effects, the object superiority effect can also be demonstrated using same–different judgements (Pomerantz *et al.*, 1977).

We have seen that the word v. letter effect appears to depend upon masking. Such a dependence also appears to obtain for the object–line effect, since McClelland (1978) has shown that the object–line effect reported by Williams and Weisstein (1978) is increased by masking with random lines. Moreover, the type of mask engenders selective effects. Single line targets are interfered with more by random line masks, whereas object targets are more vulnerable to masks containing objects. This finding, in turn, bears some resemblance to that of Jacobson (1974), who reported that words were more effectively masked by other words than by letter fragments.

There will be limits to the extent to which these analogies can fruitfully be pursued, if only because the principles of composition of printed words and of line drawings of objects differ considerably. Nevertheless, at a certain level of theorizing these findings from diverse paradigms appear to converge. One of the issues indicated by this convergence is the general conception of "perception" referred to in Section 9.2. Thus the considerations set out above can be seen as echoing, in the word recognition domain, McClelland's (1978) conclusion about object perceptions:

> If formation of a representation of an object is based upon prior formation of a representation of its parts, then how can we be able to report the identity of a line in an object under conditions in which we cannot report the same line when it is presented in isolation? While this paradox may seem compelling, it disappears *if we question the tacit assumption that the activation of a representation of a stimulus element can be mapped transparently into an overt response* (McClelland, 1978, p. 222; my italics).

The factors I have assumed to intervene between feature analysis and response decision are somewhat different from those proposed by McClelland, but the two accounts are united in their rejection of an orthodox view that amounts to a metatheory of perception (see also Henderson, 1978; Allport, 1979; Marcel, in press).

Chapter 11

Attention and Word Processing

11.1 ATTENTION AND LEVELS OF ANALYSIS

Automatic analysis of words

A commonplace observation concerning the acquisition of skills is that the attainment of a high level of competence is accompanied by a quality of automaticity. In learning to drive, many things seem to compete for our attention. Changing gear involves the combination of unrelated activities, with our feet on the pedals and a hand on the gear lever, rather like the children's game of circularly rubbing the stomach while patting the head. Having negotiated one such act of limb-stirring we may find that the fourth limb, the hand that steers the car, has been released from the directive control of the eyes: it has had to join in a synkinetic dance in sympathy with its gear-changing partner. Attending to the road ahead has been too much to do while we have been so preoccupied with the mechanics of the car itself.

With the acquisition of driving skill, these experiences are forgotten. We say that the tactics of driving have become "automatic". This has the primary implication that much of the detailed planning of actions is unconscious. Moreover, there are various extensions of the concept of automaticity. Subjectively, automatic performance is effortless (see Kahneman, 1973). Automatic actions often leave no record in memory and lacking conscious volition, they generally cannot be prevented or aborted by the agent. Finally, a measurable correlate of the effortlessness of automatic acts is their diminished tendency to compete with other ongoing activities. The skilled driver can engage in fluent conversation whilst driving. To say that an action has become automatic, of course, does not explain what has happened; it does not put an end to further questions. (See Allport (1980) for a formidable critique of automaticity as an explanatory concept.) In using the term I simply draw attention to certain attributes of performance.

It is interesting that the earliest experiments on people's ability to do two things at once often used reading as one of the tasks. Solomon and Stein (1896) investigated their own ability to combine reading with various writing tasks.

This task has recently been returned to by Neisser and his colleagues (Neisser, 1976) who have shown that after about six weeks of practice, reading is unimpaired by simultaneous writing to dictation. However, in most such experiments interest has centred on the automation with practice of the task that is to be combined with reading. It is taken for granted that the subject comes to the experiment with much of the information processing in reading already automated.

The flexibility of attention in monitoring a reading process that is largely automated was of interest to Huey (1908). Huey echoed Quantz's belief that the eye–voice span attested to the automation of early visual processes in reading. Attention did not "go ahead with the eye" but tended to hang back with the accumulated meaning. But Huey emphasized that the attention during reading could not only move back and forth over the text but also up and down through the levels of information processing—visual, phonological and semantic (cf. Huey, 1908, pp. 148–151). He held that primary memory served the fluent reader by accumulating material in a speech code to which attention could be directed in controlled search. "When a considerable amount is thus suspended, the attention may wander backward and forward to get a fuller meaning where this is needed, with no fear of losing the minor parts, which are taken care of physiologically and may be taken into the focus of consciousness at will" (p. 148).

Huey was also careful to distinguish between the role of a particular level of code in mediating stimulus analysis and the accessibility of that level of code to conscious inspection. We have already seen the importance of this distinction in the discussion of wholism, especially in the question of what role a graphemic code plays in word identification. Here Huey echoes F. Schumann in arguing that the inability to retrieve a form of representation in consciousness does not entail its absence in the "automatic functioning" of stimulus analysis mechanisms.

Conversely we may interpret the description of a reader as reading letter by letter as indicating a failure of automaticity. This is characteristic of the reading of the young child, and we may speculate that it is revealed in forms of acquired dyslexia in which the patient attempts to spell out words to be read. The automation of visual processes in the child's reading has recently attracted increasing interest, and some writers, notably LaBerge and Samuels (1974), have attempted to formulate a general theory of the development of automatic processes in fluent reading (see also Schneider and Shiffrin, 1977). Others have been concerned with the role of attention in restricted domains, such as the control of eye movements (e.g. Hochberg, 1970; Fisher, 1979). A prevalent theme in this work is that at early stages in the acquisition of reading skill most attention is concentrated on "decoding", only allowing some slight residual effort to be invested in comprehension.

An important step in the acquisition of automaticity consists of the decision to relax control. This is a compelling subjective event in various motor skills, whether it be riding a bicycle or carrying a very full cup. Various students of the child's acquisition of reading skill have suggested that the relaxation of highly controlled, serial processing may represent an important achievement. This process can be simulated in adults by means of artificial visual search tasks (Schneider and Shiffrin, 1977). Here, it has been remarked, some subjects have to be weaned off controlled, plodding search by instructions to sacrifice accuracy for speed.

In reading, the relaxation of control of lower-level processing is usually accompanied by a transfer of attention to a higher level, and this transfer of attention from, say, a letter level to a word level has been mistaken by wholistic theorists for a reorganization of the feature extraction process itself.

It is evident that in skilled reading attention can be switched between levels. Indeed, the manipulation of the level to which attention is directed, with the resulting variation in the nature and quantity of material that can be recalled, is basic to a well-known approach to memory, the so-called levels of processing approach (Craik and Tulving, 1975). Moreover, the nature of the text may attract attention to lower levels of processing that are otherwise automatic. When reading poor handwriting, so much attention may be devoted to decipherment that comprehension suffers drastically. Who has not reached the end of a scribbled essay or letter to find that, just as in the young child's battle with print, in the struggle to recognize individual words the sense has been lost almost completely? To take a very different example, the design of Augustan verse is such that attention is drawn to the phonological aspect of language, in terms of metre, rhyme, alliteration, onomatopoeia, etc. Alexander Pope's lines from *The Dunciad*

> Pensive poets painful vigils keep,
> Sleepless themselves to give their readers sleep

almost lulls us by its narcotic sounds into missing the barbed message that underlies and contrasts with the whispering phonology.

Attention can not only be *directed* down to the visual or phonological levels, it can also drift there. Most people who have occasion to read when disinclined or fatigued have caught themselves translating text into internal speech without extracting or at least retaining any sense at all.

There are at least two possible costs to automatic processing, both relating to the unmodifiable nature of such processes. First is the difficulty of "debugging" automatic processes. If something is amiss with our tennis serve we have to take the whole action sequence apart and devote attention to component responses that we cannot normally afford to be aware of. Error detection in the automatic process may also be very poor, and the amazing persistence of speech errors and spelling errors in common words must in part be attributed to the automatic processing from which they result. This holds particularly for the failure of incidental learning during reading to correct spelling difficulties (see many of the papers in Frith (1980) for a fuller discussion.)

The second cost of automatic processing is that it cannot generally be switched off when it produces an irrelevant or interfering output. Some well-known examples of such interference come from published results on speeded classification where it is found that the ability to sort stimuli according to a predefined attribute such as colour is interfered with when another, integral attribute of the stimulus such as size is varied independently. "Integrality", in this context, refers to dimensions that are bound together by virtue of the fact that objects must possess attributes on both dimensions. The problem for the perceiver seems to be that dimensions such as colour and size are packaged together automatically in the formation of descriptions of the world at the level of an object code. For this reason the machinery that serves voluntary response decisions is unable to reach back to a lower level of processing and gain access to information about these dimensions independently of each other.

In reading, this sort of interference may be manifest in another way between different levels of code. In some cases a deeper level of code than is required by the task is nevertheless derived automatically and when derived may interfere with lower-level decisions. For example, I have been able to show (Henderson, 1973) that in letter-search for a physically defined target letter, there is interference from the presence in the background of other items that are physically dissimilar but share the same name (e.g. *A* can be found faster when the background contains *e* rather than *a*). The classic form of this interference takes place at the word level in the Stroop Test. The original test (Stroop, 1935) required subjects to name the colour of ink in which a word was printed. It was shown that if the word was itself the name of a (different) colour, responding was slower and less accurate. Thus the automatic processing of a stimulus to a depth far beyond that required to determine surface colour interferes with the supposedly superficial response. Even after extended practice the interference persists quite strongly (Jensen and Rohwer, 1966). As it turns out, there is nothing peculiar about the interference between colour words and ink-colour, and since Stroop's original demonstration much ingenuity has gone into generalizing the effect to different forms of conflict.

Theoretical controversy about Stroop interference has centred on the question of the level at which processing interference is located. At least three stages have had their adherents: perceptual attention (Hock and Egeth, 1970; Biederman and Tsao, 1979), conceptual encoding (Seymour, 1977), and response decision (Warren, 1972). Attempts to adjudicate between these loci have not been conclusive, although the perceptual attention hypothesis seems to run into clear difficulties (see Stirling, 1979; see also Chapter 8).

One fundamental feature of Stroop interference seems to be that it varies with stimulus response "compatibility". Thus the strong link between the shape of a printed word and its name interferes more with the weak linkage between the ink-colour and its name, than the converse. Moreover, when the connection between word–shape and word-name is most direct (when the word is of high frequency or has been recently primed), the interference arising from this association is maximal (Warren, 1974).

Even when the relevant stimulus–response pathway is a more "natural" one than is the case for naming the colour of ink, interference may still be manifest as a consequence of processing that is wider or deeper than that required by the experimenter. This is one way in which we can regard the pseudohomophone effect in the lexical decision task. Since the work of Rubinstein *et al.* (1971) several authors have reported that pseudohomophones such as BURD and BRANE yield slower *no* decisions in the lexical decision task than do other non-words such as HOSK which do not sound like real words. This suggests that it is difficult to attend to the visual specification of a word without also being influenced by its phonology, at least in this rather artificial task where phonology is irrelevant or misleading. For some authors this failure of selectivity is entailed by the structure of the processing sequence. Thus Rubinstein *et al.* (1971) assume that a phonological representation is required to address the lexicon. For others the failure of selectivity arises not because lexical access is contingent upon phonological coding but because phonological coding is "epiphenomenal" (Coltheart, 1978). What this means, in the dual process theory of pronunciation espoused by Coltheart, is that the nonlexical route from print to sound (cf. Chapter 5) functions automatically, that is, it cannot be totally switched off.

Interference from automatic processing beyond the compass of single words can also be demonstrated. For instance Willows and McKinnon (1973) had subjects read stories in black print which was interspersed with alternating lines of irrelevant text in red print. In a subsequent test of comprehension, good readers showed more intrusions of material from the irrelevant, red lines. In this case automatic processing of material in the visual periphery incurred a cost.

So far we have discussed these examples of the costs associated with automaticity as arising out of two sorts of automatic process. First, stimulus processing takes place which is not relevant to the decision required in the experimental task. Secondly, this processing having taken place, its product cannot be ignored in arriving at a response decision. According to this account, there are two logically determined points at which interference *might* have been prevented. Taking the Stroop example, word shape might not have been processed in order to access the lexicon and, even if this occurred, the resultant conceptual or articulatory representation might not have influenced a decision about ink-colour.

It is sometimes thought surprising that a "high-level" process like lexical access by means of word shape can be accomplished fast enough to interfere with a "superficial" process such as colour naming. An alternative interpretation is that Stroop interference has little to do with the relative speed with which the competing codes are derived. Instead, this account holds that the major limitation of performance arises at the stage where the results of preconscious stimulus processing become available for conscious decision-making. The problem here is that the lexical interpretation of the word is arrived at automatically and that such higher-level codes tend to upstage their rivals in the theatre of consciousness (see also Section 10.2 on "robustness of codes").

The trouble with this view is that the notion of a higher-level code is obscure. It must be admitted that so far the concept is largely intuitive. Although the difference between, say, a graphemic and a lexical level of representation is relatively clear, it is not difficult to find cases that are less readily agreed. In such cases the argument becomes circular. The higher-level code must be the one that interferes more with the processing of the other, and this in turn must be due to its taking precedence in attracting attention.

Despite this lack of complete specifiability in applications of the attentional theory, the theory as a whole can be identified by contrast with an opposing view. I shall illustrate this by two experiments which, though drawn from quite different domains, compare subjects' ability to make decisions about two aspects of a stimulus, one global and one more analytical.

Consider a task in which a subject is asked to process the sort of letter array shown in Fig. 12. The array consists of a single, large letter composed of small elements which are themselves letters. It is possible to demonstrate Stroop interference using these arrays. Stirling and Coltheart (1977) performed such a demonstration by having subjects name the global letter as quickly as possible. The response could be made fastest when the elements from which the global letter was constructed were themselves that same letter. This condition was

Fig. 12 A letter array with independent global and analytical aspects. Example of the type of stimulus used by Navon (1977) and Stirling and Coltheart (1977).

slightly faster than one in which the elements were neutral symbols such as asterisks. Much the slowest condition was one in which the elements consisted of a different letter from the global letter that they formed.

One of the pleasing aspects of this task is that both the primary and the interfering associations are between letter-shape and letter-name. The task is therefore capable of reversal, with element naming becoming the required response. In the present view one would expect more Stroop interference for element naming, since the global character, as a potential source of interference, would be expected to compete more effectively for attention. (There are obvious limits to this: above a certain size the global character may not be "taken in" as a letter; below it the element characters may not be resolved.)

The sort of task reversal described above has been performed by Navon (1977, Experiment 3), and as would be expected, in almost any view, naming of the global form is easier than naming of the element form. Even when global and element letter are the same, instructions to name the global form lead to RTs about 100 ms faster. Moreover, for element naming there is a healthy Stroop effect: when the global letter is inconsistent with the elements, element naming is slowed by about a further 100 ms. However, for global-form naming there was no Stroop interference at all. Whether the elements were the same or different from the global letter appeared to make no difference.

Navon's interpretation differs from my own both in the general and the particular. In general terms, Navon sees results gained from such tasks as bearing upon the relative speed at which features are analysed. I prefer to see these tasks as bearing principally upon the ease with which processed attributes can be retrieved and used to make conscious decisions. At the detailed level, Navon concludes that: "the finding that attention cannot be efficiently diverted from the whole may be interpreted as a support to the notion that global processing is a necessary stage of perception prior to more fine-grained analysis" (Navon, 1977, p. 371).

A full treatment of my disagreement with Navon would require an extended analysis of such concepts as "feature analysis" and "attention", and of the word "perception" in the quotation above. Nevertheless, it is possible briefly to outline the main difficulties that I see in his order-of-encoding interpretation.

First is the difficulty of applying Navon's account consistently across Stroop-type phenomena. Need we assume that in the original paradigm word-shape is a global stimulus that must be processed *as a prior condition* for analysis of the ink colour? (If this prior condition principle were strictly adhered to, then the more difficult the global analysis, the longer before the local analysis could commence. But the implications of this seem absurd.)

A second difficulty arises out of the inconsistency between Navon's failure to find interference with the naming of global forms and Stirling and Coltheart's successful demonstration of a substantial Stroop effect in this task. This is clearly an embarrassment to Navon's theory, since his own failure to find an effect is taken as central to his argument. There are a large number of procedural differences between the two studies which might have given rise to the discrepancy, but perhaps the most promising difference is that Navon presented his stimuli briefly and non-foveally and followed them with a dot matrix mask. All of these operations might have interfered more with the saliency of the elements as compared to the global composite. The mask in particular might be expected to interfere more with awareness of elements rather than composite forms (cf. McClelland, 1978; Taylor and Chabot, 1978).

We turn now to a word-processing task in which we can observe this same contrast between an order-of-processing theory and an attentional preference theory. As before, the basic phenomenon is one in which wholes are responded to more readily than parts, but this time the parts are letters and the wholes are words.

Johnson (1975, 1977; Johnson and Marmurek, 1978) has mounted a wholistic argument already alluded to in Chapter 9. In brief, he has argued that because two whole words can be matched faster than a single letter can be detected in a word, it follows that words are first recognized as a whole and then decomposed into component letters. Clearly this theory is expressed in terms of the serial order of encoding stages, and the similarity with Navon's theory of "global precedence" is marked despite the different tasks to which the theories are applied. Both theories make strong predictions by virtue of their basis in a fixed order of processing stages, and they are correspondingly vulnerable to refutation by any evidence that information about parts is available before that on wholes. Such evidence is available in unambiguous form in the word and letter matching task, since Marmurek (1977) and Henderson and Chard (1978) have shown that the superiority of whole matches over part matches is actually reversed in simultaneous presentation. (Johnson's earlier work employed successive presentation of target and test stimuli.) Incidentally, it also appears that in circumstances in which wholes *are* matched faster than parts this has nothing in particular to do with words since I have found the same effect for unstructured letter arrays and even nonlinguistic shapes (unpublished studies). The difficulty of finding parts in wholes is a difficulty of the comparison process itself, in which there is distracting and irrelevant information. What these findings show is the difficulty of maintaining an analytic set for the comparison when stimuli are presented sequentially.

Attention and levels of search

The task of searching linguistic material for a target letter can be used to reveal the various levels of representation which a subject typically constructs when scanning words. These representations, phonological, morphemic and syntactic, appear to be used to facilitate the detection of low-level elements such as letter targets. These demonstrations serve an incidental function by showing the absurdity of interpreting all effects of higher-level information upon lower-level decisions as indicative of prior encoding of the higher-level information.

Corcoran (1966) was the first to notice that subjects searching prose for a target letter made a disproportionately high number of omission errors for the *e* in *the*. However, he erroneously interpreted this as evidence of an acoustical factor in visual search. Subsequent research has shown that omission errors in letter search through prose are related to quite complex linguistic features of the text. Frith (1979) found that the preponderance of failure to detect letter *e* occured in final-syllable unstressed *e*s. She argued that endings containing unstressed *e* are more predictable and therefore attract less attention. Smith and Groat (1979) found an interaction between word frequency and syllabic stress: most omissions were made in unstressed *e*s of high-frequency words. They also found high omission rates for the *e* in the affix *-ed* in contrast to *-ed* which is not a morphological affix (e.g. *naked*), as well as various other effects of the linguistic function of the *e*s.

Several factors indicate that omissions are not a simple consequence of the pronunciation of the target letter in its context of occurrence: *t* is more detectable in *thy* than in *the*; *a* is more detectable in *ant* than *and* (Healy, 1976; Drewnowski and Healy, 1977). Indeed the exceptionally high incidence of omission errors in the common function words *the* and *and* is evident even when the target is the entire trigram. Subjects are more likely to detect the entire trigram as part of a word (ra*ther*, h*and*le) than standing on its own as a word (Drewnowski and Healy, 1977).

Healy and Drewnowski interpret these findings as showing that very common words are read in units larger than the letter. This might at first appear to be a statement of what I have called feature analytic wholism, but this is not so. They are careful to point out that these results may not reflect the order of processing various linguistic levels of information but instead may indicate the priority of access to those levels of information once they are processed (cf. Healy, 1976, p. 241).

Indeed, Drewnowski and Healy (1977) suggest that the "reading unit" may sometimes be larger than a word. Yet it would be absurd to take this assertion as meaning that in such cases a phrase served as an primitive visual feature in pattern recognition. In fact, a similar conclusion had previously been reached in speech perception. Savin and Bever (1970) originally mounted an argument analogous to the wholistic theory of feature analysis criticized here. They showed that a listener monitoring speech could react more quickly to a prespecified syllable target than to a prespecified phoneme target and concluded that syllables are perceptually analysed first and then decomposed into phonemes. This claim is directly analogous to that made by Johnson (1975) about visual words and letters, but it is more remarkable inasmuch as speech is extended over time so that larger units occupy more time in a physical sense.

Studdert-Kennedy (1973) was one of the first to challenge the logic of this conclusion, in particular the assumption that immediately a code is formed perceptually it can be read off to make a detection response, so that relative speed of detection becomes an automatic reflection of relative speed of encoding. Studdert-Kennedy suggests the opposite conclusion, arguing that it is precisely because the analysis of phonemes is so swift, automatic and preconscious that their retrieval in awareness is so slow. The conclusion that the results in this task reflect the ease of recovery of preconsciously analysed information was reinforced by Foss and Swinney (1973), who found that *candy* was detected faster as a target than the *can* in *candy*.

Generally, results in such tasks are best understood as showing that it is easier to attend to higher levels of analysis of linguistic information and that the level to which the subject attends may be set by the nature of the target. McNeill and Lindig (1973) studied phonemes, syllables, words and even sentences and concluded that a mismatch between the target unit and the search-list unit tended to slow detection.

We are reluctantly impelled toward the general conclusion that the typical search, detection and threshold tasks cast very little light upon the order or relative speed of deriving various levels of code. In Chapter 10 I argued that the word superiority effects reflected the robustness and manipulability of levels of code rather than their speed of derivation. In this chapter I have similarly attributed findings on the speed of detection of parts and wholes to the recoverability of perceptual information in consciousness. There may be some simple tasks so transparent that response speed reflects encoding speed directly, for example, the letter-matching task studied by Posner and his colleagues. In such cases the transparency of the task may be a product of their distance from the realm of language processing.

11.2 PRECONSCIOUS AND CONSCIOUS PROCESSES

Recent studies of preconscious processing

One circumstance in which word processing can be said to be automatic or preattentive occurs when information is extracted from a word subliminally. That is, when processing is unaccompanied by a visual experience and information derived from the stimulus is not immediately available for explicit commentary by the subject. There has accumulated a large and various literature on what has come to be known as subliminal perception (see Dixon, 1971, for an encyclopaedic review). Much of the early literature is unsatisfactory, and it is the sheer weight of evidence rather than the power of individual demonstrations that warrants consideration. One of the difficulties with the earlier work is that demonstrations of subliminal perception, and more especially of perceptual defence and sensitization to emotional words, were construed within theoretical frameworks which were themselves confused, which made appeal to homunculus-like mental censors, or which imported into the perceptual domain motivational theories that had failed to find favour elsewhere. In retrospect, the controversy over subliminal perception presents a vivid illustration of how decisions about what is the case and what facts obtain are dependent upon the available theoretical context for interpreting these facts. Some years ago I remarked (Henderson, 1977) that the return to favour of the phenomena of subliminal perception had the disconcerting property of seeming to depend upon theoretical realignments in cognitive psychology rather than any development of new and compelling evidence. Notable components of this more receptive theoretical environment were the clarification of words like "seeing" and "perception"—especially the distinction between seeing as information processing and seeing as having a visual experience—and also the collapse of a hierarchical metatheory of cognition in which encoding was represented by a contingent series of stages at which information was progressively classified into increasingly abstract forms with the output of each stage recoverable in an appropriately designed laboratory task. In the five years since I made that observation it has decayed into embarrassing obsolescence: not only has new evidence of subliminal perception come into existence but subliminal stimuli have come to be almost a routine tool for studying automatic word processing. Indeed effects that are consequent upon presentation of an unreportable stimulus have provided a convergent operation for defining those difficult terms "automatic", "preattentive", and the like.

It is helpful in understanding the change in the state of evidence concerning subliminal perception to take account of two limitations that held for much of the earlier work. The primary limitation was that the evidence centred upon what the subject could report about threshold stimuli. This results in a conflict between the direction of the subject's attention to an event and the claimed subliminal status of the event. As Marcel (in press) has noted, extensive questions about events that we claim not to have detected seem odd, even in the psychological laboratory, and subjects may evolve highly specialized strategies to satisfy their questioner in this situation. A secondary difficulty arises when threshold differences are themselves the basis for arguing that subliminal perception occurred. This holds particularly for demonstrations of threshold variations in accordance with the emotional tone of a stimulus word. Although there seems little doubt that this dependency of threshold upon emotionality is not the result of any simple form of response bias, it is unsatisfactory that a concept (subliminal perception), which is defined in terms of thresholds, should be justified by means of obtained threshold differences.

Some early studies were free from these difficulties. Worthington (1964) reported an emotionality effect when the ostensible task was detection of a test patch during dark adaptation and the words were even fainter stimuli superimposed on the test patch. Results with this technique have not been consistent, however, nor has it been possible to give a persuasive theoretical account of them. A different technique in which the effect of the purportedly subliminal stimulus is studied without the threshold value of that stimulus constituting the primary datum is exemplified by work of Smith and Henriksson (1955). They studied the Zöllner illusion and reported that a square appeared distorted when it was preceded by a subliminal presentation of the grid context. However, even had this demonstration been accompanied by all the necessary controls its implications are limited and unsurprising. In any model in which the sensory evidence that underlies thresholds is represented as a continuous quantity, it is possible to conceive of a quantity of evidence that is insufficient to exceed the threshold of awareness but sufficient to summate with other sources of evidence (the square that follows) to yield visible effects. This follows as long as the state of sensory evidence is not directly available to consciousness. What we require to surprise us is to learn that our preconscious world is peopled with richer cognitive entities than subliminal converging lines. If we could show that there exist preconscious representations of such things as the meanings of words and that furthermore these representations are not just the epiphenomenal by-products of unsuccessful acts of perception but active ingredients in cognitive life, then we would have claims on the theoretician's attention. On reflection, of course, the existence of activated preconscious representations of a word's meaning is not itself surprising to anyone who has thought about how we might conceive and produce speech from a conceptual base that is itself tacit and prelinguistic. But perhaps it is surprising that such representations can be activated unconsciously through the medium of the senses. The grounds for this surprise may turn out to be as crude as the thought that much has to be done to arrive at the meaning of a visual symbol, yet the subject who fails to have a reportable experience of a stimulus feels that he has not had a chance to do anything cognitive at all.

Faced with this dilemma there seem to be two general sorts of reply. The more direct is to doubt the order in which levels of information are processed. Many students of word recognition have found it easy to believe that a representation of a word can be formed before that of its constituent letters. Perhaps it is only a little step further to the belief that semantic representations are formed at an earlier stage than the representation of lower-level visual qualities.

The alternative theoretical accommodation is one to which we have had resort in our discussion of word superiority effects and their implications. In this view, wisdom begins with the abandonment of the notion that voluntary response processes are transparent, giving a direct view of the order of stimulus-encoding stages. Whether a representation enters consciousness depends not only on whether it can be successfully encoded, but also on whether a satisfactory description of the stimulus can be assembled from the analyses of various aspects of the stimulus.

It seems clear that aspects of a stimulus do not enter consciousness as soon as they have been successfully analysed. That is to say, we must accept that the processing system is not transparent from the response side. The colour and the shape of an object do not arrive in consciousness as separate parcels as soon as they are ready. Nor can we successfully admit one to consciousness while ignoring the other, by a controlled act of attention. It was these facts of experience that obstructed the structuralists in their attempts to divine by introspection the elements of sensation. In the case of word recognition, the tendency for entry to consciousness to be contingent on the formation of a high-level description of the stimulus in "object language" results in what I have earlier called "attentional wholism". This includes the phenomena remarked upon by Pillsbury (1897) whereby a mutilated word tends to be filled out plausibly in experience.

Subliminal perception and printing

Recent work on subliminal perception, as we have anticipated, relies on the effect that a subliminal stimulus exercises upon the perception of another stimulus, itself usually supraliminal. We have already seen that such a task allows us to avoid the interpretative and the practical difficulties involved in asking the subject direct questions about the subliminal stimulus.

Such effects of one stimulus on another can readily be obtained supraliminally when some relationship exists between the two stimuli and it is generally accepted that these interactions between pairs of stimuli constitute the simplest case of contextual priming. The priming stimulus, which often is the first to arrive, provides a context. When this context is a regular one, in the sense that it represents a relationship that is part of our knowledge of the world, priming is facilitatory. In certain limited conditions, it appears that an irregular context may result in inhibitory priming. (Such priming effects are discussed further in the next chapter.)

Contextual knowledge obviously plays a considerable role in skilled reading, and it appears that word recognition is affected by both semantic context (e.g. Tulving and Gold, 1963) and syntactic context (e.g. Kolers, 1970). The question of how linguistic knowledge interacts with information from peripheral vision in the control of eye-movements is a major focus of recent research (see Levy-Schoen and O'Regan, 1979). Accordingly it is natural that some experimenters should have turned their attention to the priming effect exercised by a peripherally presented word upon a fixated word. This method was employed by Bradshaw (1974), who presented an ambiguous homograph such as PALM foveally. He found that interpretation of the homograph could be biased by the simultaneous presentation in peripheral vision of a disambiguating primer such as TREE or HAND. Moreover, this effect obtained regardless of whether the peripheral stimulus could be consciously identified.

In a major paper on preconscious processes Allport (1977, Exp. 2) investigated a similar task. In simplified terms, he compared detection of a masked, foveal word under three conditions: with a peripherally presented related primer, an unrelated primer, and no primer. The primers were presented simultaneously with the target, but 1° above it and they were masked so as to be invariably unreportable. Performance was best with no primer, slightly impaired with the related primer, and greatly impaired with the unrelated primer. At first sight these results seem to imply that all priming is inhibitory and that related and unrelated primers differ in that the latter induce more inhibition. However, the control condition against which the direction of these effects is measured is clearly inadequate, since not only is priming absent but so too is the distraction caused by an accompanying stimulus (albeit a subliminal one). Therefore it can only be safely concluded that subliminal priming involving semantic associations has occurred, and a conclusion about the direction of this effect is unjustified.

An alternative to peripheral presentation as a way of rendering the primer subliminal is to sequence primer and target quickly at the same location so as to produce backward masking of the primer by the target. This method was adopted by Pickering (1976). He had subjects make word–nonword decisions about targets which were preceded either by strings of the same or different class. The earlier, priming strings were unreportable. As in Allport's study, the priming effects were inhibitory, but due to the inadequacy of the control condition no absolute significance can be attached to this. In this case, the control condition, by preceding the target with a blank field only, may have involved less forward masking of the target by the earlier field.

Although the procedure of masking the primer with the target is appealingly simple, it is also difficult to interpret because it may involve forward and backward masking at various levels (see Turvey, 1973) as well as forward and backward priming. These possibilities are difficult to disentangle (see Naish, 1980).

The possibility of backward priming is demonstrated in a series of studies by Jacobson (1973, 1974; Jacobson and Rhinelander, 1978). In this task, the first stimulus has to be identified and the following stimulus acts as both primer and backward task. The priming stimulus cum mask is supraliminal and it is the identifiability of the preceding target word that is of interest.

Unfortunately it is unclear which of Jacobson's results are appropriately discussed in terms of masking and which in terms of priming. For example, Jacobson (1974) found that words were increasingly effectively masked by visual noise, letter fragments, nonwords and unrelated words. This could be taken as further evidence that targets are more effectively masked by masks of their own "level". Jacobson also found that masking was less severe when exercised by associated than by unassociated words. This is perhaps best construed as a rare example of backward priming, but whether this effect interacts with the masking process cannot be determined.

The most extensive investigation of subliminal priming has been conducted by Marcel (1978b, in press; Marcel and Patterson, 1978). His work began with a development of Wickens' (1972) procedure. In this task the subjects are asked to comment on a word presentation that is masked so as to be subliminal. In an attempt to obviate the difficulties inherent in this situation subjects are presented with a subsequent, supraliminal test word and asked to judge its similarity to the unseen word. By manipulating the semantic relationship between the subliminal word and the test word, Wickens was able to show that subjects had some semantic information available to them about the subliminal word and that this information could be uncovered by these indirect means. Marcel (in press, Exp. 1) extended this finding by showing that as target-mask asynchrony was reduced, the subject's judgements about visual similarity fell to chance level before his judgements about semantic similarity.

Noting the problems involved in requiring even such an indirect commentary on "unseen" stimuli, Marcel turned from this task to the subliminal priming task, using a procedure whereby the primer is followed by a pattern mask and then by the target. He demonstrated that two forms of priming known to hold for supraliminal primers also held even when the primer could not be reported (Marcel, in press, Exps 2 and 3). In the first task, Stroop interference was produced when a colour patch to be identified was subliminally primed by an incongruent colour word. Facilitation was produced when test patch and priming word were congruent. In the second task, word–nonword decisions were shown to be facilitated when a test word was primed by a semantically related primer. This effect held equally for supraliminal primers and for pattern-masked subliminal primers but did not obtain for primers rendered subliminal by energy masking (i.e. by following them with a bright flash). In a classic paper, Turvey (1973) has elaborated on the distinction between "peripheral" energy masking and "central" pattern masking.

A more complex form of priming in the lexical decision task requires chains of three words of which the middle term may be a semantically ambiguous word (a homograph). Schvaneveldt *et al.* (1976) showed that relative to a control condition in which the three words were unrelated (e.g. RIVER, DATE, MONEY) performance was impaired when the first and third word related to the two different meanings of the middle homograph (e.g. RIVER, BANK,

MONEY). That is, it took longer to affirm that MONEY is a word. However, when BANK, MONEY was preceded by an unrelated word (e.g. DAY), BANK exercised a facilitatory priming effect on the lexical decision about MONEY. A still larger facilitatory effect obtained when BANK, MONEY was preceded by a word related to both (e.g. SAVE).

These results suggest that this sort of priming is selective and produces costs as well as benefits. In a passive, nonselective model of lexical access it would be expected that presentation of BANK would automatically activate all lexical interpretations of the stimulus and consequently lead to priming of a subsequent word related to any of these interpretations. BANK would therefore invariably prime MONEY, no matter what priming effect was exercised upon BANK itself. It is conceivable in such a model that priming the appropriate sense of BANK (SAVE, BANK, MONEY) might lead to even more facilitation of MONEY by BANK than when BANK was not primed (DAY, BANK, MONEY). What is difficult to accommodate in the passive, non-selective model is any cost to inappropriate priming. Yet this is what happens in Schvenevelt *et al.*'s experiment. RIVER, BANK, MONEY leads to a slower classification of MONEY than when all three words are unrelated, so clearly the fact that there exists a sense of BANK that is associated with MONEY is not enough to produce facilitation automatically.

There are essentially two ways of dealing with this lack of automaticity in priming. We must assume selectivity either in lexical access or in priming once access has occurred. Schvaneveldt *et al.* (1976) assumed selective access. Thus RIVER leads to the selection only of the inappropriate sense of BANK. Unfortunately this should lead to no effect of BANK on MONEY. It is as if we had preceded MONEY with STREAM. However, the effect of inappropriate priming is actually deleterious, so it may be preferable to assume that lexical access is parallel and non-selective but that when one interpretation of a homograph is primed the others are positively inhibited (Warren *et al.*, 1978), with the result that a deleterious effect is exercised on an ensuing word related to the inhibited interpretation.

These results bear upon the nature of preconscious processes in two ways. First, and most directly, they bear upon what happens when we are aware of one out of several interpretations. In this case I have suggested that selection occurs after sensory information has made contact with alternative stored interpretations. Secondly, they raise the question of whether selective priming depends upon attention being paid to the primer. Marcel (1978b) has attempted to answer this question by extending Schvaneveldt *et al.*'s study to cover the case of subliminal primers.

In Marcel's study, similar chains of three stimuli were presented for lexical decision, but a major variation was introduced with respect to the second stimulus, which was either not masked, as in the Schvaneveldt *et al.* study, or rendered invisible by masking. Masking was either energy masking (following the stimulus with a bright flash) or pattern masking (following it with a pattern). Energy masking of the middle stimulus removed all priming effects caused by that stimulus, but pattern masking had quite a different effect from the energy masking or no-masking conditions. With pattern masking of the homographic words, priming effects survived, unlike the case of energy masking. Moreover, the homograph exerted a facilitatory priming effect no matter how it was biased by the first word of the chain. This contrasts with the selective effect obtained in the no-mask condition, in which the results of Schvaneveldt *et al.* were replicated.

Marcel constructs several important conclusions upon these results. First, pattern masking may interfere with a very late stage of processing in which a visible representation is assembled. This is attested to by the demonstration of any priming effect exercised by a pattern-masked word (see below). A second point, which we shall also examine further, is that the existence of a priming effect exercised by a subliminal word provides strong evidence of an automatic component in contextual priming. A third point, the contrast between the selective priming effect obtained with a supraliminal primer and the nonselective effect with a subliminal primer, suggests that consciousness entails *interpretative commitment.* Whether the stimulus be the word PALM or a Necker Cube we can only consciously entertain one interpretation at a time. In contrast, there may be no limit to the number of preconscious interpretations of the stimulus that can coexist. All these preconscious representations may exert priming influences in parallel, so that subliminal PALM may facilitate a subsequent lexical decision about either TREE or HAND (see also Tabossi and Johnson-Laird (1980) for a discussion of the locus of selective semantic interpretation).

As an aside, it is interesting to note that philosophers have sometimes found it convenient to talk of "non-epistemic seeing" (Dretske, 1969). That is, a seeing experience unaccompanied by beliefs as to what is out there. This putative state of innocence may be contrasted with the psychological view of conscious seeing as commitment to a single interpretation.

Subliminal perception and pattern masking

In experiments such as those of Marcel (1978b, in press) pattern masking is both a tool for revealing preconscious processes by screening out conscious experience and at the same time an object of curiosity in its own right due to this apparent property.

Much of the recent work on pattern masking owes its inspiration to Turvey's (1973) distinction of *peripheral* from *central* masking. In his classic series of experiments on masking of trigrams Turvey was able to distinguish between two classes of masking phenomena. Peripheral masking (or energy masking) is induced by a field which spatially overlaps the target but is structurally dissimilar from it. Such masking largely depends upon the relative energy of target and mask, and the interaction of target and mask is widely held to be located at an early (peripheral) stage of visual processing. In contrast, there is the type of masking which has come to be employed in studies of subliminal perception and is called central (or pattern) masking. It is insensitive to low-level variables such as energy and depends instead upon structural similarities between target and mask. Such masking is regarded as central not only because it can be obtained with presentation of target and mask to different eyes, but perhaps also the term "central" is associated with the fact that it is the higher-level structural features of the stimulus that determine this form of masking.

Turvey (1973, 1978) has likened peripheral masking to *integration*, in which two fields become treated as a single montage at later processing stages. This process he has contrasted with *interruption*, which is held to underlie central masking. Interruption is conceived of as the pre-empting of the target field by the mask field in competition for the "central processor". This view of central masking seems to imply that structural similarity causes competition for limited-capacity feature analysers, rather as it does in Estes' (1969) view of lateral masking between adjacent letters.

It might seem, therefore, that we can generalize this notion of central pattern masking as competition for feature-analysers to cover even higher-level interactions between target and mask. Thus, Jacobson's (1974) and Taylor and Chabot's (1978) findings that word targets are more strongly masked by word-like masks than by random letters and McClelland's (1978) finding that drawings of "objects" are more strongly masked by object-level masks than by random lines might be taken as evidence that in these cases competition was at the level of word and object analysers. However, even this rather vague hypothesis encounters difficulties.

One problem is that the present evidence on level-specific interactions between target and mask is equivocal. It seems clear that high-level targets (words, objects) are interfered with most by high-level masks, but it is less clear what the most effective mask for low level targets is (e.g. letters and lines). McClelland (1978) found that single line targets were masked about equally well by lines and by objects. Taylor and Chabot (1978) found that letters were masked slightly more by words than by letters.

A more severe problem exists, however, for any theory which locates the interaction between target and mask exclusively at the level of visual feature analysis. This problem consists in the evidence of subliminal perception, for as the studies of Allport, Jacobson, Pickering, Wickens and others show, the target which is unreportable due to masking may have been analysed to the point of semantic interpretation. This sort of evidence has led Allport (1977) and Marcel (in press) to conclude that in these cases masking interferes with the recovery in consciousness of the records of perceptual processing.

In Allport's (1977) account, conscious perception of a word depends upon the recombination of information derived from the various specialized channels for perceptual analysis. In particular it requires the coordination of an abstract lexical code with a spatial image code that contains nonlinguistic specifications of visuo-spatial properties of the stimulus. Subliminal perception arises when masking interferes with the spatial image code. This results in a "disembodied" lexical code surviving. Without its spatial image coordinates this code cannot become available to conscious scrutiny.

I have stressed the importance of the insight contained in Allport's formulation as it bears upon the need to reassemble the output of specialized analysers (the "blackboard" model) and upon the requirements of consciousness. A further advantage of the model is that it provides us with a framework for understanding the interaction between information about location and identity. For example, Allport (1977) and Shallice and McGill (1978) have shown that when an array of words is pattern-masked, subjects tend to exchange letter clusters between words in their reports. Thus *rust* and *vent* may be reported as *runt* and *vest*. This suggests that masking has interfered with quite a late stage in the reassembly of the image, after letters have been tagged for position within the word.

Despite these advantages, Allport's model is vague about many details. In particular, it does not equip us to understand selective interference between levels of information in target and mask.

Before leaving the topic of pattern masking we should consider the general question of the extent to which subliminal perception depends upon the use of pattern masking. Some recent commentators have seemed to imply that subliminal perception—the survival of semantic information about unreportable words—is exclusively the product of pattern masking. This seems highly unlikely. Many of the older studies of subliminal perception reviewed by Dixon (1971) did not employ pattern masking. Moreover, Bradshaw's demonstration of subliminal priming was obtained in a task in which visibility of the primer was reduced by perpheral presentation rather than pattern masking. This last finding leads me to speculate that the effect of peripheral presentation in this task is not only one of data-limitation but also one of bias against the peripheral stimulus, in recoverability of perceptual information. That is to say, when a display contains items at varying retinal eccentricity the diminishing visibility of items with increased eccentricity is only partly attributable to less efficient information uptake in the periphery. There also exists an additional attentional bias whereby items successfully identified in preconscious processing compete less effectively than foveal items for admission to consciousness.

Admission to consciousness

We have already considered some of the factors which may govern the admission of information to consciousness. At present it seems preferable to view these factors as tendencies, rather than as conditions which *must* be fulfilled.

Consider, for example, the hypothesis that higher-level codes have preferential access to consciousness. Clearly there are exceptions to this. We can direct our attention to lower levels, within certain limits. Proof-reading provides evidence of both the possibility and the difficulty of this. The various demonstrations of interference from irrelevant dimensions in selective attention tasks exhibit the limitations on this ability to attend to low levels of code.

Marcel (in press) has used the existence of this ability to concentrate upon a lower-level, analytic code to argue against Allport's (1977) assertion that conscious perception occurs at a stage after information from the specific analysers has been reassembled on the "blackboard". However, in Allport's model selectivity operates between consciousness and the blackboard: the blackboard does not represent the contents of consciousness; it contains the data available to consciousness via the selection machinery. Thus the difficulty, say, of attending to colour while ignoring shape or of experiencing the identity of a word without its possessing an apparent location must be regarded as properties of the blackboard.

A rather different question concerning admission to consciousness concerns the perceptual evidence required as a condition for admission to consciousness. Marcel (in press) has observed that theory here has been dominated by a strength of activation notion. It seems likely that this notion has its origin in the concept of a sensory threshold where some amount of sensory evidence or activation is required before a stimulus can cross the threshold of awareness (see, for example, Treisman, 1960). This idea probably gains reinforcement from the fact that intense stimuli are usually successful in competing for our attention. Deutsch and Deutsch (1963) gave an alternative form to this intuition in their influential model of selective attention. They postulated central recognition units that became activated by sensory evidence. However, the likelihood of a unit's output gaining access to consciousness was not immediately influenced by the strength of sensory stimulation. Instead, it depended upon the combination of the strength of stimulation of a unit with its trigger threshold. This threshold value was determined by the "importance" of the message represented by any particular recognition unit.

The notion of consciousness being accessed by recognition units when their activation exceeds some threshold value has indeed been influential and it is central to the theories of Morton (1970) and Shallice (1972). The strength of activation account meets some difficulties, however, in data reported by Marcel (in press). It will be remembered that Marcel had been able to show that a word which was masked so as to be subliminal could nevertheless exercise a facilitatory priming effect on the speed of lexical decision to a related word that followed. When that subliminal primer was repeated up to twenty times, the magnitude of the priming effect increased but the detectability of the primer itself did not. Marcel therefore argued that whereas the activation of the recognition unit representing the primer must have increased (since the priming effect increased), the likelihood of the primer gaining access to awareness manifestly did not (detection performance was unchanged). This argument rests on the assumption that increased priming indicates increased activation of the recognition unit for the primer. Defenders of the activation theory of consciousness might prefer not to concede this. However, an even simpler difficulty for a pure activation theory consists in the fact of central backward masking: if contemporary students of central pattern masking are correct in assuming that the effect of the mask is to intervene at a late stage of processing so as to deny a target access to consciousness, it appears that access must be controlled by factors other than, or in addition to, activation strength.

I believe a more general difficulty with the activation model arises due to the focus of the model upon the question of whether a stimulus gains admission to consciousness. Of course it is not really *stimuli* that enter awareness any more than it is the *eidola* of ancient perceptual theories. It is more useful to speak of interpretations as entering awareness. The trouble with the activation theory of consciousness is that it does not provide a ready way of discussing the fact that we can focus awareness on the appearance, the sound or the meaning of a word. Allport (1979) has attempted to do justice to the various aspects of a stimulus that may enter awareness by arguing that, for a stimulus to be consciously perceived, a hypothesis about some aspect of it must receive a chain of inferential support that leads back to the sensory input and integrates the various levels of processing of the stimulus. By and large, for a word to be consciously seen, the lexical interpretation has to be recombined with the spatial-pictorial code on the "blackboard" structure postulated by Allport. Presumably, however, failure to arrive at a lexical coding would still allow perception of the stimulus as a symbol array. The reassembly of features within the framework of a picture code which specifies the layout of the visual field is usually a necessary condition for awareness. We do not usually *see* entities as pure identities concerning which we have no locational specifications. (I have noted that in a page glimpsed from, say, a book falling off my knee I may occasionally apprehend a word without seeing it in any context. On reading the page through, the word is invariably found.)

Even if a pictorial specification is generally a condition of a *seeing experience*, it does not appear to be a strict requirement of the conscious stream of evoked thoughts that forms the highest level of attention in skilled reading. As Allport has noted, in such reading we are rarely aware of the visual aspect of processing. The conceptual level of representation is not consciously anchored in the visible appearance of letters or words. In this case, experiences at the conceptual level "can be constructed with adequate horizontal support links within that level" (Allport, 1979, p. 249).

Active v. passive processes and priming

We have already discussed the general question of the extent to which word processing may be said to be automatic. Certainly it appears that much of the early visual processing in word identification can take place without the necessity of attentional control. The process of lexical access itself appears, in the fluent reader, to be automatic under most circumstances. The only substantial objections to this conclusion in the word identification literature appear to come from three sources: Johnston and McClelland's (1974) finding that the word superiority effect depended on the subject adopting a whole-word attentional strategy; Aderman and Smith's (1971) finding that word superiority did not hold for an unexpected word presentation; and the related finding that word superiority effects are enhanced by blocking stimulus type (e.g. Manelis, 1974). The evidence from blocked v. randomized comparisons is not entirely consistent (see Carr *et al.*, 1978), but it does appear that word superiority effects depend to some extent on a general expectation about stimulus type and this may reflect a limit on the automaticity of word analysis. The presence of an effect of expectation has generally been taken as evidence that a process is not wholly automatic or "passive" (see below). On the other hand, Johnston and McClelland's demonstration that word identification is impaired by focusing attention on particular letters, while it has great methodological significance for studies of word superiority, may only imply that a whole-word strategy is optional when the stimulus subtends a relatively large angle.

Debate about the role of attentional control in word recognition has recently spread to include the process of contextual priming. The prevailing model of contextual priming has tended to be one in which facilitation is induced by the passive spread of activation in semantic space, so that excitation of a lexical entry results in an increased level of activation of associated entries. Such activation is held to die away fairly quickly.

A different basis for priming effects has been proposed by Posner and Snyder (1975) and by Tweedy *et al.* (1977), who pointed out that the effect of a priming stimulus might be to induce in the subject an *active* expectation for a set of stimuli that might include the following stimulus. The primary evidence for such an active process would be the dependence of the priming effect on factors that could be expected to influence expectations, notably the probability that priming will be valid (semantic relatedness). Using the lexical decision task, Tweedy *et al.* succeeded in demonstrating such an effect. They varied the proportion of occasions in which the relationship between successive words was one of semantic relatedness. The facilitatory effect of semantic relatedness on the lexical decision to the second word increased with the proportion of words which were validly primed. However, this finding establishes only that some part of the priming effect is sensitive to environmental utilities. A more detailed analysis by Neely (1977) suggests that the expectation-like component is superimposed on another, automatic priming effect. When the primer occurs very shortly before the test word (say, 250 ms), only the automatic process can take place, but with longer inter-stimulus intervals there is time for the expectation-like strategy to develop. This strategy tends to manifest itself more strongly as the subject's experience with the experiment increases and it has two symptoms. The magnitude of the priming effect depends upon the proportion of trials in which semantic relatedness obtains and inhibitory effects are manifest on trials where relatedness does not obtain. Posner and Snyder (1975) embody this last fact in a "cost–benefit" analysis of priming (see Chapter 12).

It is tempting to conclude from these results that a simple contrast can be made between active and passive priming. Passive priming depends upon the automaticity of lexical access and of consequent spreading activation. In addition to Neely's evidence it is testified to by the very existence of subliminal priming (e.g. Marcel, 1978b). Active priming is optional and may be assumed to result from expectations about the test stimulus which are relatively slow to develop and which result in inhibitory effects when the expectations are violated (unrelated primers).

This contrast of active and passive processes relies on the assumption that active processes are voluntary and their optional property is the result of the subject's choosing. However, a severe difficulty for this view of the active component in priming is beginning to emerge, for Jonasson (1978) and Humphreys (1980) have found inhibitory effects of invalid priming even when the priming stimulus was presented subliminally. Indirect evidence suggesting inhibitory effects induced by subliminal primers has also been advanced by Pickering (1976) and Allport (1977). It seems to make little sense to speak of active expectations based upon subliminal information, so the assumption that the optional, utility-sensitive component of priming depends upon conscious volition appears to be suspect.

Chapter 12

The Mental Lexicon and Reading

12.1 DEVELOPMENT OF THE CONCEPT OF A MENTAL LEXICON

The general conception of a mental lexicon as a sort of dictionary within the head seems to have arrived in psychology by a number of fairly independent routes.

One rather pervasive insight into the operation of a mental lexicon stems from the obvious fact that human language users can readily perform the function of various types of actual dictionary. Not only can we translate between the domains of print, speech and meaning, as when we produce and understand speech, read aloud, read for comprehension, write down our ideas and spell to dictation, but we can also exhibit properties of the index to our mental lexicon, as when we generate words that share a common initial phoneme (Smith and Jones, 1975), or words that rhyme or are synonymous.

The study of meaning, its representation and organization, has involved linguists (e.g. Katz and Fodor, 1963) and psychologists (e.g. Johnson-Laird, 1975) in speculating about aspects of lexical structure. Such work has tended to concentrate on relatively central aspects of comprehension without explicit treatment of questions of lexical access in the perception of written or spoken language, but recently these approaches have converged on the problem of contextual effects in sentence processing. Another convergence between the linguistic and psychological approaches occurs in concern with the morphological organization of the mental lexicon. For example, various psychological studies of perception and memory have shown that the stem of derived and inflected words is functionally salient (Kintsch, 1972; Murrell and Morton, 1974; Taft and Forster, 1975).

Behavioural concern with lexical functioning is at least as old as the nineteenth-century studies of aphasia. The pioneering work of Broca and of Wernicke indicated a functional distinction between lexical and syntactic processes. In the syndrome known as Broca's aphasia the lexicon is largely preserved and access to content words is possible, whereas access to syntactic expressions is lost. The opposite condition obtains in Wernicke's aphasia: the patient can express syntax but can only give highly limited lexical content to his utterances. Neuropsychological work implies a distinction not only between lexical and syntactic processes but also between lexical and semantic processes, or at least between the name and the meaning of a word. In anomic aphasia the patient who cannot recall a word can still recognize the object to which it refers and can usually describe its function. Often such patients paraphrase the meaning of a word while searching for the word form. In essence this is like a chronic tip-of-the-tongue condition, and as with that phenomenon it demonstrates that there are independent access routes to words and to the meanings they express. We might surmise that it is the route to a word from its meaning that is impaired in anomic aphasia (rather than the representation of words themselves), since words that cannot be recalled can generally be *recognized* amongst a set of lures as semantically appropriate.

So far we have discussed the development of the concept of a mental lexicon in relation to meanings and the production of speech. However, it is the treatment of the lexicon in relation to the perception and comprehension of language that bears most directly on the question of how reading is accomplished. Interest in this aspect of lexical access began with the postulation by Treisman (1960) of "dictionary units".

Treisman's influential formulation was actually designed to reconcile early models of selective attention to some of the known facts about dichotic listening. "Filter" theories of attention had been mildly embarrassed by the finding that subjects while shadowing the message in one ear sometimes could recognize their name amongst the unattended material in the other ear. This led Treisman to propose her well-known "attenuation" version of filter theory.

Suppose, she argued, that word recognition consists in the activation of dictionary units beyond some threshold value and that dictionary units have different thresholds of activation so as to reflect the familiarity of a word, or its importance. In this way, such words could, through experience, become more accessible, more perceptible. In addition to these fairly permanent variations in the accessibility of lexical units we could suppose that the system was responsive to temporary circumstances such as contextual constraint. Presentation of the words "I sang a . . ." would lower the threshold for the unit representing "song". Using the theoretical vocabulary of the time, Treisman (1960) speculated that such contextual effects might operate "on some kind of conditional probability basis".

Having set out these assumptions, Treisman went on to argue that if attentive *filtering* is reinterpreted in terms of a diminution of the flow of evidence ("attenuation"), we can think probabilistically of the fate of unattended words. Highly familiar or important words may still have their dictionary units triggered by the reduced flow of sensory evidence.

It is worth summarizing Treisman's (1960) achievement. With the simple proposal of dictionary units that function as evidence collectors with tunable activation thresholds, together with the further assumption that these word thresholds are permanently adjusted in accordance with word frequency (and with "importance", in some sense) and are temporarily responsive to contextual constraint, Treisman has outlined a mechanism that is capable of predicting two prevalent phenomena of word recognition: the word frequency effect and the contextual facilitation effect. More generally, her proposals specify dictionary units as the location on which converge the effects of sensory stimulation and of pre-existing linguistic knowledge.

Treisman's dictionary unit hypothesis was proposed as a solution to some of the problems facing theories of selective attention, and so the theory is understandably vague about many of the details that concern us here in the realm of language perception. Perhaps most notably it is silent on the question of the nature of the sensory evidence that is capable of activating units in the lexicon. It is also silent on what precisely are the consequences of the firing of a dictionary unit and how this is related to comprehension or the production of spoken and written forms of the word.

Some further progress on the latter question is to be found in the work of Oldfield (see, for example, Oldfield, 1966). This work brought together two great nineteenth-century lines of research, that on the neuropsychology of the aphasias and that on the chronometry of lexical access.

Oldfield drew attention to the fact that an educated person might know the meaning of about 75,000 words and can select from an admittedly much smaller working vocabulary so as to issue words in spontaneous speech at a rate of more than two per second. This competence suggested to Oldfield two general questions which are sufficiently enduring preoccupations to be worth quoting. "How is this stock or store organised, arranged and indexed? and by what means do we gain access to items in it?" (Oldfield, 1966, p. 341).

The logogen model

Through the 1960s Treisman's dictionary unit hypothesis was developed into a fuller and more explicit model of lexical access by Morton. His *logogen model* evolved in a number of papers (e.g. Morton, 1964b, 1969, 1970, 1979), remaining essentially unmodified until very recently (e.g. Morton, 1979b; Morton and Patterson, 1980).

Morton's model shares with Treisman's the conception of a recognition unit that collects and sums evidence from sensory stimulation and from the perceiver's linguistic knowledge. It shares also the notion of a tunable threshold for each unit. Moreover, as in Treisman's account, the properties of tunable thresholds are used to predict those two main classes of effect, word frequency and contextual facilitation. To these core assumptions Morton adds the following details.

(*i*) *Integration* The logogen system serves as the nexus for information about words, whether the source be reading, speech or semantic conception.

(*ii*) *Representation* Individual logogens are lexically specific. There are separate logogens for *phrase* and *frays* and, one must presume, for (river) *bank* and (piggy) *bank*. Although much of the discussion of logogens treats them as word detectors, strictly speaking, they are concerned with morphemic segments (Murrell and Morton, 1974). Moreover, as collectors of sensory information, the logogens are fairly abstract in their interests. They are, for example, indifferent to the distinction between cursive script and print. On the other hand they are only concerned with linguistic expressions, being uninfluenced by pictured concepts, for example.

(*iii*) *Output* The output of a logogen, when it fires, is a phonological pattern. Such output patterns have available to them an output buffer. (The properties of this output buffer and its rehearsal loop need not concern us here; essentially, their purpose is to provide an account of the eye-voice span and various short-term memory effects.)

(*iv*) *Evidence* The evidence accruing in a logogen sums together irrespective of source. Thus the effects of stimulus and context upon the level of activation of a logogen are additive.

(*v*) *Time constants* The stimulus evidence accruing in a logogen decays rapidly, in about one second. However, once a logogen has been critically activated (reached threshold) the threshold value for that logogen is slightly reduced and this reduction is relatively long-lasting. (This threshold reduction is, of course, the means whereby familiar words become more perceptually available. It follows from the central location of the logogen devices in the system as a whole that the word frequency effect should depend upon the frequency of reception in both reading and listening as well as the frequency of production. It is the number of times a logogen fires that determines its threshold value.)

(*vi*) *Passivity* Morton and Broadbent (1967) have laid stress upon the passivity of the system, in the sense that it does not require control by a mechanism external to the system as described. For example, no overview exists of the state of activation in the various logogens at one instant. (For contrary views, see Coltheart *et al.*, 1977; Larochelle *et al.*, 1980.)

(*vii*) *Semantics* The logogens do not contain semantic information. They merely serve as an interface, an index to the semantic system. The representation of morphemes by the logogens is therefore said to be "structural, not semantic" (Morton, 1979b). This conclusion serves incidentally to illustrate certain limitations of the dictionary metaphor.

Evaluation of the Mark I logogen model

The surprising power of the simple Treisman–Morton assumption about dictionary units that function as evidence collectors with tunable thresholds was evident into the early 1970s. There were two main advantages to the model. The first related to its success as a predictive device. Not only did it bring together the facilitatory effects of word frequency and of context in a single mechanism, but arguably the model also embodied a better account of the word frequency effect than was offered by rival theories (notably the so-called sophisticated guessing theory). The second advantage was of a much more general sort. The logogen model provided a theoretical vocabulary with which it was possible to discuss a wide range of linguistic activities, including reading, speaking and listening, as well as the more specialized phenomena of the laboratory such as the Stroop effect, the eye–voice span, and so on.

The adoption of "logogen"-language as a sort of metalanguage deserves comment. First, it is worth noting that logogen became a sort of British dialect-word for lexicon. (Taking the book not altogether randomly from my shelf, I consult the index of Coltheart *et al.*'s (1980) *Deep Dyslexia* to find 49 separate entries under "Logogen". Sampling with premeditation Gibson and Levin's (1975) *Psychology of Reading* I find 0 entries.)

This drafting of "logogen" into the metalanguage is a tribute to the early success of the logogen model; more particularly it is an indication of the fact that in the 1960s the model held the field, partly through lack of any coherent competitor. Thus Morton (1969) was justified in writing of the lack of alternative models against which the logogen model could be tested. Nevertheless, it should not pass unnoticed that the use of a term both as a neutral way of referring to a set of competences (a rough equivalent to "mental lexicon") and also as a way of denoting a particular hypothesis about the mechanism involved is an undesirable practice.

In a sense we can measure progress in the 1970s by the discovery of difficulties facing the logogen model and by the emergence of alternative conceptions of lexical access, so I shall use the Mark I logogen model as a background against which recent progress can be set.

Morton himself based a major revision of the model (Morton, 1979b) on findings that the facilitatory effect on recognition of repetition of a word only obtained with a given modality. Winnick and Daniel (1970) were the first to show that whereas word recognition was facilitated by pretraining on those same words, it was unaffected by pretraining on the semantically equivalent pictures or on verbal definitions, despite that fact that all pretraining required production of the appropriate name. This finding was followed up by Clarke (see Morton, 1979b). They also found no facilitation by pretraining that consisted in naming in response to definitions. Nor did auditory presentation of a word facilitate subsequent visual recognition. Because a fundamental tenet of the original model was that the firing of a logogen led to a reduction in its threshold, thus facilitating subsequent attempts to fire it, and because the firing of the logogen was indifferent to the source of the evidence (visual, auditory or semantic), this lack of visual facilitation when a logogen had fired in response to auditory or semantic stimulation was quite fatal to the model. In consequence, Morton (1979b) was obliged to abandon the attractive parsimony of the original formulation and proposed a logogen system Mark II, in which are posited separate input logogens for visual and auditory words and a single output logogen serving speech production. Each of these logogens is connected to the semantic system. Picture recognition is held to occur somewhere else.

Another rather specific difficulty with the original logogen model, and on the face of it also a difficulty with the revised model, has to do with the pattern of effects across three variables: stimulus legibility, associative context, and word frequency. The main problem arises from the apparently reliable finding that the effects on lexical decision RT of word frequency and stimulus legibility do not interact. They appear to be strictly additive (Stanners *et al.*, 1975; Becker and Killion, 1977). This is inconsistent with the logogen model because legibility presumably affects the rate at which evidence accrues in the logogen. Since frequency affects the amount of evidence required to fire a logogen, legibility and frequency would be expected to interact.

Recently the additive-factors logic that governs this conclusion has come under attack (Pachella, 1974; McClelland, 1979; Miller, 1979). However, the criticism of the logogen model does not depend upon the additive-factors logic. Associative context does interact in its effect with stimulus legibility. Yet the effects of context and of frequency are both supposed to arise through variation in the amount of evidence required to fire the logogen. It is therefore difficult to explain why these two factors should be differentially qualified by the legibility variable. (The interaction of legibility with context effects has been reported by Meyer *et al.*, 1975 and Becker and Killion, 1977.)

This difficulty for the logogen model is by no means trivial: frequency and context effects are the main supports on which the model rests. However, one must acknowledge that the pattern of interaction amongst these variables (and also with the repetition effect) creates a general problem for theorists.

A major attempt to circumvent these difficulties is made in Becker's *verification model* (Becker, 1976, 1979; Becker and Killion, 1977) in which lexical access is divided into two stages. The first is concerned with sensory evidence and is influenced by legibility. It operates to produce a "sensory set" of candidates. The choice from this set is made at a second "verification" stage. The verification process consists of tests on the word candidates one by one, in series. Both frequency and context affect the order in which candidates are tested. Thus the sensory set is examined in descending order of frequency.

Candidates suggested by the context, however, pre-empt the entire sensory set and are tested first.

We can now see that prediction of the additivity of frequency and legibility effects is straightforward, since these effects are located at different serial stages. The explanation of the interaction between context and legibility is somewhat more contrived. It is held to occur because words out of context are affected by legibility in the normal way (at the first stage which yields up the sensory set); words in context by-pass this stage to enter the verification set directly and are therefore unaffected by legibility.

One difficulty with Becker's approach in the verification model is that a great many strong assumptions are made about the recognition process (the serial verification process, the partition of sensory analysis from lexical search the direct testing of candidates supplied by context, etc.). Yet there is little to motivate this apparatus other than the pattern of interaction amongst the three factors discussed.

Becker's verification model incidentally exhibits another challenge to a basic principle of the logogen model. In the original logogen model it was implicitly assumed that lexical access was by direct access to a content-addressable store. This bit of computer science jargon expresses the fact that one can go directly to the exact address of a logogen from a full stimulus description. The sensory evidence leads directly to the word without intervention of a search process. In contrast, search models were pioneered by Rubinstein *et al.* (1971) and subsequently adopted by Forster (1976) as well as by Becker. In the extreme search case, the mental dictionary is held to be totally unstructured with respect to the sensory evidence for a word. Access would then involve a look-up process whereby a spelling or sound input is successively compared to each dictionary entry until a match is found. Most actual models have been less extreme and have assumed that the sensory evidence can be used to delimit a subset of the lexical entries which is then serially searched.

Although Oldfield (1966) had drawn attention to the existence of the question about the nature of the access procedure, it was not until Rubinstein's work that the implications of adopting one or other of the search/direct-access assumptions began to be explored. This exploration was associated with the development of the lexical decision task. This can be illustrated as follows.

Consider the problem of how the subject decides that a letter string that is plausible (i.e. a pseudoword) is not a real word. The extreme search model produces NO decisions as a result of exhaustive search of the lexicon. This correctly predicts the finding that NO responses in the lexical decision task are generally slower than YES responses (e.g. Rubinstein *et al.*, 1971). But it implies an absurdly cumbersome procedure, which is one reason for the adoption of limited-subset search models. The logogen model offers no account of how NO decisions are arrived at, but Forster (1976) and Coltheart *et al.* (1977) have shown how a direct-access model can be designed to yield NO decisions that are slower than YES decisions. This is achieved by postulating a deadline mechanism whereby a NO response is made if no logogen fires within a preset time interval starting at stimulus onset. (Forster and Bednall (1976) have attempted to refute the deadline approach to direct-access NO decisions, but their conclusion depends on a number of assumptions that need not be conceded.)

Another set of developments that has raised questions about the logogen model concerns the time-constants of context effects. Evidence seems to suggest various distinct time constants (see below). These include a facilitatory effect of repetition that holds over long intervals, perhaps days (e.g. Scarborough *et al.*, 1977) and a much shorter-lasting effect of semantic association that decays over a few seconds. This short-term effect of association seems to be further divisible into a high-speed automatic facilitation and a slower-acting and perhaps longer-lasting effect which may be facilitatory or inhibitory according to the subject's expectations (e.g. Neely, 1977).

Not only are these recently drawn distinctions not envisaged in the logogen model but, with the wisdom of hindsight, it also has become easier to see general deficiencies in the treatment of context through the model. For example, the distinction between repetition effects and association effects is not clearly made. Moreover, the discussion of contextual facilitation centres on the effect of sentence context but provides no explanation of how the sentence context can activate specific logogens. Consider the sentence

On the train he looked at his paper.

Morton and Long (1966) report evidence that the concluding word *paper* becomes more salient as a result of its predictability. However, a moment's reflection shows us that *paper* is only one of a very large number of plausible lexical completions (including *timetable*, *shoes*, *watch*, *companion*, *luggage*, items that have little intrinsically in common with each other). The problem here consists in the supposition that the semantic system directly primes specific lexical candidates via the logogens. This involves the system continuously in activating very large sets of lexical items. (This problem is shared by Becker's model, since context supplies candidates directly to the verification set, by-passing and pre-empting the candidates produced by sensory analysis.) Viewed in general terms, the problem arises in any model where the context-sensitive system and sensory analysis make independent contributions that converge on a central decision mechanism. Perhaps a simpler arrangement would be for the context system to operate on the candidates produced by sensory analysis. In the Morton and Long test sentence we might envisage the context system as priming, say, bisyllabic words beginning with /p/ that refer to entities that gentlemen might examine on trains. Obviously this relieves the context system of the burden of considering a staggering collection of travellers' impedimenta.

Arguments of the sort considered here are weak to the extent that they rely on the presumption that brains are constrained in their operation by avoidance of computational complexity, so it is worth mentioning a different kind of difficulty: the precise timing of contextual priming.

Morton seems to conceive of the activation of logogens by the context system as long lasting, in contrast to the rapid decay of activation from sensory sources. Thus he writes of contextual priming as acting "to maintain constant the levels of the counts in logogens affected by that context" (Morton, 1969, p. 166). Yet this would make for a very noisy system, since the priming would bias the analysis of all the subsequent words in the message unless its timing was precisely guided by syntactic analysis. The crux of the matter seems to be the limitation of the extent to which our expectations can be given lexical form.

The sensory analysis component of the logogen model merits very little comment. The logogen model, like most other models of lexical access, involves the minimum of assumptions about the nature of preliminary visual and auditory analysis of words. This has the unfortunate consequence that work on "visual processes" and work on "lexical processes" in word recognition have tended to exist in parallel but unconnected universes. However, it is not obvious that work on preliminary visual analysis places strong constraints on the form that lexical access theories might take.

One general difficulty with the treatment of sensory analysis in the logogen model is that it provides no account of the transmission of sensory "format" information about words through the system. Once a logogen fires, it transmits an abstract phonological code onwards in the system and we must assume that sensory detail about the colour, appearance and position of the word are discarded or transmitted onward by some other, unspecified system. This raises two problems: we are often capable of reporting such details (though with interesting limitations, cf. McClelland (1976) on recall of letter-case), and there must be some point in the recognition system at which the products of specialist analysis (e.g. colour, shape, lexical content) are reassembled to give the integrated percept that we experience. Allport has been one of the few authors to treat these important questions (e.g. Allport, 1977, 1979), and as he points out, these are problems not only for the logogen model but for all sequential recoding models.

In summary, using the logogen model as a framework for discussion we have been able to examine the development of our understanding of the lexicon up to the late 1970s. Our review has focused on the following issues: (*i*) the treatment of sensory pattern recognition and the problem of how we recover sensory detail; (*ii*) the operation of contextual priming at a lexical level; (*iii*) modality specificity of repetition effects and the consequent development of the Mark II logogen model; (*iv*) problems raised by the pattern of interaction between word frequency, associative context and stimulus legibility; and (*v*) the contrast between two access procedures—lexical search and direct-access.

Oldfield (1966), in the question cited toward the beginning of this chapter, posed two fundamental questions about lexical access—the nature of the access procedure and of the access code. We have seen that the logogen model involved an implicit commitment to a direct-access view of the procedure. The vagueness of the model about sensory pattern analysis precluded any explicit commitment on the form of the access code, but at least the structure of the Mark II logogen model, by postulation of separate visual and auditory logogens, renders explicit a commitment to the possibility of access via a visual code. Almost incidentally, the logogen model takes a stand on the other great current issue: whether access to the lexicon in reading is direct and visual or indirect and phonological.

12.2 THE LEXICAL ACCESS CODE

The notion that, in reading, visual information may require at some stage to be translated into a speech code for comprehension to ensue, has at least three discernible sources. (*i*) It has been observed for well over a century that reading is often accompanied by inner speech. It is but a step from this to the assumption that this transformation is a prerequisite of comprehension and but a further, apparently innocent, step to the assumption that what is required for comprehension must therefore be a requirement for lexical access itself. Although the logic of these steps was well disposed of by Huey (1908) in Chapter VII of his celebrated book, the argument continued to influence thinking. (*ii*) The ease of recognition of a letter string is quite well predicted by its pronounceability. Spoehr and Smith (e.g. 1975) have based a speech-recoding theory on this correlation. Such views are critically examined in Chapters 9 and 10. (*iii*) Speech has chronological priority over reading in intellectual development, and some would hold that it has biological priority, too. Speech is fairly effortlessly acquired, in contrast to the laboured study which reading requires, and it has therefore seemed an "efficient" arrangement for reading to be parasitic on the competence we have with spoken language. After all, it may be reasoned, when we come to reading, we already possess a lexicon that is auditorily addressable. Wouldn't it be simplest if we translated print into speech and then used the already developed, phonological addressing system? Moreover, that seems effectively to be what we suppose of the child when we teach reading. That is, we teach the child what a word "says". This view has been given a further veneer of respectability by influential linguists such as Bloomfield (1942), who have pronounced writing to be a derivation of speech, lacking any independent linguistic identity.

The end of the 1960s saw a renewal of experimental interest in this issue which had been for so long the target of free-floating speculation and dogma. Firm stands were taken in favour of the proposition that lexical access *required* speech recoding (e.g. Rubinstein *et al.*, 1971; Gough, 1972; Smith and Spoehr, 1974). Equally strong were the assertions that a visual code was a *sufficient* basis for lexical access in reading (Bower, 1970; Kolers, 1970; Baron, 1973) or even that it was a *necessary* basis (F. Smith, 1971). Others held that *either code* could serve access in reading (Meyer *et al.*, 1974), launching the dual process theory that was extensively discussed with respect to pronunciation mechanisms in Chapters 5 and 6.

In two incisive reviews Coltheart (1978, 1980b) considered and rejected the arguments made in these papers. The two major problems for this literature are that some of the tasks do not necessitate lexical access, while other tasks provide evidence of phonological recoding without any assurance that this recoding occurs *prior to lexical access*. Clearly, the reader can retrieve word phonology from the lexicon (postlexical phonology). What is at issue in this debate is whether the reader can engage in phonological recoding of orthographic information prior to consulting the lexicon (prelexical phonology) and, if so, whether this recoding plays a role in lexical access or even is a requirement for lexical access.

The reader interested in the details of these studies should consult Coltheart's reviews. In what follows I present an overview of the arguments with particular reference to the types of experimental test that have been used. To give some structure to the discussion, I start from the assumption that fluent reading involves lexical access by means of a visual code and go on to demand evidence that lexical access is ever dependent on phonological recoding. Before considering the evidence, however, it is worth briefly examining the form that prelexical phonology might take.

The prevailing assumption has been that prelexical phonology is derived from grapheme–phoneme correspondences (GPCs), and this view is taken by Coltheart (1978). If this were true, prelexical recoding could only be accomplished for regular words (if we ignore the possibility of recursive search down a list of correspondences accompanied by a lexical check of spellings; see Chapter 5.) An interesting corollary of the GPC view seems to be that direct visual access must be assumed for exception words. That is, if we assume that prelexical phonological recoding relies on GPCs and that some exception words exist that are not amenable to GPC translation, we are compelled to accept the reality of visual access to the lexicon, at least for those words.

In Chapters 5 and 6 various doubts were raised about the adequacy of a GPC mechanism as a means of arriving at word pronunciation. These considerations suggest that we should not presume the existence of a GPC route to prelexical phonology. However, there seems no doubt that, at least for some regular words, a GPC translation could be achieved and even if that translation lacked some phonological detail, such as stress assignment, it should be adequate to provide an unambiguous lexical address. To cope with the vexatious problem of exception words being given a regular, but in this case inappropriate, translation which happens to correspond to another phonological entry in the lexicon (e.g. BREAD→/brid/→*breed*) we might assume that GPC translation is only attempted for GPCs that are *marked as relatively unambiguous*. In sum, we cannot rule out on purely logical grounds the possibility of access mediated by prelexical phonology, although if translation depends upon GPCs, we are thereby committed also to the possibility of direct visual access for exception words.

In Chapters 5 and 6, I advanced lexical analogy as the preferred alternative to GPC translation. This theory is based on the assumption that all attempts to derive word phonology from written language involve the activation of a lexicon that serves the conversion of orthographic patterns into word phonology. The question for such a system is whether we can sensibly speak of anything like "prelexical" phonology. In so far as analogy theory is a *lexical* theory, it involves the assumption that phonology is stored in word (or morpheme) packages, even if these consist of structured elements (see Chapter 6). Clearly, then, it would be odd to term such phonological recoding "prelexical". However, this is not the essence of the matter, since what was intended when GPC translation was characterized as "prelexical" was phonological recoding prior to a *semantic* lexicon. The original question was whether word meanings could be arrived at by phonological recoding. The answer seems to be that lexical analogy theory is entirely neutral on the relationship between its orthographic-phonological lexicon and semantics. So there is no reason why analogy theory should not allow the possibility of phonological recoding as a prelude to gaining access to the meaning of words.

Many distinct techniques have been applied to the question of whether phonological recoding is employed in lexical access, and the principal ones are as follows:

Word-length effects

Various authors have used effects dependent on the number of letters in a word or on the number of syllables in a word as indices of phonological recoding (Forster and Chambers, 1973; Frederiksen and Kroll, 1976; Green and Shallice, 1976). As a rough generalization, letter-length effects are reliably found in naming tasks but are usually, but not invariably, absent in lexical decision tasks. Syllabic length effects are usually not obtained for words in either task (see Chapter 7 for further details and qualifications). It is the tendency for these length effects to be absent in the lexical decision task which has been used to argue that phonological recoding cannot be taking place. Unfortunately, however, no one has yet shown why prelexical phonological recoding must necessarily yield letter or syllabic length effects. To be sure, we can readily invent reasons why grapheme–phoneme translation *might* result in one or other length effect. For that matter, such length effects can more or less plausibly be attributed to other encoding stages. Only if it can be shown that such effects are a necessary product of phonological recoding will their absence in lexical decisions have potential significance.

Homophones

Our ability to read and interpret correctly the meaning of homophones such as *sail/sale* shows that some visual information must be contained in the lexicon. However, Rubinstein *et al.* (1971) have argued that homophones are disambiguated by a "spelling-check" consequent upon lexical access using a phonological code (see Chapter 5 for further discussion). Rubinstein's theory predicts that the less frequent member of a pair of homophones will yield longer RT in the lexical decision task than an equivalent non-homophone because the spelling-check is carried out first on the higher-frequency candidate. This effect has proved rather elusive. Rubinstein *et al.*'s original report of an effect was based on a poorly controlled study. Coltheart *et al.* (1977) repeated the investigation with better controls and failed to find any effect of homophony. In a further study, Davelaar *et al.* (1978) found a very small but apparently reliable effect which was abolished when the nonword stimuli sounded like English words (e.g. BRANE). They argued that naïve subjects tend to rely on phonological recoding in making lexical decisions. However, this is an optional strategy, and it is abandoned when it leads to difficulties because the nonwords include pseudohomophones like BRANE. This account is not without problems: if the homophone effect is caused by a spelling check, this same strategy could be continued even when the nonwords were pseudohomophones. The same kind of spelling check that affirms that SAIL is a legal lexical spelling will successfully reject BRANE. So it is not clear why inclusions of nonwords like BRANE should lead to the abandonment of phonological recoding.

In summary, it is clear that the homophone effect is not inevitable and therefore cannot be used as evidence that phonological recoding is mandatory. There is some evidence that the homophone effect arises through the adoption of a strategy which is optional. Whether this strategy consists in prelexical phonological recoding is not yet clear.

Another and rather different diagnostic use of a homophone test is found in experiments on phrase evaluation (Baron, 1973; Doctor and Coltheart, 1980). Interest here centres on the speed and accuracy with which subjects can decide that visually presented phrases such as SHE BLUE UP THE BALLOON are meaningless, compared with sentences such as SHE KNOW UP THE BALLOON which do not even *sound* sensible.

Baron, using adult readers, found that nonsense phrases containing a homophone-lure were rejected slightly more slowly than other nonsense phrases, but not reliably so. However, subjects did make significantly more erroneous "yes" responses to phrases containing a homophone-lure. Doctor and Coltheart studied children, unfortunately using only an accuracy measure, and found a very substantial effect on accuracy. This effect increased as age decreased.

There is no reason to accept that these studies have any bearing on the question of prelexical phonological recoding. The task requires an evaluation of the entire phrase, and meaninglessness is created by a violation of syntax across the string of words. The role of a *post*lexical phonological code in mediating comprehension has not been seriously disputed. Therefore, we can plausibly argue that, in the above example, BLUE evokes *blew* (the syntactically and semantically acceptable form) by the following steps: direct visual access to the lexical entry for *blue* automatically activates the lexically stored, whole-word phonology, this phonological pattern in turn activates (if only weakly) the lexical entry for *blew*, and that activation is sufficient on some trials to lead to an acceptance decision. Doctor and Coltheart attempt to deal with this difficulty by showing that subjects made more errors on meaningless sentences containing *nonwords* where the nonword sounded correct (SHE BLOO UP THE BALLOON v. SHE NOE UP THE BALLOON). Only the prelexical method of phonological recoding can apply to nonwords, they argue, so the greater difficulty of items that sound correct must be due to prelexical recoding.

This argument will not do at all. First, what subjects do with nonwords has no certain bearing on what they do with words. Secondly, we do not require an experiment to tell us that we are capable of synthesizing a pronunciation for a pseudohomophone like BLOO and using that code to access the lexical entry for the same-sounding real word. What this experiment adds, as indeed others have done, is simply that it is difficult to inhibit this sequence of processes when confronted with a nonword.

Pseudohomophones

A large number of investigations have reported that pseudohomohpones like BRANE (sounding like *brain*) take longer to classify as nonwords in the lexical decision task than do neutral but pronounceable nonwords like SLINT (e.g. Rubinstein *et al.*, 1971; Coltheart *et al.*, 1977; Patterson and Marcel, 1977; and Barron, 1979). The same type of stimulus comparison was also used in the phrase evaluation study of Doctor and Coltheart, described above.

Coltheart *et al.* (1977) have satisfactorily disposed of the idea that the pseudohomophone effect constitutes evidence of a role for phonological encoding in normal lexical access. One simple objection to this idea is that pseudohomophones are not real words, so their fate in the lexical decision task (which is not real reading!) has no ineluctable implication for the reading of words. Another objection can be based on the fact that nonword decisions are reliably slower than word decisions in the lexical decision task. Thus we cannot reject the possibility that whereas words are invariably accessed by means of a visual code, the decision about an item which we *fail* to find in the lexicon is slower and therefore allows time for us to synthesize a phonological code for the nonword and thus to be delayed or misled by pseudohomophones. Coltheart *et al.* (1977) express matters succinctly when they say of this effect: "It remains to be shown, however, that this is any more than an epiphenomenon."

Orthographic regularity

A potentially strong test of phonological recoding prior to access of the (semantic) lexicon consists in the effect of orthographic regularity on lexical decision time. Such a test meets the criterion of direct applicability to affirmative lexical decisions. Furthermore, regularity, as a variable, appears to bear directly on phonological regularity.

In Chapters 5 and 6, I discussed regularity effects largely in the context of naming latency tasks and favoured the hypothesis, originally advanced by Glushko (1979), that regularity effects reflect the extent to which a word's pronunciation is consistent with that of its orthographic neighbours. This implies that phonological recoding involves the activation of an orthographic-phonological lexicon. In the synthesis of a word's phonology, even when the whole word phonology is available from the word's lexical entry, it does not seem possible wholly to ignore the "noise" generated by phonologically inconsistent neighbours. In the present context, we turn to the question of whether such inconsistency also interferes with whatever decision making is required by the somewhat mysterious lexical decision task.

Coltheart *et al.* (1979) failed to find any evidence of slower lexical decisions to exception words in two experiments and concluded that access in lexical decision tasks never depends upon a phonological code. This null finding was replicated by Bauer and Stanovich (1980, Exp. 1), using the Coltheart *et al.* word set, but they argued that if consistency with the phonology of orthographic neighbours was the effective variable rather than GPC regularity, the Coltheart *et al.* word set was inappropriately partitioned, because many of the words classified as "regular" turn out to be nevertheless "inconsistent". Bauer and Stanovich went on to show that a reliable effect of consistency could be obtained for affirmative lexical decisions. Moreover, as in Glushko's study of naming latencies, regular but inconsistent words were no faster than exception words.

A number of other studies of lexical decision RT have also obtained a reliable effect of regularity/consistency with these two variables confounded. Barron (1980) reported a "regularity" effect for good but not for poor readers, and Stanovich and Bauer (1978) found a regularity effect that could be abolished by requiring the subjects to increase decision speed. This last manipulation may result in a strategy that more closely resembles normal reading (where words do not have to be distinguished from nonword lures as they do in the lexical decision task).

If we accept the existence of a sort of regularity effect mediated by consistency, this seems to offer strong support for the idea that phonological recoding can, but need not, play a role in lexical access. One way to conceptualize this role is as follows. The synthesis of a pronunciation for a letter string is probably fairly automatic, as the phenomenon of Stroop interference suggests. Suppose that this phonological representation can feed back activation to the lexical node for the word and that such activation is pooled with the visual activation. A consequence of this would be that the ancillary activation from the synthesized phonology would be available earlier and perhaps more strongly for consistent than for inconsistent words.

The idea that the phonology derived from visually presented words can contribute independently to lexical decision making receives some support from Hillinger (1980). He found that successive presentation of two rhyming words facilitated lexical decision to the second word and this effect was independent of graphemic similarity (e.g. EIGHT primed MATE). Clearly, this sort of reverberating phonology can be misleading to the extent that it activates inappropriate lexical entires, so we must either assume that this phonological feedback produces activation that is not generally strong enough to trigger a decision without additional visual evidence or else we are forced into the postulation of a supplementary spelling-check procedure to minimize false positive decisions.

Articulatory suppression

The oldest technique for investigating the role of phonological encoding in reading is one in which the reader is given a secondary task that is intended to engage fully his articulatory system so that the articulatory system is unavailable to act in support of reading. Early studies, such as those of Secor (1900), required the subject to read while whistling or while the mouth was obstructed. More recent techniques have involved biofeedback from laryngeal muscle activity Hardyck *et al.*, 1966), investigation of reading in the prelingually deaf (e.g. Doctor *et al.*, 1981) and, most commonly, use of a simple concurrent articulation task (e.g. Kleiman, 1975).

It was already clear to Huey (1908) that inner speech in reading might operate as a purely central phenomenon ("motor word-ideas . . . a combination of auditory and motor elements") and that it did not necessarily require peripheral motor activity. The implications of this insight for the articulatory suppression technique have escaped many subsequent investigators but are well brought out by Coltheart (1980b). He distinguishes the task of obtaining an articulatory representation of print from the task of executing articulatory instructions. Only the second of these can be presumed to be interfered with by the typical concurrent articulation task.

Huey (1908) expressed another fundamental insight into the role of inner speech when he attributes to it the function of providing a more stable temporary storage medium pending comprehension of a sentence (see, especially, Huey, 1908, p. 146). This theme has been developed conceptually in terms of the distinction between phonological coding as a prerequisite of lexical access (prelexical phonology) and the use of postlexical phonology as a storage medium pending comprehension.

An influential, experimental investigation of this distinction was reported by Kleiman (1975). He found that an auditory shadowing task produced similar amounts of interference in visual word-matching and in synonymity judgements but much greater interference with a rhyme judgement task. He reasoned that visual matching did not require phonological recoding. Because interference was no greater for synonymity judgements than for visual matching and synonymity judgements surely involve lexical access, there was a *prima facie* case for concluding that lexical access did not require phonological recoding. Could one be confident, though, that the shadowing task did interfered with phonological recoding? Kleiman argued that one could by virtue of the greater interference manifest in the rhyme task. Having thus seemed to establish that phonological coding was not required for lexical access, Kleiman went on to show that it did play a role in postlexical comprehension processes.

Kleiman's conclusions may be sound, but his means of arriving at them are certainly not. At least two damaging criticisms of his argument can be made. Concerning the inference drawn from the interference of shadowing with rhyme judgement, Besner *et al.* (1981) point out that it is possible, indeed likely, that rhyme judgements require postlexical phonology, so the presence of interference from shadowing cannot be used as a test of the occurrence of *prelexical* phonological recoding. The second criticism was raised by Baddeley (1979), who showed that mental load was a more effective source of interference than articulatory suppression when dealing with the influence of a secondary task upon comprehension. Since shadowing is fairly onerous, it is likely that its effect is mediated more by general load than by specific articulatory interference.

There is no good evidence that articulatory suppression interferes with prelexical phonological coding and there is some evidence specifically indicating that it does not (Besner *et al.*, 1981, Exp. 5). When lexical access has taken place and information at the word level requires to be held in temporary storage pending deeper semantic and syntactic analysis, there may be selective interference resulting from articulatory suppression. However, in this case it seems that the specifically articulatory interference is greatest not so much when comprehension is difficult but when it is necessary to retain the surface structure of the text (Levy, 1977, 1978; Baddeley, 1979).

We can now assess the conclusions to be drawn from this wealth of recent experimentation. Most of the techniques simply do not allow us to pronounce upon the question of what role phonological recoding plays in lexical access, and we must take care to distinguish the volume of claims made from the actual weight of evidence. Only the orthographic regularity manipulation seems capable of supporting strong conclusions, and even here, there is room for doubt, since it might be that regular or consistent words are set apart by some correlated but underlying property, such as age of acquisition. Moreover, there is disagreement about the existence of regularity effects. If we are correct in assuming that these disagreements can be resolved by the assumption that consistency, not GPC regularity, is the variable that influences access times, then it seems likely that the phonological "echo" produced by the automatic synthesis of pronunciation by lexical analogy produces feedback that supports lexical activation from direct visual analysis.

12.3 CONTEXT AND LEXICAL ACCESS

An assorted collection of effects

The ease with which a word can be read is influenced by previous verbal events in a wide range of circumstances. In some cases the interaction is between two presentations of the same word. In others the interaction appears to be based on a semantic or syntactic relationship between a test word and previous material. This might take the form of a semantic association between successive words, presented individually. Alternatively, the relevant circumstance might be the occurrence of a test word in a predictive sentential context. We are obliged to consider a range of time-scales over which interactions can occur as well as the variety of relationships that may obtain. Some interactions are influenced by a second's delay; others survive a delay of the test word of at least several days. Let us consider some examples.

Scarborough *et al.* (1977) have shown that lexical decision latency is reduced on the second presentation of a word even when the occurrences of the word are separated by two days. Repetition effects are not uncommon in other tasks so diverse as to imply a variety of underlying mechanisms. These include the facilitation of naming by repetition (Kirsner and Smith, 1974), a negative probe recency effect in immediate memory search (Monsell, 1979), and a response-repetition effect in choice reaction time (Rabbitt and Vyas, 1973).

Facilitation is also found in the lexical decision task when the relationship between two word-trials is not one of identity but of semantic association. Thus the "yes" response to BUTTER is faster if the previous word was BREAD than if it was NURSE (e.g. Meyer and Schvanevaldt, 1971). Recently, interest has been concentrated on the notion that such priming effects may comprise two distinct components: a rapid, automatic facilitation and a somewhat slower-acting, optional process which depends upon the subject's expectations and may be facilitatory or inhibitory (e.g. Neely, 1977).

Yet another sort of interaction between words is that which occurs within a sentence. Since the work of Tulving and Gold (1963) it has often been reported that an appropriate sentence context facilitates the recognition of a test word. Recently the priming interaction between isolated words that are semantically related and the sentence context effect have often been presumed to be varieties of the same species. However, superficially at least there are good grounds for keeping these phenomena apart and at least one theorist has vigorously argued for their distinction (Forster, 1979).

Repetition and frequency

It has often been speculated that it would be an efficient arrangement for the lexicon to be organized according to the frequency with which words are used. Such a view was expressed early in the development of the concept of the mental lexicon (e.g. Oldfield, 1966). Presumably the assumption implicit in this view is one of competition between the demands of the numerous words in our vocabulary. Thus it is assumed that by organizing the lexicon appropriately, high-frequency words can be rendered more accessible at the cost of longer delays in gaining access to the entries for rare words.

It is easy to see how this might work in serial search models of lexical access (Rubinstein *et al.*, 1971; Forster, 1976). In these models competition is incorporated in the serial order of search. If we arrange for frequent candidates to be examined *earlier* than rare ones, we have a simple mechanism for word-frequency effects. An alternative way of incorporating frequency effects within a search model is described by Landauer (1975). In his model, high-frequency words are more likely to be encountered in lexical search because they have *more* representations in the store.

These serial search models are incompatible with a finding reported by Glanzer and Ehrenreich (1979). They varied the composition of lists of words presented for lexical decisions and found that high-frequency words were responded to much faster in lists entirely composed of high-frequency words than in lists of words of varying frequency. Since the high-frequency words should come at the start of the search list irrespective of what follows, their latencies should be constant across these conditions according to the serial search model. To accommodate their effect of list composition, Glanzer and Ehrenreich propose that subjects are able to restrict their search to that portion of the lexicon containing only high-frequency words, when this is an appropriate strategy. In effect, this assumes a sort of working dictionary of common words.

In direct-access models such as the logogen theory, there is no competition between words equivalent to the competition for priority in serial search, and so the word frequency effect falls out less naturally from the direct access model. Indeed it has not been made clear what larger purpose is served by investing the logogens for higher-frequency words with lower thresholds of activation. A critic might hold that this property of the logogens is only there to account for the experimentally obtained effects of frequency.

Until recently the precise way in which word frequency becomes represented in the system has received less attention. By what means is word frequency detected?

First, it is worth mentioning some word attributes which are more or less fortuitously associated with frequency and which may become confused with frequency even though they are almost certainly not the basis of frequency effects. Since Zipf's (1935) work it has been known that common words and rare words differ in their phonemic composition. The spoken duration of rare words exceeds that of common words even when number of letters is controlled (Wright, 1979). Graphemic differences also obtain between common and rare word classes, and common words tend to resemble each other visually more than they do rare words (Landauer and Streeter, 1973).

Age of acquisition of a word is another variable associated with frequency. Lachman (1973) has suggested that "age" and frequency contribute independently to picture-naming speed, and Gilhooly and Gilhooly (1979) have claimed that age of acquisition is predictive of the accessibility of words even when frequency is taken into account. It has been suggested that later-acquired words are often defined in terms of words already known, thus priming these earlier words (Gilhooly and Gilhooly, 1979), but no convincing explanation has been offered of the persistence of such "priming" effects and it may be more fruitful to conceive of this effect as occurring in the semantic system rather than being reflected in the state of logogen thresholds. Other semantic factors associated with word frequency have been shown to influence lexical access and these include the multiplicity of meanings expressed in a word (Jastrzembski and Stanners, 1975) and its concreteness (James, 1975).

We now consider how the frequency of occurrence of a word might come to be reflected in the organization of the mental lexicon, by which I mean how frequency is detected and registered rather than the way, once registered, it influences the identification of a stimulus word. It is worth distinguishing two sorts of mechanism: (*i*) an accumulative counter which reflects frequency directly by incrementing some quantity on each encounter with a given word, and (*ii*) a recency detector which represents some aspect of the lag since the last occurrence of a given word. The recency detector is in some ways a simpler device since it only has to count up to one, though it must also have some way of measuring lag. Obviously such a recency detector only reflects frequency in a probabilistic manner. Words that have not recently been encountered are likely but not certain to be quite rare (i.e. low frequency).

A number of studies of the effects of repetition on word recognition have established the existence of a facilitatory effect of repetition. They also seem to show that this recency or repetition effect is insensitive to recurrences of a word beyond a single repetition (Scarborough *et al.*, 1977). The effect occurs over rather long lags: Scarborough *et al.* (1977) found facilitation when the occurrences of a word were separated by several days and Kolers (1976) found an effect of repeating prose a year later, though this may be quite a different sort of phenomenon.

The repetition effect is not very task-specific. For example, it obtains in lexical decision tasks whether they involve isolated words (Scarborough *et al.*, 1977) or sentence search (Dixon and Rothkopf, 1979). The effect can also be obtained in tachistoscopic threshold tasks (Murrell and Morton, 1974) and, weakly, in word-naming RT tasks (Scarborough *et al.*, 1977). Furthermore, for repetition to be effective it does not have to take place within the confines of one single task. Lexical decision is facilitated by a prior encounter with the same word in a naming RT task (Scarborough *et al.*, 1977).

There is some evidence to suggest that the repetition effect is automatic: it appears independent of the subject's expectations (Scarborough *et al.*, 1979) as well as by the long epoch over which the effect holds.

Perhaps the most interesting aspect of the repetition effect is its vulnerability to changes in stimulus format between the repeated presentations of the word. The effect survives changes in the orientation of letters (Kolers, 1976), shifts between upper and lower case (Scarborough *et al.*, 1977), and changes in handwriting (Morton, 1979b), but it is abolished by changes from an alphabetic to some other form of representation. For example Winnick and Daniels (1970) and Morton (1979b) found no facilitation across pictures and words and neither these authors nor Scarborough *et al.* (1977) found transfer from the auditory to the visual modality.

A conclusion that might be drawn from these findings is that the repetition effect takes place at a stage of processing at which an abstract description of the stimulus is used to search the lexicon. In the case of written words this abstract description would be graphemic (see also Chapter 10). If this were so, we might expect that a repetition effect would not be obtained between, say, presentations of 6 and six.

Attempts to locate the processing stage at which the repetition effect occurs and to investigate whether repetition and frequency effects take place at a common stage of processing have generally employed Sternberg's additive-factors logic, wherein an interaction between factors is taken as evidence that the factors affect a common stage, providing that performance is measured by a ratio scale (as in RT). There are numerous possible objections to this fashionable form of argument, including its restriction to models in which the stages are serial and contingent (cf. McClelland, 1979) and the fact that interactions can arise for other reasons (cf. Stanovich and West, 1979).

Despite these caveats it is of some interest to note the pattern of interactions involving frequency and repetition. There is general agreement that frequency and legibility effects are additive (Stanners *et al.*, 1975; Becker and Killion, 1977). This presents a problem, as we have seen, for the logogen model, since it seems to imply that frequency effects take place at a different stage from contextual priming effect (which interact with legibility) and if legibility is assumed to influence an early stage of processing then so must contextual priming but not frequency.

What of the relationship between frequency and repetition? Here we enter very obscure territory. Forbach *et al.* (1974) found a nonsignificant tendency for the repetition effect to be larger with low-frequency words. The same interaction was significant in the study by Scarborough *et al.* (1977). Neither the empirical state of affairs nor the appropriate interpretation is entirely clear. Scarborough *et al.* assume the reality of a frequency × repetition interaction (justifiably, in my view), but they appear to regard such an interaction as evidence for the proposition that word-frequency effects are *caused* by repetition effects. This cannot be correct: if frequency had no other basis but repetition/recency, there would be no effect of frequency with repetition controlled and no interaction of frequency with repetition. The fact that there is an independent word frequency effect and that it interacts with the repetition effect suggests that the two effects are independent factors which influence the same stage of information processing. (This is the interpretation of an interaction indicated by additive-factors logic.) A further test of this conclusion now suggests itself. If frequency and repetition effects are tied to the same processing stage, they should exhibit the same pattern of interaction with some other variable. We have established that frequency and legibility are additive factors; it follows that so should be repetition and legibility. Unfortunately no published results are available on this question, but an unpublished experiment by Besner and Swan (personal communication) did not have this predicted outcome: the finding was that the two factors interacted. It is therefore beginning to appear that the pattern of interactions across frequency, legibility and repetition is intransitive. This, in turn, shows that additive-factors logic is not an unfailing diagnostic device.

I think it can be concluded with reasonable assurance that some or all of the word-frequency effect occurs without the mediation of repetition/recency. There is no strong evidence that any of the word frequency effect is mediated by repetition but some weak evidence that they independently influence the same stage of processing (their effects appear to interact). There is also some weak evidence that word frequency effects are not located at an early stage of perception, because word frequency effects are additive with those of legibility, and conventional wisdom has it that legibility effects occur at an early stage of perception. This last finding is difficult to reconcile with models like Morton's, in which perceptual analysis and lexical access take place in a single stage (the logogen), but compatible with models like that of Becker, in which perceptual analysis and lexical search comprise successive stages. A different possibility, in which the word frequency effect is held to occur *after* lexical access, seems barely to have been explored. (Clearly such a notion would require us to revise our assumptions about the requirements of the lexical decision task.)

Finally, it is difficult to avoid the conclusion that the word frequency effect has betrayed the trust invested in it by those who believed that it would serve to reflect in a rather direct way the working of the lexical access procedure. It seems likely that the word frequency effect is a composite of various factors that influence various stages of word recognition. As a set of phenomena these provide no privileged view of the manner of lexical access.

The lexicon as a mechanism for contextual priming: an optimistic beginning

It has long been known that more can be read from a glimpse at a semantically and syntactically structured piece of text than from a random list of words. Many of the nineteenth-century students of reading treated the context of letters within a word and the context of words within a phrase as aspects of the same process. For Cattell, contextual facilitation arose because familiarity with written language enables us to apprehend material in larger units. Practice allows us to ascend through the levels of perceptual unit from the individual letter, to the word and on to the phrase. By this means we are able to compensate for certain hypothetical limits on perceptual functioning, notably the supposedly fixed limit on the number of units we can apprehend.

A different view was taken by Huey in discussing the observation that more can be read to the right than the left of the point of fixation. "The words far at the right although dimly seen, are helped into consciousness and preserved in memory by associative links from those that are clearly seen" (Huey, 1908, p. 61). Here Huey goes beyond the perceptual unit account of context effects to say something about the *mechanism* of contextual facilitation. He seems to be invoking the idea of lexical associative priming. Not only did Huey assign a role for contextual facilitation in helping words "into consciousness", he also proposed a more general role for context in the semantic interpretation of a word (e.g. his discussion of the use of context to disambiguate the word *top*, cf. Huey, p. 156).

With the advent of "information theory" in the early 1950s experimenters once again turned their interests to the effects of context on perception. In an influential early study Miller *et al.* (1951) showed that a subject's ability to identify words spoken against background noise was much greater in a sentence context than with isolated words. In accordance with the preoccupations of information theory, Miller *et al.* interpreted this effect as one of *a priori* probability. Context was held to restrict the set of alternatives from which the subject chooses. A further observation by Miller (1962) established an important point which has often seemed to be subsequently lost. In this study Miller showed that mere lexical association between successive word pairs was not a sufficient explanation of contextual facilitation since facilitation is reduced or absent when the test sentence is rearranged into an agrammatical string.

It was not long before experimenters turned to visual presentation. Tulving and Gold (1963) presented a sentence minus the concluding word and then measured the tachistoscopic duration threshold for predictable and unpredictable completions. Not surprisingly, the predictable words had the advantage, and the extent of this effect was related to the ease with which the final word could be guessed from context alone.

The early studies are far more unsatisfactory than is usually conceded, perhaps because the very general point they make is scarcely in dispute. One particular source of difficulty is the use of identification threshold as the measure. This makes it very difficult to estimate the contribution of guessing to the effect, despite attempts to control this, and it also leaves unclear the extent to which contextual facilitation depends upon degraded presentation (speech in noise, tachistoscopic display, etc.).

These studies also leave obscure the sort of predictive information which is abstracted from context, whether lexical, syntactic or conceptual. Consider the sentence: HE ATE THE .... There are syntactic grounds for expecting completion with a noun. In these terms POACHED, for example, is in violation. Association at the lexical level might lead to the expectation of a word associated with ATE. This might include FORK and, perhaps, POACHED but not LOT and certainly not CLOCK. Prediction at a deeper semantic level, given, say, a scenario of greediness confronted by a feast, might suggest LOT but not LEAST.

Not only can we envisage a variety of types of contextual information (e.g. syntactic, lexical, conceptual) operating in a variety of ways (e.g. sophisticated guessing, criterion bias), we can also conceive of these as influencing divers aspects of performance (e.g. perceptual identification, lexical disambiguation). The next development focussed on one aspect of context and one measure of performance. This was the work of Meyer and his colleagues (Meyer and Schvaneveldt, 1971; Meyer *et al.*, 1975). The measure was lexical decision latency, and the contextual information was also lexical, involving associations between isolated words.

Meyer and his colleagues showed that the time taken to affirm that BUTTER is a word is less when it has been preceded by BREAD than by NURSE. This facilitative effect dissipated as the delay between the items was increased, seeming to become undetectable after about four seconds.

Meyer *et al.* consider two possible ways in which associative facilitation might work. (*i*) Semantically similar words might require similar procedures for perceptual analysis. If such a procedure had just been employed, it might be repeated more efficiently for a short period thereafter. (*ii*) Facilitation might occur at a later stage due to a property of the lexicon. If the lexicon functions as an associative network, activation spreading from a particular location to its semantic neighbours might temporarily increase the sensitivity of the neighbouring entries to sensory stimulation.

In later work Meyer has favoured Hypothesis (*i*). Essentially, he provides two reasons (Meyer *et al.*, 1975). First, associative priming interacts with legibility. Legibility is assumed to affect an early processing stage. Therefore, on additive-factors logic, so must associative facilitation. This argument can safely be disregarded. It depends crucially on a fairly arbitrary partitioning of performance into processing stages and it depends upon the additive-factors interpretation of an interaction. Neither of these inferences is compelling. The second reason depends upon various insecure assumptions about pronunciation tasks, and it need not detain us.

Not only do the arguments in support of Hypothesis (*i*) turn out to be without force, there is also a severe difficulty with the notion that semantically similar words require similar preliminary visual analysis as a prelude to lexical access. There seems to be no other reason for supposing this to be so, and there is considerable difficulty in envisaging how prelexical semantic similarity could operate.

Hypothesis (*ii*), in which priming is due to excitation spreading between semantically related entries in the lexicon, seems to have attracted more general interest. A powerful, if indirect source of support for this hypothesis has been the widespread adoption of the spreading-activation principle on other grounds (cf. Collins and Loftus, 1975). However, the spreading-activation theory fails to predict a finding which has subsequently been reliably established: the existence of inhibitory as well as facilitatory consequences of priming.

A general theory that accommodates inhibitory as well as excitatory priming has been advanced by Posner and Snyder (1975). They proposed that two independent mechanisms underlay associative priming effects. The first mechanism resembles Meyer's spreading-activation process. It is held to be fast-acting, to yield only facilitatory excitation and to lack inhibitory consequences. The facilitatory effects dissipate quite rapidly. The operation of this process does not require conscious attention to the priming relationship, and there is no limit to the number of associations that may be activated. The second mechanism reacts more slowly, requiring an onset asynchrony of at least 300 ms between primer and test stimulus. It is called into play when the subject consciously attends to the primer as a predictive cue. Not only does this mechanism produce facilitatory effects when the primer is a valid predictive-cue, but it also produces inhibitory effect when the cuing is invalid.

The principal reasons given by Posner and Snyder for distinguishing between two underlying mechanisms were the fact that many priming conditions give rise to facilitation without evidence of inhibition and the fact that where both costs and benefits do arise, their time courses differ.

Posner's original experiments involved tasks that were not obviously connected with reading, and the priming relationship was not one of semantic association, so it was important to bring together Meyer's task and Posner's theory. This has subsequently been done in a number of studies which have explored cost–benefit functions in single-word reading tasks (Neely, 1976, 1977; Fischler, 1977; Tweedy *et al.*, 1977; Antos, 1979; Tweedy and Lapinsky, 1981). Cost–benefit functions have also been reported where priming is induced by a sentence context (Schuberth and Eimas, 1977; West and Stanovich, 1978; Fischler and Bloom, 1979; Stanovich and West, 1979; Myers and Lorch, 1980). We shall consider the problem of sentence context later.

Cost–benefit analysis and beyond

Priming experiments appear likely to enjoy the vogue in the 1980s that word-superiority experiments did in the 1970s. On this topic there has already accrued a substantial literature. I propose to treat recent work (roughly, work published since 1977) under two headings. Under the present heading I concentrate largely upon priming interactions between isolated words. Under the next heading I widen the enquiry in an attempt to see what light, if any, these experiments and the models derived from them cast upon the operation of context in continuous prose. The discussion of interactions between isolated words begins with consideration of the experimental tasks that have been employed. This is followed by a review of temporal aspects of facilitation and inhibition consequent upon priming. Finally we shall concern ourselves with the role of expectation and the predictive value of the prime.

The preponderance of studies have employed some version of the lexical decision task. A limiting case of the single-word priming paradigm that bridges the gap between single-word and sentence contexts has been employed by Spoehr and Schuberth (1980). In this Continuous Lexical Decision task, a sentence is presented as a succession of isolated words and a lexical decision required to each. To introduce some response uncertainty, nonword foils are occasionally inserted in the series. This task has the merit of being reasonably natural, within the limits imposed by decisions about whether a string of letters forms a word. If the task were converted to a naming latency one, it would not even be necessary to include nonword foils.

A more widely used version of the lexical decision task is one in which the successive trials consist of unrelated words (and nonwords) with insertion of a proportion of related pairs, adjacent in the series. However, this arrangement requires a certain temporal separation of a word from its predecessor (and potential primer), since a response is required to each stimulus in the series. To bring a word closer in time to the intended primer that precedes it, two techniques may be used. Meyer's original method was to present two stimuli simultaneously and call for a *yes* response only if both were words. An even more artificial variant involves no decision-making to the primer, which stands merely as an irrelevant predecessor of the target word. Such a procedure seems likely to evoke in the subject specially tailored strategies.

In addition to the way in which priming stimuli are introduced, the nature of the priming relationship also requires examination. It is worth stressing that two sorts of relatedness have been employed without being sufficiently distinguished. In Posner's studies, which led to the formulation of the cost–benefit model, the relationship is one of identity. This is also the case in Myers and Lorch's (1980) study of verification. More usually the relationship between primer and target is one of semantic association, following Meyer's technique. The main question arising here is whether identical primers and targets are simply to be regarded as the extreme case of semantic relatedness or whether instead the identity relationship should be treated as a repetition effect (which in a strict sense it certainly is) and classed with the long-lasting repetition effect studies by Scarborough and his colleagues.

The solution I propose is to reserve the term "repetition effect" for the long-lasting, modality-specific effect. The effect studied by Posner and by Myers and Lorch should be regarded as a limiting-case of short-term priming by association. There is some evidence that the short-term associative effect is *not* modality specific. Swinney *et al.* (1979) found that a spoken word presented for lexical decision facilitated the decision about a subsequent, visually presented associate. (It is probable that in repetition experiments such as that of Kirsner and Smith (1974) both the short-term associative effect and the long-term modality-specific repetition effect are operating.)

Another aspect of these priming experiments that needs closer scrutiny is the performance measure itself. We saw that in the studies of long-term repetition effects, lexical decision, naming and tachistoscopic threshold tasks were all employed. The same holds for priming experiments. However, it would be dangerous to fall into the assumption that these tasks yield up interchangeable measures of "word recognition". There is no reason to assume as great a degree of lexical involvement in the pronunciation and identification tasks. Dual process theory (see Chapter 6) asserts that regular words and nonwords can be assigned a pronunciation without the retrieval of lexical phonology. Moreover, at an empirical level we find smaller frequency and repetition effects in naming than in lexical decision RT. This might be taken to imply a lesser degree of lexical involvement in the naming task. Tachistoscopic threshold tasks, like naming tasks, do not logically require lexical access although, in fact, they commonly seem to involve it (cf. Henderson, 1980b). Morton's tests of the logogen model (e.g. Morton, 1979b) are exceptional in the use of threshold tasks. Unfortunately, it is difficult to be sure with this task that the primer is not inducing a simple guessing strategy.

From the foregoing it might seem that the lexical decision task is best qualified to determine the role of the lexicon in contextual effects. Coltheart (1975) has extolled the virtues of lexical decision RT in this respect. However, this task is not without difficulties, too. It remains obscure what demands are made of the lexicon in deciding that a string is a real word. Certainly this may stop short of a specific semantic identification, and in this context Neill (1979) has advanced some interesting speculations. He begins by noting certain instances of inhibitory priming (e.g. Rosch, 1975). Such inhibition he attributes to the need to suppress the "noise" created by spreading activation in certain sorts of task.[20] The lexical decision task would be expected to yield little inhibition of this type, however, since the spreading activation of semantic associates may well form a sufficient basis for affirmative responses. The point is that the lexical decision task only requires the subject to decide whether a string is meaningful, without requiring that its specific meaning be identified.

Let us consider the temporal characteristics of facilitatory and inhibitory priming. As we have seen, Posner's cost–benefit theory was originally based upon his finding that at short delays between primer and target item (say, stimulus–onset asynchrony <300 ms) only facilitation occurred, whereas with longer delays inhibitory effects were also obtained, such that the advantage enjoyed by targets that were related to the preceding primer was balanced by a roughly equal disadvantage for targets that were preceded by an unrelated primer. In these cases the RT advantage (facilitation) and disadvantage (inhibition) are determined relative to a control condition in which no primer is employed.

These findings enabled Posner to argue that facilitation developed rapidly and automatically. With longer delays, however, the subject was able to entertain conscious expectations, on the basis of the primer. These expectations were held to direct the focus of a limited capacity attentional mechanism toward a zone in the lexicon. When the primer turned out to be unrelated to the target, this zone would not contain the target and the necessity of shifting attention to the true location of the target in the lexicon incurred time costs, yielding an inhibitory effect for invalid priming.

Neely's work (1976, 1977) seemed to confirm that this temporal asymmetry between facilitation and inhibition held for words. In particular, she obtained facilitation with related primers that was not accompanied by any cost when the primer was unrelated, up to a primer–target interval (SOA) of 400 ms. Beyond that interval there was a growing cost of invalid priming. The benefits from valid priming appeared also to diminish after a delay of 750 ms, suggesting that the automatic facilitation effect decays with extended delay, as Meyer's early work had also shown.

This appears to be yet another of those deceptive high noons in the course of research on a cognitive problem. For a moment we think that reality has been glimpsed with shadowless clarity. Unfortunately, it soon became evident that rapid inhibition could be found. For example, Antos (1979) reported inhibitory effects for invalid primers that preceded the target by only 200 ms (SOA). Indeed, for nonword lexical decisions he found inhibition whether or not the primer was valid. Myers and Lorch (1980) found evidence of inhibition at SOA = 250 ms. Even in Posner's letter-matching task, rapid inhibition has been found (McLean and Shulman, 1978). Furthermore, a study by Stanovich and West (1979), which at first sight appeared to extend the Posner–Neely finding to the sentence context paradigm, turns out on further examination to be inconsistent. In their Experiment 2, Stanovich and West found only facilitation at a target delay of 150 ms, whereas at a delay of 750 ms they found both inhibition and facilitation (for invalid and valid contexts, respectively). The apparent correspondence of these values with Neely's (1977) is actually extremely puzzling, for the following reasons. Subjects were instructed to read aloud a context such as "the boy swam underneath the . . . .", and about 150 or 750 ms after the completion of vocalization of ". . . the" a final word was presented and the naming latency measured. In the above example valid priming would lead to presentation of "bridge". One difficulty is that it is unclear what aspect of the sentential context does the priming. No single lexical term is strongly associated with "bridge". We shall return to this problem below, for it is crucial to the analysis of sentential contexts. Even if we take the effective primer to be "underneath", the priming delay includes the time taken up by the articulation of "the" followed by the 150-ms blank interval. Thus the priming delay is probably a full second from primer onset and half a second from primer offset and therefore much longer than the period over which Posner and Neely found costless facilitation.

It appears that the asynchrony typically found in the development of inhibitory and facilitatory processes cannot be treated as a fixed measure of the speed with which conscious attention develops to replace automatic facilitation, and therefore the formation of a conscious expectation cannot be regarded as the cause of cost–benefit functions.

Certainly it is clear that some priming effects occur without conscious expectations operating. For example, Fischler (1977) found a facilitatory effect on the first occasion of a word being preceded by an associated primer, even though this followed 32 unrelated trials and the subject had no other reason to expect any association. Moreover, in the previous chapter we discussed several instances where a priming effect was evoked by a subliminal primer.

With the inexpensive wisdom of hindsight we can identify a weak line of argument concealed in Posner's dual-process theory. The bare bones are as follows. "Fast" priming seems to yield benefits without risk of costs when the priming is invalid. "Slow" priming yields roughly equal costs or benefits depending upon primer validity. On these empirical grounds is erected a theoretical distinction between the processes underlying fast and slow priming. We identify the mechanism of fast priming as *automatic.* The meaning of this term becomes clear only in opposition to the mechanism held to underlie slow priming. This mechanism is one which responds to *conscious expectations* by gambling on the cue validity of the primer. Most of the rest of the argument simply borrows prevalent intuitions about "conscious" processes, e.g. that they are slow to develop, that it takes a relatively long time to shift their focus ("location shifting"), and also that they have limited capacity. Costs arise in the *conscious-predictive* mode because something that can only be in one place at a time ("attention") is in the wrong place when the primer is misleading and therefore has to be relocated.

Imagine we are examining a display with a narrow-beam flashlight. If we are in the gambling mode, then after DOCTOR we may turn our light toward NURSE in the expectation that it may be the next stimulus. If, however, the unexpected stimulus CARROT arrives, we shall have to swing the torch beam all the way over from NURSE.

But wait a moment, you may say. The torch beam must surely have some odd properties. If DOCTOR primed NURSE, surely we must assume that it would prime SURGERY, HOSPITAL, etc. as well. The torch beam must indeed be many-fingered, and therefore it is unclear in what sense we may speak of it as possessing limited-capacity.

Moreover, priming is said to incur cost in so far as CARROT is processed more slowly when preceded by DOCTOR than when preceded by, say, SLINT. Yet it is not clear why it should take longer to move the torch beam from NURSE to CARROT than to switch it on in the first place. (What happens to the beam when nothing, or nothing lexical, precedes the test word. Where is it?)

Having postulated a homunculus to turn the pages of the lexicon for us, we might at least expect him to serve as a more complete explanatory device!

However, we have not yet touched upon the central difficulty. This seems to me to be the argument (*i*) that the presence of costs indicates predictive behaviour and (*ii*) that predictive behaviour entails conscious expectations. Such an argument is manifestly fallacious. Many conditioning phenomena seem to show animals capitalizing on the predictive values of environmental cues, but we do not feel impelled to suppose that this depends upon their conscious expectations.

So far we have discussed cue validity (the predictability of the test stimulus from the priming stimulus) as if it reflected exclusively the organization of semantic memory. We could put this notion to the test by arranging the series of stimuli such that the artificial contingencies of the experiment were reliably opposed to the natural semantic contingencies. Thus DOCTOR might generally be followed by CARROT, whereas TURNIP would follow NURSE. This particular experiment has not been performed, but an analogous test was reported by Neely (1977). She found that when BODY was more likely to be followed by a part of a building than by a part of the body then the subject was faster in the former case. That is, the probabilistic structure of the experiment overrode the natural associations stored in permanent memory.[21] A parallel finding has been obtained in the Stroop test by Logan and Zbrodoff (1979). They found that when conflicting trials were much more frequent than compatible trials, the classic Stroop interference was reversed and the incongruent display yielded facilitation. This effect depends upon the incongruence being predictable, e.g. GREEN *always* being written in red ink (though their version of the Stroop test was not actually the colour-word one).

These and other parallels between the Stroop task and the primed lexical decision task have led Logan (1980) to formulate a very general model of such phenomena. In this model, an evidence collector (not unlike an input logogen) combines information from different sources. These sources include the sensory analysis of the test stimulus, the transitional probabilities of the experimental sequence, and any natural semantic associations that obtain. Inhibition arises not through any *negative* effect on the rate of evidence collection by the appropriate detector, but rather because inappropriate detectors have accrued more (misleading) evidence and thus the final decision mechanism requires more evidence than it otherwise would from the appropriate detector.

Logan makes a distinction between "attentional" and "automatic" processing, but unlike Posner's distinction this is not explicitly coordinated with the conscious/unconscious dichotomy. Instead, Logan appears to regard natural semantic relationships (DOCTOR–NURSE) as automatically processed, whereas the accommodation to artificial experimental contingencies requires attention. It is not clear to me whether the automatic/attentional distinction contributes anything to the model over and above the simpler distinction between natural semantic associations and predictabilities due to the arrangement of contingencies within experiments.

Sentence context and fluent reading: towards some general conclusions

The literature to which I now turn is peculiarly difficult to organize. It contains important inconsistencies of fact which cannot yet be resolved. Indeed, there are even good grounds for disputing whether any facilitatory effect of sentence context obtains if the task closely resembles normal reading, with undegraded text and no special delays between onset of context and of test item. There are also major theoretical disagreements. On one hand, orthodox opinion holds that the effects of sentence context are but an extension of those obtained with isolated words. In both cases lexical access for the test word is facilitated by the "top-down" action of an appropriate context. In this view, any differences between the action of single-word and sentence contexts require only a minor accommodation on the part of the orthodox theory. At an opposite extreme lies the view of sentence context as qualitatively distinct in its effect from that of isolated words, a position often associated with the denial of any important role for sentence context in facilitating lexical access.

A common consequence of such upheavals is the re-examination of assumptions about what is happening in the experimental tasks. This type of reappraisal has taken two forms in the present debate. At a general level, there has been speculation about the form that context naturally takes in fluent reading and how this is reflected in laboratory tasks. More specifically, the two prevalent tests of lexical access have been critically scrutinized, i.e. the lexical decision and naming tasks.

I mention these difficulties not in the hope of engaging the reader's sympathies but rather to warn him that the expository scheme I have followed is, even more than usually, one imposed on the material rather than discovered in it.

I begin with the dry matter of experimental paradigms, first with the general contrast of single word and sentence contexts, then with the rival claims of the lexical decision and naming latency tasks to be simple and direct reflections of the process of lexical access. From this I turn to the central idea that sentential context acts to facilitate lexical access. This is treated in three portions. First, I consider and reject the notion that lexical association plays an important role in mediating the effects of sentence context. Secondly, I examine the notion that an appropriate sentence context induces expectations that lead to facilitation of lexical access for the test word. The difficulties facing this view are less intractable than those facing the spreading lexical activation view but none the less they are considerable, and I argue against a general role for such a mechanism.

Thirdly, I discuss alternative conceptions of how sentential context might influence performance. This closes my review of the question as far as it concerns lexical access, but I conclude with a brief look at other roles for context in the interpretation rather than the identification of words.

Questions about paradigms

Sentence context is generally regarded as a more worthy object of scrutiny than the context provided by a single, preceding word. There seem to be two related but distinguishable reasons for this judgement. One appeals to ecological validity. The world (or at least the world of books) is composed of sentences, and it is to them that the cognitive machinery is likely to have adapted. Conversely, a subject going about his normal business with sentences is unlikely to be engaged in the conduct of strategies specially contrived to meet the circumstances. In short, what we discover may be expected to have some general significance.

Presumably, then, it would be the occasion for celebration if we found that accounts of priming effects amongst isolated words could successfully be extended to cover sentence context. The corollary, however, is that if the effects of single-word and sentence context point in different directions, we must assume that the latter point at some greater psychological truth.

This argument may seem incontestable but it is worth noting two reservations. First, it depends what we are bent on investigating. If we wish to determine the facilities afforded by the mental lexicon and if the single-word priming task but not the sentential context task reflects their operation, then it is the single-word task that we should prefer. Secondly, the rhetoric of ecological validity does not sit comfortably on a task in which we present the subject with a display such as JOHN ATE THE . . . and then after a brief pause ask him whether PIE is a word or not.

The other reason for treating sentence context as the primary form of context is that much of the literature on contextual facilitation is focussed on the psychology of reading. This is not universally the case, however. Posner's original formulation of the cost–benefit theory of priming was directed at attentional issues with no special reference to language processing. Indeed, it might be argued that the importation of that theory into the realm of sentence processing has failed to take sufficient account of the nature of linguistic predictabilities.

Let us transfer our attention from the nature of the context to the tasks used to test for context effects. The earliest experiments on sentence context employed tachistoscopic identification and this test continues to be used in some single-word priming studies, but almost all recent work on the effects of sentence context has utilized either the naming latency task or the lexical decision latency task. (I exclude, in this statement, work on sentence interpretation as distinct from word identification and lexical access. This distinction is discussed more fully at the close of this chapter.)

The naming latency task has one strong advantage: it is a natural task for the subject to perform. Moreover, it does not require the subject to treat the test word in a very different manner from the preceding context. Against this must be set certain difficulties. The primary of these is that oral reading does not logically require lexical access. It may in fact often or even always involve lexical access, but this cannot be presumed. In Chapters 5 and 6 as well as earlier in this chapter we have discussed theories of the translation of print into sound. I shall not recapitulate these issues here but only remind the reader that many theorists have postulated some role for a nonlexical process that translates print into sound. Even models that do not contain such translation processes, such as the lexical analogy theory, require us to complicate and qualify the notion of lexical access.

There are also technical difficulties with the naming task. The response is a relatively complex one, although only its onset is involved in yielding the latency measure. Furthermore, anticipatory guessing responses are difficult to identify.

The lexical decision task is a rather more mysterious creature. The question it poses—whether a string of letters forms a real word—cannot be said to be a natural one. The inclusion of nonword lures like SLINT may force a deeper visual analysis of real-word neighbours like SLANT than would normally be the case in reading text. Worse still, there is no guarantee that this strange task does not recruit strategies that are altogether peculiar to it.

Typically, the lexical decision latency for a highly familiar word is about 100 ms greater than the naming latency (e.g. Forster and Chambers, 1973; Frederiksen and Kroll, 1976). For rare words the difference may be over twice as great. If we assume that in naming highly familiar words the lexicon is often if not always, consulted, we may enquire what extra processes occupy the more extended time taken by lexical decisions. One obvious answer is that the decision process itself may be quite burdensome. Unfortunately that suggests that some experimental effects are likely to be located at the decision stage itself. For example, authors have postulated various sorts of post-access checks (e.g. Mitchell and Green, 1978; Rubinstein *et al.*, 1971). On the other hand a different difficulty presents itself in the possibility that lexical decisions depend on a deeper form of lexical processing than the mere activation of an entry in the input lexicon. James (1975), Morton (1979a) and Patterson (1979) have argued that lexical decisions involve a degree of semantic processing.

These questions about the nature of the experimental tasks assume importance for two reasons. One is that as purported measures of lexical access their examination exposes the disturbing vagueness of the underlying concept of lexical access. The other is that some authors (e.g. Forster, 1981) have suggested that the two tasks reveal different effects of sentence context.

Does a sentence context facilitate lexical access?

The traditional view, which holds that spread of excitation amongst lexical associates leads to facilitation of lexical access for words embedded in an appropriate sentence context, seems to be objectionable on both logical and empirical grounds.

The logical, or perhaps linguistic, grounds are as follows. It seems clear that in most sentences the constraints that exist are not due to associations between particular lexical terms. Take the sentence NEWTON WAS HIT ON THE HEAD BY THE .... Even disregarding agrammatical completions such as WALKED, the difference between plausible and implausible completions is not accountable in terms of lexical associations between the final word and some preceding word.... APPLE is plausible and ... LAUGHTER or ... TURNIP implausible not because of some natural category embracing HIT or HEAD and APPLE and embodied in the structure of the lexicon. On the contrary, LAUGHTER is implausible because we know it is not capable of this sort of agency. TURNIP is implausible because although a turnip is as capable as an apple of striking one on the head, it is more difficult to construct a scenario for flying turnips than for flying apples (apples grow in trees above our heads; inanimate objects fall more often than they rise). Besides, in this case we have episodic knowledge: we knew what fell on Newton.

Once again, it is bracing to discover what progress we can make simply by taking thought. However, at this point it also becomes necessary to consult reality. After all, it might be true that contextual facilitation only holds for sentences which *are* characterized by lexical associations (e.g. THE BOY HIT THE *BALL* WITH THE *BAT*).

We can safely disregard this possibility because examination of studies which have shown facilitatory effects of a sentence context, both in vision (e.g. Schuberth and Eimas, 1977; West and Stanovich, 1978) and in hearing (e.g. Morton and Long, 1976), reveals that in most of the sentences the test word has no special lexical association with an earlier term in the sentence. Moreover, Miller's early studies of context had shown that an agrammatical rearrangement of the words of a sentence would not induce facilitation.

It therefore seems that we can disregard lexical spreading-excitation as a fundamental mechanism for facilitating lexical access in the reading of sentences. This conclusion immediately sets sentence context apart from the literature on interactions between successive, isolated words.

What, then, characterizes the relationship between the test word and its context in experiments on sentences where facilitation has been reported? The simplest answer seems to be the predictability of the test word from the whole context. That is, test words that exhibit facilitation tend to be those that subjects provide as the most likely completion for an incomplete sentence (this predictability is often called "dominance"), and accordingly, we must turn our attention next to prediction as a mechanism for contextual facilitation in sentence reading.

An important advance in the study of the role of predictability was made in the work of Fischler and Bloom (1979). They showed that an incomplete sentence context facilitated a subsequent lexical decision only when the test word was a highly probable completion of the sentence. Context had no effect on appropriate but less likely completions. Inappropriate (nonsensical) completions showed inhibitory effects that were much larger than the facilitatory effect for likely completions. Indeed, facilitatory effects were only obtained for completions that were predicted on over 90% of occasions. This implies that for a given context facilitation only extends to a single lexical item. This conclusion differs sharply from that reached about single-word contexts, where priming effects appear to extend widely (e.g. Fishler, 1977).

These findings have been confirmed by Forster (1981). Using the lexical decision task, he found a similar pattern across predictable, unpredictable and inappropriate completions for a naming task, but in this case the facilitatory effect for the highly predictable completions did not approach significance. Moreover, Kleiman (1980) has shown that lexical decisions are fastest for the most commonly given completions, although owing to the lack of a control condition it cannot be determined whether this effect is truly one of facilitation.

Some authors (e.g. Stanovich, 1981) have argued that these effects can be accommodated in the cost–benefit framework advanced by Posner and Snyder. On first examination this idea might seem promising. It will be remembered that the essence of that theory was that costs or benefits are produced, depending on whether a limited-capacity, conscious process or expectation is fulfilled or not in the completion. Some of the gross symptoms of this mechanism appear to exist in the data cited. There are indeed costs and benefits. "Limited capacity" is exhibited in the restriction of facilitation to the most likely completion. Finally, it is the conformity of the completion to expectation that yields facilitation. Despite this *prima facie* case, there are a number of serious objections to the proposition that the subject is gambling on his conscious predictions and this gambling exercises its effect upon lexical access time for the test word.

First, there is evidence that the subject's strategy is not under intentional control. Fischler and Bloom (1979) found that the subject still exhibited the effects even when instructed to ignore the context. This suggests a degree of automaticity in the mechanism, a conclusion endorsed by Swinney *et al.* (1979).

A more severe difficulty lies in the balance of costs and benefits. In most studies, the magnitude of facilitation effects is considerably smaller than that of the inhibitory effects. Indeed, in some studies, inhibition is obtained without the compensation of any reliable amount of facilitation (Stanovich and West, 1979, Exp. I; Fischler and Bloom, 1980; Forster, 1981).

Furthermore, the subject's gamble does not promise to be a very rewarding one. Gough and Hillinger (1980) point out that predictable words tend to be high-frequency words, for which lexical access is generally supposed to be facile, anyhow. As Fischler and Bloom (1980) have suggested, it is probably inefficient to restrict attention to a single predicted completion. (People who helpfully complete our sentences for us in conversational exchanges serve as a constant reminder of the inefficiency of that particular psycholinguistic guessing game.) The force of these points is to imply that a focussed gambling strategy is unlikely to serve the reader well outside the laboratory, where the sentence completions are not arranged by a benevolent experimenter.

However, the single most damaging objection is the one mentioned by Fischler and Bloom (1979) when they ask why there is no evidence whatsoever of inhibition for completions that are appropriate (i.e. not nonsensical) *but very unpredictable*. This finding appears to lie beyond the reach of the gambling theory, and some radical reformulation of how predictions bias lexical accessibility would be needed to accommodate it.

Perhaps there is something fundamentally wrong with the notion that sentence context typically acts to facilitate lexical access in normal reading. To re-examine this notion we shall focus on the phrases "in normal reading" and "facilitates lexical access".

The most obvious ways in which the typical experimental test of sentence context effects differs from normal reading is that the test stimulus is often degraded by masking and the contextual frame often precedes the test word as a discrete and leisurely precursor. For these reasons, critics have suggested that facilitation effects may be artifacts of the experimental situation. Consider, first, the effects of degrading the legibility of the test stimulus.

It is well established that context effects are enhanced in poorer readers (e.g. Biemiler, 1977–1978; Schvaneveldt, Ackerman and Semlear, 1977; West and Stanovich, 1978; Perfetti *et al.*, 1979; see Spoehr and Schuberth, 1980, for a review). This fact is of some interest in itself, but it has also suggested to some authors that a deficiency in lower-level reading processes may lead to a greater reliance on conceptually driven processes (e.g. Stanovich, 1981). Of course it is an oversimplification to assume that the effects of degrading the legibility of the test word are to convert the normal reader into a backward reader, but nevertheless stimulus degradation may have the effect of encouraging conceptually driven processes and thus enhancing context effects.

Some support for this view is to be round in Forster's (1976) report that a reliable facilitatory effect of context could only be obtained when the test word was subjected to backward masking. A similar finding was obtained by Stanovich and West (1979). In their Experiment 1 the effects of context were small and unreliable with high-legibility displays, but when the visual contrast of the display was reduced, context effects were substantial and reliable. In contrast, their Experiment 2 showed no interaction between context effects and legibility; even with high-legibility displays a substantial context effect was obtained. It is worth noting that *both* of these experiments have outcomes that are inconsistent with the idea that context facilitates lexical accession in normal reading: in Experiment 1 there is no reliable context effect with undegraded test words; in Experiment 2 there is no interaction of degradation with context, as there should be if both variables influence access time.

Although it is not possible to resolve all the empirical inconsistencies which present themselves in this area, we must try to reach some conclusions. First, I suggest that it cannot safely be concluded that using high-legibility test words is sufficient, by itself, to abolish context effects. A number of studies show reliable effects for undegraded words, and even those that render unreliable effects when degradation is removed (Forster, 1976; Stanovich and West, 1979, Exp. 1) exhibit effects which are in the expected direction. A second matter that is probably more crucial is the frequent *failure* to obtain any interaction between stimulus legibility and the context effect (Stanovich and West, 1979, Exp. 2; Mitchell and Green, 1980; Schuberth, Spoehr and Lane, 1981). Perfetti and Roth (1981) have reported that an interaction between context and legibility obtained only when legibility was reduced to a point where errors become common. In the only other report of a significant interaction, Stanovich and West (1979, Exp. 1) do not cite error rates, but it is notable that the degradation effect is very large, increasing latencies from 466 to 736 ms in the no-context condition. We shall return to the relationship between legibility and context shortly when we consider the possible locus of sentence-context effects.

Apart from stimulus degradation, the other aspect of experiments on sentence-context effects which deviates markedly from the conditions of normal reading is the presentation of prior context often as a separate event and for a relatively long time. Such a procedure seems likely to induce strong expectations in the reader. Moreover, Mitchell and Green (1978) have argued that contextual processing which may operate too slowly to influence normal reading has the opportunity to influence performance when the test word is delayed.

It does appear that as the delay between context and test word begins to approximate that of fluent reading, contextual facilitation diminishes or is absent. Fischler and Bloom (1980) used rapid sequential visual presentation (RSVP) of context and test words and found that contextual facilitation was marginal at slower rates and absent at fast rates of presentation. This contrasts with the facilitation obtained by Fischler and Bloom (1979) when the context could be inspected for several seconds. It is notable that the small and often unreliable effects reported by Forster (1981) were obtained with the RSVP procedure. A similar absence of reliable facilitation was found by Stanovich

(1981) in his final experiment, in which he attempted to minimize delay of the test word. Lastly, Mitchell and Green (1980) found no facilitation in a rapid, continuous lexical decision task.

In summary, the conclusion we have reached about facilitatory effects of a sentence context is that such effects do not characterize normal reading. Facilitatory effects found in the laboratory are the product of unnatural conditions such as severe degradation of the visual appearance of the test word or delay of the test word. Even under these circumstances facilitation tends to be restricted to words that are unambiguously predictable from the context. It is to be doubted whether such facilitatory effects are due to hastening of the process of lexical access for the test word. The fact that facilitation, when it occurs, tends to combine additively with degradation (save when legibility is very severely impaired) seems to imply that these effects take place at different processing stages. It is notable too that word frequency, which interacts with context in single-word priming (e.g. Becker, 1977), combines additively with the effects of a sentence context (Schuberth and Eimas, 1977). Yet it is generally assumed that frequency effects are the product of the lexical access procedure.

From these observations it seems incontrovertible that effects of a sentence context differ sharply from those to be found in single-word priming. With a sentence context, facilitation is much more elusive, it is confined to highly predictable completions and the effect does not usually interact with legibility or word frequency. Moreover, as we have seen, neither the spreading lexical activation hypothesis nor the cost–benefit prediction hypothesis generalizes successfully from single-word studies to sentence-context studies. There are probably two reasons for this. (*i*) The factors that make for predictability of a word in a sentence are not ordinarily reducible to associations between word pairs. The fate of behaviouristic word-chaining approaches to language should remind us of this. (*ii*) Single-word priming operates at asynchronies as small as 40 ms (Fischler and Goodman, 1978). In contrast, the semantic predictabilities within a sentence probably become available relatively slowly. Given that perceptual processes in reading (including lexical access) are fairly swift and "automatic", sentential constraints probably do not become available in time to influence them. Such constraints are more likely to influence processes at the semantic interpretation level itself.

It is interesting to speculate whether the lack of perceptual facilitation by sentence context in reading sets reading apart from listening. The earliest studies of sentence-context effects were those of Miller on speech intelligibility. Moreover, the Treisman–Morton dictionary-unit models treated speech and writing indifferently. Since then, experimental work on sentence context effects has diverged into one or other modality, as if ears and eyes were connected to different psychologists. (The interested reader can pursue recent work on speech in Morton and Long, 1976; Blank and Foss, 1978; Marslen–Wilson and Welsh,

1978.) I shall not digress into the domain of speech other than to observe that it seems possible that top-down processing plays a much larger part in the perceptual processing of speech than it does in reading.

Before leaving this topic, we must briefly consider inhibitory effects of a sentence context. It may seem paradoxical to devote extensive space to the elusive facilitatory effects induced by a predictive context and to mention only briefly the ubiquitous inhibitory effects that are induced by an inappropriate context—especially as many experiments yield inhibitory effects alone (e.g. Fischler and Bloom, 1980; Mitchell and Green, 1980, Exp. 1; Forster, 1981). However, this is entirely due to the persistent theoretical yearnings for facilitatory effects.

The simplest interpretation of inhibitory effects is that advanced by Fischler and Bloom (1979, 1980). They assume that facilitation is only induced when the test word is delayed and highly predictable but that inhibition of an inappropriate test word is rapidly generated and is extremely difficult to avoid. Since the set of possible, semantically anomalous completions is generally large, such inhibition must, perforce, fan out to a vast number of items. Fischler and Bloom (1980) suggest that such relatively automatic inhibition would serve as a valuable indication to the reader that his construction of a consistent interpretative model of the sentence meaning had failed.

There are two difficulties with this idea. First, it is not clear why incongruity (inhibition) should be detected so much faster than congruity (facilitation). To this we might respond that the detection of incongruity may be based on a more superficial examination of sentence meaning. Alternatively, we might conclude that incongruity is not detected faster, it merely has attentional priority.

Secondly, Forster (1981) has shown that the inhibition of inappropriate completions obtains even when the context is very *unfocussed* (e.g. THEY WERE ALL BUSY LOOKING FOR . . .). The effect, however, is sharply reduced in magnitude. This implies that the access thresholds would have to have been raised for a very large set of words. It might be preferable to assume that the inhibition occurs *after* lexical access for the test word has been achieved and is specific to that word-meaning.

Lexical access and semantic interpretation

It has been widely supposed that the effects of word frequency, repetition and context reflect the process of lexical access and that these effects can be assessed through performance on word identification, word naming and lexical decisions. It has been possible to discuss many of these issues without being very explicit about what is meant by lexical access, but the discussion has also served to expose the vagueness of the term. One difficulty is that the term is partially specified by its employment in a number of models. For example, the models of Morton, Forster and Becker all make assertions about aspects of the process of lexical access. At a vaguer level, the dual-process theory of pronunciation embodies assumptions about aspects of lexical functioning in making the distinction between lexical and nonlexical routes. Vaguer still are the assumptions about lexical access made in theories of the word-superiority effect.

Some, but not all, of these vaguenesses result from differing conventions about the extension of the term—for example, how much of the perceptual analysis of a word to include in the hypothetic stage called "lexical access", or how much of the unpacking of semantic information from a lexical entry to include. Our expectation about, say, the interaction of legibility with factors that are held to reflect the access process will depend upon such definitions.

The foregoing discussion of lexical access has largely been conducted from the point of view of the student of perceptual processes in reading. The perspective of those primarily interested in comprehension processes is likely to be different.

Tabossi and Johnson-Laird (1980) distinguish between three aspects of lexical functioning. First, the lexicon serves the perceptual identification of words in the stream of discourse. I have argued that sentence context normally exercises little influence on this level of lexical functioning, but it must be admitted that a persuasive semantic context can sometimes induce us to experience and supply a word that is not present in the text. Moreover, it seems that this is most likely to happen when the word suggested by the context visually resembles the word actually present in the text. (This is suggested by Pillsbury's (1897) work but the problem has been largely neglected subsequently.) The fact of intrusional errors induced by context does not, in itself, establish that when the candidate word supplied by context is the same word which is physically present, perception will be facilitated. The latter outcome can be obtained in the laboratory, as we have seen, but it probably does not commonly occur in attentive, fluent reading. Lexical access is generally too swift and effortless to be influenced by semantic interpretation processes of the sort that handle sentence comprehension. For these processes to interact we must delay the test word and perhaps degrade its legibility, that is, we must shift the normal balance in favour of the semantically driven process.

A second, deeper level of lexical functioning is described by Tabossi and Johnson-Laird. At this level the general sense of a word is retrieved from the lexicon. This is most clearly illustrated in the case of homographs like BRIDGE (*structure* or *card-game*), but the process is not confined to homographs. A considerable literature has accumulated around the use of context in disambiguation (e.g. Conrad, 1974; Cairns and Kamerman, 1975). It is generally conceded that ambiguous sentences take longer to construe (see Clark and Clark, 1977, for a review), so there is time to bring to bear interpretations that arise out of sentence processing. It is widely assumed that all the senses of an ambiguous word are retrieved when sensory activation takes place and that contextual information is used to select an appropriate sense (e.g. Marcel, 1978b). In this view, context influences a fairly late stage of processing. In the perceptual literature on word recognition this stage would be said to occur after lexical access, since that literature equates "lexical access" with Tabossi and Johnson-Laird's first level of lexical functioning.

In the third level, a specific sense of the word is supplied, according to the relevance of particular semantic features (e.g. *diamond* as cutting agent and as jewellery; *cook* as boil and as fry). This level, too, is susceptible to contextual influence (Barclay *et al.*, 1974; Tabossi and Johnson-Laird, 1980). Indeed, without context this level of interpretation could scarcely be sustained. It is interesting to note that for this level of interpretation we reserve a phrase based on print and not speech. Thus, we speak of "giving an appropriate reading" to a sentence But then despite the primacy of spoken over written language it is the eye that has always served as a metaphor for the enquiring intelligence. No doubt you see what I mean . . .

Notes

1 Other epigraphers, however, have denied the pictographic origin of modern writing. Schmandt-Besserat (1978) has argued that the Sumerian ideographs—a key stage in the development of writing—originated from the widespread use of clay tokens as a record-keeping device. The employment of drawings of these tokens linked the two stages.

2 The problem of how to classify the Semitic consonantal script has considerably exercised scholars (cf. Edgerton, 1952; Gelb, 1963). The important point, I suggest, is to avoid using the term "alphabetic" to describe a script that uses one sign for each syllabic segment, albeit in a way that signals the identity of the syllable-initial consonant.

3 It has sometimes been suggested that the idealized spectrographs used for speech synthesis omit invariant features that are present in natural speech. Cole and Scott (1974) make such a claim for the spectrographic pattern known as the *burst*. However, it seems likely that the form taken by a burst is as context-dependent as that of a transition (cf. Wintz *et al.*, 1972).

4 An analogy suggests itself here with the rapid loss of conscious access to certain figural properties of printed words. McClelland (1976) and others have shown that in tachistoscopic word identification experiments subjects have poor immediate recall of the case in which letters were presented. Yet in other tasks which do not require explicit recall of case information, tacit knowledge can be demonstrated (e.g. Kirsner, 1972).

5 This type of matching had previously been employed by Guthrie (1973).

6 Makita's attribution of the high level of literacy in Japan to the properties of the Kana syllabary has a face validity which has perhaps led to rather uncritical acceptance. It might just as well be the simple syllabic structure of the spoken language that matters. Furthermore, Steinberg and Yamada (1978) have shown that Japanese preschool children find it easier to learn Kanji signs than Kana. Also, if Taylor (1980) is correct about the high level of literacy in Korea, this must be attributed to quite different causes, because the Hangul alphabet/syllabary is highly complex, if ingenious.

7 A difficulty encountered by all attempts to characterize English orthography in terms of a set of rules should become evident in the course of this historical prelude. Our spellings evolved over a thousand years of pressure from military conquest, pronunciation drift, printing technology, spelling reformers, and a host of other factors, both principled and accidental, including downright mistakes. An abstract and ahistorical set of rules cannot be expected to capture the product of such a process in any detail.

8 Analogy-based pronunciation mechanisms are discussed in some detail in Chapter 5.

9 Solso *et al.* (1979) have published a type count (which they term "versatilities") for the bigrams and trigrams appearing in the Kucera and Francis (1967) word corpus.

10 This is an appropriate juncture at which to protest about two undesirable aspects of syndrome-naming in neuropsychology. One is the sheer proliferation of names for a given syndrome, which merely creates confusion for readers of the literature. The second, which also threatens to confuse the authors themselves, is the tendency to give to syndromes a name which expresses the author's interpretation of the *nature* of the disability. This makes it more than usually difficult to keep apart facts and their theoretical interpretations.

11 Since these words were written, similar comments have been published in an interesting review of the syndrome by Marcel (1980). He makes three main points about the reading errors. (*i*) The errors suggest that application of GPC rules is quasi-random, yet it is unclear why this so often results in a real word being produced. (*ii*) Many errors cannot be attributed to the use of any legal GPC, however exceptional: e.g. *applaud* → appollo. (*iii*) There is a striking resemblance between errors in surface dyslexia and those made by normal children learning to read.

12 Other discussions of visual similarity errors in deep dyslexia can be found in Coltheart (1980), Morton and Patterson (1980) and Shallice and Warrington (1975).

13 Both Coltheart (1980) and Saffran *et al.* (1980) have advanced the hypothesis that the symptoms of deep dyslexia arise because the patient has lost direct access to the left-hemisphere lexicon and relies upon a less efficient and complete lexicon located in the right hemisphere. In this view, the various types of error made by these patients are a product of this reliance on a right-hemisphere lexicon that plays little role in normal reading. Since, *ex hypothesi*, deep dyslexics lack direct access to the lexicon that largely serves normal reading, the relevance of the syndrome to the question of direct access in normal reading is circumstantial.

14 Shallice and Warrington (1980) appear to imply a model of phonographic translation in which segments of various size are used as the units of translation but the model is not explicitly described.

15 The KW cluster appeared briefly in Middle English only to be replaced by the Romance spelling QU. *Kwashiorkor* is a foreign borrowing adopted for technical (medical) purposes and ignored by *OED*.

16 Hochberg (1970) was one of the first to formulate a distinction between two sources of information guiding the eye: peripheral vision and cognitive prediction. A good collection of recent papers on the control of eye movements is to be found in the first section of Kolers *et al.* (1979).

17 There are more technical difficulties attaching to Biederman and Tsao's argument, not least of which is the use of a between-subjects design taken together with evidence that the Chinese subjects were slower in the colour-naming and word-naming control conditions. Moreover, Smith and Kirsner (in press) report a failure to replicate.

18 To speak of a "left-hemisphere advantage" is to label the effect according to what we have inferred has happened rather than to what we have determined empirically. What the experimenter has done is to compare performance with stimulus presentation to the left and the right of the visual field. It would be much more conservative therefore to speak of visual field advantages. Against this must be set the low S–R compatibility involved in connecting statements about presentation field with inferences about brain hemispheres. For readers unused to laterality debates this is often confusing, and because those readers are on the side of the angels (ultimate lateralization) I abandon propriety on their behalf. For an interesting discussion of the difficulties involves in interpreting field advantages, see Marshall (1973).

19 Since this was written, I have received from McClelland and Rumelhart (1980) a report of an elaborate mathematical model which they have constructed and used in simulation studies. This develops in detail notions like those described here. I find it difficult to evaluate the undoubtedly successful predictions of a model containing so many parameters whose values are arrived at by *post hoc* juggling. The test of the model must be its ability to generate new and successful predictions.

20 To the tasks considered by Neill it may be worth adding visual search tasks in which the time taken to find a specific word target is increased when background items belong to the same semantic category (Henderson and Chard, 1977). This sort of effect is usually described as a facilitatory effect of category difference, but it may be more appropriate to interpret it as an inhibitory effect of semantic homogeneity.

21 There is an amusingly wild comparison to be made here with work on "the generality of the laws of learning" (Seligman, 1970). The pragmatic learning of humans in the priming task, with the subject accommodating to artificially arranged contingencies that override natural associations, contrasts with the difficulty of conditioning animals to unnatural associations.

References

Adams, M. J. (1979). Models of word recognition. *Cognitive Psychology* **11**, 133–176.

Aderman, D. and Smith, E. E. (1971). Expectancy as a determinant of functional units in perceptual recognition. *Cognitive Psychology* **2**, 117–129.

Ades, A. E. (1974). How phonetic is selective adaptation? Experiments on syllable position and vowel environment. *Perception and Psychophysics* **16**, 61–66.

Albrow, K. H. (1972). *The English Writing System: Notes Toward a Description.* London: Longman.

Allard, F. and Henderson, L. (1976). Physical and name codes in auditory memory: the pursuit of an analogy. *Quarterly Journal of Experimental Psychology* **28**, 475–482.

Allport, D. A. (1977). On knowing the meaning of words we are unable to report: the effects of visual masking. *In* S. Dornic (Ed.) *Attention and Performance* **6**. Hillsdale, N.J.: Lawrence Erlbaum Associates.

Allport, D. A. (1979). Word recognition in reading: a tutorial review. *In* P. A. Kolers, H. Bouma and M. Wrolstad (Ed.) *Processing of Visible Language*. Vol. 1. New York: Plenum Press.

Allport, D. A. (1980). Attention and performance. *In* G. L. Claxton (Ed.) *New Directions in Cognitive Psychology*. London: Routledge and Kegan Paul.

Alpern, M. (1971). Effector mechanisms in vision. *In* J. A. King and L. A. Riggs (Ed.) *Woodworth and Schlosberg's Experimental Psychology* (3rd edit.). New York: Holt, Rinehart and Winston.

Anderson, I. H. (1937). Eye movements of good and poor readers. *Psychological Monographs* **4**, 1–35.

Anderson, S. R. (1974). *The Organization of Phonology*. New York and London: Academic Press.

Antos, S. J. (1979). Processing facilitation in a lexical decision task. *Journal of Experimental Psychology: Human Perception and Performance* **5**, 527–545.

Asayama, T. (1914). Cited in Lyman, Kwan and Chao (1938) *q.v.*

Baddeley, A. D. (1979). Working memory and reading. *In* P. A. Kolers, M. Wrolstad and H. Bouma (Ed.) *Processing of Visible Language*. New York: Plenum Press.

Baker, E., Berry, T., Gardner, H., Zurif, E., David, L. and Veroff, A. (1975). Can linguistic competence be dissociated from natural language functions? *Nature* **254**, 509–510.

Baker, R. G. (1980). Orthographic awareness. *In* U. Frith (Ed.) *Cognitive Processes in Spelling*. London and New York: Academic Press.

Baker, R. G. and Smith, P. T. (1976). A psycholinguistic study of English stress assignment rules. *Language and Speech* **19**, 9–27.

Barclay, J. R. (1972). Non-categorical perception of a voiced stop: a replication. *Perception and Psychophysics* **11**, 269–273.

Baron, J. (1973). Phonemic stage not necessary for reading. *Quarterly Journal of Experimental Psychology* **25**, 241–246.

Baron, J. (1975). Successive stages in word recognition. *In* P. M. A. Rabbitt and S. Dornic (Ed.) *Attention and Performance 5*. London and New York: Academic Press.

Baron, J. (1977a). Mechanisms for pronouncing printed words: use and acquisition. *In* D. LaBerge and S. J. Samuels (Ed.) *Basic Processes in Reading: Perception and Comprehension*. Hillsdale, N.J.: Erlbaum.

Baron, J. (1977b). What we might know about orthographic rules. *In* S. Dornic (Ed.) *Attention and Performance 6*. Hillsdale, N.J.: Erlbaum.

Baron, J. and Strawson, C. (1976). Use of orthographic and word-specific knowledge in reading words aloud. *Journal of Experimental Psychology: Human Perception and Performance* **2**, 386–393.

Baron, J. and Thurston, I. (1973). An analysis of the word superiority effect. *Cognitive Psychology* **4**, 207–228.

Baron, J., Treiman, R., Freyd, J. and Kellman, P. (1980). Spelling and reading by rules. *In* U. Frith (Ed.) *Cognitive Processes in Spelling*. London and New York: Academic Press.

Barr, J. (1976). Reading a script without vowels. *In* W. Haas (Ed.) *Writing without Letters*. Manchester: Manchester University Press.

Barron, R. W. (1979). Reading skill and phonological coding in lexical access. *In* M. M. Gruneberg, R. N. Sykes and P. E. Morris (Ed.) *Practical Aspects of Memory*. New York and London: Academic Press.

Barron, R. W. (1981). Development of visual word recognition: a review. *In* T. G. Waller and G. E. MacKinnon (Ed.) *Reading Research: Advances in Theory and Practice*, Vol 2. New York and London: Academic Press.

Barron, R. W. and Henderson, L. (1977). The effects of lexical and semantic information on same-different visual comparison of words. *Memory and Cognition* **5**, 566–579.

Barron, R. W. and Pittinger, J. B. (1974). The effect of orthographic structure and lexical meaning on same-different judgements. *Quarterly Journal of Experimental Psychology* **26**, 566–581.

Bauer, D. W. and Stanovich, K. E. (1980). Lexical access and the spelling-to-sound regularity effect. *Memory and Cognition* **8**, 424–432.

Becker, C. A. (1976). Allocation of attention during visual word recognition. *Journal of Experimental Psychology: Human Perception and Performance* **2**, 556–566.

Becker, C. A. (1979). Semantic context and word frequency effects in visual word recognition. *Journal of Experimental Psychology: Human Perception and Performance* **5**, 252–259.

Becker, C. A. and Killion, T. H. (1977). Interaction of visual and cognitive effects in word recognition. *Journal of Experimental Psychology: Human Perception and Performance* **3**, 389–401.

Bellugi, U. and Fischer, S. (1972). A comparison of sign language and spoken language. *Cognition* **1**, 173–200.

Benson, D. F. and Geschwind, N. (1969). The alexias. *In* P. U. Vinkel and G. W. Bruyn (Ed.) *Handbook of Clinical Neurology*, Vol. 4. Amsterdam: North Holland.

Besner, D., Alcott, D. and Parry, P. (1979). Deep dyslexia and the right hemisphere hypothesis: evidence from the FBI and the KGB. Unpublished MS. University of Reading.

Besner, D. and Coltheart, M. (1979). Ideographic and alphabetic processing in skilled reading of English. *Neuropsychologia* **17**, 467–472.

Besner, D., Daniels, S. and Slade, C. (in press). On the reading of ideograms. *British Journal of Psychology*.

Besner, D., Davies, J. and Daniels, S. (1981). Phonological processes in reading: the effect of concurrent articulation. *Quarterly Journal of Experimental Psychology* **33A**, in press.

Besner, D. and Jackson, A. (1975). Same-different judgements with words and non-words: a word superiority/inferiority effect. *Bulletin of the Psychonomic Society* **6**, 578–580.

Biederman, I. (1972). Perceiving real world scenes. *Science* **177**, 77–80.

Biederman, I. and Tsao, Y-C. (1979). On processing Chinese ideographs and English words: some implications from Stroop-Test results. *Cognitive Psychology* **11**, 125–132.

Biemiler, A. (1977–78). Relationship between oral reading rates for letters, words and simple text in the development of reading achievement. *Reading Research Quarterly* **13**, 223–253.

Bjork, E. L. and Estes, W. K. (1973). Letter identification in relation to linguistic context and masking conditions. *Memory and Cognition* **1**, 217–223.

Blank, M. A. and Foss, D. J. (1978). Semantic facilitation and lexical access during sentence processing. *Memory and Cognition* **6**, 644–652.

Bliss, C. K. (1965). *Semantography-Blissymbolics*. Sydney: Semantography-Blissymbolics Publications.

Bliss, C. K. (1976). *Mr. Symbol Man*. Sydney: Semantography-Blissymbolics Publications.

Bloomfield, L. (1933). *Language*. New York: Holt, Rinehart and Winston.

Bloomfield, L. (1942). Linguistics and reading. *The Elementary English Review* **19**, 125–130.

Bolinger, D. L. (1946). Visual morphemes. *Language* **22**, 333–340.

Bouma, H. (1971). Visual recognition of isolated lower case letters. *Vision Research* **11**, 459–474.

Bower, G. H. (1970). Reading by eye. *In* H. Levin and J. P. Williams (Ed.) *Basic Studies in Reading*. New York: Basic Books.

Bradley, H. (1919). *On the Relations between Spoken and Written English*. Oxford: Clarendon Press.

Bradley, L. and Bryant, P. E. (1978). Difficulties in auditory organization as a possible cause of reading backwardness. *Nature* **271**, 746–747.

Bradshaw, J. L. (1974). Peripherally presented and unreported words may bias the perceived meaning of centrally fixated homograph. *Journal of Experimental Psychology* **103**, 1200–1202.

Bradshaw, J. L. and Nettleton, N. C. (1974). Articulatory interference and the mown-down heterophone effect. *Journal of Experimental Psychology* **102**, 88–94.

Broadbent, D. E. (1967). Word frequency effect and response bias. *Psychological Review* **74**, 1–15.

Broadbent, D. E. (1971). *Decision and Stress*. London and New York: Academic Press.

Broadbent, D. E. (1977). The hidden preattentive processes. *American Psychologist* **32**, 109–118.

Broadbent, D. E. (1979). Review of N. S. Sutherland (Ed.) *Tutorial Essays in Psychology 1*. *Quarterly Journal of Experimental Psychology* **31**, 367–368.

Broadbent, D. E. and Broadbent, M. (1977). General shape and local detail in word perception. *In* S. Dornic (Ed.) *Attention and Performance 6*. Hillsdale, N.J.: Erlbaum.

Brooks, L. (1967). The suppression of visualization by reading. *Quarterly Journal of Experimental Psychology* **19**, 289–299.

Brooks, L. (1977). Visual pattern in fluent word identification. *In* A. S. Reber and D. L. Scarborough (Ed.) *Toward a Psychology of Reading*. Hillsdale, N.J.: Erlbaum.

Brooks, L. (1978). Non-analytic correspondences and pattern in word pronunciation. *In* J. Requin (Ed.) *Attention and Performance* 7. Hillsdale, N.J.: Erlbaum.

Bruder, G. A. (1978). Role of visual familiarity in the word-superiority effects obtained with the simultaneous-matching task. *Journal of Experimental Psychology: Human Perception and Performance* **4**, 88–100.

Bryant, P. E. and Bradley, L. (1980). Why children sometimes write words which they do not read. *In* U. Frith (Ed.) *Cognitive Processes in Spelling*. London: Academic Press.

Bryden, M. P. and Allard, F. (1976). Visual hemifield differences depend on typeface. *Brain and Language* **3**, 191–206.

Buswell, G. T. (1920). An experimental study of eye–voice span in reading. *Supplementary Educational Monographs* No. 17. Chicago: University of Chicago.

Cairns, H. S. and Kameraman, J. (1975). Lexical information processing during sentence comprehension. *Journal of Verbal Learning and Verbal Behavior* **14**, 170–179.

Calfee, R. C., Chapman, R. and Venezky, R. (1972). How a child needs to think to learn to read. *In* L. W. Gregg (Ed.) *Cognition and Learning in Memory*. New York: Wiley.

Carr, T. H., Davidson, B. J. and Hawkins, H. L. (1978). Perceptual flexibility in word recognition: strategies affect orthographic computation but not lexical access. *Journal of Experimental Psychology: Human Perception and Performance* **4**, 674–690.

Carr, T. H., Lehmkuhle, S. W., Kottas, B., Astor-Stetson, E. C. and Arnold, D. (1976). Target position and practice in the identification of letters in varying contexts: a word superiority effect. *Perception and Psychophysics* **19**, 412–416.

Carr, T. H., Posner, M. I., Pollatsek, A. and Snyder, C. R. R. (1979). Orthography and familiarity effects in word processing. *Journal of Experimental Psychology: General* **108**, 389–414.

Carroll, J. B. (1972). The case for ideographic writing. *In* J. F. Kavanagh and I. G. Mattingly (Ed.) *Language by Eye and by Ear*. Cambridge, Mass.: M.I.T. Press.

Carroll, J. B. and White, M. N. (1973). Word frequency and age of acquisition as determinants of picture naming latency. *Quarterly Journal of Experimental Psychology* **25**, 85–95.

Cattell, J. M. (1885). The inertia of the eye and brain. *Brain* **8**, 295–312.

Cattell, J. M. (1886). The time taken up by cerebral operations. *Mind* **11**, 220–242, 377–392, 524–538. Reprinted in Poffenberger (Ed.) *James McKeen Cattell*. New York: Basic Books, 1973.

Chall, J. (1967). *Learning to Read: the Great Debate*. New York: McGraw Hill.

Chambers, S. M. and Forster, K. I. (1975). Evidence for lexical access in a simultaneous matching task. *Memory and Cognition* **3**, 549–559.

Chomsky, C. (1970). Reading, writing and phonology. *Harvard Educational Review* **40**, 287–309.

Chomsky, N. (1957). *Syntactic Structures*. The Hague: Mouton.

Chomsky, N. (1965). *Aspects of the Theory of Syntax*. The Hague: Mouton.

Chomsky, N. (1968). *Language and Mind*. New York: Harcourt Brace Jovanovich.

Chomsky, N. and Halle, M. (1968). *The Sound Pattern of English*. New York: Harper and Row.

Christie, W. M. (1974). Some cues for syllable juncture perception in English. *Journal of the Acoustical Society of America* **55**, 819–821.

Clark, H. H. (1971). The importance of linguistics for the study of speech hesitations. *In* D. L. Horton, and J. J. Jenkins (Ed.) *The Perception of Language*. Columbus, Ohio: Charles Merrill.

Clark, H. H. and Clark, E. V. (1977). *Psychology and Language: an Introduction to Psycholiguistics*. New York: Harcourt Brace Jovanovich.

Cohen, G. and Freeman, R. H. (1978). Individual differences in reading strategies in relation to handedness and cerebral asymmetry. *In* J. Requin (Ed.) *Attention and Performance* 7. Hillsdale N.J.: Erlbaum Associates.

Cole, R. A. and Jakanik, J. (1978). Understanding speech: how words are heard. *In* G. Underwood (Ed.) *Strategies of Information Processing*. London: Academic Press.

Cole, R. A., Rudrucky, A. I. and Zue, V. (1978). How to read visible speech. Paper presented to the Psychonomic Society Conference, San Antonio.

Cole, R. A. and Scott, B. (1974a). The phantom in the phoneme: invariant characteristics in stop consonants. *Perception and Psychophysics* **15**, 101–107.

Cole, R. A. and Scott, B. (1974b). Toward a theory of speech perception. *Psychological Review* **81**, 348–374.

Collins, A. M. and Loftus, E. F. (1975). A spreading-activation theory of semantic processing. *Psychological Review* **82**, 407–428.

Coltheart, M. (1977). Critical Notice of Gibson, E. J. and Levin, H. "The Psychology of Reading". *Quarterly Journal of Experimental Psychology* **29**, 157–167.

Coltheart, M. (1978). Lexical access in simple reading tasks. *In* G. Underwood (Ed.) *Strategies of Information Processing*. London and New York: Academic Press.

Coltheart, M. (1980a). Deep dyslexia: a right hemisphere hypothesis. *In* M. Coltheart, K. Patterson and J. C. Marshall (Ed.) *Deep Dyslexia*. London: Routledge and Kegan Paul.

Coltheart, M. (1980b). Reading, phonological recoding and deep dyslexia. *In* M. Coltheart, K. Patterson and J. C. Marshall (Ed.) *Deep Dyslexia*. London: Routledge and Kegan Paul.

Coltheart, M. and Coltheart, V. (1972). On Rumelhart's model of visual information processing. *Canadian Journal of Psychology* **26**, 292–295.

Coltheart, M., Davelaar, E., Jonassen, J. T. and Besner, D. (1977). Access to the internal lexicon. *In* S. Dornic (Ed.) *Attention and Performance 6*. Hillsdale, N.J.: Erlbaum.

Coltheart, M., Besner, D., Jonassen, J. T. and Davelaar, E. (1979). Phonological encoding in the lexical decision task. *Quarterly Journal of Experimental Psychology* **31**, 489–507.

Coltheart, M., Patterson, K. and Marshall, J. C. (1980). *Deep Dyslexia*. London: Routledge and Kegan Paul.

Conrad, C. (1974). Context effects in sentence comprehension: a study of the subjective lexicon. *Memory and Cognition* **2**, 130–138.

Conrad, R. (1964). Acoustic confusion in immediate memory. *British Journal of Psychology* **55**, 75–84.

Corcoran, D. W. J. (1966). An acoustic factor in letter cancellation. *Nature* **210**, 658.

Cosky, M. J. (1976). The role of letter recognition in word recognition. *Memory and Cognition* **4**, 207–214.

Cosky, M. J. (1980). Word length effects in word recognition: evidence from word meaning latency data. Unpublished MS. St Olaf College, Maine.

Craik, F. I. M. and Tulving, E. (1975). Depth of processing and the retention of words in episodic memory. *Journal of Experimental Psychology: General* **104**, 268–294.

Craik, K. (1948). *The Nature of Explanation.* Cambridge: Cambridge University Press.

Cutler, A. (1980). Syllable omission errors and isochrony. *In* H. W. Deckert (Ed.) *Temporal variables in speech—Studies in honour of Frieda Goldman-Eisler.* The Hague: Mouton.

Cutting, J. E. (1977). The magical number two and the natural categories of speech and music. *In* N. S. Sutherland (Ed.) *Tutorial Essays in Psychology* Vol. 1. Hillsdale, N.J.: Erlbaum.

Davelaar, E., Coltheart, M., Besner, D. and Jonasson, J. T. (1978). Phonological recoding and lexical access. *Memory and Cognition* **6**, 391–402.

Day, J. (1977). Right-hemisphere language processing in normal right-handers. *Journal of Experimental Psychology: Human Perception and Performance* **3**, 518–528.

Déjerine, J. (1891). Sur un cas de cécité verbale avec agraphie suivi d'autopsie. Cited in Hécaen and Kremin (1976).

Deutsch, J. A. and Deutsch, D. (1963). Attention: some theoretical considerations. *Psychological Review* **70**, 80–90.

Dixon, N. F. (1971). *Subliminal Perception: the Nature of a Controversy.* London: McGraw-Hill.

Dixon, P. and Rothkopf, E. Z. (1979). Word repetition, lexical access, and the process of searching words and sentences. *Journal of Verbal Learning and Verbal Behavior* **18**, 629–644.

Doctor, E. A. and Coltheart, M. (1980). Children's use of phonological encoding when reading for meaning. *Memory and Cognition* **8**, 195–209.

Doctor, E., Coltheart, M. and Jonasson, J. T. (1981). Aspects of reading and learning to read. Unpublished MS. Birkbeck College, London.

Dodd, B. (1976). The phonological systems of deaf children. *Journal of Speech and Hearing Disorders* **41**, 185–198.

Dodd, B. (1980). The spelling abilities of profoundly deaf children. *In* U. Frith (Ed.) *Cognitive Processes in Spelling.* London and New York: Academic Press.

Dodd, B. and Hermelin, B. (1977). Phonological coding by the prelingually deaf. *Perception and Psychophysics* **21**, 413–417.

Downing, J. (Ed.) (1973). *Comparative Reading.* New York: MacMillan.

Dretske, F. I. (1969). *Seeing and Knowing.* Chicago: University of Chicago Press.

Drewnowski, A. and Healy, A. F. (1977). Detection errors in *the* and *and*: evidence for reading units larger than the word. *Memory and Cognition* **5**, 636–647.

Dunn-Ranklin, P. (1978). The visual characteristics of words. *Scientific American* **238**, 122–130.

Dykstra, R. (1966). Auditory discrimination abilities and beginning reading achievement. *Reading Research Quarterly* **1**, 5–34.

Edgerton, W. F. (1941). Ideograms in English writing. *Language* **17**, 148–150.

Edgerton, W. F. (1952). On the theory of writing. *Journal of Near Eastern Studies* **11**, 287–290.

Egeth, H. and Blecker, D. (1971). Differential effects of familiarity on judgements of sameness and difference. *Perception and Psychophysics* **9**, 321–326.

Ehri, L. C. (1979). Linguistic insight: threshold of reading acquisition. *In* T. G. Waller and G. E. MacKinnon (Ed.) *Reading Research: Advances in Theory and Practice* Vol. 1. New York and London: Academic Press.

Ehri, L. C. (1980). The development of orthographic images. *In* U. Frith (Ed.) *Cognitive Processes in Spelling*. London and New York: Academic Press.

Eichelman, W. H. (1970). Familiarity effects in a simultaneous matching task. *Journal of Experimental Psychology* **86**, 275–282.

Eimas, P. D. (1975). Auditory and phonetic coding of the cues for speech: discrimination of the /r–l/ distinction by young infants. *Perception and Psychophysics* **18**, 341–347.

Ellis, A. W. (1979). Speech production and short term memory. *In* J. Morton and J. C. Marshall (Ed.) *Psycholinguistics Series*, 2. London: Elek.

Ellis, H. D. and Shepherd, J. W. (1974). Recognition of abstract and concrete words presented in left and right visual fields. *Journal of Experimental Psychology* **103**, 1035–36.

Endo, M., Shimizu, A. and Hori, T. (1978). Functional asymmetry of visual fields for Japanese words in Kana writing and random shape-recognition in Japanese subjects. *Neuropsychologia* **16**, 291–298.

Erdmann, B. and Dodge, R. (1898). *Psychologische untersuchungen über das lesen*. Halle: Niemeyer.

Erikson, D., Mattingly, I. G. and Turvey, M. T. (1973). Phonetic activity in reading: an experiment with Kanji. *Haskins Laboratories Status Report on Speech Research* **33**, 137–156.

Estes, W. K. (1972). Interactions of signal and background variables in visual processing. *Perception and Psychophysics* **12**, 278–286.

Estes, W. K. (1975). The locus of inferential and perceptual processes in letter identification. *Journal of Experimental Psychology: General* **104**, 122–145.

Estes, W. K. (1979). Perceptual processing in letter recognition and reading. *In* E. C. Carterette and M. P. Friedman (Ed.) *Handbook of Perception* Vol. 9. New York and London: Academic Press.

Estes, W. K., Bjork, E. L. and Skaar, E. (1974). Detection of single letters and letters in words with changing versus unchanging mask characteristics. *Bulletin of the Psychonomic Society* **3**, 201–203.

Evett, L. and Humphreys, G. W. (1981). The use of abstract graphemic information in lexical access. *Quarterly Journal of Experimental Psychology* **33A**, in press.

Firth, I. (1972). Components of reading disability. Unpublished doctoral dissertation. University of New South Wales, Australia.

Fischler, I. (1977). Associative facilitation without expectancy in a lexical decision task. *Journal of Experimental Psychology: Human Perception and Performance* **3**, 18–26.

Fischler, I. and Bloom, P. (1979). Automatic and attentional processes in the effects of sentence contexts on word recognition. *Journal of Verbal Learning and Verbal Behavior* **18**, 1–20.

Fischler, I. and Bloom, P. A. (1980). Rapid processing of the meaning of sentences. *Memory and Cognition* **8**, 216–225.

Fischler, I. and Goodman, G. O. (1978). Latency of associative activation in memory. *Journal of Experimental Psychology: Human Perception and Performance* **4**, 455–470.

Fisher, D. F. (1979). Understanding the reading process through the use of transformed typography: PSG, CSG and automaticity. *In* P. A. Kolers, M. E. Wrolstad and H. Bouma (Ed.) *Processing of Visible Language 1*. New York: Plenum Press.

Fodor, J. A., Bever, T. G. and Garrett, M. F. (1974). *The Psychology of Language*. New York: McGraw-Hill.

Forbach, G., Stanners, R. and Hochaus, L. (1974). Repetition and practice effects in a lexical decision task. *Memory and Cognition* **2**, 337–339.

Forster, K. I. (1976). Accessing the mental lexicon. *In* E. C. T. Walker and R. J. Wales (Ed.) *New Approaches to Language Mechanisms*. Amsterdam: North Holland.

Forster, K. I. (1979). Levels of processing and the structure of the language processor. *In* W. E. Cooper and E. C. T. Walker (Ed.) *Sentence Processing: Psycholinguistic Studies Presented to Merril Garrett*. Cambridge, Mass.: M.I.T. Press.

Forster, K. I. (1981). Priming and the effects of sentence and lexical contexts on naming time: evidence for autonomous lexical processing. *Quarterly Journal of Experimental Psychology* **33A**, in press.

Forster, K. I. and Bednall, E. S. (1976). Terminating and exhaustive search in lexical access. *Memory and Cognition* **4**, 53–61.

Forster, K. I. and Chambers, S. M. (1973). Lexical access and naming time. *Journal of Verbal Learning and Verbal Behavior* **12**, 627–635.

Foss, D. J. and Blank, M. A. (1980). Identifying the speech codes. *Cognitive Psychology* **12**, 1–31.

Foss, D. J. and Swinney, D. A. (1973). On the psychological reality of the phoneme: perception, identification and consciousness. *Journal of Verbal Learning and Verbal Behavior* **12**, 246–257.

Frederiksen, J. R. (1976). Decoding skills and lexical retrieval. Presented at Psychonomic Society Conference, St Louis.

Frederiksen, J. R. and Kroll, J. F. (1976). Spelling and sound: approaches to the internal lexicon. *Journal of Experimental Psychology: Human Perception and Performance* **2**, 361–379.

French, M. A. (1976). Observations on the Chinese script. *In* W. Haas (Ed.) *Writing without Letters*. Manchester: Manchester University Press.

Freund, A. (1975). Word and phrase recognition in speech processing. *In* D. W. Massaro (Ed.) *Understanding Language*. New York and London: Academic Press.

Frith, U. (1976). How to read without knowing how to spell. Paper presented to the British Association, Lancaster, 1976.

Frith, U. (1979). Reading by eye and writing by ear. *In* P. A. Kolers, M. E. Wrolstad and H. Bouma (Ed.) *Processing of Visible Language 1*. New York: Plenum Press.

Frith, U. (Ed.) (1980). *Cognitive Processes in Spelling*. London and New York: Academic Press.

Fromkin, V. A. (1973). *Speech Errors as Linguistic Evidence*. The Hague: Mouton.

Garrett, M. F. (1975). The analysis of sentence production. *In* G. H. Bower (Ed.) *The Psychology of Learning and Motivation*, Vol. 9. New York and London, Academic Press.

Gelb, I. J. (1963). *A Study of Writing* (second edit.). Chicago: University of Chicago Press.

Gelb, I. J. (1974). Records, writing and decipherment. *Visible Language* **8**, 293–318.

Geyer, J. J. (1970). Models of perceptual processes in reading. *In* H. Singer and R. B. Ruddell (Ed.) *Theoretical Models and Processes of Reading*. Newark, Del.: International Reading Association.

Gibson, E. J. and Levin, H. (1975). *The Psychology of Reading*. Cambridge, Mass.: M.I.T. Press.

Gibson, E. J., Pick, A. D., Osser, H. and Hammond, M. (1962). The role of grapheme–phoneme correspondence in the perception of words. *American Journal of Psychology* **75**, 554–570.

Gibson, E. J., Shurcliff, A. and Jonas, A. (1970). Utilization of spelling patterns by deaf and hearing subjects. *In* H. Levin and J. P. Williams (Ed.) *Basic Studies on Reading*. New York: Basic Books.

Gilhooly, K. J. and Gilhooly, M. L. (1979). Age-of-acquisition effects in lexical and episodic memory tasks. *Memory and Cognition* **7**, 214–223.

Glanzer, M. and Ehrenreich, S. L. (1979). Structure and search of the internal lexicon. *Journal of Verbal Learning and Verbal Behavior* **18**, 381–398.

Gleitman, L. R. and Rozin, P. (1973). Teaching reading by use of a syllabary. *Reading Research Quarterly* **8**, 447–483.

Gleitman, L. R. and Rozin, P. (1977). The structure and acquisition of reading I: relations between orthographies and the structure of language. *In* A. S. Reber and D. L. Scarborough (Ed.) *Toward a Psychology of Reading*. Hillsdale, N.J.: Erlbaum.

Glushko, R. J. (1979). The organization and activation of orthographic knowledge in reading aloud. *Journal of Experimental Psychology: Human Perception and Performance* **5**, 674–691.

Glushko, R. J. (1980). Cognitive and pedagogical implications of orthography. *In* J. Kavanagh and R. Venezky (Ed.) *Orthography, Reading and Dyslexia*. Baltimore, Md: University Park Press.

Golding, W. (1955). *The Inheritors*. London: Faber and Faber.

Goldman-Eisler, F. (1961). Hesitation and information in speech. *In* C. Cherry (Ed.) *Information Theory*. London: Butterworths.

Gough, P. B. (1972). One second of reading. *In* J. P. Kavanagh and I. G. Mattingly (Ed.) *Language by Eye and by Ear*. Cambridge, Mass.: M.I.T. Press.

Gough, P. B. and Cosky, M. J. (1977). One second of reading again. *In* N. J. Castellan, D. B. Pisoni and G. R. Potts (Ed.) *Cognitive Theory*, Vol. 2. Hillsdale, N.J.: Erlbaum.

Gough, P. B. and Hillinger, M. L. (1980). Learning to read: an unnatural act. *Bulletin of the Orton Society* **30**, 1–17.

Goldscheider, A. and Müller, R. F. (1893). Zur Physiologie und Pathologie des Lesens. *Zeitschrift für klinischen Medizin* **23**, 131–167.

Green, D. W. and Shallice, T. (1976). Direct visual access in reading for meaning. *Memory and Cognition* **4**, 753–758.

Greene, J. (1972). *Psycholinguistics*. Harmondsworth: Penguin.

Groff, P. (1975). Shapes as cues to word recognition. *Visible Language* **9**, 67–71.

Grumach, E. (1976). The Cretan scripts and the Greek alphabet. *In* W. Haas (Ed.) *Writing without Letters.* Manchester: Manchester University Press.

Guthrie, J. T. (1973). Reading comprehension and syntactic responses in good and poor readers. *Journal of Educational Psychology* **65**, 294–299.

Haas, W. (1969). On "spelling" and "spelling reform". *In* W. Haas (Ed.) *Alphabets for English.* Manchester: Manchester University Press.

Haas, W. (1970). *Phonographic Translation.* Manchester: Manchester University Press.

Haas, W. (1976). Writing: the basic options. *In* W. Haas (Ed.) *Writing without Letters.* Manchester: Manchester University Press.

Hall, R. A. (1961). *Sound and Spelling in English.* New York: Chilton.

Halle, M. (1969). Some thoughts on spelling. *In* K. S. Goodman and J. T. Fleming (Ed.) *Psycholinguistics and the Teaching of Reading.* Newark: International Reading Association.

Halle, M. (1972). On a parallel between conventions of versification and orthography: and on literacy among the Cherokee. *In* J. F. Kavanagh and I. G. Mattingly (Ed.) *Language by Ear and by Eye.* Cambridge, Mass.: M.I.T. Press.

Hanna, P. R., Hanna, J. S., Hodges, R. E. and Rudorf, E. H. (1966). *Phoneme–Grapheme Correspondences as Cues to Spelling Improvement.* Washington: US Dept of Health, Education and Welfare.

Hansen, D. and Rogers, T. S. (1973). An exploration of psycholinguistic units in initial reading. *In* K. S. Goodman (Ed.) *The Psycholinguistic Nature of the Reading Process.* Detroit: Wayne State University Press.

Hardyck, C. D., Petrinovich, L. F. and Ellsworth, D. W. (1966). Feedback of speech muscle activity during silent reading: rapid extinction. *Science* **154**, 1467–1468.

Hardyck, C., Tzeng, O. J. L. and Wang, W. S-Y. (1977). Cerebral lateralisation effects in visual half-field experiments. *Nature* **269**, 705–707.

Hatta, T. (1977). Recognition of Japanese Kanji in the left and right visual fields. *Neuropsychologia* **15**, 685–688.

Hatta, T. (1978). Recognition of Japanese Kanji and Hirakana in the left and right visual fields. *Japanese Psychological Research* **20**, 51–59.

Havens, L. L. and Foote, W. E. (1963). The effect of competition on visual duration threshold and its independence of stimulus frequency. *Journal of Experimental Psychology* **65**, 6–11.

Hawkins, H. L., Reicher, G., Rogers, M. and Peterson, L. (1976). Flexible coding in word recognition. *Journal of Experimental Psychology: Human Perception and Performance* **2**, 235–242.

Healy, A. (1976). Detection errors on the word *the*: evidence for reading units larger than letters. *Journal of Experimental Psychology: Human Perception and Performance* **2**, 235–242.

Hécaen, H. and Kremin, H. (1976). Neurolinguistic research on reading disorders resulting from left hemisphere lesions: aphasic and "pure" alexias. *In* H. Whitaker and H. A. Whitaker (Ed.) *Studies in Neurolinguistics* Vol. 2. New York and London: Academic Press.

Henderson, A., Goldman-Eisler, F. and Skarbek, A. (1965). Temporal patterns of cognitive activity and breath control in speech. *Language and Speech* **8**, 236–242.

Henderson, A., Goldman-Eisler, F. and Skarbek, A. (1966). Sequential temporal patterns in spontaneous speech. *Language and Speech* **9**, 207–216.

Henderson, L. (1973). Effects of letter-names on visual search. *Cognitive Psychology* **5**, 90–96.

Henderson, L. (1974). A word superiority effect without orthographic assistance. *Quarterly Journal of Experimental Psychology* **26**, 301–311.

Henderson, L. (1975). Do words conceal their component letters? A critique of Johnson (1975) on the visual perception of words. *Journal of Verbal Learning and Verbal Behavior* **14**, 648–650.

Henderson, L. (1977). Word recognition. *In* N. S. Sutherland (Ed.) *Tutorial Essays in Psychology* Vol. 1. Hillsdale, N.J.: Erlbaum.

Henderson, L. (1978). Pandemonium and visual search. *Perception* **7**, 97–104.

Henderson, L. (1980a). Wholestic models of feature analysis in word recognition: a critical examination. *In* P. A. Kolers, H. Bouma and M. Wrolstad (Ed.) *Processing of Visible Language, 2*. New York: Plenum Press.

Henderson, L. (1980b). Is there a lexicality component in the word superiority effect? *Perception and Psychophysics* **28**, 179–184.

Henderson, L. and Chard, M. J. (1976). On the nature of the facilitation of visual comparisons by lexical membership. *Bulletin of the Psychonomic Society* **7**, 432–434.

Henderson, L. and Chard, M. J. (1978a). Semantic effects in visual word detection with visual similarity controlled. *Perception and Psychophysics* **23**, 290–298.

Henderson, L. and Chard, M. J. (1978b). *Word Recognition*. Final report to the SSRC on grant No. HR 3301.

Henderson, L. and Chard, M. J. (1980). The reader's implicit knowledge of orthographic structure. *In* U. Frith (Ed.) *Cognitive Process in Spelling*. London and New York: Academic Press.

Henderson, L., Coltheart, M. and Woodhouse, D. (1973). Failure to find a syllabic effect in number-naming. *Memory and Cognition* **1**, 304–306.

Henderson, L., Henderson, S. E. and Shine, J. (1979). A test of the sub-program retrieval theory of speech preparation latencies. Unpublished paper presented to the Experimental Psychology Society, York, April, 1979.

Henderson, L., Chard, M. J. and Clark, A. (1981). Preparation and speech programming in rapid reading and reciting. *Canadian Journal of Psychology* **35**, 224–243.

Herrmann, D. J. and McLaughlin, J. P. (1973). Language habits and detection in very short term memory. *Perception and Psychophysics* **14**, 483–486.

Hillinger, M. L. (1980). Priming effects with phonemically similar words: the encoding-bias hypothesis reconsidered. *Memory and Cognition* **8**, 115–123.

Hinshelwood, J. (1899). *Letter, Word and Mind-blindness*. London: Lewis.

Hirata, K. and Osaka, K. (1967). Tachistoscopic recognition of Japanese letter materials in left and right visual fields. *Psychologia* **10**, 7–18.

Hochberg, J. (1968). In the mind's eye. *In* R. N. Haber (Ed.) *Contemporary Theory and Research in Visual Perception*. New York: Holt, Rinehart and Winston, 1968.

Hochberg, J. (1970). Components of literacy: speculation and exploratory research. *In* H. Levin and J. P. Williams (Ed.) *Basic Studies on Reading*. New York: Basic Books.

Hock, H. S. and Egeth, H. E. (1970). Verbal interference with encoding in a perceptual classification task. *Journal of Experimental Psychology* **83**, 299–303.

Holbrook, M. B. (1975). A comparison of methods for measuring the inter-letter similarity between capital letters. *Perception and Psychophysics* **17**, 532–536.

Holden, M. H. and MacGinitie, W. H. (1972). Children's conception of word boundaries in speech and print. *Journal of Educational Psychology* **63**, 551–557.

Holmes, J. M. (1978). Regression and reading breakdown. *In* A. Caramazza and E. B. Zurif (Ed.) *Language Acquisition and Language Breakdown: Parallels and Divergences.* Baltimore: Johns Hopkins Press.

Huey, E. B. (1908). *The Psychology and Pedagogy of Reading*. Reprinted 1968. Cambridge, Mass.: M.I.T. Press.

Humphreys, G. W. (1978). The use of category information in perception. *Perception* **7**, 589–604.

Imura, T. (1943). Aphasia: characteristic symptoms in Japan. *Journal of Psychiatric Neurology* **47**, 196–218.

Jacobson, J. Z. (1973). Effects of association upon masking and reading latency. *Canadian Journal of Psychology* **27**, 58–69.

Jacobson, J. Z. (1974). Interaction of similarity to words of visual masks and targets. *Journal of Experimental Psychology* **102**, 431–434.

Jacobson, J. Z. and Rhinelander, G. (1978). Geometric and semantic similarity in visual masking. *Journal of Experimental Psychology: Human Perception and Performance* **4**, 224–231.

Jakobson, R., Fant, C. G. M. and Halle, M. (1961). *Preliminaries to Speech Analysis: the Distinctive Features and their Correlates.* Cambridge, Mass.: M.I.T. Press.

James, C. T. (1975). The role of semantic information in lexical decisions. *Journal of Experimental Psychology: Human Perception and Performance* **1**, 130–136.

James, W. (1908). *Psychology*. Vol. 1. New York: Holt, Rinehart and Winston.

Jastrzembski, J. and Stanners, R. (1975). Multiple word meanings and lexical search speed. *Journal of Verbal Learning and Verbal Behavior* **14**, 534–537.

Jensen, A. R. and Rohwer, W. D. (1966). The Stroop colour-word test: a review. *Acta Psychologica* **25**, 36–93.

Jevons, W. S. (1871). The power of numerical discrimination. *Nature* **3**, 281–282.

Johnson, N. F. (1975). On the function of letters in word identification: some data and a preliminary model. *Journal of Verbal Learning and Verbal Behavior* **14**, 17–29.

Johnson, N. F. (1977). A pattern-unit model of word identification. *In* D. LaBerge and S. J. Samuels (Ed.) *Basic Processes in Reading: Perception and Comprehension.* Hillsdale, N.J.: Erlbaum.

Johnson, N. F. and Marmurek, H. H. C. (1978). Identification of words and letters within words. *American Journal of Psychology* **91**, 401–415.

Johnston, J. C. (1978). A test of the sophisticated guessing theory of word perception. *Cognitive Psychology* **10**, 123–153.

Johnston, J. C. and McClelland, J. L. (1973). Visual factors in word perception. *Perception and Psychophysics* **14**, 365–370.

Johnston, J. C. and McClelland, J. L. (1974). Perception of letters in words: seek not and ye shall find. *Science* **184**, 1192–1193.

Johnson-Laird, P. N. (1975). Meaning and the mental lexicon. *In* A. Kennedy and A. Wilkes (Ed.) *Studies in Long Term Memory*. London: Wiley.

Johnson-Laird, P. N. (1977). Psycholinguistics without linguistics. *In* N. S. Sutherland (Ed.) *Tutorial Essays in Psychology* Vol. 1. Hillsdale, N.J.: Erlbaum.

Jonasson, J. T. (1978). Unpublished experiment cited in Coltheart (1978).

Jonides, J. and Gleitman, H. (1972). Conceptual category effect in visual search: O as a letter or as a digit. *Perception and Psychophysics* **12**, 457–470.

Juola, J. F., Leavitt, D. D. and Choe, C. S. (1974). Letter identification in word, nonword and single-letter displays. *Bulletin of the Psychonomic Society* **4**, 278–280.

Kahnemann, D. (1973). *Attention and Effort.* Englewood Cliffs, N.J.: Prentice Hall.

Katz, J. J. and Foder, J. A. (1963). The structure of a semantic theory. *Language* **39**, 170–210.

Kay, J. and Marcel, A. J. (1981). One process, not two, in reading aloud: lexical analogies do the work of nonlexical rules. *Quarterly Journal of Experimental Psychology* **33A**, in press.

Kershner, J. R. and Gwang-Rong Jeng, A. (1972). Dual functional hemisphere asymmetry in visual perception: effects of ocular dominance and post-exposural processes. *Neuropsychologia* **10**, 437–445.

Kinchla, R. (1977). The role of structural redundancy in the perception of visual targets. *Perception and Psychophysics* **22**, 19–30.

Kinsbourne, M. (1971). The minor cerebral hemisphere as a source of aphasic speech. *Archives of Neurology* **25**, 302–306.

Kintsch, W. (1972). Abstract nouns: imagery versus lexical complexity. *Journal of Verbal Learning and Verbal Behavior* **11**, 59–65.

Kirsner, K. (1973). An analysis of the visual component in recognition memory for verbal stimuli. *Memory and Cognition* **1**, 449–453.

Kirsner, K. and Smith, M. C. (1974). Modality effects in word identification. *Memory and Cognition* **2**, 637–640.

Klapp, S. T. (1976). Short-term memory as a response preparation state. *Memory and Cognition* **4**, 721–729.

Klapp, S. T., Anderson, W. G. and Berrian, R. W. (1973). Implicit speech in reading, reconsidered. *Journal of Experimental Psychology* **100**, 368–374.

Klapp, S. T. and Wyatt, E. P. (1976). Motor programming within a sequence of responses. *Journal of Motor Behavior* **8**, 19–26.

Klatzky, R. L. and Atkinson, R. C. (1971). Specialization of the cerebral hemispheres in scanning for information in short-term memory. *Perception and Psychophysics* **10**, 335–338.

Kleiman, G. M. (1975). Speech recoding in reading. *Journal of Verbal Learning and Verbal Behavior* **24**, 323–339.

Kleiman, G. M. (1980). Sentence frame contexts and lexical decisions: sentence acceptability and word relatedness effects. *Memory and Cognition* **8**, 336–344.

Klima, E. S. (1972). How alphabets might reflect language. *In* J. F. Kavanagh and I. G. Mattingly (Ed.) *Language by Eye and by Ear.* Cambridge: M.I.T. Press.

Kolers, P. A. (1970). Three stages of reading. *In* H. Levin and J. P. Williams (Ed.) *Basic Studies in Reading.* New York: Basic Books.

Kolers, P. A. (1971). Eye–voice span or response bias? *In* D. L. Horton and J. J. Jenkins (Ed.) *The Perception of Language.* Columbus, Ohio: Charles Merrill.

Kolers, P. A. (1976). Reading a year later. *Journal of Experimental Psychology: Human Learning and Memory* **2**, 554–565.

Kolers, P. A., Wrolstad, M. E. and Bouma, H. (Ed.) (1979). *Processing of Visible Language 1.* New York: Plenum Press.

Kroll, J. F. (1976). Does the lexicon contain orthographic neighbourhoods. Paper presented to the Psychonomic Society, St Louis.

Krueger, L. E. (1979). Features versus redundancy. *Journal of Experimental Psychology: General* **108**, 125–130.

Krueger, L. E. and Shapiro, R. G. (1979). Letter detection with rapid serial visual presentation: evidence against word superiority at feature extraction. *Journal of Experimental Psychology: Human Perception and Performance* **5**, 657–673.

Kučera, H. and Francis, W. N. (1967). *Computational Analysis of Present-day American English*. Providence, R.I.: Brown University Press.

LaBerge, D. and Samuels, S. J. (1974). Towards a theory of automatic information processing in reading. *Cognitive Psychology* **6**, 293–323.

Lachman, R. (1973). Uncertainty effects on time to access the internal lexicon. *Journal of Experimental Psychology* **99**, 199–208.

Landauer, T. K. (1975). Memory without organization: properties of a model with random storage and undirected retrieval. *Cognitive Psychology* **7**, 495–531.

Landauer, T. K. and Streeter, L. A. (1973). Structural differences between common and rare words: failure of equivalence assumptions for theories of word recognition. *Journal of Verbal Learning and Verbal Behavior* **12**, 119–131.

Larochelle, S., McClelland, J. L. and Rodrigues, E. (1980). Context and the allocation of resources in word recognition. *Journal of Experimental Psychology: Human Perception and Performance* **6**, 686–694.

Lashley, K. S. (1951). The problem of serial order in behavior. *In* L. A. Jeffress (Ed.) *Cerebral Mechanisms in Behavior*. New York: Wiley.

Lehiste, I. (1977). Isochrony reconsidered. *Journal of Phonetics* **5**, 253–263.

Levin, H. and Kaplan, E. L. (1970). Grammatical structure and reading. *In* H. Levin and J. P. Williams (Ed.) *Basic Studies on Reading*. New York: Basic Books.

Levin, H. and Kaplan, E. L. (1971). Listening, reading and grammatical structures. *In* D. L. Horton and J. J. Jenkins (Ed.) *The Perception of Language*. Columbus, Ohio: Charles Merrill.

Levy, B. A. (1977). Reading: speech and meaning processes. *Journal of Verbal Learning and Verbal Behavior* **16**, 623–638.

Levy, B. A. (1978). Speech analysis during sentence processing. *Visible Language* **12**, 81–101.

Levy-Schoen, A. and O'Regan, K. (1979). The control of eye movements in reading. *In* P. A. Kolers, M. E. Wrolstad and H. Bouma (Ed.) *Processing of Visible Language 1*. New York: Plenum Press.

Liberman, A. M., Cooper, F. S., Shankweiler, D. P. and Studdert-Kennedy, M. (1967). Perception of the speech code. *Psychological Review* **74**, 431–461.

Liberman, I. Y., Shankweiler, D., Liberman, A. M., Fowler, C. and Fischer, F. W. (1977). Phonetic segmentation and recoding in the beginning reader. *In* A. S. Reber and D. L. Scarborough (Ed.) *Toward a Psychology of Reading*. Hillsdale, N.J.: Erlbaum.

Liberman, I. Y., Liberman, A., Mattingly, I. G. and Shankweiler, D. (1980). Orthography and the beginning reader. *In* J. Kavanagh and R. Venezky (Ed.) *Orthography Reading and Dyslexia*. Baltimore, Md: University Park Press.

Lindsay, P. H. and Norman, D. A. (1977). *Human Information Processing*. New York and London: Academic Press.

Logan, G. D. (1980). Attention and automaticity in Stroop and priming tasks: theory and data. *Cognitive Psychology* **12**, 523–553.

Logan, G. D. and Zbrodoff, N. J. (1979). When it helps to be mislead. *Memory and Cognition* **7**, 166–174.

Lotz, J. (1972). How language is conveyed by script. *In* J. F. Kavanagh and I. G. Mattingly (Ed.) *Language by Eye and by Ear*. Cambridge, Mass: M.I.T. Press.

Lyman, R. S., Kwan, S. T. and Chao, W. H. (1938). Left occipito-parietal brain tumour with observations on alexia and agraphia. *Chinese Medical Journal* **54**, 491–516.

McLean, J. P. and Shulman, G. L. (1978). On the construction and maintenance of expectancies. *Quarterly Jounal of Experimental Psychology* **30**, 441–454.

McClelland, J. L. (1976). Preliminary letter identification in the perception of words and nonwords. *Journal of Experimental Psychology: Human Perception and Performance* **2**, 80–91.

McClelland, J. L. (1977). Letter and configurational information in word identification. *Journal of Verbal Learning and Verbal Behavior* **16**, 137–150.

McClelland, J. L. (1978). Perception and masking of wholes and parts. *Journal of Experimental Psychology: Human Perception and Performance* **4**, 210–223.

McClelland, J. L. (1979). On the time relations of mental processes: an examination of systems of processing in cascade. *Psychological Review* **86**, 287–330.

McClelland, J. L. and Johnston, J. C. (1977). The role of familiar units in perception of words and nonwords. *Perception and Psychophysics* **22**, 249–261.

McClelland, J. L. and Miller, J. (1979). Structural factors in perception. *Perception and Psychophysics* **26**, 221–229.

McClelland, J. L. and Rumelhart, D. E. (1980). An interactive activation model of the effect of context in perception. Part 1. San Diego: Center for Human Information Processing Report 91, April, 1980.

MacKay, D. G. (1972). The structure of words and syllables: evidence from errors in speech. *Cognitive Psychology* **3**, 210–227.

MacNeilage, P. and Ladefoged, P. (1976). The production of speech and language. *In* E. C. Carterette and M. P. Friedman. *Handbook of Perception* Vol. VII. New York and London: Academic Press.

McNeill, D. and Lindig, K. (1973). The perceptual reality of phonemes, syllables, words and sentences. *Journal of Verbal Learning and Verbal Behavior* **12**, 419–430.

Mae, C. C. (1976). Even Chinese ideograms are phonologically coded in STM. Paper presented at the Annual Conference on Language Development. Boston University, 1976. Cited in Taylor (1981).

Makita, K. (1968). The rarity of reading disability in Japanese children. *American Journal of Orthopsychiatry* **38**, 599–614.

Manelis, L. (1974). The effect of meaningfulness in tachistoscopic word perception. *Perception and Psychophysics* **16**, 182–192.

Marchbanks, G. and Levin, H. (1965). Cues by which children recognise words. *Journal of Educational Psychology* **56**, 57–61.

Marcel, A. J. (1978a). Prerequisites for a more applicable psychology of reading. *In* M. M. Grunberg, P. E. Morris and R. N. Sykes (Ed.) *Practical Aspects of Memory*, London and New York: Academic Press.

Marcel, A. J. (1978b). Explaining selective effects of prior context on perception: the need to distinguish conscious and pre-conscious processes in word recognition. *In* J. Requin (Ed.) *Anticipation et Comportement*. Paris: Editions du CNRS.

Marcel, A. J. (1980). Surface dyslexia and beginning reading. *In* M. Coltheart, K.

Patterson and J. C. Marshall (Ed.) *Deep Dyslexia*. London: Routledge and Kegan Paul.

Marcel, A. J. (in press). Conscious and unconscious reading: the effects of visual masking on word perception. *Cognitive Psychology*.

Marcel, A. J. and Patterson, K. (1978). Word recognition and production: reciprocity in clinical and normal studies. *In* J. Requin (Ed.) *Attention and Performance* 7. Hillsdale, N.J.: Erlbaum.

Marmurek, H. H. C. (1977). Processing letters in words at different levels. *Memory and Cognition* **5**, 67–72.

Marsh, G., Desberg, P. and Cooper, J. (1977). Development changes in reading strategies. *Journal of Reading Behavior* **9**, 391–394.

Marshall, J. C. Some problems and paradoxes associated with recent accounts of hemispheric specialization. *Neuropsychologia* **11**, 463–470.

Marshall, J. C. (1976). Neuropsychological aspects of orthographic representation. *In* R. J. Wales and E. Walker (Ed.) *New Approaches to Language Mechanisms*. Amsterdam, North Holland.

Marshall, J. C. and Newcombe, F. (1966). Syntactic and semantic errors in paralexia. *Neuropsychologia* **4**, 169–176.

Marshall, J. C. and Newcombe, F. (1973). Patterns of paralexia: a psycholinguistic approach. *Journal of Psycholinguistic Research* **2**, 175–199.

Marshall, J. C. and Newcombe, F. (1977). Variability and constraint in acquired dyslexia. *In* H. Whitaker and H. A. Whitaker. *Studies in Neurolinguistics* Vol. 3. New York and London: Academic Press.

Marslen-Wilson, W. D. and Welsh, A. (1978). Processing interactions and lexical access during word recognition in continuous speech. *Cognitive Psychology* **10**, 29–63.

Martin, S. E. (1972). Non-alphabetic writing systems: some observations. *In* J. F. Kavanagh and I. G. Mattingly (Ed.) *Language by Eye and by Ear*. Cambridge, Mass.: M.I.T. Press.

Mason, M. (1975). Reading ability and letter search time: effects of orthographic structure defined by single-letter positional frequency. *Journal of Experimental Psychology* **104**, 146–166.

Mason, M. (1978a). From print to sound in mature readers as a function of reader ability and two forms of orthographic regularity. *Memory and Cognition* **6**, 568–581.

Mason, M. (1978b). The role of spatial redundancy in grapheme recognition: perception or inference? *Journal of Experimental Psychology: Human Perception and Performance* **4**, 662–673.

Massaro, D. W. (1973). Perception of letters, words, and nonwords. *Journal of Experimental Psychology* **100**, 349–353.

Massaro, D. W. (1975a). Language and information processing. *In* D. W. Massaro (Ed.) *Understanding Language*. New York and London: Academic Press.

Massaro, D. W. (1975b). Preperceptual images, processing time, and perceptual units in speech perception. *In* D. W. Massaro (Ed.) *Understanding Language*. New York and London: Academic Press.

Massaro, D. W. (1975c). Primary and secondary recognition in reading. *In* D. W. Massaro (Ed.) *Understanding Language*. New York and London: Academic Press.

Massaro, D. W. (1975d). *Experimental Psychology and Information Processing*. Chicago: Rand McNally.

Massaro, D. W. (1979). Letter information and orthographic context in word perception. *Journal of Experimental Psychology: Human Perception and Performance* **5**, 595–609.

Massaro, D. W. and Klitzke, D. (1977). Letters are functional in word identification. *Memory and Cognition* **5**, 292–298.

Massaro, D. M. and Klitzke, D. (1979). The role of lateral masking and orthographic structure in letter and word recognition. *Acta Psychologica* **43**, 413–426.

Massaro, D. W. and Schmuller, J. (1975). Visual features, preperceptual storage, and processing time in reading. *In* D. W. Massaro (Ed.) *Understanding Language*. New York and London: Academic Press.

Massaro, D. M., Venezky, R. L. and Taylor, G. A. (1979). Orthographic regularity, positional frequency and visual processing of letter strings. *Journal of Experimental Psychology* **108**, 107–124.

Massaro, D. W., Taylor, G. A., Venezky, R. L., Jastrzembski, J. E. and Lucas, P. A. (1980). *Letter and Word Perception*. Amsterdam: North-Holland.

Matthews, M. L., Weisstein, N., Williams, A. and Baron, J. (1976). The ubiquitous word-superiority effect. Unpublished MS. University of Guelph, Ontario.

Mayzner, M. S. and Tresselt, M. E. (1965). Tables of single-letter and digram frequency counts for various word-length and letter-position combinations. *Psychonomic Monograph Supplements* **1**, 13–32.

Mayzner, M. S., Tresselt, M. E. and Wolin, B. R. (1965a, b, c). Tables of trigram, tetragram and pentagram frequency counts for various word-length and letter-position combinations. *Psychonomic Monograph Supplements* (a) **1**, 33–78; (b) **1**, 79–142; (c) **1**, 145–185.

Meyer, D. E. and Schwaneveldt, R. W. (1971). Facilitation in recognising pairs of words: evidence of a dependence between retrieval operations. *Journal of Experimental Psychology* **90**, 227–234.

Meyer, D. E., Schwaneveldt, R. W. and Ruddy, M. G. (1974). Functions of graphemic and phonemic codes in visual word recognition. *Memory and Cognition* **2**, 309–321.

Meyer, D. E., Schwaneveldt, R. W. and Ruddy, M. G. (1975). Loci of contextual effects on visual word recognition. *In* P. M. A. Rabbitt and S. Dornic (Ed.) *Attention and Performance 5*, London and New York: Academic Press.

Mezrich, J. J. (1973). The word superiority effect in brief visual displays: elimination by vocalisation. *Perception and Psychophysics* **13**, 45–48.

Miller, G. A. (1962). Decision units in the perception of speech. *IRE Transactions in Information Theory* **8**, 81–83.

Miller, G. A. (1972). Contribution to general discussion. *In* J. F. Kavanagh and I. G. Matingly (Ed.) *Language by Eye and by Ear*. Cambridge, Mass.: M.I.T. Press.

Miller, G. A., Bruner, J. S. and Postman, L. (1954). Familiarity of letter sequences and tachistoscopic identification. *Journal of General Psychology* **50**, 129–139.

Miller, G. A., Galanter, E. and Pribram, K. H. (1960). *Plans and the Structure of Behavior*. New York: Holt, Rinehart and Winston.

Miller, G. A., Heise, G. A. and Lichten, W. (1951). The intellegibility of speech as a function of the context of the test materials. *Journal of Experimental Psychology* **41**, 329–335.

Miller, J. (1979). Cognitive influences on perceptual processing. *Journal of Experimental Psychology: Human Perception and Performance* **5**, 546–562.

Mitchell, D. C. and Green, D. W. (1978). The effects of context and content on immediate processing in reading. *Quarterly Journal of Experimental Psychology* **30**, 609–636.

Mitchell, D. C. and Green, D. W. (1980). Contextual effects in continuous reading. Paper presented to the BPS Conference on reading, Exeter, 1980.

Miura, T. (1978). The word superiority effect in a case of Hiragana letter strings. *Perception and Psychophysics* **24**, 505–508.

Miyawaki, K., Strange, W., Verbrugge, R., Liberman, A. M., Jenkins, J. J. and Fujimura, O. (1975). An effect of linguistic experience: the discrimination of [r] and [l] by native speakers of Japanese and English. *Perception and Psychophysics* **18**, 331–340.

Monsell, S. (1978). Recency, immediate recognition memory and reaction time. *Cognitive Psychology* **10**, 465–501.

Morais, J., Cary, L., Alegria, J. and Bertelson, P. (1979). Does awareness of speech as a sequence of phones arise spontaneously? *Cognition* **7**, 323–331.

Morton, J. (1964a). The effects of context upon speed of reading, eye movements and eye-voice span. *Quarterly Journal of Experimental Psychology* **16**, 340–355.

Morton, J. (1964b). Grammar and computation in language behaviour. *International Audiology* **3**, 216–225.

Morton, J. (1969). Interaction of information in word recognition. *Psychological Review* **76**, 165–178.

Morton, J. (1970). A functional model for memory. *In* D. A. Norman (Ed.) *Models of Human Memory*. New York and London: Academic Press.

Morton, J. (1979a). Word recognition. *In* Morton, J. and Marshall, J. C. (Ed.) *Psycholinguistics Series 2*. London: Elek.

Morton, J. (1979b). Facilitation in word recognition: experiments causing change in the logogen model. *In* P. A. Kolers, M. Wrolstad and H. Bouma (Ed.) *Processing of Visible Language I*. New York: Plenum.

Morton, J. and Broadbent, D. E. (1967). Passive vs. active recognition models or Is your homunculus really necessary? *In* W. Wathen-Dunn (Ed.) *Models for the Perception of Speech and Visual Form*. Cambridge, Mass.: M.I.T. Press.

Morton, J. and Long, J. (1976). Effect of transitional probability on phoneme identification. *Journal of Verbal Learning and Verbal Behavior* **15**, 43–51.

Morton, J. and Patterson, K. (1980). A new attempt at an interpretation, or, an attempt at a new interpretation. *In* M. Coltheart, K. Patterson and J. C. Marshall (Ed.) *Deep Dyslexia*. London: Routledge and Kegan Paul.

Moscovitch, M. (1976). On the representation of language in the right hemisphere of right-handed people. *Brain and Language* **3**, 47–71.

Muraishi, S. (1972). Acquisition of reading Japanese syllabic characters in pre-school children in Japan. Twentieth International Congress of Psychology, Tokyo, 1972.

Muraishi, S. (1976). The reading ability of pre-school children in Japan. *In* J. E. Merritt (Ed.) *New Horizons in Reading*. Newark: International Reading Association.

Murrell, G. and Morton, J. (1974). Word recognition and morphemic structure. *Journal of Experimental Psychology* **102**, 963–968.

Myers, J. L. and Lorch, R. F. (1980). Interference and facilitation effects of primes upon verification processes. *Memory and Cognition* **8**, 405–414.

Naish, P. (1980). The effects of graphemic and phonemic similarity between targets and masks in a backward visual masking paradigm. *Quarterly Journal of Experimental Psychology* **32**, 57–68.

Navon, D. (1977). Forest before trees: the precedence of global features in visual perception. *Cognitive Psychology* **9**, 353–383.

Neely, J. H. (1976). Semantic priming and retrieval from lexical memory: evidence for facilitatory and inhibitory processes. *Memory and Cognition* **4**, 648–654.

Neely, J. H. (1977). Semantic priming and retrieval from lexical memory: roles of inhibitionless spreading activation and limited-capacity attention. *Journal of Experimental Psychology: General* **106**, 226–254.

Neill, W. T. (1979). Switching attention within and between categories: evidence for intracategory inhibition. *Memory and Cognition* **7**, 283–290.

Neisser, U. (1967). *Cognitive Psychology*. New York: Appleton-Century-Crofts.

Neisser, U. (1976). *Cognition and Reality*. San Francisco: W. H. Freeman.

Nooteboom, S. G. and Cohen, A. (1975). Anticipation in speech production and its implications for perception. *In* A. Cohen and S. G. Nooteboom (Ed.) *Structure and Process in Speech Perception*. Berlin: Springer Verlag.

Novik, N. (1974). Parallel processing in a word-nonword classification task *Journal of Experimental Psychology* **102**, 1015–1020.

Oden, G. C. (1979). A fuzzy logical model of letter identification. *Journal of Experimental Psychology: Human Perception and Performance* **5**, 336–352.

Ohala, J. (1974). Experimental historical phonology. *In* J. Anderson and C. Jones (Ed.) *Historical Linguistics II: Theory and Description in Phonology*. Amsterdam, North Holland.

Oldfield, R. C. (1966). Things, words and the brain. *Quarterly Journal of Experimental Psychology* **18**, 340–353.

O'Neil, W. (1972). Our collective phonological illusions: young and old. *In* J. F. Kavanagh and I. G. Mattingly (Ed.) *Language by Eye and by Ear*. Cambridge, Mass.: M.I.T. Press.

Otto, H. and Pizillo, C. (1970). Effect of intralist similarity on kindergarten pupils' rate of word acquisition and transfer. *Journal of Reading Behavior* **3**, 14–19.

Paap, K. R. (1975). Theories of speech perception. *In* D. W. Massaro (Ed.) *Understanding Language*, New York and London: Academic Press.

Pachella, R. G. (1974). The interpretation of reaction-time in information-processing research. *In* B. Kantowitz (Ed.) *Human Information Processing: Tutorials in Performance and Cognition*. Hillsdale, N.J.: Erlbaum.

Paivio, A. (1975). Perceptual comparisons through the mind's eye. *Memory and Cognition* **3**, 635–647.

Panofsky, E. (1939). *Studies in Iconology*. New York: Harper and Row.

Park, S. and Arbuckle, T. Y. (1973). Ideograms versus alphabets: effects of script on memory in "biscriptal" Korean subjects. *Journal of Experimental Psychology: Learning and Memory* **6**, 631–642.

Patterson, K. E. (1979). What is right with deep dyslexia patients? *Brain and Language* **8**, 111–129.

Patterson, K. E. (1981). Neuropsychological approaches to the study of reading. *British Journal of Psychology* **72**, 151–174.

Patterson, K. E. and Marcel, A. J. (1977). Aphasia, dyslexia and the phonological coding of written words. *Quarterly Journal of Experimental Psychology* **29**, 307–318.

Pei, M. (1965). *The Story of Language*. Philadelphia: Lippincott.

Perfetti, C. A., Goldman, S. R. and Hogaboam, T. W. (1979). Reading skill and the identification of words in discourse context. *Memory and Cognition* **7**, 273–282.

Perfetti, C. A. and Roth, S. F. (1981). Some of the interactive processes in reading and their role in reading skill. *In* A. Lesgold and C. Perfetti (Ed.) *Interative Processes in Reading*. Hillsdale, N.J.: Erlbaum.

Pickering, J. (1976). The perception of familiar stimuli *Perception* **5**, 251–264.

Pillsbury, W. B. (1897). A study in apperception. *American Journal of Psychology* **8**, 315–393.

Pisoni, D. B. and Lazarus, J. H. (1974). Categorical and non-categorical modes of speech perception along the voicing continuum. *Journal of the Acoustical Society of America* **55**, 328–333.

Pisoni, D. B. and Tash, J. (1974). Reaction times to comparisons within and across phonetic categories. *Perception and Psychophysics* **15**, 285–290.

Pollatsek, A. and Carr, T. H. (1979). Rule-governed and wholistic encoding processes in word perception. *In* P. A. Kolers, H. Bouma and M. Wrolstad (Ed.) *Processing of Visible Language* Vol. 1. New York: Plenum Press.

Pollatsek, A., Well, A. D. and Schindler, R. M. (1975). Familiarity affects visual processing of words. *Journal of Experimental Psychology: Human Perception and Performance* **1**, 328–338.

Pomerantz, J. R., Sager, L. C. and Stoever, R. J. (1977). Perception of wholes and of their component parts: some configurational superiority effects. *Journal of Experimental Psychology: Human Perception and Performance* **3**, 422–435.

Posnansky, C. J. and Rayner, K. (1977). Visual-feature and response components in a picture-word interference task with beginning and skilled readers. *Journal of Experimental Child Psychology* **24**, 440–460.

Posner, M. I. (1969). Abstraction and the process of recognition. *In* G. H. Bower and J. T. Spence (Ed.) *The Psychology of Learning and Motivation* Vol. 3. New York and London: Academic Press.

Posner, M. I. (1970). On the relationship between letter names and superordinate categories. *Quarterly Journal of Experimental Psychology* **22**, 279–287.

Posner, M. I. and Snyder, C. R. R. (1975). Attention and cognitive control. *In* R. L. Solso (Ed.) *Information Processing and Cognition: The Loyola Symposium*. Hillsdale, N.J.: Erlbaum.

Premack, D. (1976). *Intelligence in Ape and Man*. Hillsdale, N.J.: Erlbaum.

Pulgram, E. (1976). The typologies of writing systems. *In* W. Haas (Ed.) *Writing without Letters*. Manchester: Manchester University Press.

Purcell, D. G. and Stanovich, K. E. (1982). Some boundary conditions for a word superiority effect. *Quarterly Journal of Experimental Psychology* **34A**, in press.

Purcell, D. G., Stanovich, K. E. and Spector, A. (1978). Visual angle and the word superiority effect. *Memory and Cognition* **6**, 3–8.

Quantz, J. O. (1897). Problems in the psychology of reading. *Psychological Monograph Supplements* Vol. 2, No. 1.

Rabbitt, P. M. A. and Vyas, S. (1973). What is repeated in the "repetition effect"? *In* S. Kornblum (Ed.) *Attention and Performance 4*. New York and London: Academic Press.

Rayner, K. (1975). The perceptual span and peripheral cues in reading. *Cognitive Psychology* **7**, 65–81.

Rayner, K. (1976). Developmental changes in word recognition strategies. *Journal of Educational Psychology* **68**, 323–329.

Reddy, R. (Ed.) (1975). *Speech Recognition: invited papers presented at the IEEE symposium.* New York and London: Academic Press.

Reddy, R. and Newell, A. (1975). Knowledge and its representation in a speech understanding system. *In* L. W. Gregg (Ed.) *Knowledge and Cognition.* Potomac, Md: Erlbaum.

Reicher, G. M. (1969). Perceptual recognition as a function of meaningfulness of stimulus material. *Journal of Experimental Psychology* **81**, 274–280.

Rosch, E. (1975). Cognitive representations of semantic categories. *Journal of Experimental Psychology: General* **104**, 192–233.

Rosner, J. and Simon, D. P. (1971). *The auditory analysis test: an initial report.* Learning Research and Development Center, University of Pittsburgh.

Rozin, P., Bressman, B. and Taft, M. (1974). Do children understand the basic relationship between speech and writing? The mow motorcycle test. *Journal of Reading Behavior* **6**, 327–334.

Rozin, P. and Gleitman, L. R. (1977). The structure and acquisition of reading II: the reading process and the acquisition of the alphabetic principle. *In* A. S. Reber and D. L. Scarborough (Ed.) *Toward a Psychology of Reading.* Hillsdale, N.J.: Erlbaum.

Rozin, P., Poritsky, S. and Sotsky, R. (1971). American children with reading problems can easily learn to read English represented by Chinese characters. *Science* **171**, 1264–1267.

Rubinstein, H., Lewis, S. S. and Rubinstein, M. A. (1971). Evidence for phonemic recoding in visual word recognition. *Journal of Verbal Learning and Verbal Behavior* **10**, 645–657.

Rumelhart, D. E. (1976). Toward an interactive model of reading. CHIP report no. 56, University of California, San Diego.

Rumelhart, D. E. (1977). *An Introduction to Human Information Processing.* New York: Wiley.

Rumelhart, D. E. and Siple, P. (1974). Process of recognizing tachistoscopically presented words. *Psychological Review* **81**, 99–118.

Saffran, E. M. (1980). Reading in deep dyslexia is not ideographic. *Neuropsychologia* **18**, 219–223.

Saffran, E. M. and Marin, O. S. (1977). Reading without phonology: evidence from aphasia. *Quarterly Journal of Experimental Psychology* **29**, 515–526.

Saffran, E. M., Schwartz, M. F. and Marin, O. S. M. (1976). Semantic mechanisms in paralexia. *Brain and Language* **3**, 255–265.

Saffran, E. M., Bogyo, L. C., Schwartz, M. F. and Marin, O. S. M. (1980). Does deep dyslexia reflect right-hemisphere reading? *In* M. Coltheart, K. Patterson and J. C. Marshall (Ed.) *Deep Dyslexia.* London: Routledge and Kegan Paul.

Sakamoto, T. and Makita, K. (1973). Japan. *In* J. Downing (Ed.) *Comparative Reading.* New York: Macmillan.

Sasanuma, S. (1974). Kanji versus Kana processing in alexia with transient agraphia: a case report. *Cortex* **10**, 89–97.

Sasanuma, S. (1975). Kana and Kanji processing in Japanese aphasics. *Brain and Language* **2**, 369–383.

Sasanuma, S. (1980). Acquired dyslexia in Japanese: clinical features and underlying mechanisms. *In* M. Coltheart, K. Patterson and J. C. Marshall (Ed.) *Deep Dyslexia*. London: Routledge and Kegan Paul.

Sasanuma, S. and Fujimura, O. (1971). Selective impairment of phonetic and non-phonetic transcription of words in Japanese aphasic patients: Kana vs. Kanji in visual recognition and writing. *Cortex* **7**, 1–18.

Sasanuma, S., Itoh, M. K. and Kobayashi, Y. (1977). Tachistoscopic recognition of Kana and Kanji words. *Neuropsychologia* **15**, 547–553.

Sasanuma, S. and Monoi, H. (1975). The syndrome of Gogi (word-meaning) aphasia: selective impairment of Kanji processing. *Neurology* **25**, 627–632.

Savin, H. B. (1975). What the child knows about speech when he starts to learn to read. *In* J. F. Kavanagh and I. G. Mattingly (Ed.) *Language by Eye and by Ear*. Cambridge, Mass.: M.I.T. Press.

Savin, H. B. and Bever, T. G. (1970). The nonperceptual reality of the phoneme. *Journal of Verbal Learning and Verbal Behavior* **9**, 295–302.

Scarborough, D. L., Cortese, C. and Scarborough, H. S. (1977). Frequency and repetition effects in lexical memory. *Journal of Experimental Psychology: Human Perception and Performance* **3**, 1–17.

Scarborough, D. L., Gerard, L. and Cortese, C. (1979). Accessing lexical memory: the transfer of word repetition effects across task and modality. *Memory and Cognition* **7**, 3–12.

Schendel, J. D. and Shaw, P. (1976). A test of the generality of the word-context effect. *Perception and Psychophysics* **19**, 383–393.

Schmandt-Besserat, D. (1978). The earliest precursor of writing. *Scientific American* **238**, 38–47.

Schneider, W. and Shiffrin, R. M. (1977). Automatic and controlled information processing in vision. *In* D. LaBerge and S. J. Samuels (Ed.) *Basic Processes in Reading: Perception and Comprehension*. Hillsdale, N.J.: Erlbaum.

Scholes, R. J. (1971). *Acoustic Cues for Constituent Structure*. The Hague: Mouton.

Schuberth, R. E. and Eimas, P. D. (1977). Effects of context on the classification of words and nonwords. *Journal of Experimental Psychology: Human Perception and Performance* **3**, 27–36.

Schuberth, R. E., Spoehr, K. T. and Lane, D. M. (1981). Effects of stimulus and contextual information on the lexical decision process. *Memory and Cognition* **9**, 68–77.

Schvaneveldt, R., Ackerman, B. P. and Semlear, T. (1977). The effect of semantic context on children's word recognition. *Child Development* **48**, 612–616.

Schwartz, M. F., Saffran, E. M. and Marin, O. S. M. (1980). Fractionating the reading process in dementia. *In* M. Coltheart, K. Patterson and J. Marshall (Ed.) *Deep Dyslexia*. London: Routledge and Kegan Paul.

Scragg, D. G. (1974). *A History of English Spelling*. Manchester: Manchester University Press.

Secor, A. (1900). Visual reading. *American Journal of Psychology* **11**, 225–236.

Seligman, M. E. P. (1970). On the generality of the laws of learning. *Psychological Review* **77**, 406–418.

Seymour, P. H. K. (1977). Conceptual encoding and locus of the Stroop effect. *Quarterly Journal of Experimental Psychology* **29**, 245–265.

Seymour, P. H. K. (1979). *Human Visual Cognition*. West Drayton, Middlesex: Collier Macmillan.

Seymour, P. H. K. and Jack, M. V. (1978). Effects of visual familiarity on "same" and "different" decision processes. *Quarterly Journal of Experimental Psychology* **30**, 455–470.

Seymour, P. H. K. and Porpodas, C. D. (1980). Lexical and non-lexical processing of spelling in developmental dyslexia. *In* U. Frith (Ed.) *Cognitive Processes in Spelling*. London and New York: Academic Press.

Shaffer, L. H. and Hardwick, J. (1968). Typing performance as a function of text. *Quarterly Journal of Experimental Psychology* **20**, 360–369.

Shaffer, L. H. and Hardwick, J. (1970). The basis of transcription skill. *Journal of Experimental Psychology* **84**, 424–440.

Shallice, T. (1972). Dual functions of consciousness. *Psychological Review* **79**, 383–393.

Shallice, T. and McGill, J. (1978). The origins of mixed errors. *In* J. Requin (Ed.) *Attention and Performance*, 7. Hillsdale, N.J.: Erlbaum.

Shallice, T. and Warrington, E. K. (1975). Word recognition in a phonemic dyslexic patient. *Quarterly Journal of Experimental Psychology* **27**, 187–199.

Shallice, T. and Warrington, E. K. (1980). Single and multiple component central dyslexic syndromes. *In* M. Coltheart, K. Patterson and J. C. Marshall (Ed.) *Deep Dyslexia*. London: Routledge and Kegan Paul.

Shankweiler, D. and Liberman, I. Y. (1972). Misreading: a search for causes. *In* J. F. Kavanagh and I. G. Mattingly (Ed.) *Language by Eye and by Ear*. Cambridge, Mass.: M.I.T. Press.

Shannon, C. E. (1948). A mathematical theory of communication. *Bell System Technical Journal* **27**, 379–423.

Simon, D. P. and Simon, H. A. (1973). Alternative uses of phonemic information in spelling. *Review of Educational Research* **43**, 115–137.

Sinclair, A., Jarvella, R. J. and Levelt, W. J. M. (Ed.) (1978). *The Child's Conception of Language*. Berlin: Springer-Verlag.

Smith, A. (1966). Speech and other functions after left dominant hemispherectomy. *Journal of Neurology, Neurosurgery and Psychiatry* **29**, 467–471.

Smith, E. E. and Haviland, S. E. (1972). Why words are perceived more accurately than nonwords: inference versus unitization. *Journal of Experimental Psychology* **92**, 59–64.

Smith, E. E. and Spoehr, K. T. (1974). The perception of printed English: a theoretical perspective. *In* B. H. Kantowitz (Ed.) *Human Information Processing: Tutorials in Performance and Cognition*. Potomac, Md: Erlbaum.

Smith, F. (1969). Familiarity of configuration vs. discriminability of features in the visual identification of words. *Psychonomic Science* **14**, 261, 263.

Smith, F. (1971). *Understanding Reading*. New York: Holt, Rinehart and Winston.

Smith, G. J. W. and Henriksson, M. (1955). The effect on an established percept of a perceptual process beyond awareness. *Acta Psychologica* **11**, 346–355.

Smith, M. C. and Kirsner, K. (1982). Language and orthography as irrelevant features in colour–word and picture–word Stroop interference. *Quarterly Journal of Experimental Psychology* **34A**, in press.

Smith, P. T. (1980). Linguistic information in spelling. *In* U. Frith (Ed.) *Cognitive Processes in Spelling*. London and New York: Academic Press.

Smith, P. T. and Baker, R. G. (1976). The influence of English spelling patterns on pronunciation. *Journal of Verbal Learning and Verbal Behavior* **15**, 267–285.

Smith, P. T. and Groat, A. (1979). Spelling patterns, letter cancellation and the processing of text. *In* P. A. Kolers, M. E. Wrolstad and H. Bouma (Ed.) *Processing of Visible Language 1*. New York: Plenum Press.

Smith, P. T. and Jones, K. F. (1975). Phonemic organization and search through long term memory. *In* P. Rabbitt and S. Dornic (Ed.) *Attention and Performance V*. New York and London: Academic Press.

So, K., Potter, M. C. and Friedman, R. B. (1977). Chinese characters, English words, and drawings: naming and understanding. Unpublished MS., M.I.T.

Solomons, L. and Stein, G. (1896). Normal motor automatism. *Psychological Review* **3**, 492–512.

Solso, R. L., Barbuto, P. F. and Juel, C. L. (1979). Bigram and trigram frequencies and versatilities in the English language. *Behavioral Research Methods and Instrumentation* **11**, 475–484.

Spector, A. and Purcell, D. G. (1977). The word superiority effect. *Perception and Psychophysics* **21**, 323–328.

Sperling, G. (1960). The information available in brief presentations. *Psychological Monographs* **74**, no. 11.

Spoehr, K. T. (1978). Phonological encoding in visual word recognition. *Journal of Verbal Learning and Verbal Behavior* **17**, 127–141.

Spoehr, K. T. and Schuberth, R. E. (1980). Processing words in context. *In* O. Tzeng and H. Singer (Ed.) *Perception of print: reading research in experimental psychology*. Hillsdale, N.J.: Erlbaum.

Spoehr, K. T. and Smith, E. E. (1973). The role of syllables in perceptual processing. *Cognitive Psychology* **5**, 71–89.

Spoehr, K. T. and Smith, E. E. (1975). The role of orthographic and phonotactic rules in perceiving letter patterns. *Journal of Experimental Psychology: Human Perception and Performance* **1**, 21–34.

Stanners, R. F., Jastrzembski, J. E. and Westbrook, A. (1975). Frequency and visual quality in a word-nonword classification task. *Journal of Verbal Learning and Verbal Behavior* **14**, 259–264.

Stanovich, K. E. (1981). Attentional and automatic context effects in reading. *In* C. Perfetti and A. Lesgold (Ed.) *Interactive Processes in Reading*. Hillsdale, N.J.: Erlbaum.

Stanovich, K. E. and Bauer, D. W. (1978). Experiments on the spelling-to-sound regularity effect in word recognition. *Memory and Cognition* **6**, 410–415.

Stanovich, K. E. and West, R. F. (1979). Mechanisms of sentence context effects in reading: automatic activation and conscious attention. *Memory and Cognition* **7**, 77–85.

Steinberg, D. and Krohn, R. (1975). The psychological validity of Chomsky and Halle's vowel shift rule. *In* R. Koerner, J. Odmark and J. Shaw (Ed.) *The Transformational-Generative Paradigm and Modern Linguistic Theory*. Amsterdam: John Benjamins.

Steinberg, D. and Yamada, J. (1978–79). Are whole word Kanji easier to learn than syllable Kana? *Reading Research Quarterly* **14**, 88–99.

Sternberg, S. (1969). The discovery of processing stages: extensions of Donders' method.

In W. G. Koster (Ed.) *Attention and Performance II.* Amsterdam: North Holland.

Sternberg, S., Monsell, S., Knoll, R. L. and Wright, C. E. (1978). The latency and duration of rapid movement sequences: comparisons of speech and typewriting. *In* G. Stelmach (Ed.) *Information Processing in Motor Control and Learning.* New York and London: Academic Press.

Stirling, N. (1979). Stroop interference: an input and an output phenomenon. *Quarterly Journal of Experimental Psychology* **31**, 121–132.

Stirling, N. and Coltheart, M. (1977). Stroop interference in a letter naming task. *Bulletin of the Psychonomic Society* **10**, 31–34.

Stroop, J. R. (1935). Studies of interference in serial verbal reactions. *Journal of Experimental Psychology* **18**, 643–662.

Studdert-Kennedy, M. (1973). The perception of speech. *In* T. A. Sebeok (Ed.) *Current Trends in Linguistics 12.* The Hague: Mouton.

Sugishita, M., Iwata, M., Toyokura, Y., Yoshioka, M. and Yamada, R. (1978). Reading of ideograms and phonograms in Japanese patients after partial comissurotomy. *Neuropsychologia* **16**, 417–426.

Swinney, D. A., Onifer, W., Prather, P. and Hirshkowitz, M. (1979). Semantic facilitation across sensory modalities in the processing of individual words and sentences. *Memory and Cognition* **7**, 159–165.

Tabossi, P. and Johnson-Laird, P. N. (1980). Linguistic context and the priming of semantic information. *Quarterly Review of Experimental Psychology* **32**, 595–603.

Taft, M. and Forster, K. I. (1975). Lexical storage and retrieval of prefixed words. *Journal of Verbal Learning and Verbal Behavior* **14**, 638–647.

Tanaka, T. (1977). Development of letter recognition. *Japanese Journal of Psychology* **48**, 49–53.

Taylor, G. A. and Chabot, R. J. (1978). Differential backward masking of words and letters by masks of varying orthographic structure. *Memory and Cognition* **6**, 629–635.

Taylor, G. A., Miller, T. J. and Juola, J. F. (1977). Isolating visual units in the perception of words and nonwords. *Perception and Psychophysics* **21**, 377–386.

Taylor, I. (1980). The Korean writing system. *In* P. A. Kolers, M. Wrolstad and H. Bouma (Ed.) *Processing of Visible Language* Vol. 2. New York: Plenum Press.

Taylor, I. (1981). Writing systems and reading. *In* T. G. Waller and G. E. MacKinnon (Ed.) *Reading Research: Advances in Theory and Practice.* New York and London: Academic Press.

Teng, E. L. and Sperry, R. W. (1973). Interhemispheric interaction during simultaneous bilateral presentation of letters or digits in commisurotomized patients. *Neuropsychologia* **11**, 131–140.

Theios, J. and Muise, J. G. (1976). The word identification process in reading. *In* N. J. Castellan and D. Pisoni (Ed.) *Cognitive Theory* Vol. 2. Hillsdale, N.J.: Erlbaum.

Thompson, M. C. and Massaro, D. W. (1973). The role of visual information and redundancy in reading. *Journal of Experimental Psychology* **98**, 49–54.

Thorndike, E. L. and Lorge, I. (1944). *The Teacher's Word Book of* 30,000 *Words.* New York: Columbia University.

Thorndike, R. L. (1973). *Reading Comprehension: Education in Fifteen Countries.* New York: Wiley.

Tinker, M. A. (1965). *Bases for Effective Reading*. Minneapolis: University of Minnesota Press.

Treisman, A. M. (1960). Contextual cues in selective listening. *Quarterly Journal of Experimental Psychology* **12**, 242–248.

Treisman, A. M., Squire, R. and Green, J. (1974). Semantic processing in dichotic listening: a replication. *Memory and Cognition* **2**, 641–646.

Tulving, E. (1972). Episodic and semantic memory. *In* E. Tulving and W. Donaldson (Ed.) *Organization of Memory*. New York and London: Academic Press.

Tulving, E. and Gold, C. (1963). Stimulus information and contextual information as determinants of tachistoscopic recognition of words. *Journal of Experimental Psychology* **66**, 319–327.

Tulving, E. and Madigan, S. (1970). Memory and verbal learning. *Annual Review of Psychology* **21**, 437–484.

Turvey, M. T. (1973). On peripheral and central processes in vision: inferences from an information-processing analysis of masking with patterned stimuli. *Psychological Review* **80**, 1–52.

Turvey, M. T. (1978). Visual processing and short term memory. *In* W. K. Estes (Ed.) *Handbook of Learning and Cognitive Processes* Vol. 5. Hillsdale, N.J.: Erlbaum.

Tweedy, J. R. and Lapinski, R. H. (1981). Facilitating word recognition: evidence for strategic and automatic factors. *Quarterly Journal of Experimental Psychology* **33A**, 51–60.

Tweedy, J. R., Lapinski, R. H. and Schvaneveldt, R. W. (1977). Semantic context effects on word recognition: influence of varying the proportion of items presented in an appropriate context. *Memory and Cognition* **5**, 84–89.

Tzeng, O. J. L., Hung, D. L., Cotton, B. and Wang, W. S-Y. (1979). Visual lateralization effect in reading Chinese characters. *Nature* **282**, 499–501.

Tzeng, O. J. L., Hung, D. L. and Garro, L. (1978). Reading the Chinese characters: an information processing view. *Journal of Chinese Linguistics* **6**, 287–305.

Underwood, B. J. and Schultz, R. W. (1960). *Meaningfulness and Verbal Learning*. Philadelphia: Lippincott.

Vachek, J. (1966). Some remarks on writing and phonetic transcription. *In* E. P. Hainf (Ed.) *Readings in Linguistics*. Chicago: Chicago University Press.

Velletri-Glass, A., Gazzaniga, M. and Premack, D. (1973). Artificial language training in global aphasics. *Neuropsychologia* **11**, 95–104.

Venezky, R. L. (1970). *The Structure of English Orthography*. The Hague: Mouton.

Venezky, R. L. and Calfee, R. C. (1970). The reading competency model. *In* H. Singer and R. B. Ruddell (Ed.) *Theoretical Models and Processes of Reading*. Newark: International Reading Association.

Venezky, R. L. and Massaro, D. W. (1979). The role of orthographic regularity in word recognition. *In* L. Resnick and P. Weaver (Ed.) *Theory and Practice of Early Reading*. Hillsdale, N.J.: Erlbaum.

Walker, W. (1969). Notes on native writing systems and the design of native literacy programs. *Anthropological Linguistics* **11**, 148–166.

Wang, W. S-Y. (1973). The Chinese language. *Scientific American* **228**, 50–60.

Warren, R. E. (1972). Stimulus encoding and memory. *Journal of Experimental Psychology* **94**, 90–100.

Warren, R. E. (1974). Association, directionality and stimulus encoding. *Journal of Experimental Psychology* **102**, 151–158.

Warren, R. E., Warren, N. T., Green, J. P. and Bresnick, J. H. (1978). Multiple semantic encoding of homophones and homographs in contexts biasing dominant or subordinate meanings. *Memory and Cognition* **6**, 364–371.

Warren, R. W. (1971). Identification times for phonemic components of graded complexity and for spelling of speech. *Perception and Psychophysics* **9**, 345–349.

Weir, R. and Venezky, R. L. (1968). English orthography—more reason than rhyme. *In* K. S. Goodman (Ed.) *The Psycholinguistic Nature of the Reading Process.* Detroit: Wayne State University Press.

Weisstein, N. (1973). Beyond the yellow-Volkswagen detector and the grandmother cell. *In* R. L. Solso (Ed.) *Contemporary Issues in Cognitive Psychology: the Loyola Symposium.* Washington: Winston.

Weisstein, N. and Harris, C. S. (1974). Visual detection of line segments: an object superiority effect. *Science* **186**, 752–755.

Wernicke, C. (1874). Der aphasische Symptomenkomplex. Breslau: Cohn and Weigert. Translated in R. S. Cohen and M. W. Wartofsky (Ed.) (1966). *Boston Studies in the Philosophy of Science* Vol. 4. Dordrecht: Reidel.

Wertheimer, M. (1923). On objects as immediately given to consciousness. Translated in J. Herrnstein and E. G. Boring (Ed.) *A Source Book in the History of Psychology.* Cambridge, Mass.: Harvard University Press.

West, R. F. and Stanovich, K. E. (1978). Automatic contextual facilitation in readers of three ages. *Child Development* **49**, 717–727.

Whaley, C. P. (1978). Word-nonword classification time. *Journal of Verbal Learning and Verbal Behavior* **17**, 143–154.

Wheeler, D. D. (1970). Processes in word recognition. *Cognitive Psychology* **1**, 59–85.

White, M. J. (1969). Laterality differences in perception: a review. *Psychological Bulletin* **72**, 387–405.

Wickens, D. D. (1972). Characteristics of word encoding. *In* A. W. Melton and E. Martin (Ed.) *Coding Processes in Human Memory.* Washington: Winston.

Wijk, A. (1966). *Rules of Pronunciation for the English Language.* Oxford: Oxford University Press.

Wijk, A. (1969). Regularized Inglish. The only practicable solution of the English Spelling Reform Problem. *In* W. Haas (Ed.) *Alphabets for English.* Manchester: Manchester University Press.

Williams, A. and Weisstein, N. (1978). Line segments are perceived better in a coherent context than alone: an object-line effect. *Memory and Cognition* **6**, 85–90.

Willows, D. M. and McKinnon, G. E. (1973). Selective reading: attention to the "unattended" lines. *Canadian Journal of Psychology* **27**, 292–304.

Winnick, W. A. and Daniel, S. A. (1970). Two kinds of response priming in tachistoscopic recognition. *Journal of Experimental Psychology* **84**, 74–81.

Wintz, H., Scheib, M. E. and Reeds, J. A. (1972). Identification of stops and vowels for the burst portion of /p,t,k/ isolated from conversational speech. *Journal of the Acoustical Society of America* **51**, 1309–1317.

Worthington, A. G. (1964). Differential rates of dark adaptation to taboo and neutral stimuli. *Canadian Journal of Psychology* **18**, 257–268.

Wright, C. E. (1979). Duration differences between common and rare words and their implications for the interpretation of word frequency effects. *Memory and Cognition* **7,** 411–419.

Yamadori, A. (1975). Ideogram reading in alexia. *Brain* **98,** 231–238.

Yamadori, A. and Ikumura, G. (1975). Central aphasia in a Japanese patient. *Cortex* **11,** 73–82.

Yik, W. F. (1978). The effect of visual and acoustic similarity on short-term memory for Chinese words. *Quarterly Journal of Experimental Psychology* **30,** 487–494.

Young, A. W., Bion, P. J. and Ellis, A. W. (1980). Studies towards a model of laterality effects for picture and word naming. *Brain and Language* **11,** 54–65.

Zaidel, E. (1978). Lexical organisation in the right hemisphere. *In* P. Buser and A. Rougeul-Buser (Ed.) *Cerebral Correlates of Conscious Experience.* Amsterdam: Elsevier.

Zeitler, J. (1900). Tachistoscopic untersuchungen über das Lesen. *Philosophische Studien* **16,** 380–463.

Zipf, G. F. (1935). *The Psycho-biology of Language: an Introduction to Dynamic Philology.* New York: Houghton Mifflin.

Author Index

First-named authors only are listed.

Subject Index